THE CONSTITUTION OF ANCIENT CHINA

The Princeton-China Series

DANIEL A. BELL, *SERIES EDITOR*

The Princeton-China Series aims to publish the works of contemporary Chinese scholars in the humanities, social sciences, and related fields. The goal is to bring the work of these important thinkers to a wider audience, foster an understanding of China on its own terms, and create new opportunities for cultural cross-pollination.

The Constitution of Ancient China by Su Li, edited by Zhang Yongle and Daniel A. Bell, translated by Edmund Ryden

Traditional Chinese Architecture by Fu Xinian, edited by Nancy Steinhardt, translated by Alexandra Harrer

Confucian Perfectionism: A Political Philosophy for Modern Times by Joseph Chan

A Confucian Constitutional Order: How China's Ancient Past Can Shape Its Political Future by Jiang Qing, edited by Daniel A. Bell and Ruiping Fan, translated by Edmund Ryden

Ancient Chinese Thought, Modern Chinese Power by Yan Xuetong, edited by Daniel A. Bell and Sun Zhe, translated by Edmund Ryden

The Constitution of Ancient China

Su Li

Edited by Zhang Yongle &
Daniel A. Bell

Translated by Edmund Ryden

PRINCETON UNIVERSITY PRESS

PRINCETON & OXFORD

Published by Princeton University Press
41 William Street, Princeton, New Jersey 08540
6 Oxford Street, Woodstock, Oxfordshire OX20 1TR

press.princeton.edu

Jacket art courtesy of Shutterstock

Library of Congress Cataloging-in-Publication Data

Names: Su, Li, 1955– author. | Zhang, Yongle, editor. | Bell, Daniel (Daniel A.), 1964– editor. |
      Ryden, Edmund, translator.
Title: The constitution of ancient China / Su Li ; edited by Zhang Yongle and Daniel Bell ;
      translated by Edmund Ryden.
Description: Princeton, New Jersey: Princeton University Press, 2018. |
      Series: The Princeton-China series | Includes bibliographical references and index.
Identifiers: LCCN 2017023088 | ISBN 9780691171593 (hardcover : alk. paper)
Subjects: LCSH: Constitutional history—China. | Culture and law—China. |
      China—Politics and government—History. | China—History.
Classification: LCC KNN2090 .S826 2018 | DDC 342.3102/9—dc23
LC record available at https://lccn.loc.gov/2017023088

British Library Cataloging-in-Publication Data is available

This book has been composed in Miller.

Printed on acid-free paper. ∞

Printed in the United States of America

10 9 8 7 6 5 4 3 2 1

CONTENTS

EDITORS' ACKNOWLEDGMENTS

THE EDITORS THANK Professor Zhu Suli and his four commentators for their contribution to this productive intellectual dialogue. Thanks are also due to Professor Jiang Shigong, who participated in the workshop on Su Li's manuscript in late 2013 and contributed insightful perspectives; to the Department of Philosophy at Tsinghua University, which hosted this workshop; to anonymous referees for Princeton University Press who wrote constructive and insightful reports on an earlier draft of this book; to Tsinghua University, which provided the project funds for the translation; to our logistics assistant, Dr. Cao Chengshuang; to Zhang Hantian, who proofread the footnotes and bibliography; and, last but not least, especially to our brilliant translator, Dr. Edmund Ryden, and to our thoughtful and efficient editor at Princeton University Press, Rob Tempio.

Editors' Introduction

Zhang Yongle & Daniel A. Bell

CHINA'S ECONOMIC PROSPERITY has brought increasing interest in the future of its political system. In this context, the Chinese constitution has gradually become a focus of public attention. Among contemporary Chinese legal scholars, Zhu Suli's studies on the ancient Chinese constitution occupy a unique position. His approach, radically different from the mainstream, gives rise to many new findings with deep implications for understanding contemporary China. (As Zhu Suli often uses "Su Li" as his pen name, he will be referred to as Su Li hereafter.)

Before the twentieth century, imperial China never had a written Constitution defining major aspects of political life. In the early twentieth century, in an effort to be recognized as a modern state, China imported the Western civil law tradition, in which lawyers were trained to deal with written laws. Although the great constitutional monarchist Yan Fu at that time understood constitution as the fundamental structure of physical bodies and social organizations, and applied the concept to the interpretation of China's ancient political institutions,[1] the understanding of the constitution as a written text still dominated China's constitutional minds. The concatenation of new revolutions further set aside the ancient Chinese legal tradition. Because of this rupture, to contemporary Chinese constitutional lawyers, ancient Chinese politico-legal institutions seem more remote than German *Grundgesetz* (Basic Law) or the U.S. Constitution. Similarly trained in the civil law tradition, Chinese legal historians rarely call the ancient Chinese politico-legal institutions they study "constitutional." In contrast, Su Li focuses on a series of ancient institutions and practices beyond legal texts, and calls them "constitutional." Although he could lean on Western intellectual traditions that encompass ancient institutions and practices in constitutional history—for example, the Greek notion of πολιτεία,[2] Walter Bagehot's interpretation of the British constitution,[3] or Rudolf Smend and Carl Schmitt's notion of *die Verfassung*[4]—in contemporary China the attempt to do this is an intellectually pathbreaking adventure.

This is merely one of the many intellectual adventures Su Li has attempted. In China, his intellectual reputation reaches far beyond legal circles. It is widely recognized that he has made groundbreaking contributions to the sociology of law, law and economics, and law and literature in China. He reinterprets Mao Zedong's and Confucius's insights about human nature and social institutions using the academic discourse of social sciences;[5] he repeatedly reminds readers of China's internal complexity. Like Richard Posner—one of his favorite contemporary scholars—he often crosses the border and tests the nerves of other legal scholars by challenging established doctrines in constitutional, civil, criminal, administrative, and intellectual property law and other disciplines.

Su Li was born in Anhui Province on 1 April 1955 and served in the People's Liberation Army between 1970 and 1976. Like Justice Oliver Wendell Holmes, who once served in the U.S. Army, he stands ramrod straight, even now in his sixties. After more than five years' service as a mapping and surveying soldier, he parlayed his military experience into employment. In 1978, the second year after resumption of the college entrance exam following the end of the Cultural Revolution, he was admitted to the Department of Law of Peking University. After his graduation in 1982, he served in the Guangdong customs office for two years, and then returned to Peking University as a graduate student in the history of Chinese legal thought. In 1985, he went to the United States and studied first at McGeorge School of Law at the University of the Pacific in California, and later at Arizona State University. He earned LL.M. (1987, U.S. business tax law), M.A. (1992, U.S. legal system), and Ph.D. (1992, interdisciplinary studies of law) degrees before returning to Peking University in 1992 to teach in the Department of Law. He served as dean of the School of Law from 2000 to 2010.

Su Li experienced nearly the entire process of the reconstruction of the legal academic tradition after the Cultural Revolution. After 1949, China systematically imported the Soviet legal tradition, but during the Cultural Revolution, even this tradition was partially suppressed, not to mention Western liberal or social democratic traditions. During Su Li's period of undergraduate studies—a crucial time for the reconstruction of China's legal academic tradition—law students still studied Soviet legal theory, but they were increasingly attracted to Western legal thought. As China moved toward a market economy, Soviet legal discourse gradually lost favor. Legal thought from the United States, Europe, and Japan provided new sources for academic progress. It is almost a tacit consensus among legal scholars that China should follow Western developed countries in the reconstruction of its legal system.

In 1992, Su Li was one of the few law professors in China with a doctorate from the United States. Against the natural expectation that he would promote American mainstream legal and political doctrines, Su Li attracted the attention of academia as an antimainstream scholar. In 1996, four years after his return to China, he published his first book, *Fazhi Jiqi Bentu Ziyuan* (法治及其本土资源, *Rule of Law and Its Indigenous Resources*).[6] While most of his colleagues were discussing how to speed up the transformation of Chinese society by transplanting more Western legal institutions, Su Li openly doubted the feasibility, or even desirability, of doing this. Western legal institutions and doctrines, as he remarks, are "local knowledge" (a term he borrows from the American anthropologist Clifford Geertz) that may not satisfy or fit the needs of Chinese society, especially its rural segment. The urgent task is to study the concrete shape and needs of Chinese society, and uncover "indigenous resources" for China's rule of law.

In *Rule of Law and Its Indigenous Resources*, the chapter on Zhang Yimou's movie *The Story of Qiu Ju* (秋菊打官司) is the most influential piece. In this film, the village chief, impatient with Qiu Ju's husband for his curse of failing to father sons, kicks him in the testicles. Qiu Ju, pregnant at that time, asks the village chief to apologize. After being bluntly refused, Qiu Ju appeals to higher authorities, one level after another, for official intervention to force the village chief to apologize for his misdeed. Before long, Qiu Ju goes into a difficult labor. The village chief calls on a few young men, who carry Qiu Ju to the hospital tens of miles away, where she delivers her child safely. The village chief's assistance, which goes beyond his official duty, restores the balance between the two families. However, the legal system responds to Qiu Ju's petition belatedly, charging the village chief with intentional injury. The police apprehend the chief, leaving Qiu Ju deeply perplexed. She expects no more than an apology from the village chief, but the system prescribes imprisonment. Su Li remarks that Qiu Ju is certainly ignorant of the law, but her expectation has a solid basis of legitimacy in rural China. Her perplexity implies the tension between the social logic of rural society and the formal legal system deeply influenced by the modern West.

To understand Qiu Ju's expectation and perplexity, Su Li turned to Fei Xiaotong (1910–2005), one of the founding fathers of China's sociology and anthropology. Fei's *From the Soil: The Foundations of Chinese Society* presents an influential interpretation of the social life of China's preindustrial rural communities.[7] In a society based on face-to-face interaction between people familiar with each other, punishment is administered with an eye to restoring the social relation of interdependence. In contrast, in a society of strangers, officials do not have to consider how punishment will fix the social balance between them. For Qiu Ju, an apology from the village chief is sufficient to restore the status of her family in the village. Although the chief kicks the husband, his help in Qiu Ju's childbirth restores the balance between the two families. However, the legal system of the state has no idea of the concrete interaction between the two families. Su Li points out that the "universal" system of legal discourse, deaf to Qiu Ju's appeal, has its own limitations. Rule of law in such a huge and complex country cannot be successful without understanding Qiu

Ju's expectation and perplexity. Therefore, it behooves legal theorists in China to uncover the indigenous resources of rule of law in China.

Su Li's idea of indigenous resources inspired fierce debates. Critics from both the left and the right attacked his notion of indigenous resources as a token of nostalgia for preindustrial rural society. But this charge is probably too simplistic. Su Li refuses the truth claimed by believers of modernization, not because he attempts to find a different version of truth in the remote past. Rather, as an antifoundationalist, he is almost instinctively suspicious of all kinds of claims to universality. As the Chinese translator of Foucault's *Nietzsche, Genealogy, History*, Su Li often quotes Nietzsche's remarks about truth and Foucault's analysis of "discourse/power" in his own works. From an antifoundationalist perspective, it doesn't make any sense to believe there is something foundational in the remote past. Therefore, his notion of "local knowledge" and "indigenous resource" may have more affinity to the present than the past. Contemporary China is characterized by unbalanced development—highly urbanized, advanced regions coexisting with poor, self-sustained preindustrial villages. Su Li emphasizes that these different regions may need different approaches to governance, and argues that the belief of most lawyers that "the more modern, the better" is a hegemonic way of thinking.

If *Rule of Law and Its Indigenous Resources* announces Su Li's approach, *Song Fa Xia Xiang* (送法下乡, *Sending Law to the Countryside*), published in 2000, best illustrates his approach in a series of empirical studies.[8] In this book, based on elaborate investigation and interviews at basic-level courts in rural China, Su Li depicts the disparity between primary judges in rural China and the legal formalism in textbooks. Many basic-level courts in rural China are characterized by their embeddedness in the local society. Judges care more about substantive justice as recognized by the concrete community; in terms of legal reasoning, judges are usually consequentialists who reach a conclusion before considering legal inference, application, and argumentation. They tailor the facts of the case according to their moral intuition, so as to facilitate the legal application leading to a given result. They solve the central issue of the dispute, but also care deeply about peripheral issues, such as the enforcement of the judgment, in order to eradicate the origins of the dispute from the local community. In this solid study, Su Li urges his colleagues to keep China's complexity in mind and not to denounce local practices from a static ideal of the rule of law, but to understand the legitimacy of these practices in their own social contexts.

Sending Law to the Countryside provoked a wave of research on rural China's judicial practices and pushed China's sociology of law and legal anthropology forward significantly. However, Su Li's emphasis on the inner diversity and complexity of China also invites a question: How are China's diversity and complexity integrated into a large political entity? Obviously, mere research on grassroots society is insufficient to answer this question.

In *Daolu Tongxiang Chengshi* (道路通向城市, *The Road to the City*), published in 2004, Su Li provides a primary answer to the question and anticipates his later study of the ancient constitution of China.[9] The last part of this book discusses the constitution of the People's Republic of China (PRC). However, Su Li's interest lies not in how the constitutional text was written and interpreted but in the actual process of state building. This chapter investigates not only some general problems of the twentieth century, including national independence, social revolution, and modernization, but also how a series of particular conditions, such as the size of the country, unbalanced development, peasant revolution, and "feudal tradition" (in the Marxist sense), influenced the Chinese form of constitution and constitutional development. Su Li especially reinterprets Mao's *On the Ten Major Relationships* as a classic work in understanding the constitutional relationship between the central and local governments. In China, the history of the party and constitutional law are two fields that rarely communicate with each other. Su Li's study exemplifies how to use documents in the history of the party to conduct constitutional studies.

If the need to study judicial practices in rural China pushes Su Li to use Fei Xiaotong and the Confucian tradition, the need to understand the integration of the big country compels him to reinterpret Mao. His generation, growing up in an environment full of Mao's quotations, is very familiar with Mao's ideas. However, after the Cultural Revolution, many instinctively denounced Mao as the opposite of rule of law. In Su Li's view, the integration of political community is the basis of the rule of law. The Communist Revolution integrated this fragmented country and laid a political foundation for China's rule of law. Mao, as the most important leader of the party, should be taken seriously in legal studies. Su Li's approaches to Confucius and Mao are very similar: he is interested in the political function of Confucianism and Maoism, rather than the discourses the two thinkers used to construct their systems of thought. In other words, intellectual history or the history of ideas is never his interest. Confucianism gained a prominent position because of its successful response to a series of social and political needs. Similarly, Maoism is notable not as a belief system, but as a systematic response to many of the fundamental problems of modern China.

In terms of theoretical tools in research, Su Li is fond of cost-benefit analysis from law and economics. As the main Chinese translator of Richard Posner's works, he appreciates Posner's use of economics in the analysis of legal problems, and attempts to apply cost-benefit analysis to the study of constitutional history. From this theoretical tool, we can judge that his approach to history is necessarily etic rather than emic.[10] For him, the discourse or rhetoric that historical actors used might serve their actions but rarely reflects the real function of their actions in the society. An outsider can use the analysis of utility to penetrate their discourses to reach a more comprehensive explanation. This preference resonates with Su Li's Nietzschean suspicion of truth—of course, one may legitimately wonder whether Nietzsche would trust economics. But at least Su Li does not claim that his cost-benefit analysis is a privileged approach to another form of truth.

The intellectual distance between *The Road to the City* and the current book on the ancient Chinese constitution is actually not too vast. But this potential had not been actualized until he stepped down from his position as dean of the Peking University School of Law in 2010. Su Li worked for a time as a visiting professor in Xinjiang and Tibet. In the wide-open spaces of Inner Asia with its diverse cultures, he decided to launch a project to depict the ancient constitution of China. He produced and published a series of articles on different aspects of China's ancient constitution. His writings in this book represent only a part of his scholarship on this subject. But we are confident that they have crystallized his most important ideas on the subject.

Su Li's Depiction of China's Ancient Constitution

This book captures five pieces written by Su Li: one introduction, three related articles, and a response to the four commentators. Due to limited space, we omit his influential studies on the institution of emperorship,[11] the configuration and regulation of military power,[12] the internal integration of small agricultural communities,[13] and so on.

INTRODUCTION: THE EFFECTIVE
CONSTITUTION OF ANCIENT CHINA

In the introduction, Su Li announces that the subject of his study is "effective constitution," rather than constitutional law on paper. The former consists of a series of institutions and practices, which, evolving in response to changing social and historical conditions, integrate different parts of China into a whole. Some of these institutions and practices may be stipulated by written laws, some may guide specific cases of administrative and legal decision as principles or rules, but most of them just live in and shape Chinese politico-legal practices subliminally. The unwritten is often more important than the written.

The "effective constitution" can be prescriptive in two senses: one is in the sense of complying with the so-called universal values: liberty, democracy, human rights, rule of law, constitutionalism, and so on. But the other sense is more important: these institutions and practices are indispensable for the peaceful life of the people of this vast land, and are therefore desirable and good. This inference indicates Su Li's pragmatic and consequentialist tendencies. In other words, he tends to evaluate an institution primarily by the actual benefits it brings in the long run, which may include unintended consequences, rather than by the normative justification by its designers and proponents. His frequent use of the word "peace" may give the audience a Hobbesian impression. There are similarities, but essentially his notion of peace goes much deeper than mere preservation of life.

Su Li divides the structure of the "effective constitution" of ancient China into three interrelated levels. The first level is the constitution of individual social life, referring to the generation of cooperation and order in small agricultural communities. Su Li attaches the Confucian conception of *Qi Jia* (齐家, regulating the family) to this level. The second level is how to constitute a unified, large politico-cultural community above those small agricultural communities that lack horizontal contact with and recognition of one another. This entails not only a strong central government, but also the willingness and capacity of the politico-cultural elites to go beyond their hometowns to participate in state affairs, so as to maintain a stable dynasty, a huge state that can provide the people with peace and acquire their respect in return. Su Li attaches the Confucian conception of *Zhi Guo* (治国, governing the state) to this level. The last level is how to extend the politico-economic-cultural influence of the dynasty in the central plains characterized by agricultural civilization and to suppress the influence of the nomadic civilization in the north. In Su Li's eyes, this is exactly what the Confucian conception of *Ping Tianxia* (平天下, bringing peace to the world under heaven) signifies.

CENTRAL-LOCAL RELATIONSHIP AND GEOPOLITICAL CONSIDERATIONS IN CHINA'S ANCIENT CONSTITUTION

A large state with diverse peoples, religions, and cultures is difficult to administer and always at risk of falling apart. Therefore, the relationship between the central government and local constituent entities is crucial. In this book, Su Li views the feudal system of the Zhou dynasty as an early attempt to build the constitution of a large state. However, as the historical conditions evolved, the feudal system was finally abandoned and the new unitary system under the emperor became the new principle. The commandery and county system (郡县制), also known simply as the commandery system, plays the crucial function of integrating different localities of the country into an overarching entity.

Then, Su Li proceeds to the geopolitical considerations in China's division of administrative areas. To consolidate the central government and curb centrifugal forces on the local level, ancient rulers of China divided administrative areas prudently. They may have divided a culturally homogeneous area into two pieces or merged culturally heterogeneous areas into a single province.

Finally, Su Li also briefly analyzes the problem of *Ping Tianxia* (平天下), which aims at providing a basic institutional framework to settle conflicts between an agricultural dynasty and the surrounding nomadic peoples. The issue sometimes arises as a special form of the relationship between the central government and local entities.

Through these analyses, Su Li argues that the unitary system, resulting from a long trial-and-error process, is the only feasible option for agricultural China.

It would be absurd to reduce this institution to the ambition of the emperor or the ignorance and servility of his subjects. Readers familiar with modern Chinese intellectual history can easily detect the political implications of this conclusion: for Su Li, radical critics of China's past political system since the late Qing era were usually motivated by the contemporary need for political mobilization, but their critique rarely truthfully presented the functionality of the political system in China's past.

THE STANDARDIZATION OF LANGUAGE
AS CULTURAL CONSTITUTION

The operation of the imperial bureaucracy across a vast territory always requires effective and efficient means of communication. From the Qin dynasty on, the bureaucracy was staffed by intellectual elites selected from their localities but sharing a unified script system and approximately similar pronunciation. The forms of writing and pronunciation, therefore, became a crucial part of China's "cultural constitution." Su Li gives high praise to the Qin dynasty's unification of the script system, based on the judgment that the standardization of Chinese characters became the basis of China's bureaucratic governance. The unified script system provided infrastructure for effective communication between the central authority and its agents in far-flung territories. With a unified script, the intellectual elites could also transcend their parochial identity and find their new role in a dynasty and a civilization.

Although the script has been unified since the Qin dynasty, the pronunciation of Chinese characters varies from one place to another. Many dynasties promoted a certain phonetic system as their Mandarin (官话), which differed from the local dialects and was generally used by politico-cultural elites. Although the scholarly literature has paid little attention to the importance of the standardization of pronunciation in Mandarin, Su Li has elevated it to the status of "cultural constitution." With Mandarin, politico-cultural elites could communicate directly about public affairs, major events, and important historical literature.

The standardization of the script and the phonetic system was the basis of nationwide Confucian education, which integrated the literati in different geographical locations in a transgenerational cultural community. On the cultural level, this gave rise to a "social contract" among generations of literati and maintained the transmission of the ancient institutional and cultural tradition to new generations.

MERITOCRACY AND THE SELECTION
OF POLITICO-CULTURAL ELITES

To integrate the vast empire, there should be a system to select elites from different localities to staff the various levels of bureaucracy. Although the Zhou dynasty and later Confucian thinkers highlighted genetic relationships, the efficacy and efficiency of governance were always the primary concern in political practices. As time went on, the significance of genetic relationships further declined and consensus in favor of meritocracy emerged.

In a vast empire, the selection of elites is primarily a matter of institution rather than of the knowledge and integrity of the selectors. Major social forces of different localities or dominant classes would try to influence the selection of political elites through formal or informal channels. A nationally uniform institution of elite selection would inevitably lead to tension between the central government and other social forces. Su Li traces the development of China's institution of elite selection, from selection (推举) to recommendation (察举) and finally to the imperial examination system (科举制), and analyzes how the institution has adjusted in response to the politico-social-cultural conditions of different periods and how it embodies political rationalization.

Since a written exam cannot accurately convey the virtue of prudence required for political governance, there must be other supplementary mechanisms. For example, many dynasties promoted officials with rich experience in local governance to important ministry positions. Su Li provides an overview of these institutions in chapter 3.

Finally, to integrate diverse localities and peoples, the institution of elite selection has to consider regional balance and social mobility. In this sense, the institution shares much in common with the representative system arising in medieval Europe and prospering in the modern era. Some dynasties were ruled by ethnic minorities from Inner Asia. This led to some variation in the institution of elite selection.

Comments

WANG HUI

Professor Wang Hui from Tsinghua University is a prominent scholar of Chinese literature and intellectual history. He notices that Su Li has made a methodological turn from constitutional text to effective constitution, which overcomes the conventional approach of legal interpretation that treats Western constitutions as models for the Chinese constitution. With a new definition of "effective constitution," Su Li could discuss a set of institutions conventionally regarded as anticonstitutional (e.g., the feudal system, the emperor as an institution) or irrelevant to constitution (e.g., the standardization of characters, measures, and transportation).

Although Wang Hui appreciates Su Li's methodological turn, he has reservations regarding his functionalist approach. As he points out, Su Li takes the successfully constituted civilizational state as a given premise and from there deduces structure and functions. However, a civilizational body has not only material means of production, legal institutions, languages, and other functional elements, but also beliefs, rituals, systems of knowledge, cosmological visions, and so on. The classical constitution of China cannot be reduced to a set of structural-functional relationships appealing to the taste of modern social sciences. The becoming and evolution of institutions happened in a world of meanings. Without understanding the dimensions of meaning, it is hard to fully appreciate the significance of the institutions.

To illustrate his own approach, Wang Hui explores the evolution of ancient China's cosmology, and interprets the changes to China's major institutions from the pre-Qin era, through the Han and Tang dynasties, to the Song. His study highlights that cosmology, beliefs, and systems of knowledge are also active forces that shape political life and can help us understand the cultural foundation underlying China's institutions.

LIU HAN

Liu Han, a young constitutional law scholar from Tsinghua University, locates Su Li on the contemporary intellectual map and acknowledges his contributions to urging Chinese legal scholars to rethink the meaning of "constitution," not as a modern, liberal, normative conception, but in its original, constitutive, descriptive sense.

Liu Han concurs with Wang Hui that Su Li's structural functionalism pays insufficient attention to the problem of legitimation and the dimension of politico-cultural meaning. Liu Han uses Su Li's study of the institution of the emperor (which was discussed in our workshop at Tsinghua University but omitted from this book) as an example: Su Li explains clearly that the emperor plays a crucial role in the integration of a vast empire, but this integrating function is possible only when the emperor maintains the respect of his subjects. Legitimation, therefore, is the basis of function. Ignoring the dimension of legitimation, it would be difficult to understand the end of the monarchy and the rise of new forms of upper-level leadership in the twentieth century. Although Su Li's approach can grasp the functional continuity between emperor and party secretary, it may not be able to depict the rupture and continuity in legitimation.

WU FEI

Wu Fei, a philosopher from the Department of Philosophy at Peking University, also appreciates Su Li's attempt to theorize the ancient constitution of China, but criticizes him for downplaying Confucian ideas in his picture of ancient China. China, as Wu Fei points out, is not simply a state, but a civilization— which comprises more than the institutions of a state. By focusing merely on those institutions, Su Li risks reducing a rich civilization to a state. His perspective is modern, too modern.

Wu Fei points out that although a state machine characterized by bureaucracy under imperial leadership came into being during the Qin and Han dynasties, the spiritual core of the civilization remained a ritual system based on the fiction of the patriarchal clan system in the Western Zhou dynasty. In an age when the patriarchal feudal system of the Zhou dynasty had already collapsed, Confucians of the Han dynasty reinterpreted Zhou institutions in their reconstruction of Confucian textual learning and attached the spirit of these reinterpreted institutions to Han institutions. However, in Su Li's interpretation, this dimension is reduced to a function to construct a vast state and govern it effectively, and therefore loses its richness.

ZHAO XIAOLI

Zhao Xiaoli, a scholar from Tsinghua Law School, believes that Su Li's research on ancient Chinese constitution is important not only as historical scholarship but also as a shortcut to understanding the constitution of the PRC. To demonstrate this point, Zhao Xiaoli returns to the Preamble to the 1982 Constitution, which begins with a historical narrative: "China is a country with one of the longest histories in the world. The people of all of China's nationalities have jointly created a culture of grandeur and have a glorious revolutionary tradition." Zhao Xiaoli points out that the Common Program of 1949 and the 1954, 1975, 1978, and 1982 Constitutions all start with historical narrative. The Preamble to the 1982 Constitution implies that the Chinese people have a "glorious revolutionary tradition," and that the revolutions since the 1840s are the continuation of this tradition. This indicates a new version of temporality different from conventional Constitutions. It contains all three dimensions of time: past, present, and future. Revolution does not mean cutting off history and dismantling all of the culture of the past, but only purging the tradition's rotten parts. Revolution also gives rise to new cultural elements. This constitutional temporality recognizes the present as the continuation of the past rather than its opposite.

Zhao Xiaoli further points out that Su Li has discussed the similarities between contemporary and past constitutional problems. For example, in the 1980s, with the dissolving of the people's commune, the state retreated from the countryside and a system of "self-governance" was established at the village level. Therefore, the Confucian problem of *Qi Jia*, defined by Su Li as the effort to organize the everyday life of small communities, returned to contemporary China. In the absence of direct state regulation, peasants have to coordinate social relations in their own communities by themselves, in a way comparable to the way their ancestors did in premodern society. Based on these analogies, a study of the past can shed light on our present situation.

Su Li's Response to Commentators

In his response, Su Li answers not only the questions raised by these four commentators but also those he anticipates from readers.

Regarding the potential assertion that his research is not historical enough, Su Li responds that it is intended not as historical research but as a theoretical undertaking guided by theories of social science. He is not interested in the philosophy of history or abstract political or social theories—the latter often have an innate teleological tendency, aiming at discovering universal historical law or trends, and often overrate universality. His research belongs to the tradition of empirical social science, although it may lack systematic data or statistical analysis; his primary theoretical interest lies in the historical particularity, rather than universality, of China's ancient constitution.

Wang Hui emphasizes the historicity and disparity of the lifeworlds of different periods, and Su Li acknowledges this historicity and disparity, but he believes that they are not very significant in this project. From his point of view, the three structural issues that Confucians consider—*Qi Jia*, *Zhi Guo*, and *Ping Tianxia*—have existed since the Western Zhou period and arose repeatedly in subsequent dynasties. China's institutions respond to these questions under different conditions. It is the similarity of the questions that elicits similar answers.

In response to Wang Hui's doubt that he identifies structures and functions retrospectively based on the mature shape of the Chinese state, Su Li responds that the institutions he discusses are the products of a long trial-and-error process. In other words, different dynasties have attempted to constitute and reconstitute China under given conditions; although there are many small differences, it is possible to distill some common institutional principles from their practices. Su Li even remarks, borrowing from Ronald Coase's economic theory, that it is possible to compare China to a large enterprise and to learn from the following questions: How did this enterprise arise? What are its institutional conditions? What institutions and practices may reduce its internal organizational costs? The approaches to studying an enterprise can be applied to a larger unit of analysis, such as an empire.

Now it is easy to understand why Su Li cares little about the world of meanings, especially the Confucian ideas of civilization. His response to Wu Fei and Liu Han could be phrased as follows: he works as a social scientist, aiming at explanation rather than interpretation. Su Li recognizes that Confucianism played a very important integrating function, providing ancient China with a constitutional/political/legal theoretical paradigm, a sacred constitutional discourse. In this sense, the integrating function is related to the belief. However, he is not sympathetic to the Neo-Confucian attempt to restore the status of Confucianism as a privileged official doctrine. As a pragmatist, he cares about how Confucianism responded to the questions raised by the practices of governance, rather than its self-promotion.

At the same time, Su Li doesn't believe that Confucianism can explain the historical particularity of China's ancient constitution. This particularity derives not from abstract culture, but from the concrete problems arising from the production and life of the people on this land, conditioned by the natural geographical and climatic conditions and the corresponding modes of production. To prevent flooding along the Yellow River and the invasion of nomadic peoples from the north, it was necessary to organize the scattered, self-sustaining peasants. This collective interest of survival gave rise to a central authority and fueled its expansion. Confucianism legitimated this system through a set of symbols and meanings, but it cannot explain how it came into being. Here we can clearly see the influence of historical materialism on his arguments.

Finally, Su Li elaborates on the concept of constitutionalism understood as an undertaking to limit the power of government by a constitution, especially a written Constitution. Su Li contends that he doesn't reject this concept in general. However, as a pragmatist and consequentialist, he believes it is still a local concept. He is not sure whether the application of this concept could improve social conditions in China. He even remarks: "it was not the text of the U.S. Constitution that created the great United States of America, but rather the course of American history brought a sacred luster to the U.S. Constitution."[14] From his perspective of effective constitution, every country has its own particular constitutional problem that cannot be answered by self-claimed universal methods or undertakings. Sometimes it is even unnecessary to consider the experiences of other countries.

Su Li and all of his commentators share the historical sense that there is a strong continuity between China's past and present. But this does not mean that they believe China's contemporary political system also primarily aims at integrating agricultural communities. As the collective founder and leader of the system, the Communist Party of China has been very industry-oriented from the beginning. Many parts of China's political institutions are designed to speed up industrialization and urbanization. Almost seventy years after the PRC's founding in 1949, China now has the largest manufacturing industry in the world. What is constant is political leaders' awareness of the difficulty of running a large country and achieving political integration. Even with an urbanization rate as high as 57.35 percent by 2016, China still faces enormous centrifugal forces from different aspects of society: the wealth gap between urban and rural areas, tension between different social classes, potential and actual religious and ethnic conflicts, and so on. Fear of chaos persists among political leaders and policy makers. Su Li and his commentators completely understand this fear, although they do not share a single approach in response.

Further Intellectual Implications

As Zhao Xiaoli properly points out, China has such a strong sense of historical continuity that even revolutions were conducted with reference to historical precedents in the remote past. Hence, Samuel Huntington's reminder that modernization doesn't equal Westernization can be easily understood and accepted in China.[15] Su Li and his commentators are the carriers of a cultural confidence that the Chinese are capable of finding the path and institutions best for themselves. It would be misleading to call them cultural conservatives—after all, they have different opinions on the future of the Confucian legacy. For example, while Wu Fei cherishes the Confucian tradition, Wang Hui is more interested in China's future-oriented revolution in the twentieth century, which has some spiritual connection with the Daoist and Buddhist tradition reinterpreted by the modern revolutionary intellectual Zhang Taiyan. But they all believe that the study of ancient China has direct practical and intellectual implications for contemporary China.

For readers unfamiliar with Chinese history, this book provides a very useful shortcut to understanding China's ancient constitution. Su Li stresses that his work is not historical research but rather social scientific theoretical research. Thus, he provides a highly concise "stick figure" of ancient China, crystallizing his theoretical reflections. Readers may obtain an overview of the ancient Chinese constitution and understand its function in a short time, without being overwhelmed and confused by too many historical details.

For those already familiar with ancient Chinese history, this book can be read as a contemporary reflection on Chinese history with a unique historical background. One may ask, why do Su Li and his commentators deal with Chinese history in such a way? Would such a discussion have been possible twenty years ago? Ten years ago? In fact, the birth of such a work requires many conditions, including the confidence brought by China's economic revival as well as a significant knowledge reserve about Western constitutional experiences and theories. Both conditions are indispensable. Without the former, familiarity with the West might only strengthen a cult of the West; without the latter, confidence might lapse into *sterile Aufgeregtheit* (sterile excitement), as Georg Simmel would call it.

It is still too early to conclude whether Su Li's attempt in this book can lead to an enduring new academic tradition of constitutional theory in China. But he is not the only scholar who has made this kind of attempt. In the twentieth century, Chinese intellectuals borrowed constitutional theories from Japan, Germany, Britain, the United States, France, the Soviet Union, and even Switzerland, but China's political institutions have evolved at their own pace, often leaving theorists surprised. Their bewilderment may be due to irrational practice, but surprise is often a token of incomprehension of reality. The gap between imported theories and the Chinese reality, as a problem to be addressed, is attracting innovative minds in China.

If China's march to revival is not interrupted in the future, sooner or later there will be an "independence movement" in constitutional theory, giving birth to new theoretical paradigms capable of explaining China's actual political practices together with the constitutional experiences of other countries in the world. Su Li's work is an important instigating effort for this intellectual independence movement. His successes and failures in this book will become food for future thinkers.

Introduction

Su Li

The state is an accident, the fruit of human action and not the result of any human planning.[1]

—ADAM FERGUSON, *AN ESSAY ON THE HISTORY OF CIVIL SOCIETY*

TO ASSIST READERS, I must briefly discuss three issues in the guise of an introduction.

The first is the meaning of the term "constitution" in my writings, and why I should so define it and use it. In answering these questions we come up against the second issue—namely, the historical geoclimatic conditions to which China was responding and the special nature of the constitution it created in response. Given that the book is confined to part of my research on the constitution of historical China, and to prevent any misunderstandings or lacunae of comprehension, this book will not attempt to do full justice to my analyses. The third section will simply outline the basic train of thought and ideas of the other pieces that are not included in this book.

Two Meanings of the Word "Constitution"

The root of the word "constitution" (English/French; German *Konstitution*), according to an English dictionary, is "to constitute," meaning "to make up" or "to form." That is, what was previously scattered or existed as isolated units unrelated to others is brought together into one whole. In this sense, and without giving a precise definition of the state, we can say that any state is formed in this way. The people of a given plot of land may belong to one country or to various countries. Therefore, a given plot of land may be a state or may be divided into many states, or it may simply be part of a larger state. From this consideration, along with a consideration of historical material, I further argue that a long-term, stable state is one where the people of some land, for the benefit of all (the public or common good), have come together in various ways. Howsoever unified or diverse the levels or forms of this governance are, overall they are what the economy, society, and culture of this place can support.[2]

The formation of such a state naturally requires the contributions of many people, that is, many individuals and groups must deliberately seek various goods, not necessarily—and in early human history it was never so—coming from an enlightened, conscious, and systematic effort to create or form a state according to a long-term plan or with united coordination, but generally as a response to problems that simply had to be dealt with. Some of these efforts and ways of acting were effective and therefore were preserved; others were ineffective and were quickly set aside and replaced. In addition, some of no particular value happened to remain in place, and others that were effective and very necessary in the past became redundant as time went by and could be disposed of or retained at will. The ways of acting that were respected by human beings and retained over a long period of time became institutions, laws, and customs. At least in the early period, in English "constitution" could also refer to the assemblage of actual laws, institutions, and customs that bring a system of political governance into existence.[3]

But from another angle, the formation of a state may be viewed as the result of self-conscious, rational effort. If we were to cut history into sections and use a scientific worldview, and go along in part with the rise and creation of the form and political body of European nation-states, this point of view would gradually be in the ascendency. These forms of effort have become more and more commonplace and are even seen as the norm. The Preamble to the U.S. Constitution is a classic example: "We the people of the United States, in order to *form* a more perfect union . . ." (emphasis mine). Therefore, they took one set of laws that at least some people at the time or their representatives thought embodied important goals, institutions, principles, and norms and wrote them down in a document to remind subsequent generations to remain loyal to these forms. This document is thence called a Constitution. The word comes from these circumstances whether or not it bears judicial significance or is formative of the state as such.

In modern times the great economic, political, and cultural influence of the United States and the various countries of Europe has led to this type of written Constitution becoming increasingly prevalent, to the extent that for many people who have come under the influence of this modern tradition the written Constitution has become the premise and foundation for the formation of the political society that is the state. The term "constitution" has taken on a normative sense: only that which is done in accordance with certain goals, principles, or norms is "constitutional." What is not so may be termed, juridically, "unconstitutional," such that the marking of such a distinction has become necessary for the very existence of the state—that is, the state is functionally "constitutional."[4] Once this document is used as the basis for laws, there arises a new field in the study of law: constitutional law.

The meaning of this term and the processes it refers to constitute a range of knowledge with its own rationality and necessity. But the problem is that many states were not produced or formed by a written document either directly or indirectly. If we were not restricted to the definition of today's international law, then historical states would almost all be what Mencius described as a political body having land, people, and politics.[5] Such states did not need recognition from any other state. They were also long-lasting, real, and actual political bodies. In fact, most important countries in the world were not formed as a result of a written Constitution. And how long those states—we are not talking about dynasties or governments—that were really formed by a written Constitution can survive is a question, and not something that can be assured by a written Constitution. There have been some constitutions that people in general and even legal specialists believed to be reasonably good, which nonetheless failed to maintain their states when faced with major problems. Out of respect, I do not name those states that copied the U.S. Constitution. Yet everyone knows that the Weimar Constitution was unable to prevent the rise of the Third Reich and the disaster that befell the German people. In fact, I want to propose a counterfactual argument: even if the Weimar Constitution had allowed for judicial review, it could not have saved Germany.[6]

There are some states that do not have a written Constitution or a document that goes by the name of "Constitution" and yet function reasonably well. First, consider the United Kingdom. There is no way you can suppose a Constitution to exist on the basis of the Magna Carta alone, even if this document, which was observed by King John for only nine weeks, is the first statute of constitutional rank in the country.[7] This situation is not only in the past. The state of Israel was founded in 1948 and still has no Constitution. Moreover, if you want to be persnickety, the United States provides an awkward example. Did the country really only begin with the 1787 U.S. Constitution? Or was it the 1791 Bill of Rights? If so, then what is the Declaration of Independence? How should one deal with the years between 1776 and 1787?[8] In fact, the U.S. Supreme Court has publicly declared that the United States existed before the American Constitution, and it was not the Articles of Confederation of the thirteen states or the U.S. Constitution but America's success in achieving victory over the United Kingdom that created the United States.[9]

The "constitution" I am studying is thus first to be read in the root sense as "constituting." Although the central government of the People's Republic of China was formed in 1949 on the basis of what was recognized at the time as of provisional constitutional effect, the Common Program,[10] this China was formed throughout history. What constituted its existence and development was not one or several normative statutes, but the uninterrupted realization, throughout the course of history, of political powers including those of the central plain and the frontiers—powers which, over a long period of sometimes bitter struggle, proved to be effective and therefore were able to survive, and which, along with changes in sociohistorical conditions, constantly progressed and accumulated a whole series of basic institutions and practices. Some of these institutions and practices are laws; some of them, however, are perhaps principles or norms that direct executive or judicial decisions, but most of them in the actual practice of political and legal activity in historical China have impregnated Chinese society and people's everyday life, working in a hidden and silent way to make these people Chinese as well as shaping and forming China. They form an effective constitution.

But this does not imply that the effective constitution has no normative significance. It still may play two roles of normative significance. The first may be said to correspond to the normative significance of what today are referred to as universal values, such as liberty, democracy, participation, and rights. I believe that one only has to examine the long history of China to be able to identify some notions that are consonant with these standards. But I do not intend to take part in such an interrogation.

But these features of an effective constitution have an additional role that I believe to be genuinely of normative significance. It is that, for the broad spread of people living peaceably on this land, these institutions and practices cannot be replaced, or virtually cannot be replaced. Therefore, this sense is worth pursuing and is a good one, even though in the twenty-first century there are some ways of acting that some Chinese people consider not good, or not necessarily good, or even very bad. But I do not intend to discuss good or bad at an abstract level or in absolute terms. In my view, the fundamental function of any institution is to improve the lives of people in their concrete environment. What matters is not whether the evidence for these institutions is such as to leave one speechless.

Unlike today's constitutional law, which can be used by a judge, this effective constitution to which I am referring normally is not a matter of rule of law. But since these institutions and practices are of irreplaceable determinative significance in the formation, unification, and effective governance of ancient China—they support and complement one another—not only influencing the rise and fall of this historical China to a considerable extent, but also shaping the institutional framework and principles of other laws of the time, they may be called fundamental or basic laws. The reason is quite simple: no eggs remain whole when the nest is overturned. If a "state" loses its framework, all other laws have no meaning, either for the legislator or for those called to obey. (Suppose that the North had not won in the American Civil War; not only would there not have been the Thirteenth, Fourteenth, and Fifteenth Amendments to the Constitution, but there would have been no United States, at least not the present nation stretching from the Great Lakes to the Gulf of Mexico.) Taking this into consideration, in Chinese I use the term "constitution" to refer both to the action of constituting and to the fundamental institution. This is much the same as the terms that Chinese people generally use when they refer to "politics and law" (*zhengfa*) or to the "political setup" (*zhengzhì*).[11]

But this does not mean that the constitution of historical China is thereby not a constitutional law that can be put into practice. In fact, people often understand law as norms, but the implementation of law comprises both institutions and customary precedents, including the discretionary power of law-executors, law proper, and informal laws.[12] Thus in value terms one can truly say that the constitution of historical China itself is the fruit of constitutional practice. But I do not think it is necessary to fight for a ticket that says "constitutionalism."

The Special Nature of China's Constitutional Question

A constitution refers to a basic political-legal setup by which any state is formed and continues to run normally. However, each country has its own features; in some cases there are big differences. Therefore, any given constitution must both respond to the general questions of all mankind—whether peace for Hobbes or protection of life, liberty, and property for Locke—and follow the specific natural geoclimatic conditions and the constraints of the resources of the state. The real trouble is not some overall goal, but rather the sequence of concrete goals that are worth valuing given the particular conditions available, and how to realize these goals in the most effective way possible within those conditions. There will always be some people who will get more or who will be considered as getting too much, which will provoke disputes over right and wrong and even lead to revolution. In general, when natural geoclimatic and other resources are much the same, allowing people to choose, over a long period of time, the basic setup and constitution of the people in one area will in the end be unlike those of people in another, such that in their eyes the differences may seem to be very great indeed, but seen in another way, they may be pretty minor. The small-scale agricultural village institutions of the middle and lower reaches of the Yellow River in China could not really be strong and violent, nor could they be purely transmitters or copiers of polite culture but were rather like the natural geographical conditions of the surrounding area. But in the south, which also received the same Confucian education, the shape of the villages and the social organization were very different from those in the middle and lower reaches of the Yellow River. For this reason, although there were many differences, Plato and Aristotle both thought, in ancient Greece, that there were only two types of constitution possible (orthodox and abnormal), and that there were only three possible models of leadership (monarchy, oligarchy, and majority rule). And later generations all thought Greek politics was that of the city-state. The thirteen colonies of British North America seemed in the eyes of their contemporaries to be very different from one another and likewise the various countries of the European Union look very different on close examination, but the former came together and formed the United States of America and the latter united in the name of the European Union because they in fact had much in common.

Yet, viewed from natural geoclimatic conditions, historical China was not like Athens or Sparta, England or France, or the United States. The setting of historical China in the heart of East Asia was very different from the Mediterranean region, or big areas such as Europe and North America, in terms of natural geoclimatic conditions. When I discuss the constitution of historical China, I am talking about the institutions and ways of acting created by the people of East Asia, especially those living along or bordering on the middle and lower reaches of the Yellow River. I do so in reply to a series of practical difficulties that have arisen because of these important differences at the level of actual practice.

What arose in the middle and lower reaches of the Yellow River was a continental agricultural civilization. In comparison with the civilization that arose in the Mediterranean basin, the agricultural civilization of China had an origin that covered a wide sweep of territory that was far from the sea. Furthermore, along the east coast of China there are few islands or peninsulas. Sailing is not easy, and the dangers of the open sea are much greater. To facilitate and promote agriculture, the villages founded were generally not big—about the same size as a Greek city-state—and were scattered over a broad swath of land marked by the Yellow River. At least in the early stages, these rural villages were so widely scattered that they had no reason or possibility of producing a polity with borders at the level of a state. The people of the time belonged to very small villages, which were economically self-sufficient. Apart from marriage and the acquisition of necessities such as salt and iron, the life of these people was one where "the sounds of cock and dog could be heard, and even up into old age the people never meet each other" (*Daodejing* 80).

This kind of continental agricultural civilization may perhaps not require an external central political authority to unify and govern it. India's civilization, which is even older than China's, never established one unifying dynasty before the Turkic Mongol people established the Mughal empire in the sixteenth century. Furthermore, China's oldest poetry is said to reflect this question among the agricultural people at the origins of Chinese political governance.[13]

Yet there are three factors that may have led to the emergence of a public authority transcending the villages. First, at times there may have been conflict between the villages themselves. To resolve this, a public authority higher than that of the villages as a whole would be required. This kind of problem could occur in any society where there was a high density of people and where a society lacking resources might emerge. The middle and lower reaches of the Yellow River were just such a region. But of greater importance were the other two factors that belong to historical China alone, and it is more probable that it was these that brought about the establishment of a public authority that transcended the villages over the broad area from the plain at the central pass (in west-central Shaanxi) east to the plain in the middle and lower reaches of the Yellow River.

The first of these two factors was management of the Yellow River. This long river is prone to flooding, which is a serious threat to the farmers on both banks.[14] Yet management of such a big river is difficult. It cannot be done by any one village alone or even by a number of riverine villages joining together. It requires the joint and coordinated efforts of the people in the middle and lower reaches of the river. This requires a strong force that can overrule the local interests of the villages or even the area and is provided by a political leader and political organization.[15] And indeed, records relevant to this are found in history. Yu (禹), the first, mythical, emperor of the first Chinese dynasty, is described as leading the people for many years to manage the water and finally succeeding. Before the Great Yu, his father, Gun (鯀), tried to manage the waters for nine years but failed. Yu handed the throne to his son Qi (启), and thus began to place the world under heaven (天下) under his household. From then on, management of the water was always a major political task for later generations of Chinese.[16]

The greatest institutional requirement lay in the external forces that pushed down on the plowed land of the middle and lower reaches of the Yellow River, that is, how to resist the northern pastoral peoples effectively and prevent their incursions or else maintain peace with them and avoid war, and so provide the basic order that would allow countless ordinary people to go about their productive lives.

The geophysical shape of ancient East Asia was quite complicated, which is what gave rise to various civilizations. In the plain of the central pass and the middle and lower reaches of the Yellow River an agricultural civilization arose; in the south and southwest there was a scattered montane agricultural civilization. But in the west and northwest there was a marked difference from the very scattered agricultural society of the central plain. There from the border of the northern part of the central plain across the vast grasslands up to Siberia roamed many nomadic pastoral peoples who arose at about the same time as the civilization of the central plain. When the agricultural and pastoral civilizations met and began to compete for resources, conflict was inevitable. Inasmuch as history records, from the earliest years of the Western Zhou onward the agricultural and pastoral civilizations were constantly in conflict, which began to comprehensively and forcefully shape the civilization of the central plain, with its political governance and the formation of its dynastic organization.[17] In later generations there were many pastoral peoples who one after another

under heaven (天下), the daily happiness, life, and health of each individual are related to those of the whole body. However, self-sufficient farming life lacks commerce, and so each village is generally small; many are formed by one extended family or several such families. The problem of the formation and upkeep of the common body of the village may, therefore, be described by the Confucian concept of "regulating the family."

The second level is how to form a unified political-cultural body that transcends the village. In traditional rural society where people know only their own village and locality—they are inward looking—there will be no push from within to form a common political, economic, and cultural body, even when the level of common cultural elements is high. Should they actually form such a common political body, then because the people of each area lack sufficient communication, links, and recognition, it will easily break apart. In fact, throughout history in Eurasia many empires have arisen, but they all had great difficulty in lasting and never rose again once they broke apart. Therefore, to ensure that countless rural villages should in some way or another constitute a common body, there must be integration. There must be a strong central authoritarian government that implements relevant measures, but the political elite of each place must also be allowed to transcend their district of birth and both want and have the ability to take part in state affairs and political governance to establish a unified and stable dynasty, a large state, that will provide people with basic peace and so win widespread recognition—adherence—from the people. Given the very broad extent of the Yellow River and the conflict between agricultural and pastoral civilizations, the complexity of the terrain, and poor communications, it was very difficult to set up and govern this state. This is the problem of "governing the state."

The third level of formation as seen from the Confucian tradition is to take the agricultural civilization of the central plain as the center and actively integrate the people of the little states scattered across the south, bringing them into the political and cultural tradition with its center in the agricultural civilization of the central plain. With expanded borders in all directions and richer resources and manpower, an effective defense and even attack on the pastoral peoples in the north will widen the political, economic, and cultural influence of the dynasties of the central plain, or by other means of contact, such as a peaceful acceptance of tribute or even annexation of territory, the central plain's agricultural civilization will maintain peace with the northern pastoral peoples and prevent the constant recurrence of "men's heads hanging from the horse's bridle and women carried off on the saddle."[22] But from the practical point of view of historical China, or from the point of view of a historical bystander, the problem is the integration of the agricultural civilization of the central plain and the pastoral civilization of the north. Experience shows that the northern pastoral peoples were always shaping Chinese civilization, not only by their incursions into the central plain, but also by their adoption and adaptation of the Confucian tradition, bringing with them a whole series of new factors into Chinese civilization. This level of the constitutional question is that of "bringing peace to the world under heaven."

Summary

What is most crucial and requires the most creativity among these three levels of constitution (following on from what has been said in the previous section) is the constitutional problem posed by the second level.

First, the common body of the rural villages cannot by itself be a response to the organizational aspects of this constitutional problem, nor can it produce this organization out of its own resources. The common body of the villages is usually based on relationships of consanguinity and kinship or on frequent communication and cooperation within villages. It has its own order of self-development, but this order can transcend small-scale society, based on consanguinity or supposed consanguinity or personal relationships, only with difficulty. Therefore, it cannot provide the political order that is required by, and is effective for, the formation of a large-scale common body. It cannot provide a sufficient vision of a state order—at least not what the historical dynasties from the Qin and Han onward supplied.[23]

A small agricultural economy also has difficulty producing a commercial town of any size, and has difficulty in producing a political culture that can extend its influence to the surrounding area. It is even more difficult for it to give rise to one or several states that have strong economic, political, and cultural power radiating from an urban center.[24] To facilitate farming and limit expenditures on land and transportation, Chinese agriculture was not only highly intensive but also small in scale. Even though such a form of village demanded a strong organization, yet although it might maintain internal order and leave villagers unhindered in peacetime, come chaos, a natural or manmade disaster, village society could crumble, be scattered, and be lost. Even the lowest level of social order is impossible. Naturally, agricultural villages, whether singly or in federation, have no way of providing the organizational strength that could bring peace to the world.

Logically, for people and organizations to transcend a given locality there must be some government, court, or public force that has a cohesive political and social strength to serve as the core of society. From the experience of dynasties through the ages, the answer to this constitutional problem was a local core political elite group, recruited not only from the agricultural Han area but equally from the northern pastoral zone or other areas with minority peoples. By taking advantage of the benefits offered by heaven, earth, and humankind, and with a strong and effective political organization and military power, it could defeat any other political and military groups that competed with it and bring about the first complete unification of this vast area. It could provide the basic common goods, peace, and order for the people of each district and so gradually win their adherence, by which they expressed their assent. The vast plain and the agricultural and other peoples on it were able to constitute a China that normally had the center of its political governance in the central plain. It then adopted all kinds of measures to actively attract the political and cultural elite of every place in the whole country to share in the political and social governance and bring it about through all kinds of political, economic, and cultural measures. People who had been highly scattered and did not have or need any links gradually formed a broad and basic cultural and political identity, sharing basic social norms and constituting a common body that was basically political and cultural or civilizational.

This does not mean that historical China did not have a high regard for constitutional issues such as the organizational structure of political governance or the separation of powers. For ancient China, this was not the primary concern. The primary concern was how to form and maintain this huge political, economic, and cultural body, how to shape and constitute this common body from the political, economic, and cultural angles. The organizational structure and form of monarchic government was simply a means to achieve this fundamental goal. But this does not mean that this was a weakness on the part of China's ancient politicians and thinkers. In fact, it is wholly in line with what Plato and Aristotle have to say about the constitution of city-states. A lot of people today are very concerned about the number of rulers a state has, but they do not believe that this number is of any special significance to the constitution of the city-states. In addition, given the geographic and cultural conditions of ancient China, there were not many practical organizational structures to choose from. In short, neither majority rule nor even oligarchy was possible.

This constitution should also be as simple to run as possible. Although the coercive power of the state could not be too weak, one still had to avoid the overuse of *laws*, which amount to "social norms supported by the coercive power of the state." This is another reason that I am concerned about constitution rather than constitutional law. It is not out of love, but because the state's capacity to absorb resources was limited, its capacity to acquire information was limited, and the resources it did acquire had to be used to govern the state and bring peace to the world under heaven. Therefore, except when it was absolutely necessary, the power of the emperor did not extend down to the rural districts. The order and institutions that agricultural society developed of its own accord were respected, and these institutions of rural society supported the state in performing the limited management that it had to undertake. It was also through institutions that the farmers who would never otherwise have met, even though they lived in close proximity, could cooperate. This was to be so not only for neighboring communities with similar geographical conditions and agricultural means of production leading to a common civilization. One also had to consider the various tribes and peoples in different areas of dissimilar nature—resulting from the collective impact of geoclimatic factors—such that they would at least live in peace with one another. In simple terms, the great difference between the constitution of historical China and the ancient city-states of Greece or the modern nation-states of Europe was that the latter were common political bodies formed on the basis of a preexisting society or nation, whereas the former had no economic or social community body that covered the whole area that could serve as a premise for shaping a society or political body in which there was mutual interchange and complementarity.

This is what determined the constitution of ancient China. From the beginning it was, and had to be, a large state, in order to bring together and integrate many diverse local cultures in the constitution of an agricultural society. It was the constitution of a civilization. Moreover, at least from the Western Zhou onward, and even having endured the severe constitutional revolutions of the Spring and Autumn, Warring States, and Qin and Han eras, the constitutional issues of regulating the household, governing the state, and bringing peace to the world under heaven never changed. Even though dynasties succeeded one another, and severe disasters struck, and the minority peoples of the north invaded the central plain many times, the constitution that began to emerge in the Qin-Han period for the most part continued, transcending the dynasties, building up, adjusting, and being revived. The questions it answered where virtually always those of regulating the household, governing the state, and bringing peace to the world under heaven of agricultural China, right up to the second half of the nineteenth century, when China faced a change of game that had not been seen for millennia and began to undergo a great reconstitution.[25]

In the course of this history and in such a vast area, the people of this land tried out various microscopic, midsized, and macroscopic institutions, using the natural and human institutions and cultural resources then available. There were failures. Some constitutional ideas were generally accepted by the political elite of their time but were only popular prejudices or even constitutional decorations, and some were "constitutional stupidities," the most striking being Wang Mang's (王莽)[26] return to the past.[27] But although some initially failed, like the commanderies and counties of the Qin, in the long run they showed that they were not the autocratic will or whim of the ruler or persons in power, but were suited to the constitution of this great state with the force to last through time and space. They had profound rationality and sociohistorical evidence, and sufficient social consensus to uphold the judgments of the holders of power and embody the collective feelings, desires, and dreams that won a leading role in society, even if these feelings, desires, and dreams were quite bad for some groups that were not in positions of power. Through this one can see that a constitution is not a natural law full of moral warmth, nor is it human effort constantly progressing toward some ultimate moral goal. At least at times, or perhaps it is always so, it is a law of necessity that upholds the state in the long term or for a special period of time.[28]

To meet the limits of space, in this book I do not discuss, first, some of the highly influential constitutional shifts of early China (before the Spring and Autumn period), such as why there was a shift from a legendary abdication in favor of persons with talent to a later hereditary monarchy, or from succession by younger brothers to inheritance by the eldest son, or the economic, political, and social changes that influenced these shifts. Second, regulating the household as a means of governance in agricultural villages and rural areas was, in my view, the greatest constitutional contribution of Confucianism to historical China. It was also a key part in the formation of the bureaucracy. But these are outside the scope of this book. Third, China's imperial system itself also has a whole series of special issues related to monarchy, unlike those of the West and of great theoretical interest, which will not be discussed in this book. Fourth, I have also omitted discussion of the military institutions related to the formation of historical China, the economic institutions of a large state, and the dubious question of citizenship and the related question of distributional justice.

The next three chapters in this book deal with three related questions of governing the state as applied to historical China. In the Western tradition and in Western constitutional research, these questions rarely attract much attention. The first is the political formation of historical China's borders: from this one can understand how, at the constitutional level, historical China dealt with geopolitical questions that easily arise and were even bound to arise. Second, to ensure that the bureaucracy at the center of power governed according to law, historical China had a cultural system of integration of constitutional significance, including a unified script, Mandarin Chinese, and, on this basis, the creation of a group of elite persons whose outlook transcended the limitations of their native district and civilizational roots. Third, historical China attracted a political and cultural elite that participated in the institutions of political governance and their changes, including three forms of civil service examination, and in these institutions there was an implicit consideration of local representation. Many of the constitutional institutions and measures discussed in this introduction belong to history, but they may continue to exist as the evidence of historical experience out of which theoretical questions can be drawn. They will challenge our interpretations, and at certain times it may be that they still have some practical significance.

Part I

with bordering tribes entering into the central plain, gradually bringing about an integration of peoples, by the Qing dynasty China's borders encompassed an area of thirteen million square kilometers and a population of 450 million. Therefore, on the basis of the size of its territory and population, this broad area of land called China from the Western Zhou onward showed an overall tendency to seek the kind of administration a large state needs. In general, since the foundation of the empire by the Qin and the Han, it never lost the status of a large state with centralized power unifying many peoples. The main dynasties generally ruled for two to three hundred years and, objectively speaking, provided a long period of peace for ordinary people. From this we may postulate that the people of this land had their own inherent and sustained reasons for creating the administration of a large state, since from an empirical point of view the administration of this large state was created by the dynasties and politicians throughout history. It was something that they imposed on the people of this area.

A large state is not a small state writ large; the administrative requirements of a large state are not the same as those of a small state. While not denying the special wisdom and organization of some small states wedged between large states—the practical wisdom of the ancient Greek city-states is indeed widely consulted by scholars of many countries even today—Aristotle also recognized that the population of a city-state could not be too large, since the larger it became the more difficult it was to administer.[10] A god would be required to do so. Who could really believe that it might be more difficult to administer Singapore, Nauru, or Tonga than China, the United States, or India? Would a more complex form of organization be required? Even if both large and small states have their own peculiar problems, this only implies that in the matter of administration of states there can hardly be any "common standard for any place surrounded by four seas," some kind of magical administrative panacea.

In fact, because the area covered is very broad—something implied by the notion of a large state—it will encompass many different kinds of terrain that might even be separated geographically or topographically. The means of production in the diverse areas will differ, and so there will be many cultural groups, dialects, and writing systems. Although these need not lead to cultural barriers, they quite probably will tend in that direction. It is hard to please all tastes, and so with more tribes and peoples the chances of differences leading to conflict are greater. Indeed, even among a people who share one common culture, even among members of the same society or community, an increase of population will necessarily lead to greater separation of interests and even to contradictions and divisions.

Hence, the greatest difference between large and small states must surely lie in their constitution (Constitution/formation). Small states, such as the Greek city-states, have no problem with different levels of administration, but in large states there is clearly a need for some kind of administrative hierarchy, and so there is what might be termed the issue of "the relationship between the center and the peripheries." The existence of this issue gives rise to the danger of possible separation of certain peripheral areas, which invariably implies war, as in the Civil War in the United States or the referendum on Scottish independence of 2014.[11] Furthermore, unlike island states, continental states face the issue of why there should be one state rather than many. Why is it that some rivers and mountain ranges constitute political boundaries and others do not? At least in some cases, these boundaries must be created by human administrations rather than by nature.

The first issue that constitutes a problem here is how historical China became a geographically large state. One might say that historical China was gradually built up in the course of history, but what history or what modern state has not previously faced different periods and levels of history in one way or other, including clan-based, village-based, tribal-based, even state-based incorporation, absorption, and integration? Without being the chosen people of God or enjoying the blessings of a leader, how is it that there can be a China that has lasted for three thousand years since the Western Zhou in this territory? Is this simply an accident of history? Why has history not shown a similar preference for the Xiong-nu (Huns), who once held sway over the northern part of the central plain, or some other great people of the continental steppe of Eurasia, or the Greeks, who were roughly contemporaneous with the Western Zhou and the Spring and Autumn and Warring States periods in China, or even the later Macedonia? Besides the idea of undertaking military conquest, there is also the issue of holding onto power. Alexander the Great created the Macedonian Empire, which straddled the Eurasian landmass and North Africa, but when he died the empire split into several parts. This is rather similar to what happened a century later on the death of the Second Emperor of Qin. But the point is that shortly afterward, the Han succeeded the Qin and created an even larger empire that lasted for four hundred years, through the Western and Eastern Han dynasties. The same scenario was played out again and again before the present formation of China, whereas Macedonia never again appeared in history.

A large state is not the product of a wide and fertile terrain. An abundance of natural resources would seem to imply that a larger population could survive in a given area, but it cannot guarantee that these people will get along harmoniously or respect one another or form and maintain a sufficiently large population that they can establish and sustain a long-lasting, peaceful, united, and large state. The vast expanse of continental Africa is far greater than the plains of East Asia, yet it has never given rise to a large state on the scale of the Han or the Tang. Even at the time of the Roman Empire it would be very difficult to say that Central and Western Europe enjoyed the peaceful and unified rule of a large state, since not only were there constant wars, there were, even more important, divisions that are still manifest in today's European Union. It was only after its "discovery" by Europeans that the fertile land of North America produced a large state. Throughout history there have been several empires in the Eurasian landmass, including the Mongol Yuan dynasty, which entered into Chinese history, but all have passed when the wind blew them away. In terms of being a territorial state/civilization, and not just a civilization like ancient India or Arabia, and one that has continued as a large state, historical China, it would seem, is the only contender.

Vast distances and complex terrain will obviously weaken the administrative power of the center over the peripheries and lead one to the reasonable hypothesis that, without the support of an outstanding and effective organization along with the length of time in office, alertness, and wisdom in constitutional practice of a ruling class, then the very size itself will play against their being able to form a state, or at least if one happened to be formed then they would not be able to continue ruling it for long. Of course, the constitution of any state must come about as the product of basic political, economic, military, and cultural components; there is no such thing as a unique hidden weapon. Therefore, this chapter concentrates on examining the constitutional framework that encouraged, sustained, and expanded historical China so that it became a large state, and in particular on a *broad understanding* of the relationship of the center to the periphery.

The next section discusses the feudal system of the Western Zhou. This should not be taken as meaning that the relationship between the Son of Heaven and the feudal states was one of the center to the periphery.[12] Rather, I have good reason to place it in the context of a broad theoretical framework of the relationship between the center and the periphery and to analyze it as such. I shall look at it as constituting the earliest attempt to create the constitutional setup of a large state and as establishing the conditions for the later conversion into the commandery system (郡县制). Even in the Qin and Han, the feudal system was highly regarded for a time and served as one choice for the constitution of a large state, but based on a cost-effective analysis it was rejected or at least set aside as a form of political practice. The third section will consider the significance and role of the commandery system for the political constitution of ancient China. The fourth section discusses the geopolitical considerations that played a role in the administrative divisions of historical China. Faced with a large country encompassing many different forms of terrain and seeking to prevent separation or division and to strengthen the central government, the central authorities needed to adopt certain constitutional measures to deal with these considerations. Yet such considerations and practices are completely absent from Western constitutional practice and the academic tradition. The focus of the fifth section is another basic issue in the constitutional tradition of historical China, namely, that from the Western Zhou on, there was the additional remit of "bringing peace to the world under heaven," which went beyond administering the central, agricultural region ("administering the state"); that is, it was necessary to provide a basic structural framework to regulate potential conflict between an agricultural China and the surrounding peoples. Although this issue is not directly equivalent to the relationship between the center and the periphery, it was at least sometimes in history formulated as parallel to this relationship. Finally, I draw a conclusion.

The Feudal System during the Western Zhou

The Chinese of a later time generally depict the commandery system as having provided historical China with its strongest and most powerful form of centralized power appropriate to the constitution of a large state, but the first attempts to draw up this constitutional framework should be traced back to the feudal divisions of the Western Zhou, for three reasons. First, the landmass under the rule of the five emperors of early legends was comparatively small and the Xia and Shang were still states composed of villages or leagues of villages, whereas the Western Zhou was—or, rather, more closely resembled—a large state with a political class. Second, counting from the decision by King Ping to move the capital east in 771 BC, the royal power of the Zhou Son of Heaven went into decline. The feudal states struggled fiercely among themselves, but before this the feudal system provided the Western Zhou with more than 270 years of stable political order. Third, no feast lasts forever. Any structure created by human beings is bound to succumb to history. Long and short are merely relative. What matters is to what extent the feudal system contributed to the constitution of a large state and whether that contribution was irreplaceable in its own time.

For this reason alone, the contribution of the feudal system of the Western Zhou to the constitution of historical China should not be underestimated. Although the Xia and the Shang had already held sway over a sufficiently broad territory, they did not exercise territorial jurisdiction or rule based on territory. Rather, towns and their hinterland constituted "hot spots" that had no clearly defined boundaries. That villages were granted the status of "fief" under the Xia and Shang was far more a matter of recognition of the political reality of a confederation of villages. In contrast, historical records inform us that in the early years of the Western Zhou, a whole series of new factors were added to those constituting the organization of the state. In addition to confirming that the lower reaches of the River Wei and the middle reaches of the Yellow River came under the direct rule of the special central area, the royal domain, the Zhou Son of Heaven, "set up the feudal princes and split the land among the people." He divided all of the land outside the royal domain into many parcels of various sizes based on the population living there and placed his relatives or meritorious ministers as fief holders, leaving some villages unconquered.

He established states ruled by princes of the blood and other states ruled by others.[13] The fiefs of the Western Zhou brought to the earlier "separate" and "established" entities a new order that gradually led to the creation of a class and body of fief-holding princes.[14]

This implies, first, that the Zhou Son of Heaven was actively pursuing a form of direct political power and not simply passively recognizing the actual power of existing tribes or leaders. The use of "separate" and "established" entities shows that the highest ruling layer of the Western Zhou had the same awareness of how politics could be used to shape a state as did the Xia and the Shang and, more important, made efforts to begin this system. Second, although they lacked sovereignty, the feudal princes had land, people, and a political establishment and thus in these respects were very like modern states. The land and people held by the feudal states all came from the Zhou Son of Heaven. Since the power of governance of the feudal princes could not be rescinded and also came from the Zhou Son of Heaven, they too belonged to this one body. Third, the "establishment" of the princes led to the creation of a new level of political units and bodies and formed a political system for the empire centered on the Zhou Son of Heaven. The very creation of a large number of feudal states of royal blood and of others administered by meritorious ministers led to a relationship between the Zhou Son of Heaven and the feudal states that, in a broad sense, is of a center to the periphery. The Zhou Son of Heaven became the prince of the feudal lords, unlike in the Xia and Shang, when the king was merely the leader of the feudal lords. Fourth, the existence of graded "fiefs" is itself an indication of the rationalization of this system. Fifth, exchanges on the frontiers, whether of tribes or of dependent states, including military conflict, also led the so-called barbarian peoples beyond the fringes of the central area—the Rong, Di, Man, and Yi—to enter into the "world under heaven" of the Zhou.[15] Therefore, all of this attests to the political awareness of the upper echelon of political leaders in the early years of the Western Zhou and a new understanding of political order at that time, as well as a new way of thinking about how to rule the empire. Behind these ideas, it is clear that the Zhou Son of Heaven had sufficiently strong economic and political might to enforce his plans and ideas for the country. "Under the wide heaven, there is no land which is not the king's; within the land's sea-coasts, there is no one who is not the king's subject." This expresses not only the constitutional self-awareness and perspective of the Western Zhou but also, and more important, its active, conscious, clear political and constitutional practice. Thus, this is the earliest record of the political constitution of a large state.

It must be recognized that the feudal states of the early Western Zhou were not countries with clearly defined borders. There was a clear distinction, however, between the state and the wilds outside the direct rule of the Zhou king and the feudal states. The cities and their hinterland occupied by the king and the feudal lords were called "states," whereas what lay beyond was called "wilderness." People who lived in the states were people of that state, whereas those outside were "barbarians" in the original sense of this word. In the early years, this clear distinction between states and wilderness was not so explicit, since the Western Zhou had not yet become a complete territorial state. The core framework and strength of its political administration tended to rely more on various blood relationships. The relationship of the Zhou king and the feudal lords to their states was limited to that of states based on the state-wilderness distinction.[16]

Things being so, the idea of "separation" of territories and their people already shows that political administration had *begun* to move in the direction of territorial jurisdiction over people. The structure of this system, founded by the Western Zhou, already provided the conditions for the creation of a territorial state. At least by the Spring and Autumn period, the distinction between state and wilderness had gradually disappeared in the case of the feudal states. "When the rituals are lost [in the state], look for them among the barbarians": this statement indicates that the culture of the states already had a great influence on the wilderness.[17] Border conflicts among the central feudal states had already brought it about that their frontiers were tightly interlocked. This in itself is a sign that the feudal kings' territorial understanding and the effectiveness of their rule over their states had grown in strength, which shows, in turn, that China had already completed the transition from being governed by clan law to becoming historical China.[18]

The Western Zhou consciously discarded clan law and blood relationships as a means for establishing the organization of a large state. It cannot be overlooked that the Western Zhou granted feudal princely status to a number of meritorious ministers, thus creating states that did not share the royal bloodline. This step amounts to rewarding the capacity and loyalty of an elite and is a first step on the road to developing a meritocracy.[19] In the context of the times, this indicates a breaking away from the principle of clan law. It is an exception. Indeed, it may even be termed an infringement of the then "rule of law," the ritual order. Yet, later history shows that this was a great precedent precisely because it violated the principle of the ritual order of a law derived from clan-based relationships.

But the politicians of the Western Zhou looked not just to what was before their eyes. What they had to consider and do was actually much greater. In such a large territory, which handicapped transportation and transmission of information, the feudal states, each ruling in its own time, lacked sufficient political, economic, and cultural exchange as well as sufficient common interests and need for interdependence for them ever to meet, not even once. Could such a structure last for long? Time would gradually, and in the end completely, dilute the close ties that had begun in blood relationships, in theory leading clan law relationships to cede to territorial ones—actually, relationships of interest. Conflict over interests among the feudal states would necessarily give rise to struggles for land, people, wealth, status, and power. A constitutional framework buttressed by blood relationships would certainly collapse. With a clear understanding of this distant yet concealed danger, a great, farsighted politician, the Duke of Zhou, while taking feudal clan law as his foundation, created an orthodox state ideology, namely, the rites of Zhou, as a support for the constitution of his time. Thanks to rituals enacted at fixed times in honor of distant ancestors, he aimed to renew and reawaken and thus strengthen the recognition of the blood relationships with the Zhou royal house and thereby promote unity.[20] Even if he did not think this would be effective forever, as a first step it was a response to present realities and current issues, because, as the saying goes, "in the long run we will all be dead."

In this sense, the rites of Zhou virtually amount to the constitutional norms and theory universally shared and accepted by the then ruling class. This was not only a case of the individual's belief that "without studying the rites there is nothing to stand on," but also, even in the entertainments practiced by the feudal princes, there were to be no infringements of the rites of Zhou; as Confucius said, "If this is acceptable, then what can ever be unacceptable?" Even more important, the feudal states not of the royal bloodline were also obliged to observe the same rites. This implies that the Zhou rites only *appeared* to be clan law; in fact, they went beyond it.

This all happened in the eleventh century BC during the Western Zhou in a territory of around 1.5 million square kilometers. It can be said, with reason, that this was the earliest time in human history that an attempt was made to establish the horizontal distribution of political power necessary to a large state. It is the earliest manifestation of a relationship between the center and the periphery ever created by humankind. From the Western Zhou until the early years of the Spring and Autumn era, this setup remained in place and in large measure maintained stability and thus can be identified as a viable form of constitution for that time.

It is true, however, that "there is no form of organisation that can be founded on love."[21] Even the love of kith and kin could not sustain the practice of the rites of Zhou. The brilliant designs and political ideology of the Duke of Zhou could not hope to maintain the fight against the ravages of time forever, much less contend against the onslaught of vested interests founded on blood relationships. It was not only that elder and younger brothers, uncles and nephews who, in name at least, were part of the clan, quarreled with one another—disagreement leading to strife and even war, assassination, and usurpation—but also that this, in turn, led to others relying on their own political might to struggle for power, position, and other related benefits. During the Spring and Autumn and Warring States periods, rebellious ministers and rapacious sons were everywhere to be found.[22] The statement that "the rites were in disarray and music corrupt" implies that China at the time was no longer able to continue to govern according to the feudal system under clan law.

The most striking and most important feature of the constitutional framework of the whole state was the relationship between the center and the periphery. This had to be changed. Perhaps this is the first reform in the administration of China as a large state, and the most important one in Chinese history.

Many thinkers suggested ways of reforming the constitution. The basic plank of the Confucians was "to follow the old norms without error and without fail," or what modern legal scholars would describe as "following precedent," the aim being to keep in check the excesses of Realpolitik. On the basis of their idealized view of the Western Zhou, they proposed the core constitutional principle of their own ideal state: "When the world under heaven has the Way, then rites, music, war, and punishments proceed from the Son of Heaven."[23] The two key points in this program were that all administrative regulations and laws must be united, and that they should all originate from the Son of Heaven, that is, from the central administration.

The more pragmatic Legalists advocated a legal centralism for the whole country, as did the Confucians, and, even more important, after reflecting on the political experience of the rationality and failure of Western Zhou feudalism, they proposed a more refined solution to the issue of the relationship between the center and the periphery that would be necessary for the administration of a large state: a separation of powers such that "while governance reaches to the four quarters, yet the key is in the centre. The sage grasps the key and the four quarters carry it out."[24] This solution encapsulates a further important principle that is found in ancient China's constitution—a political elite drawn from the *whole country*, even though it had to wait for several centuries before other measures had been put in place to ensure that it could begin to be implemented.[25] The eclectic philosophy of *Mr Lü's Spring and Autumn Annals* explicated the pithy saying "there is no greater disaster than the lack of a Son of Heaven" as follows: "There must be a Son of Heaven in the world under heaven and so there is only one. The Son of Heaven must grasp the One to hold all in his hand. Unity brings ordered rule; division produces chaos." Or, again, "Unity brings ordered rule; difference produces chaos; unity leads to stability; difference to peril."[26] For *Mr Lü's Spring and Autumn Annals*, the core issue is to reestablish a unique sovereign political power for the state as well as its real control and political sway over the whole world under heaven.

Commanderies, Counties, and Other Measures of Centralized Rule

It was not only thinkers who thought about this problem; even before that, new structures began to emerge, far more practical and concrete. Toward the close of the Spring and Autumn period, out of necessity, there were already several reforms happening that today we might describe as being of constitutional significance, based on a drawing together of the strands of history. To cope with an expansion of their territory, the states of Qin, Jin, and Chu had already developed some new political units—commanderies and counties. The princes of the feudal states directly appointed officials with the authority and capacity to represent the princely administration over these units. They did not follow the earlier practice of naming feudal ministers who then ruled the territories in their own names.

At first this was simply a matter of necessity and applicable to certain special areas. By the Warring States era, the boundaries of the feudal states had expanded greatly, either by absorbing small states on their borders or by colonizing wastelands. It was very difficult to continue using the feudal system to guarantee these border territories since the feudal states were unlikely to allow any degree of autonomy to areas for which they had sacrificed many men and gone to great expense either to conquer or to cultivate. They would much prefer to turn these new lands into efficiently managed parts of their own states, on which they could rely for the direct transfer and maintenance of state resources. To prevent the loss of these new lands, they might need to make military preparations to fight off any potential covetous rivals or even engage in constant tit-for-tat warfare until they had overcome all opposition and rebellion. All of this required a strengthening of the organizational level of political control over these newly acquired territories. It was necessary to send trusted and capable persons to take control of both military and political affairs.

The ever-growing political and military confrontations among the feudal states during the Warring States period also brought about the reform that was the institution of commanderies and counties. Pragmatic political practices obliged states to remake their administration. It had to be more rationalized and more centralized, strengthening the direct, effective political control of the center over the periphery. They had to be able to unite, coordinate, and effectively move officials and shuffle resources, both personnel and in kind, within the state. Failure to do so would make it impossible to wage large-scale warfare, whether offensive or defensive.[27]

An additional factor leading to political reform of the feudal states was that, at the time, some of the rulers of the states had themselves risen from the rank of ministers of the same states. Through political adroitness or by collusion with other ministers, they had jointly seized hold of the state or administered it alone. An example of the former is to be found in the separation of the state of Jin into three parts—Zhao, Wei, and Han—while the latter is exemplified by the state of Qi. The new princes who had grasped power in this way were not going to allow their own ministers to play the same game and therefore would not allow their ministers' political power to become strong enough to threaten them. The history of their own usurpation taught them to examine the loopholes in the original structure, reform the structure, remake the distribution of power, and affirm the authority of the center.

Whether from expediency or careful reflection, or by imitation, or even because unreformed states were simply destroyed, the system of commanderies and counties was gradually adopted as the basic form of organization of all the states. The head of a commandery or county was commissioned by the prince and held power that the prince could revoke at any moment. The criterion for choice was no longer a blood relationship. It might not even be one of political integrity. Ability and expertise counted for more. Altogether, this led the princes to know their men and appoint them wisely for the purposes of administering the polity. The political mandate strengthened the power of the center over the periphery. In the competition between the various systems used in the states during the Spring and Autumn and Warring States periods, the system of commanderies and counties undoubtedly held the upper hand over the feudal system of clan law insofar as it could better guarantee an effective and stable rule for the princes and an effective use of personnel in political, economic, and military competition. The principles of political organizational efficiency and parsimony completely superseded the seemingly milder relationships of clan law.

After the establishment of the Qin Empire, the structure of commanderies and counties was erected in the whole country and became one of the most enduring forms of constitution in China's later history. Yet at the time the Qin united the six states, perhaps out of respect for history or respect for precedent, or owing to the ongoing influence of a political ideology based on the rites of Zhou, many politicians considered or advocated feudalism and once even tried to coerce the First Emperor himself. In the eyes of many politicians, who were neither stupid nor conservative, although the commandery and county system had its merits, it was only an expedient used in the political struggles of the warring states and once a new royal dynasty was established, the orthodox tradition lay in the feudal system of the clan law. Tradition is an unobserved and overwhelming conservative force. As a constitutional practice, feudalism had already faded from the scene, but as an old constitutional ideology, a habit, a tradition, its influence was still enormous, so much so as to virtually rule over the constitutional thought of all political thinkers of the time and become their preferred choice. It was the highly rational Li Si, with his clear awareness of the long-term consequences of feudalism and his logical deduction from the manifest history of the states before his eyes, who perceptively pointed out that feudalism would sooner or later lead to complete chaos in the empire and would certainly result in wars between the states and thus undo the work of unification that the First Emperor had done. To appoint feudal princes of his own blood had been the one thing that the ambitious First Emperor sought to do in making an irrevocable change for the world and in ensuring that everything came from himself and a completely new beginning was made. Li Si's perspicacity and consequentialism led the emperor to decide to divide the empire into thirty-six commanderies.[28]

Looking back, one might say that the First Emperor and Li Si were per-haps not good politicians, but there is no doubt that they were great poli-ticians. The basic structure of the relationship between the center and the periphery that they created was to last in China for more than two thousand years, an achievement that itself is testimony to their greatness. Yet greatness grows with time and needs to be nourished by achievements. The ancients could not possibly live through such a long period of time! Faced with the fact that the dynasty collapsed with the Second Emperor, at least for a time, (prag-matic) politicians had great difficulty in really believing in the superiority of the structure of commanderies and counties. The political power that emerged after peasant uprisings at the fall of the Qin, whether in Chu or Han, whether led by politicians or by high-ranking generals, for differing reasons chose or were forced to choose the feudal system.[29]

To consolidate his own power and prevent smoldering wicks from bursting into flame and engulfing the empire in chaos, the pragmatic politician Liu Bang, who became Emperor Gao of the Han, passed laws by which generals who surrendered first to him (i.e., rebel generals!) were made vassal kings if they were successful in battle. He eliminated the best-led and best-equipped armies under the high generals Han Xin, Ying Bu, and Peng Yue. He estab-lished an order that "those not of the house of Liu who made themselves kings were to be attacked by the people of the empire."[30] After this, the early Han did reflect on the role that feudalism could play in consolidating central au-thority and decided that the central government should send out officials in residence to the feudal states who would be the effective rulers of the states. But the cachet of the family name indicates that Liu Bang's constitutional thought remained stuck in tradition. He also believed that blood relationships were more important than commanderies and counties in maintaining and consolidating the rule of the dynasty.

It takes a major obstacle to make you stop in your tracks! Later there erupted a constitutional war that was to last nearly a half century and respond to the demand to reform the constitution at the practical level. Jia Yi (ca. 200–168 BC), Chao Cuo (d. 154 BC), and Zhufu Yan (d. 126 BC) offered proposals for constitutional reform to the central government in 172, 155, and 127 BC, calling for "reassigning the feudal princes so as to reduce their power,"[31] "tak-ing commanderies away from feudal kings,"[32] and "promulgating gracious commands,"[33] respectively. These were all geared toward a single purpose: to destroy the feudal kings' political and economic power, to weaken or break the feudal kings' political and economic grasp of their states, and to replace the imperial power with court-appointed officials. Whatever name was em-ployed, the goal was to completely remove the kings' authority to rule their ap-portioned states.

Yet the constitutional experiences of the United States, later, and of ancient China both alert us to the fact that constitutional disputes may not remain at the level of argument alone (though they may do so), sometimes unavoidably leading to war.[34] In comparison with political practice, even the boldest constitutional debate may prove too innocuous. The Han court hoped to use constitutional reform to prevent war, but the reform measures adopted by Chao Cuo led to, or at least advanced, the outbreak of war. The rebels of the seven states in revolt adopted the slogan "cleaning the prince's latrines," but, more important, they wanted constitutional reform, a change in the relation of the center and the periphery. The central government beat a hasty retreat and gave in to their demands, having the advocate of war against the barbarians, Chao Cuo, clad in court robes and chopped in half at the waist in public, but peace could not be bought back. Once constitutional talk and political plans both failed to deliver peace, war was the only option. Standing along with the victors in this constitutional reform was not the goddess of law, Athena, but the famous general Zhou Yafu. The winner was not an abstract constitutional value but a very practical, strong, political, economic, and military force.

It was a feat of arms not a battle of wits that defeated the power of local feudal rule and completely dispersed the last signs of superstition the early Han politicians had invested in the feudal system. A centralized government with commanderies and counties was the only possible form of rule. Although this could not bring an end to history or guarantee everlasting peaceful rule, given what ancient China was, only this form of constitution could *better* prevent division, civil war, and separatism provoked by the major flaws besetting the political framework of the state. When Emperor Wu of the Han promulgated Confucianism as the sole philosophical school, he went one step further in providing the central authority with an ideology. The Han adopted the institutions of the Qin and brought about a great reform in the constitution of historical China by comprehensively dealing with the relationship of the center and the periphery.

The basic feature of the system of commanderies and counties lay in that the head of the executive of each level of government was directly appointed in the name of the emperor by the central government and could be removed in the same way at any time. All the power held by the appointees came from the center; posts were not hereditary, nor could they be handed over to others. It was also forbidden to serve in one's native district and equally forbidden to remain in any one post for a long time. In the Han dynasty, subordinates were chosen and appointed by the mandarin from among local people. Later, some of these had themselves to be selected by the center. In this way, a system was established that more effectively provided checks and balances and mutual reinforcement. Under this system, mandarins had no interest in, and little possibility of, forming a tight network of personal relationships in their jurisdiction during their time in office. To rule effectively, they had to rely on local officials and so needed to make an effort, and had the capacity to do so, to win their support. On the other hand, to control the locality and their subordinates effectively, from time to time they also had to call on and rely on the authority of the central government. In this way, though they might be far removed from direct supervision by the central government for a long period of time, ruling independently in some remote spot—something that was unavoidable in a large country such as ancient China—nonetheless, no mandarin, provided he was not simultaneously in charge of the troops, the nomination of local officials, or local finances, could easily initiate division or bring about separatism.

Given this state of affairs, dynasty by dynasty, the central government continued to hold examinations, exercise supervision, and even send special observers to reinforce control over the periphery. For instance, in the Han dynasty, the center expedited an inspector of commanderies or a recording inspector of commanderies. Each commandery and county would send officials to supervise the counties and districts. Through these examinations and supervision, the central government was able to reach out to the grassroots with greater facility and guarantee uniformity of state administrative orders, which was a help in maintaining political stability and economic development. Relying on this system, every level of local government was at least carrying out its own form of separation of powers with checks and balances (the executive, military, and supervisory).

The system of commanderies and counties brought about a widespread weakening of the dangers of separatism inherent in the feudal system. This does not mean that this system or any other form of constitutional framework based on central control could guarantee that the risk of separatism could never again arise. It is not possible to rely purely on the law to uphold a system for any length of time without any political vision or practical wisdom. Still less is it possible to create a system that will withstand all forms of manmade or natural disasters such as wars or floods. Later history shows that if the central government lacks experience or ability, or has no long-term vision or is politically inept, or there are internal squabbles for power within the court and influence peddling, or there is insufficient regulation of subordinate, local officials, or there are invasions of peoples over the borders, or even if natural disasters and hunger lead to large-scale peasant uprisings, then the central authorities will be subject to division, separation, and the chaos of war. Human calculations cannot compete with those of heaven. No rule is forever and no rule can be expected to be relied on forever, even if it is a constitutional institution that guarantees stability through rain or shine.[35]

After the fall of the Han, China was divided many times, but after each division a new political force always arose to restore unity and reestablish the country. Based on lessons learned from the previous dynasty, the new one would move one step further and ensure a better political foundation for the administration of this large state. Even though later eras did not use the terminology of commanderies and counties, yet by drawing together the principles and framework of historical China they reproduced in fact the model of the commanderies and counties. For this reason, it can be said that "all genera-tions implement the policies and laws of the Qin."[36]

Geopolitics and Administrative Divisions

Not only was historical China a vast land, the geography and climate of its various regions were also very diverse. In fact, they are more diverse than those of any other country in the world, including any European or North American country. Thus, the means of production in each area naturally differ. Economic, social, and cultural development is uneven. In a self-sufficient rural economy, it would be difficult to build a large, multiethnic state, and even if this were done it would be exceedingly difficult to maintain it. Separation and divisions could easily occur.[37]

Furthermore, the vast distances and geographical features of the land have had a lasting influence on the formation and administration of historical China, which goes beyond any given dynasty. "Taking the land of one genera-tion to create the shape of more than a thousand years" is no exaggeration.[38] For this reason, "any country must rely on its mountains and rivers." At least since the Western Zhou, geopolitical considerations had already entered into the field of vision of politicians, thinkers, and military strategists. Typical po-litical strategists (纵横家) such as those of the Warring States era, whether arguing for horizontal (east-west) or vertical (north-south) alliances, or what-ever party's interest they were upholding, did not make suggestions or plans simply along abstract, rational lines. Rather, they paid careful attention to the geographical factors that bore on the political, economic, and military issues of the state they were in and its neighbors. The main reason Qin was able to unite the six states was that geographical Qin "lay at the headwaters of the world under heaven and so controlled the fate of the world under heaven." "Enclosed on all four sides by mountains and rivers, its geographical features gave it supremacy over the world under heaven."[39] Many of the measures im-plemented after Qin had united the country, such as extending the Great Wall, repairing roads, or constructing the Lingqu canal, all sought geopolitical ad-vantages and achieved notable geopolitical results.[40]

For this reason, subsequent politicians usually adopt a geopolitical view when assessing the constitution of a large state. This has become the norm in planning and implementing China's constitution. The various emperors, prime ministers, and other officials have all had to make an effort to famil-iarize themselves with China's topography, because this is relevant to how the various levels of political power throughout the country can be handled administratively, and how to get in touch with the barbarians living beyond the frontiers. The respective strengths of the periphery and center, the weight accorded to the borders and the heartland, the apportioning of military forces to the borders, the sources of state taxes, as well as the delimitation of local administrative boundaries and the various customs and peoples of each area are all important.[41] Moreover, these considerations must, as far as possible, be translated into the design of concrete administrative measures and political policy options. Domestic geopolitical considerations have, therefore, always played an important role in the implementation of China's ancient constitution.[42] This applies both to the earlier feudal system and the later commanderies and counties, where geopolitical considerations play a role.

For instance, such considerations affect the choice of a site for the capital city. It seems that any state with two or more political, economic, and cultural centers will have to face this question. But many dynasties in historical China, bar those that only sought control of border areas, placed their capitals in the north or northwest of the central plain, at, or close to, the center with its more developed economy and better transportation, so as to organize and regulate the forces of each part of the whole state in response to important political and military concerns. From this center, thanks to secure transportation, there would be access to grain, people, and other material goods. Overall, two important geopolitical considerations may be identified. The first is the possibility of knowing in a timely manner about incursions by the northern nomadic peoples and responding to them. The second is that from the center it was easier to control the east and south by both military and political means. This was aimed at using the geographical site of the capital to guarantee the important political, military, economic, and cultural influence of the central government on the periphery, which was a help in ensuring that state directives were met and political integration achieved. A typical example is provided by the early Han, when the issue was whether to choose a capital within Shaanxi or Luoyang. A geopolitician of the time discussed the issue as follows:

> Liu Jing said to Emperor Gao, "The capital should be within the Pass (i.e., in Shaanxi)." The emperor questioned this. The grand ministers of left and right were all from Shandong and most of them supported Luoyang as the capital. "Take Luoyang. In the east there is Chenggao, in the West Mount Yao and Lake Min. It lies south of the Yellow River and faces the Yi and Luo Rivers. Its defences are sufficiently reliable." Marquis Liu said, "Even though Luoyang has these advantages, yet it is small and covers less than several hundred *li*. Its fields are poor and it is surrounded on all four sides by enemies. It is not a place for deploying armies. Whereas the area within the Pass has Mount Yao and the Hangu Pass on the east, and Mount Long and Shu on the west. Its fertile spare land stretches for a thousand *li*. In the south is the plenty of Ba-Shu (=Sichuan), in the north the advantages offered by the pastures of Huyuan. It is enclosed on three sides and so can be defended. It is only open on the east, from where it can control the feudal lords. If the feudal lords are secure, the grains of the empire can be transported

by the Yellow River and Wei River, and sent west for the capital. If the
feudal lords rebel, you can go down the river and transport enough sup-
plies with you. This is 'a golden city of a thousand *li*, a heavenly town.'
The proposal of Liu Jing is correct." Therefore from that day Emperor
Gao decreed the capital should be in the west.[43]

From this it can be seen that the factors that led Emperor Gao of the Han
to choose a city within the Pass rather than Luoyang were a whole series of
geographical features with implications for military security and access to economic resources, as well as in-depth strategic considerations. These all com-
bine to support the core geopolitical consideration: providing more effective
military control over the newly united but still unstable areas in the east and
south of the country.

This in fact became a constant abstract constitutional principle. Even
when peripheral areas split the power, it would still remain the overriding
concern. The most typical and well-known case is that of the dialogue between
Zhuge Liang and Liu Bei at Long Zhong. Zhuge Liang analyzed the natural
geographical environment of each part of the whole country and assessed the
main forces within the empire, confirming Liu Bei in his invasion of the southwest as part of a long-term military strategy so that he could build a state
in what is now Sichuan.[44] Although after the Eastern Jin, China's economic
center gradually began to move south of the Yangtze, the various dynasties—
except those that sought to rule only a small corner of the country—still continued to place the capital in the north of the central plain. This was largely so
as to maintain the stability of the northern frontier. This had great significance
for effective political control and administration of the whole country, even if
it demanded the transportation of a large quantity of resources from south
of the Yangtze to the north at great cost. For this reason, dynasties from the
central plain or that took control of the plain all placed their capitals along
the imperial canal, especially in Beijing, so much so that it is said of the Ming,
"the Son of Heaven kept the gate of the state."

The administrative division of historical China also imbibed geopolitical considerations. It was not simply a separation of power between central
and local government. It served as a means of checks and balances on adjoining large administrative zones—even feudal states. It thus weakened the
possibility of latent separatism by local governments within the one large
state and reinforced the stability and security of the centralized system of
government.

One of the typical examples of this is the elimination of feudal territories in
the borders. In the early years of the Western Han, kings not of the royal surname were gradually eliminated and Liu Bang set up his own relatives as vassal kings in a desire to protect the dynasty. Very soon, however, the economic
power of some of the feudal states in the south grew, posing an economic and

political threat to the centralized structure of the early Han. The Han emperors first used the advice of people such as Jia Yi and Chao Cuo, or carved up the territory of the feudal lords by assigning land to even more persons, thus step by step weakening the strength of the feudal states, or they deliberately looked for the "faults" of the feudal states and took the opportunity to abolish several of them or reduce them in size. After the Rebellion of the Seven States was put down and given that some of the large feudal states had "several dozen towns and territory of a thousand square *li*" and thus posed a threat to the central authorities, Emperor Wu of the Han adopted the suggestion of Zhufu Yan and ordered all the feudal states to enfeof their relatives while all vassal kingdoms were forced to become feudal states, such that they would no longer have the strength to rebel against their superior. Moreover, they were subject to the commandery and came under the administrative authority of the central government. In this way the problem of the feudal lords that had beset the central government since the foundation of the Han dynasty was resolved.

Administrative divisions are drawn up so as to make the task of administration easier, but it is not so clear how their merits can be measured. For instance, division of feudal states into small parcels increases the levels of administration, and the more levels there are, the more certain it is that the central government will encounter the problem that "the tip of the arrow from the strongest bow will, in the end, be unable to pierce the finest silk of the state of Lu." Decrees and supervision from the center will have difficulty in reaching down to the lowest echelons. A proliferation of administrative divisions will give rise to administrative areas that are too small. A small local government may be unable to manage effectively, and on its own, problems that pertain to it. If the higher level of government is obliged to use a uniform policy for all, then this implies a loss of the significance of having a lower level of government. If local governments are allowed to go their own way and cooperate among themselves, then this may in some way lead to an increased risk of division. Even more important, an effective hierarchical administration also requires relatively stable layers and areas of administrative responsibility. This is conducive to local officials adopting the best policies for their local situation and to the central administration in its supervisory role. When there are too many layers or areas of administration, then it is easy to decline all responsibility. This shows that there should be an organized separation of powers.[45] Even fixed administrative boundaries may yet lead to hidden and unpredictable dangers. For example, it is quite possible that as the economy develops, the center of a country may shift, or the population may move, or some given area may produce an especially important commodity, leading to an increase in the economic might of a given area such that it poses a threat to the central government. In a particular political-social environment, it is highly possible that ambitious political-military leaders may emerge, as happened with the emergence of the state of Wu in the early Han. Once something like this happens, the vast distances and challenging topography of a large state make defense difficult. Conditions are ripe in the periphery for separatism of a sort that is largely beyond the scope of an ancient military-political power to overcome or even avoid.

This helps to explain the constitutional significance of two basic administrative principles of historical China—"mountains and rivers are convenient" and "the teeth of the dog match each other."[46] The former principle underlines that administrative boundaries should respect geophysical areas since natural geographical units are a strong influence in forming a common social awareness within their domain and determining the economic, social, and cultural assets of the inhabitants. Thus, respect for the natural areas delimited by natural features helps to prevent or avoid any clash of interest between people of different areas and thus assists in the effective government of each area. The latter principle is a deliberate attempt to use the drawing of administrative boundaries as a means of overcoming the implications of the former principle, that is, the use of local geographical advantages to induce separatism. This latter principle takes into account the formative force of local political, economic, and cultural features, and reacts so as to uphold the political unity and effective administration of the whole country. This is a necessary and probably requisite measure that is effective and of constitutional significance, one that a traditional large agricultural state, especially one that has complex geographical features, must take.

The earliest example of the dog's teeth principle may be traced back to the Qin dynasty. To enable the Qin army to effectively control the Lingnan area, which was the last area to be conquered, the farthest from the political core of the Qin court and the most inaccessible, Qin placed Guiyang County (now Lian County of Guangdong Province) in the south of Lingnan under the Changsha Commandery (now Hunan Province), and Tan city (now within the limits of Huaihua, Hunan Province) in the north of Lingnan under the Xiang Commandery (now Guangxi Province). At first glance, this type of administrative division without any regard for natural geography seems extremely foolish. But in a place where mistakes should certainly not appear, either it is an incomprehensible mistake or—the best explanation—it is not a mistake and may even reflect very wise administrative design, namely, that this administrative interlocking is undertaken to prevent the rise or formation of any geographical separatism within Lingnan. In fact, even a hundred years after the demise of the Qin, when Emperor Wu of the Han began to pacify the state of Southern Yue, which had declared independence at the end of the Qin, he was able to succeed in part because he relied on this seemingly stupid administrative measure with regard to Tan city such that the Han army entered Xiang Commandery in Lingnan very rapidly and accomplished unification of the whole country under the Han.[47]

Geopolitical considerations apply not only to the drawing of administrative boundaries in mountainous regions but also in the plain, and were used not

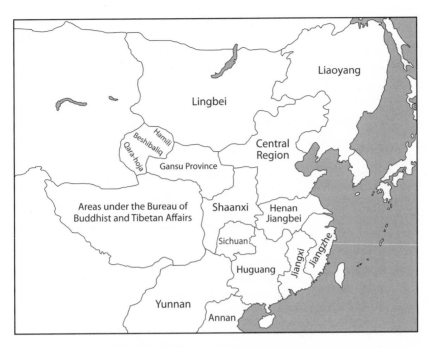

MAP 1. Administrative regions under the Yuan dynasty

only for the commanderies and counties but also, in the Han, for the feudal states. They were applied when the first Han emperor was seeking to control the minority peoples on the borders, and also were used by the various rulers of the central plain descended from the border peoples to prevent the dominance of the Han Chinese. (This will be discussed in the next section.) In fact, from the point of view of logic and even more from empirical evidence, more rulers of the central plain who came from border areas were weak than strong in comparison with rulers from the Han people and thus, in the interests of maintaining unity, gave—indeed had to give—more attention to geopolitical considerations when they drew up administrative boundaries.

The best example is that of the administrative divisions established under the Yuan dynasty. The Yuan dynasty was established by the Mongols, who were administratively much weaker than the later Manchu, who set up the Qing dynasty. According to Zhou Zhenhe, the Yuan provinces were not drawn up in the way that the Han, Tang, and Song had set up their divisions and showed no respect at all for the important mountains and rivers that had been used in the past: the Qinling mountains, the Huai River, the Nanling mountains, the Taihang mountains. None of the Yuan provinces formed one unit either geographically or culturally. Shaanxi Province crossed the Qinling mountain range and reached into the Han plain. Huguang Province included Hunan and Hubei and stretched across the Nanling mountain range as far as

Guangxi. Jiangnan Province also crossed the Nanling range into Guangdong. Henan-Jiangbei Province crossed both the Yellow River and the Huai River from north to south. Zhongshu Province lay both east and west of the Taihang mountains and included the three very different terrains of the Shanxi plateau, the north China plain, and the hilly region of Shandong. Jiang-Zhe Province ran from the Jiangnan plain down into the mountains of Fujian. Sichuan Province was the only area that resembled a traditional four-sided state with natural boundaries, but since the northern part of the central Han area now belonged to Shaanxi, the Qinling mountains no longer formed its natural defense and therefore Sichuan could not benefit from its geographical advantages.[48]

This strategy is to be seen not only on the macro scale but also at the micro level. It applies to both domestic and foreign affairs. One small example can suffice as an illustration. Between Guangdong and Fujian provinces, at the intersection of the East China Sea and the South China Sea, lies the small island of Nan'ao (南澳岛), 130 square kilometers in size. Control of the maritime area offshore from Guangdong and Fujian was of great strategic significance in history. Yet the administrative appurtenance of this island constantly shifted. Under the Qin and Han, it belonged to Southern Yue (today's Guangdong). But from the Liang dynasty (502–57) and through the Tang and Song (618–1279), Nan'ao was always placed under Fujian. Under the Qing (1644–1911), Nan'ao belonged to both Fujian and Guangdong simultaneously. Indeed, even the army camps on the island were split, that in the north belonging to Fujian, that in the south to Guangdong. The administrative division cut the island into two halves, even bisecting the military.

We can understand these difficulties only from a geopolitical angle. Although it would be difficult to prove, it seems that the shifts in jurisdiction in the early years may well have had to do with the island's remoteness from the political center in the north and the relative independence of Fujian and Guangdong. Although the Qin controlled Southern Yue, it as yet exercised no real power there.[49] Hence, from a political-military standpoint, Qin had good reason to leave Nan'ao under Southern Yue, when necessary expeditions could be mounted from Southern Yue against Fujian and Guangdong. By the sixth century, China's political, economic, and cultural center began to move east. At that time, Zhejiang and Fujian came under central control even more than Guangdong. Thus, Nan'ao became a strategic maritime point for exercising military and political control over Guangdong. The special administrative status of Nan'ao under the Qing, especially in military terms, locked Fujian and Guangdong closely together on the domestic front, though perhaps the more important factor is that of foreign affairs since the armies of both provinces were obliged to work, along with the islanders, in defending a place that was both easy to attack and difficult to defend since it was from the southeastern coastal region that ever-growing threats began to be made.

The real purpose of ensuring that administrative boundaries interlock is to establish checks and balances. However, geography or natural features or administrative regions themselves will not automatically lead to checks and balances. Therefore, the crucial point of geopolitics is not in the geography but in the politics. That is, in reflecting on, analyzing, and responding to political issues, one should never lose sight of geographic space or other geographical features that may be relevant. Furthermore, in the later history of China these geopolitical considerations always take into account the central government as their premise. It is only in such a system that administrative boundaries established according to geopolitical considerations may strengthen or weaken any given political possibility. Should the administrative or military heads of any two neighboring districts be father and son, friends, fellow townsmen, or teacher and student, and if they value their private relationship more than their loyalty due to the state or its representative—the throne or the emperor— the interlocking of administrative divisions will be meaningless. On Nan'ao island, the question is not whether it was necessary or sufficient to have two separate military camps. Rather, the issue was to have two military camps that were not dependent on each other.

Therefore, given the basic system of a central authority, the interlocking of administrative boundaries that remain firm over a long period results in the system itself being able to survive for a very long time. The system is intended not for one particular person, but for any superior official with local jurisdiction. For anywhere that harbors a latent political risk, the central government does not need to adjust administrative boundaries; it simply needs to supply the appropriate officials for the posts available, or at least to renew the military forces in adjoining districts and to enhance the supremacy of real political military power.

Thus, Nan'ao island is an example of an unseen power where boundaries interlock. In fact, in historical China, such forms of interlocking were common, as military jurisdictions and executive jurisdictions were completely separate systems but there was interlocking rather than overlap at the local level. This is what formed the mutual checks and balances, like having two forms of leadership.[50] In particular cases, administrative boundaries were altered (either in emergencies or on a long-term basis). In some places or areas, either as a general rule or in specific cases, the same official would hold both administrative and military responsibility. It was even such that the interlocking had economic significance, which was used to correct the balance of economic and political power between administrative regions so that each would balance and correct the other, to prevent the political and cultural elite of any district from getting politically jealous. Furthermore, the balance of economic power of the localities would be of help in ensuring the political balance of all places within the state.[51] For this reason, at many times, historical China witnessed many instances of administrative boundaries that seemed, or even were, inappropriate from the perspective of economic construction.[52]

The constitutional importance of geopolitical considerations in the drawing up of administrative boundaries for historical China was such that under the concentration of power at the center, faced with the concrete complexities of geography, topography, economics, society, and culture of *this particular* large agricultural state, effective political issues for the unity of China were transformed into technical issues of administrative management. One only has to compare a map of the topography of America or Europe with that of China and add to this the past or even present administrative map of China and that of America or the map of African states, to realize the particularity of the administrative divisions of China.

Administration of the Frontiers and Integration of Minority Nationality Areas

One major difference between ancient and modern states was that the former had frontier areas and lacked clear boundaries.[53] The frontier is an area. It is a geographic notion and yet it has more than geographic significance. It does not merely imply that a given district is far removed from the center of state governance, since it also has an implicit political, economic, and cultural significance. A frontier is at the limit of the reach of a state's political control and administration. The strength that comes from the sovereign—in ancient China this was the imperial court or the emperor who represented that court—has already been considerably weakened by the time it reaches the frontier. The spatial distance of political administration and the various levels of administration bring it about that the influence of the political center is unclear on the frontier in the face of the challenges and competition that arise from the various political and nonpolitical factors (though it may still have some measure of political impact). The competitor may be a small local political power, but it may very probably be another large-scale political power that wields sufficient political and military power and likewise also controls the same broad frontier region. If it is the latter, then behind the political competition, even military struggle, there is often some competition that pertains to the economy, culture, or even civilization, such as the competition between an agricultural and a pastoral civilization. A frontier is, then, often an area in which two or more political forces struggle to define their administrative control. It may belong to either of them, but neither has yet attained a monopoly of political control over this area.

Historical China has always had such frontier areas surrounding its central plain. These areas constitute a threat to the civilization of the central plain. Yet they can also be areas into which the civilization of the central plain might spread. Therefore, the outstanding politicians and thinkers of historical China through the centuries in their reflections on China never thought just of the central plain but would always (or even always had to) pay attention to the frontier areas and their peoples, considering the conflicts and exchanges between the frontier peoples and those of the central plain. From the Western Zhou onward, there existed the highly abstract notion of "governing the state (治国)" and "bringing peace to the world under heaven (平天下)." In fact, even in the Spring and Autumn era, the geographical scope of "China" as such was very restricted, normally to the central plain, and excluding areas that at the time still constituted part of the world under heaven such as Qin, Chu, Wu, and Yue.

The idea of "bringing peace to the world under heaven" naturally cannot avoid a discussion of military questions.[54] But of still greater importance is the question of long-term political governance, as, for example, was mentioned previously with reference to Alexander the Great and his state of Macedonia. Therefore, in order to understand the geographical construction of the border areas of historical China, one must first understand the special local administrative methods adopted on a long-term basis by the dynasties throughout history, including those founded by peoples from the border areas, for the frontier areas. These administrative methods for the frontier, although different from those generally applied in the central plain, nonetheless served the same function. They not only protected and upheld the dynasty that held power in the center but also, by their application over time, led to many of the peoples in the frontier regions gradually becoming assimilated into the Chinese nation. The original frontier thus could cease to be the frontier. And precisely because of this, administrative measures that may at first glance seem to be rather remote, subordinate, irregular, and local were in fact part of the constitution of the central authority of ancient China. What is related to the administration of the border areas of historical China also has to do with the constitutional integration of the frontier areas. Therefore, in this book, "the state" and "the world under heaven" are used merely to understand a notional framework of historical China and should not be read as clearly defined areas.[55]

The border areas of ancient China were vast, and clearly each had its own geographical conditions. Through the centuries, the state power of the dynasties varied in strength, and the opponents this state power competed with in the frontier regions also varied. The most urgent questions of administration of the frontiers differed over time. Likewise, there were many changes and evolutions in the administrative framework by which each dynasty responded to the administration of the frontiers. Students of the administrative framework of historical China with regard to the frontiers have many different ideas, and all are right.[56] Based on the level of the central government's trust, control, or integration of its frontier areas, one may broadly define three abstract categories of frontier.

The first is where the central government has already established effective control over the frontier and exercises a semi-military control to manage the area. In the various commanderies on the northern border during the Han dynasty, there was a subordinate official of the military-political office, an inspector whose real task was in fact to administer the border by a kind of military rule that brought unity and strength to the defense against the Xiongnu. At the same time, fixed regulations were set up to administer the region, creating all the necessary conditions for a real commandery. The Han also set up a military official under the military commander of the capital who was specifically responsible for dealing with minority peoples who surrendered to the Han court. This official gradually took on the task of administering the minority peoples and the "special area" that was on a different level from the commanderies. There was also a military administrative district under the Han and Tang called the protectorate-general. The western protectorate-general under the Han was on the same level as a commandery, but its subordinate divisions were not the ordinary counties but rather several tens of small states in the western region under military supervision. In the early years of the Tang, a Pacifying the West big protectorate-general was set up to the south of Tianshan and the northern protectorate-general to the north. The southern protectorate-general used military means to supervise the various small "states" south of Tianshan, whereas in the north counties were established that were the same as those in the rest of China. The Tang also extended the protectorate-general system to other border areas. In Liaodong and Korea, it set up the Pacifying the East protectorate-general; in the north, it set up the Shan Yu and Pacifying the North large protectorate-general. In the center and north of what is now Vietnam, it set up the Pacifying the South (Annam) middle protectorate-general, and in the southwest, the Upholding Tranquility protectorate-general. The Shan Yu, Pacifying the North, and Pacifying the South protectorates-general all had counties under them, much like the districts of the central plain.[57]

The second level is those regions where minority peoples govern and that have a comparatively closer economic and cultural relationship with the central government. Some scholars describe this kind as being either *fan* (藩, dominions serving as a fence around the central area) or *shu* (属, dominions dependent on the central government).[58] Of these two, the *fan* areas had a closer relationship to the central government, and the *shu* a more distant one. But over the long course of history the definitions of *fan* and *shu* are not so fixed; they are even quite unstable. In the Qing dynasty, the *fan* were the areas under the Superintendence Office, such as Mongolia, Xinjiang, and Tibet. In the early years of the Qing, the government's control over these areas was not the same as its control over the interior, but by modern times these areas had become part of China's territory. *Shu* refers to those countries such as Korea, Annam, and Burma that maintained tributary relationships with the dynasties of the central plain throughout history. Before the modern era at least some of these dependent states, at certain times, enjoyed very close relationships with the central government. Only after the coming of the modern era and as a result of many changes in international forces did they become independent nation-states.

The third level is those bordering national political powers that did not enter into a vassal or tributary relationship with the dynasty of the central plain. Historically, they are often referred to as "enemy" countries, but the meaning is not that of opposition, nor is there any negative sense of enmity. Rather, they are counterforces or matching forces. According to the proper sense of the term these political authorities had no relationship with the central political authorities of historical China at the constitutional level.[59] If they did, it was more in the sense of diplomatic relations today. Strictly speaking, they cannot be considered as frontier areas to the central government.

But the above discussion is simply an analysis at the conceptual level. Over the long course of history, as many powers rose and fell in the extended continental mass of East Asia, there was never a time when some dynasty or political power always had the upper hand. Therefore, the frontiers of each dynasty or political power were always subject to change. This holds not just for once-formidable "enemy states" such as the Xiongnu (匈奴), Tujue (突厥),[60] or Western Qiang (西羌), which when the power of the central plain was sufficiently strong were either partially or wholly subject to it and so became *fan* or *shu* of China. Sometimes the central government set up what resembles militarily supervised special administrative zones over territory that came under the jurisdiction or control of these powers, making them the frontiers of the central plain.[61] There were even some "enemy states" that for a time became very strong, such as Nanshao in Yunnan and its successor state of Da Li. This was conquered in the Yuan dynasty and by the Ming and Qing had become a province under effective direct rule from the central government.

But history does not all go in one direction. At specific times, very strong border powers did arise, forcing the dynasty in the central plain, not just temporarily but even for long periods, to use many methods to bring these enemy states to vassalage, even to the extent of ceding territory to them. Frontier areas that were originally under the effective control of the central dynasty, and even in some cases that had already been divided into commanderies and counties or departments and prefectures and brought wholly under the central administrative body, would be newly conquered by the bordering powers and occupied, or the central government would be forced to cede them to the bordering power, as with the Sixteen Prefectures of Yan and Yun. From this they became "old states" of the dynasties of the central plain or the dynasties that were content to rule over only part of China.

Besides using military districts to control the frontier area, the policy adopted by the central government of historical China in responding to the border people and their political power was basically that of "carrot and stick."[62] The "stick" was the use of military force to hold them down; the "carrot" was to entice them with the promise of economic benefits. It was a policy that was both hard and soft. But in practice the policy was neither unyielding nor fixed; it took account of local customs following the injunction of the *Record of*

Rites: "Improve their education; do not alter their customs; smooth out their politics; do not change their habits."[63] One could say that this was a case of local autonomy.

The earliest way of doing things was to establish a special administrative body in a given border area and to take the seat of the chief of each tribe as the basis for establishing departments and counties, allowing the local people's leader to establish a hereditary government. The classic example is to be found in the carrot-and-stick prefectures and departments set up by the Tang dynasty in the northwest.[64] When the Yuan dynasty was ruling the minority areas of the southwest it set up a similar system of headmen, so that each of the border tribes maintained, or basically maintained, its original socioeconomic system, method of organization, administrative bodies, religious faith, customs, and cultural traditions. The leader of each tribe was recognized as the political uniting force for that area and was granted the right, if he wished, to hereditary succession to the post of headman, becoming a support and even replacement for the Yuan court in ruling over the border areas. Apart from political adherence to the central imperial dynasty, economically speaking, there was a fixed tax, corvée, and fealty to the court, but all other affairs were left to the autonomous administration of the local headman.[65]

Although the methods may differ, taken in the abstract they were created as a substitute in cases where the central government of the central plain, owing to political, financial, and cultural constraints, was unable to employ the normal administrative systems in ruling over the border areas. For this reason, the central government ruled over, but did not administer, the border peoples and tribal districts, or rather, it governed them in name only. The advantage of this was that, while recognizing the difference between the Han Chinese and the barbarians as a basis, it first created and upheld unity and peace over a broad sweep of the border area. "One country, two systems," or even many systems, was beneficial not only to the political and economic development of the center and the frontier but also to the intercourse between peoples, and created the conditions for their future integration.

Yet the ruling powers through the generations were very much aware of the problems that this system of rule left behind, or could give rise to. First, the central government's allowing hereditary succession in the frontier districts meant that the political loyalty of the upper classes was not guaranteed. Should the control exercised by the center weaken or external forces intervene or increase, then the subordinates might become too powerful and even head toward separatism. This would affect not just the borders but also the interior. Second, even if the hereditary rulers of the frontiers maintained political loyalty to the central government, the system itself entrenched the political, economic, and social authority of the leading aristocracy. There was a lack of free movement in society, such that the lower echelons, in particular, gained nothing from the arrangement. From this it follows, third, that this was not only at variance with the basic constitutional tradition of historical China, which stressed rule by meritocracy, but also unhelpful for the constitutional integration of the feudal officials of the border area into a multinational state.

Considering the deficiencies of the governance of the border areas, when all the various conditions are taken into account and added up, or even simply to meet the urgent exigencies of some major event affecting the government, central governments through the years would shift from a policy of ruling but not administering to one of indirect rule, or even one using the normal administrative apparatus of direct rule.

A classic example of this is the headman system set up by the Yuan in the southwest. The Yuan dynasty itself was founded by a border people who set up a central authority in the central plain. Their ruling classes had a severe lack of capable administrators, but at the same time they did not trust the Han Chinese as officials, especially on the southwestern border. Hence, the situation differed from the prefectures and departments set up according to the Tang policy of "carrot and stick." In the area farthest from the political center of the dynasty, the southwest, the Yuan established autonomous headmen. This was not only a concession to the leaders of the southwestern tribes but also a measure to hold down the Han.

For this reason, after the Yuan, the Ming partially continued the headman system. On the basis of the size of territory under each hereditary headman, the Ming set up three kinds of nonmilitary officials: barbarian prefect, barbarian department magistrate, and barbarian county magistrate. This setup went some way toward bringing the barbarian officials into the officialdom of the Ming government. It weakened their local character and strengthened their administrative nature. It led to the later policy, enacted in Yunnan and Guizhou, of "moving barbarians into the normal track," that is, changing the hereditary barbarian officials into officials sent out on a rotating basis by the court, and thus strengthened control over the southwestern border.

The policy of moving barbarians into the normal track was the first major constitutional revolution undertaken by the center to resolve the question of administering the southwestern frontier. But because of pressure from Mongolia in the north of China, the Ming government was unable to use a similar policy on a large scale outside the southwest. Indeed, the policy was largely directed against the important barbarian officials; lesser officials found their power actually enhanced.[66]

Another border people that entered the central plain and established a dynasty, the Qing, continued and greatly expanded the shifts that the Ming had begun, reaching a peak under the Yongzheng Emperor, and linked to a series of political, economic, and social changes.[67] To speed up the policy of moving the barbarians into the normal track, the Qing government even launched several wars against the minority peoples of Yunnan, yet even up to the 1911 Revolution, the barbarian officialdom in many localities had still not ended.[68]

This was not only because the capacity of the central government was limited, but also because the implementation of the policy of moving the barbarians into the normal track caused the Qing government to realize that there were vast differences in the natural geography and human culture of the various areas in China's southwest, and that to impose a uniform policy was simply inappropriate.[69]

Conclusion

Although at times there was disorder, or rump states content to rule over a portion of the country, if the standard is not set just by recognition of the central dynasty but also by the expansion and, in particular, the long-term stability of the borders, then the borders of historical China were as a whole expanding and secure. In this respect, the relations between the center and the periphery for historical China were successful from a constitutional point of view. The basic structure and implementation of governance of the frontiers of historical China and integration of the localities were for the most part effective. After the Tang, the main reason for the expansion of the frontiers of historical China was the integration of peoples brought about by the Mongolian and Jurchen peoples from the north establishing dynasties in the central plain, leading to a reconstruction of China's borders. But the various regimes founded in the central plain by the northern peoples, as well as the Yuan dynasty, and particularly the Qing, in their political administration of the whole country basically continued the way of thinking and constitutional arrangement of the centralized authority of the Qin and the Han.

This shows that there is good reason to assert that "the hundred dynasties all implemented the institutions and laws of the Qin." This cannot be explained away as a result of the ambition of emperors through the years to "make the world under heaven their home," or as a thousand-year folly of countless Chinese people who lacked the creativity or imagination to produce some other system. The simplest explanation is probably that this system was the best practicable choice available to ancient agricultural China. There was no competitor or replacement. Furthermore, so long as the central government made no major errors of policy, and provided that all other conditions were generally stable—including no climatic or natural disasters or external political forces—then, given the agricultural economy as a foundation, the political framework of this central authority and the administrative organization that corresponded to it, from a theoretical point of view, was possible and, from a practical point of view, was indeed so. Although not continuously, for a comparatively long period this framework supplied ancient China with peace based on unity and brought it about that, insofar as the technology of the time permitted, a large agricultural state was able to flourish and become strong.

The central authority of historical China was always seeking readjustment and improvement and went through changes of terminology—commanderies, departments, circuits, and provinces—as well as changes to the permanence or temporary nature of administrative boundaries, and also microscopic adjustments to the separation and reunification of the military, administrative, supervisory, and fiscal levels from the central government to those of local government. Whatever the case, whether or not there were such shifts and adjustments, one thing that stands out as a political phenomenon is that ever since the Northern Song reestablished and perfected the central powerhouse, ancient China never again saw an internal revolt caused by separation of power at the local level, nor was there any separation that led to a dynasty being replaced. The only thing that happened was that border people invaded (setting up the Yuan and the Qing) or there was other social unrest (such as agricultural riots at the end of the Yuan and of the Ming), which led to a change of dynasty. Whether this proves that the system of central authority was effective and complete is worth asking.

A classic proof comes from the Qing, a dynasty set up to rule China by a border people. But even up to the end of the Qing, external threats and internal chaos were very, very serious. The Han Chinese armies that pacified the Taiping Revolt were private armies—the Xiang and Huai armies—that grabbed a lot of power both in the center and on the periphery. But before the 1911 Revolution the central government of the Qing could still exert effective control over the peripheries. The rebels sought to draw Han Chinese officials to their side with calls for a "greater sense of the nation" illustrated by slogans such as "expel the Tartars."[70] But the high officials of Han nationality on the frontiers did not take this opportunity to engage in separatism for the areas under their control. This was not simply out of blind loyalty to the Qing royal family but, rather, probably because they had a view that went beyond narrow Manchu vassalage versus Han nationalism. They were politically and personally loyal to the constitutional framework of the central authority of a civilization that was both ancient and new. At least to some extent, this may be attributable to a traditional constitutional ideology with which they had grown up.

Some of the tributary nations of traditional China, such as Korea, Annam, and Burma, became separate and independent states in modern times. Other tributary states like the Ryuku Islands came and remain under Japanese control. But this cannot, at least not fully, be attributed to errors of policy or application on the part of the Qing court with regard to frontier administration. Much more fundamental is the fact that, from the nineteenth century onward, China was faced with a great revolution the likes of which had not been seen for millennia. The rise of powerful states brought to the countries and political authorities of East Asia a marked change. Heading a large agricultural state, the Qing government was at first powerless, and then incapable, to respond effectively to this great global revolution, which posed a challenge to historical

China's constitution.[71] In the face of the challenge, the late Qing court lost not only tributary nations but also a great part of its own territory, such as Taiwan, and finally rule over China itself. But to attribute all this to the system of border administration or even to elevate it to the lack of the all-around panacea of a democratic Constitution is to go too far.

Reflecting on the victory of the commandery-county system over the feudal system can also help us understand the constitutional revolutions China has had to face in modern times. The victory of the Qin-Han commandery-county system does not mean that the feudal system of the Western Zhou was a complete failure, still less a mistake from the beginning, which should never have happened. The incessant wars between the princely states in the Spring and Autumn and Warring States eras do indeed show that the feudal system was no longer able to create the peace, stability, and order that the people hoped for in this land at that time. It implies that they needed to create a new constitutional format.

The Western Zhou was indeed a peak moment in China's ancient society. Its "establishing the many feudal princes and dividing up the land for the people" not only was a case of constitutional innovation by which "there was a new foundation for an ancient nation" but also brought about integration of the various peoples and tribes in the areas under Zhou rule. "When looked at in the light of the Way" (*Zhuangzi: Autumn Floods*), the feudal system of the Western Zhou represents the political elite of the central plain in those times, which beside the use of military might, established political unity—"to even their politics"—and was the earliest attempt to provide a constitution for a vast state. The Western Zhou feudal system was the best form of concentration of power that was practically possible at the time, just as today the European Union is the best form of centralized authority that can be achieved, even if it is not the ideal form of centralized power for European states.

Even though the Western Zhou constitution finally broke apart, this does not mean that it failed. The Western Zhou left behind a great agricultural state. The rites of Zhou provided a constitutional template for this large agricultural state and facilitated the implementation of a constitution for a large state. Even the wanderings of the political elite among the various states during the Spring and Autumn and Warring States eras were exchanges on the political, economic, and cultural levels oriented to the whole country. Many aberrant forms of Chinese characters as well as ways of writing were to a large extent unified; speech was improved in the exchanges of the political elite, producing a "refined language." Without these foundations, the unification of the script under the Qin would not have been possible. Likewise, the Qin court's "officials as teachers" and "law for teaching" (*Hanfeizi: Five Vermin*) would have been impossible.

Hence, the criterion for assessing the system of historical China is not whether it was always so and hence is "universal," nor whether it matches some theory or other, nor whether it meets some unsubstantiated but beautiful prospective ideal, but whether, at a given historical time and within the various economic and social constraints of the time, it fully utilized all the resources that it could use and imagine to produce the best possible political and social conditions for people's lives and the emergence and growth of a large state. And, moreover, *only it could do this!*

A realizable constitution for a great state is an important condition for its emergence and growth, but it is not the only, or a sufficient, condition for this to occur. A system, even a constitution, is not God. In this world, there is indeed no system that, relying on its own resources alone, can suffice to ensure the long-term peaceful existence of a state. For this to happen, in addition to the system, there must be the support of economic, social, and cultural factors, including prudence on the part of political rulers as well as wise and timely responses to important questions of government. At the least, one should not commit too many great errors and one may even need assistance from heaven: "a fair breeze and timely rain."

Since this is so, we may conclude this chapter with a purely academic question: why does contemporary academic discussion of China's constitution lack any discussion of China's geopolitical considerations and practicalities beyond a reference to feudalism and commanderies and counties? Given that this thread of thought has had a long-lasting and profound influence on historical China's constitution and that, in the world of Chinese historical studies, relevant theories and reflections, publications, and writings have a long history that still have considerable influence today, why have they not influenced studies of the constitution?[72] This in itself is an issue that deserves consideration in the academic world. The main reason could be that the leading contemporary language and models used in talking about China's constitution come from a European and North American tradition. Although there were some—albeit superficial from the point of view of ancient China—geopolitical analyses and discussions in ancient Greece and Rome,[73] because of the geographical features of Europe and North America as well as the nature of those countries, plus the fact that the international system dominated by Europe and North America has produced geopolitical studies at an international level, it is no longer necessary to reflect on the geopolitics within a state at a constitutional level. This is, of course, merely a hypothesis or something said in a hurry, but it does point out that theories about the constitution of contemporary China could draw on the experience of historical China, even if to do so may first be a challenge to the scholarly self-confidence of contemporary China's legal scholars.

CHAPTER TWO

Ancient China's Cultural Constitution

A UNIFIED SCRIPT AND MANDARIN CHINESE

Su Li

Speech without writing will not run far.

— CONFUCIUS[1]

The Lord ... said, "So they have been forming themselves into one nation, speaking the same language! This is only a beginning. Now they are making this [the tower of Babel], later I am afraid there will be nothing that they cannot do."

— GENESIS 11:6

Definition of the Problem

The border areas of historical China were vast. Once a centralized authority had been set up, it could never do more than use military force to control them, that is, it used military might to establish and sustain political unity. Yet, since ancient times, China has also practiced civic rule—unified political governance under a central authority—rather than military might. Civic rule is not only a matter of executive governance based on written law codes and ancestral statutes (constitutional precedents); it is also very much like what Weber described as "bureaucracy" and "a legitimate authority supported by professional bureaucrats."[2]

Therefore, the significance of reading and literacy is obvious. For the training and formation of a political and cultural elite, indeed even just to create one generation after another of people with political ideals, feelings, and imagination who would have a greater sense of belonging to their state and civilization, and not just to their birthplace, residence, or the agricultural society in which they lived, literacy was of the utmost importance. It was also very important for the governance of this vast territory by means of an executive organization run by a political and cultural elite chosen through examinations, which could ensure that the commands of the central authority were implemented, thus constantly expanding the influence of the political organization and culture of historical China. Reading and writing were from the beginning at the root of China. They relate to China's constitution; indeed, they may be described as *constituting* ancient China's cultural constitution.

This was especially so in historical China. Unlike most laws, the basic role of a constitutional institution is to constitute a common political body, a state, *on the basis of a common social body*. This is done by means of the arrangement of various formal institutions and the public goods they produce to strengthen the political and cultural cohesiveness of the common body. The states of Europe were at first based on cities, whereas those of modern times are based on nations. When the United States was formed, it was through the union of thirteen North American colonies. This goes to prove that when these states were formed, the common social body that was to form their basis was by and large already in existence. The tradition of state theory and constitutional research extrapolated from these examples can pass over, and indeed it generally omits, this prepolitical constitution or preconstitutional question and runs straight to the question of state institutions or organizational arrangements.[3] But as was said in the previous chapter, in the vast territory that is today called China there were countless small-scale rural villages scattered around, and even though an agricultural economy and geographical proximity would bring the people to share many things in common, self-sufficiency and poor communications brought it about that "the people could reach old age and die without having met each other" (*Daodejing* 80). Also, the height of the mountains and size of the rivers gave rise to many peoples and many tribes. It would be very difficult to say that they were one body. The common body was shaped by the dynasties throughout history on the basis of politics, the economy, the military, and culture.

This chapter focuses on the unification of the script and its two aspects: reading and speaking. The first is a matter of literacy, whereas the second largely has to do with the language used by ancient readers (officials) to communicate with one another. But this has nothing to do with the right to education in Mandarin Chinese or any other such constitutional linguistic rights, nor is it a matter of how literacy might change a person's destiny. This chapter will show why reading and literacy were very important *for China*.

Unification of the Script

Many researchers have pointed out that the appearance of writing and of politics cannot be separated. Writing is essential for unified governance since through its spokespeople a political center is able to promulgate regulations over a large area.[4] China's ancient oracle bone script and bronze inscriptions recorded important affairs of state, whether sacrifices, wars, natural disasters, or unusual astronomical phenomena. The territory of both the Shang and Zhou dynasties was already quite large.[5] Their main institution was feudalism, a special kind of separation of powers, but there were always some political affairs such as suppressing rebellion or cooperating to oppose the incursions of the northern pastoral people, which required coordination among the feudal states to arrive at unified action. Therefore, it was inevitable that coordination and management were carried out through information transmitted in writing. During the Spring and Autumn and Warring States eras of interstate warfare, for domestic affairs such as administering their commanderies and counties, the states needed a means of communication that would cross space and time, and efficiently organize and coordinate precisely unified political and military action. Even if one cannot say that the possession of writing implies a large state, writing is essential to establish a state with a unified administration. Up to now all societies that lack writing are merely tribal societies.

Writing is an aid to the unification of laws and institutions, to a situation where commands and prohibitions are obeyed and an efficient bureaucracy can be set up. It also assists the accumulation and gathering of the political experience of each place and even of many people across time and space. Therefore, from the Spring and Autumn period on, writing was widespread and common in all the feudal states, including—among the students recruited by Confucius—the rites (including laws) spread down to the common folk, and including all the written laws promulgated by the various states.[6] These things all indicate a strengthening of civil government.

In addition to the need for large-scale familiarity with writing to help its maintenance and transmission, the written words themselves also pose several problems. First, written words can be used to overcome the gaps of time and space, but time and space can also shape and distort them. A large state is more likely to encounter the problem of lack of uniformity in script. In a small state, especially a city-state, there is only one political and economic center, and so writing can easily be concentrated and monopolized by the temple. Indeed, the cultural elite will want to congregate at this place and even without any extra effort will communicate among themselves and so bring uniformity and regularity to writing. But a large state has vast frontiers, communication is poor, and the economic and social development of each place will be comparatively independent. Several political and economic centers will easily develop, and inevitably so. When writing spreads down from the center and is used by the community of the political and cultural elite of each economic and cultural center, then it will easily lead to the independent development of the script and even to rejection of the script of other people. As time goes by and the script spreads further, what was once a united script will in time cease to be uniform.

All changes in the form of Chinese characters, whether borrowing homophones, creating new characters, or combining characters, must all first have their origin in the customs shaped in each region. Given the lack of communication between regions, many accidents, such as mistaken characters and lacunae in texts, could all have first occurred in a given area—"mistakes are many and are handed down"—and so they become independent versions.

Second, a large state that carries out its administration efficiently through writing is also demanding of the script. To ensure communication and preservation of archives, the characters cannot be as difficult or complicated as those on the oracle bones or bronze inscriptions. The characters must be simplified and writing must be fluent. But in a large state such as China the simplification of the characters must first come about in peripheral areas, and so it may be that the script in each region will vary. If there is a lack of sufficient communication between regions, then the simplifications of each locality will ossify over time such that within the region writing will spread more quickly and more broadly but communication between regions will become more difficult to the point of becoming impossible.[7]

The effective communication of the script across regions, therefore, requires a certain force or institutions that from time to time unify the script and ensure its standardization. This, however, is something that rural society, with its native self-sufficiency, is unable to supply and hence it cannot shape the institutions to standardize a script on the national level by itself. Once local elites have started to use and transmit their own variants of the script, then over time they will reformulate the political and cultural identity of each region and hence be unable to support or even to maintain the political unity of the whole state. When the Qin united China and founded a centralized rule, this problem became especially important and relevant.

But there is one other problem. In a small state, central authority is perhaps that of one man or of a family clan. The Qin and Han dynasties were large states with vast frontiers that could not truly be ruled by one emperor alone, however much his authority was centralized or even "tyrannical." He had to rely on the political elite and so set up a bureaucratic system that distributed responsibilities down the hierarchy from the center to the localities. This had to be, and necessarily was, highly rationalized administration, and a rationalized administration will certainly regulate the bureaucracy and unify local government. It must have one law code. It must not only lay stress on the organization of institutions and due process, but also value the formality of legal records and legal documents. Only in this way will "laws run and prohibitions be effective," only then can "one evaluate what is done by assessing the roles assigned," only then can there be the rule of a centralized authority that lives up to its name.[8]

Therefore, the unification of the script carried out by the Qin is of constitutional significance for the political governance of agricultural China and its formation by means of this governance. Moreover, this significance is not limited to the Qin. One might say that because the script was unified it was possible to achieve the shift from the Chineseness (*huaxia*) of the village states of the governance of the Shang and Zhou to the state with broad frontiers of political China, and it also allowed a unified government with written laws to become a real option for political governance. From the center down to the localities not only was it possible to rely on officials trained in administration of the law and in a law that had become a tool by which the center oversaw its officials, but as the laws and regulations in the uniform script spread more among the people, it was enough for officials to use laws unfairly in matters of importance for some of the people to be able to directly appeal to the imperial authority regarding them for acting against institutions or laws, and so there emerged the "appeals to the throne" or "appeals to the capital."[9] In this sense, the civil government of ancient China led to an expansion of rule by law, and rule by law must be carried out through writing—even if you say that this rule by law *does not embody the value it has today.*

History records that the first step in the unification of the script was unifying the characters, bringing uniformity and normalizing the various forms of characters that had formed in the feudal states and local areas and abolishing regional peculiarities. The second step was in fact even more important. It was to completely do away with the former standard large seal script of the bronze inscriptions and replace it with a script based on the characters used in the state of Qin. The new script relied on consultation on the characters used in the six other states, and it adopted the small seal script as the official script. In actual practice, however, great use was made of simplifications, and the scribal script, which was easier to use and more efficient, was taken as the norm for public documents.[10] This was perhaps the most important national standard of ancient China.

Yet the most important step was perhaps the third. In the process of unifying the script and on the basis of this script, there arose a community of professional specialists, officials who were adept at using this standardized script and who thereby communicated important political, legal, and military affairs of state. Thanks to them, unification of the characters truly became an institution that brought life. In wartime, they were dispersed among the people and spread news like wildfire. As soon as peace came, they could reorganize on the back of the new government and continue to multiply and spread of their own accord. This corps of officials with such vitality and this institution could use its own product to ultimately edit the diverse forms of the characters found in each region.

This proves that unification of the script is not simply a matter of individual literacy or the spread of culture in society! Rather, it is first and foremost a matter of establishing a cultural community, from the center to the peripheries, among all levels of government administrative officials and their key assistants, all the important generals in the army and their important aides, as well as all the elites throughout the whole country being prepared or having the ability to take part in government of the state. Even across time and space, they could still communicate and, in the process, get to know one another better, learning to share similar ideas and to trust and rely on one another. With this community based on the common recourse to writing for communication, they were able to implement the decrees and laws of the center promptly, write prompt reports, gather information and record it—information that had to do with important news about political governance from every place in the whole country—and efficiently delete, or very greatly reduce, errors and discordant voices in the communication of information and its storage. In the exercise of civil administration through the centuries, they gradually formed and shared a professional ethics and a political-cultural loyalty to Chinese civilization and not simply to a given emperor or dynasty. They would share similar value judgments, modes of work, and an institutional environment. Hence, they became a professionalized and specialized community of the political and cultural elite that took as its natural profession political governance and administration.

With this professionalized, specialized, and departmentalized bureaucracy, and a bureaucratic institution, even if the Qin and later dynasties seem to be, from a constitutional point of view, a case of imperial rule—and indeed, it was often the case that a decree from the emperor (especially the founder of a dynasty) ruled all—any state decision was in practice the fruit of participation by many more of the political elite. This participation was conducted not only through meetings, discussions, or other forms of face-to-face communication, but also via a whole variety of written means. The participants, therefore, might be scholars of all levels from anywhere in the state, from within the system or outside it. The Chinese emperor, therefore, could not have been an isolated tyrant as people in China today imagine him to have been. The latter model is more like the image in the West of the absolute monarch of the later Middle Ages or the early modern period. Even if it was the case that the emperor had the last word, this was like on the battlefield when the commanding general orders an advance or a retreat. It is a requirement of the institutional position held and not an expression of some personal despotism: the system does not allow anyone else to deputize for one. It is not that there is no physical obstacle. Whether it was a matter of waiting for the emperor's decision or the many bits of information that would support his decision, or sorting out all the various sources of information to resolve an issue up to the final carrying out and realization of the decision, the participation of the elite scattered across the country was required at all levels. Thanks to writing, the accumulation of knowledge did not need to rely on persons. It could still cross boundaries of time and space. At least in part, it was possible to rely on writing to accomplish a task.

On the other hand, because the elite were scattered from the center to the peripheries at all levels, to the farthest corners of the empire, this bureaucratic community was itself virtually the authoritative centralized institution. Their existence and service in the departments maintained the running of the central institution. This centralized bureaucratic system, with its long-term stability, was also able to strengthen the political and cultural cohesiveness of the whole of society. The elite culture could seep down and attract other currents and the cultural investment of ordinary people, so the number of scholars would increase, and not only surround and support the court or the central government, but also in certain, or even most, matters become the medium of exchange of information between the state and the people, saving the officials or government the expense of communicating information to the people, leading to a pattern of joint governance and complementarity between the emperor and the gentry.[11] Thanks to this, the political outlook of unity fostered in the Qin and Han times gradually led to the realization under later dynasties of a peaceful, rational large state with a vast population and a historically unprecedented uniformity under the governance—according to the rule of law—of a political and cultural elite. The institution of a unified script was partly responsible for bringing this about.

Thus, we might also be able to understand this from another angle and ask why the Qin in its time declared that "ministers should be seen as teachers."[12] It may not be only because the Qin adopted a Legalist culture. It could wholly be because at a time when knowledge was not yet widespread, the Qin court had to employ all the scholars as officials—rather like the "intellectualization" of Chinese cadres in the early 1980s—for it to be able to establish a central government system that relied on writing to function. "Liu Xiang had not studied when he was young": perhaps because the scholars of his time, apart from the nobles, had basically all been absorbed into the civil bureaucracy of the Qin.

As a by-product, a unified script would certainly also lead to another political shift: a reflective and thoughtful politics, or what Weber termed a rational politics. As communication in writing increased, it would necessarily bring it about that officials at all levels would gradually develop refined habits of expression, reading, and writing, obliging people to continue to raise their attentiveness to new heights, to a profound study and reflection and understanding of characters, paying attention to accurate communication and refined taste, and so fostering an ability of consummate literary expression and its accompanying understanding of written characters. This ability is a help by which people can overcome the limits of time and space. Understanding and sharing come from different areas and times and, along with different personal experiences, allow the direct experience of previous generations and other people to become the indirect experience of many readers. This would not only shape a sense of belonging and identity, it would also greatly promote Chinese civilization, not only politically, but also in terms of literature.[13]

All of this can be seen naturally. We may even include literary works, literary contacts, and literary creations that seem to have nothing to do with politics. Everything could be transformed into a form of political soft power, such that once scholars had entered into this tradition they could oppose it only with great difficulty. Writing itself does not in fact have any attraction for the reader. The attractive force of writing comes from the thoughts and feelings of the people recorded in writing, the subjective and objective worlds of literary expression, the comprehensiveness, depth, detail, and originality of expression. Without Confucius, Mencius, Laozi, and Zhuangzi, there would be no *Spring and Autumn Annals* or *Book of Odes*. Chinese characters alone do not suffice to construct the Chinese civilization of the Spring and Autumn and Warring States periods, and there would naturally not be the glamour of this civilization. Without the *Iliad* and the *Odyssey*, without Plato and Aristotle, there would basically not be the ancient Greece we can imagine and be fascinated by. Therefore, a civilization that is sustained by writing will not only attract individual scholars, but also indirectly attract illiterate people in distant, far-off, and remote places, and in this way it became a very special form of manifestation of the integration and formation of Chinese politics, society, and culture. Indeed, it even attracted people outside Chinese civilization, attracting those who had never been to China. Over East Asia and some parts of Southeast Asia, Chinese civilization had enormous influence, and although commerce and trade may have been a factor, the greatest impression was left by works of literature.

With a unified script it was possible to have the later systems for selecting the political and cultural elite through writing, be it the poetry of the Tang or the operas of the Yuan, or the different types of essay and especially the imperial exams, which we shall discuss later in detail and which deserve to be described as truly great.[14]

The Significance of Unified Speech

The constitutional significance of a uniform script has been publicly recognized throughout history. Yet, on reflection, for the formation of historical China, this is only one part of its cultural constitution that could be supported and guaranteed by a formal state institution. Of greater importance and of greater difficulty to manage effectively by means of formal institutions is speech. Speech is intimately related to writing, but its users are far more numerous and it changes easily and in many ways. The significance of unified speech—Mandarin Chinese—for the construction and maintenance of historical China has been much neglected.

"In the beginning there was only one language; everyone spoke the same language" (Genesis 11:1). This statement broadly applies to the situation in early China. The "state" in the time of the Xia, Shang, and Zhou dynasties is said to have been composed of villages or alliances of villages. From this we can deduce that the ruling classes of these dynasties shared the same, or a similar, language, such as the "refined speech" mentioned by Confucius.[15] Yet as the community expanded and the territory increased, newer communities and offshoot political communities would be brought into or separated away from the main body. They would be scattered around and, although not cut off, yet be in areas that would only rarely interact. Owing to many attendant circumstances, speech would separate and deviate from the norm. As each new form developed in isolation, the common stock of the original language would certainly be torn apart. Without any corresponding regular communication, influence, or correction, each offshoot linguistic community might repel others and vice versa. Even if the written script were unified, it is enough that transportation and communication were inconvenient to bring it about that there would be no way to ensure that the spoken language of the ordinary people in each area would remain the same. Changes in speech influence writing. Not only does speech have a manifest influence on phonetic scripts, it also influences a nonphonetic script. For instance, the Chinese character 冇 (read *mou* in Cantonese and meaning "has not") after a long time was not written the same way everywhere.

Under modern conditions, the people of a comparatively large area, whose speech may not all be the same, will be helped by the strong political force and economic force of the central government—abetted by commercial interests and personal contacts between different places—to form a multinational state even though this may be a seedbed for future separatism. In ancient times, when communication between people was highly inconvenient and the state was founded on an agricultural economy, the radiating influence of the political, economic, and cultural center was very limited, and this would cause a lot of hassle. It is unthinkable that one could simply rely on a written script to maintain a stable political and cultural community *over a long period of time*.

A classic example is that of the Roman Empire. At its height the empire flourished, but as its borders expanded, Latin, which was originally simply the local language and writing of Rome, was taken by the Roman army to every province and widely used throughout the whole of Europe. But the empire soon weakened, its frontiers were reduced, and it fell. Even though Latin was retained as a written language by the political, religious, and cultural elite of Europe for as much as a thousand years and in some fields is still in use today, in the original heartland of the Roman Empire, the north coast of the Mediterranean, which was not far away from Rome and where communication by sea and land was very convenient, after only some few hundred years, each place evolved its own dialect. The original Latin-speaking community was torn apart. Once speech changed, the phonetic script in which it was recorded also changed. At first different accents, dialects, and even languages emerged, and then there were communities with different scripts and even with different cultures, until there were nations each with its own language and script. Inasmuch as other political and economic conditions allowed, even or only thanks to external divisive forces, in the modern era there appeared a whole set of independent nation-states.[16]

Chinese characters are ideographic and not directly linked to pronunciation. To a great extent, the written characters are independent of any pronunciation, and even if the difference in pronunciation in various areas is very marked, the written characters will not be affected. This has helped Chinese characters to continue without relying on pronunciation and to develop independent of sound. People who do not share the same dialect in any way whatsoever but do share the use of Chinese characters can communicate with one another through the characters. To a limited extent, this has helped in the formation and maintenance of a circle bound by Chinese characters that is not the same as the circle bound by spoken Chinese. The former is a weaker form of a community sharing a common script.

The unified script is simply a help though. The maintenance of a culture of Chinese characters has no means of resisting disruption from radical, long-term, and comprehensive political and economic forces. Scholars from China, Japan, and Korea, all East Asian countries that in the course of history have shared the use of Chinese characters and other forms of institutional culture, are able to communicate to a certain extent through the written script. However, this merely constitutes a circle bound by Chinese characters. Japan has never formed a political or cultural community with China. The Korean Peninsula, which used Chinese characters extensively, is geographically contiguous to China, is near China's developed eastern region, and has always had a close political and economic relationship with China, has, because of first becoming a Japanese colony and then due to the outside political and economic influences during the Cold War, been divided since the end of the Second World War into two separate states. This just goes to show that the capacity for maintenance of unity relying only on a unified script is limited.

The politicians of historical China could not, of course, have known of things that would happen in the future, but they could still directly feel, grasp, and understand the great importance of this issue to ancient China's constitution and politics. China had vast frontiers and a difficult terrain and innumerable self-sufficient agricultural communities, poor communications, and little contact between peoples. Since time immemorial, each place in China has had its own dialect. One needed only to cross a mountain or river and the spoken language would be different. It was no problem for rural communities, which were limited to their own space and time, that "no one could talk of snow and ice" or "no one could talk of the sea." However, for the political construction and effective administration of a large agricultural state and the long-term maintenance of peace, dialectical separatism, even if not a direct threat, was at least a problem that had to be addressed.

The normal course of agricultural society is to remain content with one's lot. This is a help toward the formation of a stable, small-scale village community, but it cannot of itself create a state like the ancient China of the Qin and Han dynasties, a community with one civilization. In fact, it could result in a pervasive hassle for language and writing and be an obstacle in the formation and administration of a large state. First, a small-scale agricultural community communicates orally and does not need writing; second, since each little locality was self-sufficient, this would inevitably lead to the formation of dialects; and, third, the easily recognized and used standard for a rural community is its own dialect, and it would not use the writing system of the whole country. This implies that rural China certainly had many offshoot linguistic communities. Most of the ordinary people knew only their own dialect, making it difficult to form a national identity. Dialects would also increase the cost of economic, political, and cultural communications between places within the whole state, naturally also creating further difficulties for the economic, political, and cultural integration of the various places and minimizing and even nullifying the role played by a unified script in ensuring unification. As soon as external or internal political, economic, or cultural conditions allowed, some dialectical communities might split away from this historical China, and this might give rise to large-scale warfare.

To strengthen China's political and cultural integration and formation, it was necessary—in addition to a unified script—to pay attention to, revive, motivate, and change daily speech, which is by nature hard to regulate. In an ancient agricultural society it is impossible to enforce a uniform spoken language, nor is it necessary, since, except in the face of natural or manmade disasters or when people leave home, contented rural farmers could pass all their lives meeting no one who spoke another language. Only a few scholars have read books and are literate and know that there is a world beyond their own and have ideas about themselves and the family, the state and the world that differ from those of the vast majority of farmers. They alone have ideals or a view of the China dream. If age, health, and finances permit, they may even pursue ideals and perhaps on a long-term basis gain their living in a place with an unfamiliar dialect. It is only then, and *for them alone*, that the lack of a spoken language in which to communicate becomes a real problem.

A unified script is already of some assistance to scholars, but it is hardly convenient to communicate only in writing. It is of low efficiency, and so it is difficult to enjoy profound, detailed, or complex communication. Indeed, my own experiences of communicating at a scholarly level with Japanese and

Korean scholars leads me to believe that although it is possible, the result of such communication is far more that it increases and thus reinforces the cultural divide between the two parties and does not create a cultural identity.

The biggest problem lies in the political administration of the state. If a Cantonese scholar were unable to communicate with people outside Guangdong Province and with Chaozhou or Shaoguan speakers within the province itself, then his political prospects would be severely limited. Even if he were brilliant, how could the emperor call on him for advice or speak to him in private? How could he communicate with court officials from other provinces and places? He could also not be employed outside his native province, or even in other parts of his own province, unless he took an interpreter, needing a new one in each place. Yet how could a government institute such interpreters and guarantee their political loyalty? This simply takes us back to the original issue.

This thought experiment only goes to show that without a common form of speech that scholars of all places share, the centralized authority that has existed since the Qin and Han would have been quite unable to function. Even if you can read, you would not have any more practical ability to participate in the governance of the whole state—either at the central or local level. As soon as dialects prevented the political and cultural elite of each place from entering the court and taking the road to the palace bureaucracy, they could not belong to the elite of this state or court. They would be forced to return to and remain sheltered in their own hometowns.

However, literacy would not make much sense in the home villages of a rural community.[17] People would have no reason to invest in reading and writing. It would be of more use to join wholeheartedly in the dialect cultural community of that place. Even people who could read would be interested only in local affairs and not in political, economic, military, cultural, or social affairs of significance to the whole state. They would not be concerned with the territory of the whole state, with its customs and peoples, because none of these would have any real or imaginary direct interest for them since it would be very difficult for them to have any real or deep connection.

This problem, finally, relates to China as a whole. Scholars who are concerned for only their home region are unable to carry the empire in their hearts. They cannot, and also have no reason to, "first make the concerns of the world under heaven their own and then allow the joys of the world under heaven to be their own joys." Even the cleverest scholar would be outstanding only in his own place and region, rather than being a distinguished person from Guangdong or Shanxi or Shanghai but *belonging to China*.

For at least some scholars, whose way ahead was impeded by limitation to a dialect, a greater danger would be that, thanks to their potential and ability, they would try to create a new script for their dialect on the basis of an existent script or even make up a wholly new script. Once such a person was seen as the creator of the local language and script, then from being a potential carrier of the Chinese script, he would become someone engaged in splitting apart the same script. People who originally could have integrated Chinese culture and politics would instead have divided Chinese culture and politics. The greater their creative power, the greater the risk would be. This is, of course, speculation, but the history of other countries does provide such examples.[18]

The preceding analysis simply proves that in this highly complex land, with many places where economic life suffers from poor communication and there are many nationalities and various peoples, for the formation, on the theoretical level, of a political and cultural China, besides a unified script, there must be a common form of speech and unity must rely on a common spoken language.

Yet from considerations of feasibility and effectiveness, historical China required only a bottom line of a linguistic community that was mostly reserved for the political and cultural elite. This linguistic community need only assist and effectively include the script-based community of the uniform script, and be able to effectively link the political and cultural elite of each place, because only these people could leave their home regions and come up against the problem of linguistic incomprehension.

Furthermore, since it was before the modern era, all spoken forms of speech could simply be transmitted orally. They could not avail themselves of scientific technology to record them or transmit them. Therefore, this linguistic community had to be able to generate itself within the given social conditions of the time. This obviously needed the political unity of the state to serve as a powerful controlling force, yet it could not be done by direct support from the state.

This requires us to adopt a constitutional viewpoint from which to understand the Mandarin speech that evolved and developed in ancient China.[19] This is also an unashamedly great constitutional system, institution, and measure. To form and uphold an efficient and united political governance, China's political and cultural elite used many ways and paths consciously and subconsciously seeking to take Chinese characters as the foundation and create a common speech different from any one dialect and that would basically serve for oral communication among the political and cultural elite. Although the Chinese language constantly changed and formed new offshoots, the striving at different times in history for a standard pronunciation—in retrospect we can see these as different forms—led in the direction of affirming a speech for oral communication among the scholars of the whole country. In the struggle for life in history, the party that had the force to win out in the end was Mandarin Chinese.

Yet phonetic research shows that in the Yuan, Ming, and Qing dynasties there were different forms of Mandarin in a broad sense, and each was used in government.[20] From a linguistic or phonetic point of view, or from today's *Putonghua* (普通话), the phonetic differences among these forms of seemingly inaccurate so-called blue-green Mandarin (i.e., with a heavy provincial accent) were enormous. Merely from a linguistic angle or even without any particular reason or justification, these forms of Mandarin were not dialects. But this purely linguistic point of view overlooks the most important constitutional function and social significance of Mandarin. For speakers of Mandarin, for the political and cultural formation of China, the standard for determining what was Mandarin was not in uniformity or proximity to uniformity of sound but rather in linguistic use and function, namely that the users could understand and communicate with one another and parties could engage in conversation.

Mandarin did not need to serve for everything. Local food and drink, and highly localized customs, because they were of no importance to the formation of China as a whole, could not be discussed in Mandarin, but this was not a problem. The really important role of Mandarin was for communication about affairs the mandarins/officials were concerned with, that is, public affairs, important political, social, historical, and cultural affairs that were of significance to ancient China, and the relevant important historical materials.[21] Two scholars who had not yet met but who had been trained in a similar political and cultural background, even if they had heavy local accents, by using Mandarin and with some good guesswork to pick out a few key sounds, would be able to communicate and discuss orally and even debate the wisdom of ancient Chinese scholars and relate it to affairs of state and affairs of their office.

Not only was the whole country not united in speech, there was not even a standard form of the speech used by the mandarins. Moreover, Mandarin was not the speech of the ordinary people.[22] We can deduce that spoken Mandarin was very closely linked to the written script and much more loosely connected to local customs and affairs. It could hardly have been a normalized or standardized form of a dialect. Instead, it would have more probably been a form of speech that was closely linked to the literary language of the classics. This spoken language would need to be able to talk about politics, society, rites, and laws and so would be adapted to discussing such topics. It would be closely connected to the tradition and resources of knowledge shared by China's political and cultural elites. If not related to the Confucian school, then it would at least be related to the Hundred Schools of the Masters; it would be at least concerned with—if not solely focused on—Confucian classics, historical records, philosophical writings, and miscellaneous works. The knowledge that was already crystalized in written form in the classics was the most appropriate material for exposition and discussion in Mandarin Chinese. From this we may deduce that what was relevant to discussion in Mandarin was anything related to the classics and the common problems that the political and cultural elite faced at different times over a long period of time in the course of China's history, such as how to regulate one's household, the state, and the world under heaven. This relationship between Mandarin and the classics and the constraints it imposed easily led to the formation in the conservatism of "fidelity to the past" displayed by the ancient political and cultural elite of

China. This was not necessarily the result of an abstract cultural conservatism. Rather, it was more probably because right from the start the knowledge transmitted in Chinese characters and in Mandarin Chinese was classical and elitist and not a popular or secular discourse.[23]

Even if what follows is merely tentative, we can explain the traditional Chinese family and tutor-based pedagogy as follows: the tutor rarely explained the meaning of the text; he stressed recitation. This tradition is found in China even up to the present time. Not only did early reading classes use recitation, but also the pupils were asked to learn the texts by heart and recite them out loud.[24] In fact, there is no empirical research to support recitation and rote learning as being more helpful for the memory and other scholarly abilities than understanding and silent reading, except for the multiplication tables, given that in China teachers of arithmetic do not require their pupils to recite and learn mathematical formulas by heart. Hence, one reasonable supposition is that recitation helps the teacher to supervise and correct the pupils' pronunciation, whereas with a phonetic script there is no great need for supervision and correction.

Recitation is a form of social memory and a corrective institution for the normalization of the pronunciation of Chinese characters. In a society that lacks other techniques for recording or transmitting the sounds of Chinese characters, recitation will ensure that the Mandarin pronunciation of the characters will have a social impact in certain communities and families so that what is transmitted by ear may influence the next generation. When I was young, every morning my uncle said, "To study and practice regularly: is that not a pleasure (reading *yue*)!" Twenty years later, my mother, who was illiterate, could still correct me and tell me to read *le* as *yue*. Thanks to so many such unconscious actors, at a time when people were highly dispersed, the Mandarin pronunciation of Chinese characters may well have been passed on in this way. The transmission of this linguistic culture is already completely independent of the various activities of the relevant persons, independent of their subjective pursuits or personal feelings and knowledge.

The Formation and Maintenance of Mandarin Chinese: A Hypothesis

The greatest difficulty that Mandarin raises is this: in such a vast country, even if only among the scholars, how could a form of speech be created that was widely used even if not always standardized? Later we will consider the question of how Mandarin was maintained and spread. Only in later years did it win support from, and forceful promotion by, the state.[25] Any first effort must have encountered insuperable obstacles to its being carried out and supervised.

From an empirical point of view, it is not possible to find the origin of Mandarin. Nor is it possible to use empirical data to set up a reliable institutional system to maintain the operation of Mandarin. This section relies only on current historical records to reflect on the way of experience, and sketch a possible institutional system, even though it cannot be the real one, that might account for the appearance and continuity of Mandarin. By throwing a brick so as to attract a piece of jade, I hope that I can inspire scholars to pay attention to this question and undertake research into it.

Any premise regarding the origin of Mandarin must be tentative. In a place that is sufficiently broad and for which communication is reasonably convenient, there would be a large enough community of persons linked by blood or marriage who would share a language that was highly similar, though there might be particular accents. Compared to surrounding communities, this one would have a higher level of socioeconomic development and might even form the ruling group of that area. As a result, its language would not only lead to internal cohesion within the group, but also be culturally attractive to other groups and enjoy political leverage. The activities of this group would have already led to the common use and tradition of a vibrant, living, and expanding language that had never been broken over a long period of time.

This supposed origin, in empirical terms, can generally be said to be that of the Chinese people for a long period of time, when they were farming the land, competing, and even slaughtering one another in the lower reaches of the Yellow River. We might suppose that the clan rulers of the Xia, Shang, and Zhou would use the language of this people as the official language of their court, their Mandarin Chinese. The area controlled by these three dynasties in their collective rule of more than fifteen hundred years was largely the same for each, and so although the Mandarin of later generations has both redundancy and omissions, overall it was reinforced. Of particular importance was the Western Zhou. Not only did the Son of Heaven himself enfeof a large number of his relatives and a few able ministers, sending them out to various places, but each feudal prince in turn enfeofed others, whether or not this was the intention and plan of the Zhou Son of Heaven.[26] Objectively speaking, this amounted to making the language and pronunciation used every day by the ruling class of the Western Zhou the standard, official language and in a flash spreading it throughout the country to every locale and so winning for it a significant number of users in the land.

There is indirect evidence for this supposition and deduction. In the Spring and Autumn period, Duke Huan of Qi was able "to bind the feudal princes of the nine regions in the one world under heaven." Confucius was waiting for any one of the feudal princes to come and study under him so as to found the Eastern Zhou. In the Warring States period, the strategists Su Qin and Zhang Yi were able to travel to all the states and bind them in north-south or east-west alliances, and a few "foreigners" among the political elite, such as Shang Yang, were able to participate effectively in the core political decisions of non-native states because the linguistic tradition was already firmly established in the central plain.[27] Later on, in the thirteen hundred years between the Qin and the Northern Song, excluding a break of two hundred years when the Eastern Jin moved the capital city to Nanjing, the dynasties consistently chose Chang'an, Luoyang, or Kaifeng as their capital. The long-term stability of the political, economic, and cultural center assisted in maintaining the basic stability of this one common language, which then radiated out over the surrounding areas.

But there must also have been other factors at work. There must be some more important social reasons that would cause people, at least the scholars, scattered among various dialectical areas, to not lose contact with the center over a considerable period of time despite wars, chaos, and the distances of space and time. The central plain had to show sufficient political, economic, and cultural achievements to create its own political and cultural radiance and attract scholars to consciously and willingly take the linguistic tradition of the central plain as their standard for correcting the languages of each place. It was also necessary to discover, rely on, and consciously strengthen some conservative features of Chinese pronunciation and so oppose the inroads of the dialects. On this basis it was also necessary to form a microcosmic institution dealing with the pronunciation of Chinese and a means of recording it, forming an institutional system of language and speech to which scholars from every region could appeal, even though they were highly separated from one another, to independently correct their pronunciation of the Chinese characters and so join the living tradition of the Chinese language, which in principle would seem originally to have been something that could only have been transmitted orally. As the scholars of every place sought to shape their ability in Mandarin Chinese, the regions they could serve expanded, and thus, without officials being aware of it, the area in which Mandarin was used grew.

In ancient agricultural China, it was, in theory, completely impossible to fulfill the conditions just described. But reality is more miraculous than we could possibly imagine. Given that China has always had a broad tradition of Mandarin speech, even though I am not able to link causes and effects, based on the fact that Mandarin exists, it is possible to conclude that ancient China was able to cross the mountains of the north and the rivers of the south and create the social foundations that gave rise to and maintained Mandarin Chinese, creating the complex active organization by which Mandarin emerged and has continued to exist, although up to now no one has explained it clearly or convincingly.[28]

Over millennia and across vast spaces, it may be that ancient China was able to shape and maintain a common pronunciation of Mandarin, first, owing to the hieroglyphic nature of Chinese characters. This made it such that, based on Chinese characters, the Chinese language may have constructed a geographic-cultural community that did not simply rely on pronunciation. From this it advanced to the possibility of establishing a historical cultural community based on the characters that transcended time and continued to be full of life. In other words, even though the language of each region was different from others, at least for a rather long period of time they may well have formed a political and cultural community based on the unified script. Its hieroglyphic nature considerably weakened the influence dialects could have on the characters so that the characters could be used without being linked to the pronunciation of any given locale. The Chinese language is not the spoken language of any particular place, yet it can become the dialect of every place and even the vehicle of pronunciation of the characters in every time and age. This means that the pronunciation of Chinese characters would seem to transcend space and time. Even if the phonetic reading of a Chinese character may disappear from daily speech in many or even all areas, such as the use of the entering tone in modern Mandarin Chinese, the characters formerly associated with this tone still exist and are still used by later generations.

A second, concomitant advantage of an abstract pronunciation is that, overall, it weakens the natural antipathy the local elite feel toward an unfamiliar tongue. In daily life, someone could feel antipathy toward Shanghainese, Cantonese, or even Pekinese, but it is hardly likely that he would feel antipathy toward the *Putonghua*, which does not belong to any particular area. At times it may seem as if someone felt antipathy toward *Putonghua*, but in fact this is an antipathy toward the person speaking, who does not belong to the same community as the person who feels the antipathy.

Third, as was mentioned earlier, the repository of Chinese characters accumulated in the course of a long history tended to lend to the characters as a whole a cultural aura of mystery, solemnity, and veneration. This is a real form of soft power and to a very great extent it was able to effectively prevent people from using dialects to create local cultures inspired by particularism and splittist influences.[29] It could effectively rule out the independent development of localization, which could all too easily happen with a hieroglyphic script and would lead in the direction of the production of minority nationality scripts.[30]

Another feature that assisted in the creation and maintenance of the unity of the Chinese language was how Chinese characters are formed. Xu Shen's *Explanation of Words and Characters* divides the ways of making Chinese characters into six kinds: indicator graphs, pictographs, form and voice compounds, etymonic compounds, graphically and etymonically related pairs, and phonetic loan characters. Later scholars determined that the third type was the most common. The *Explanation of Words and Characters* records 10,516 Chinese characters, of which form and voice compounds number 8,545, more than 80 percent. This implies that the number of homophones in Chinese is vast and that a person needs to recognize and be able to read reasonably accurately only a thousand commonly used Chinese characters to be able to "see the character and read one [phonetic] half" or "know [i.e., read] the character by knowing one [phonetic] half" and so guess how to read characters he has not yet learned.[31] If the fourth and sixth types are added, the number of phonetic characters is even higher. This feature of Chinese characters is useful for teaching and for self-study, and especially helpful for learning correct pronunciation. In the abstract, we might even say that, taken as a whole, Chinese characters are a record of the phonetic information of each character, with the result that the pronunciation of many homophones does not need to be learned through oral transmission. This feature not only makes it easier for scholars to use Mandarin, which is based on the pronunciation of the characters, but also means that spoken Mandarin, which is supported by Chinese characters, has an advantage over dialects that lack a supporting script or could never have such script, and thus Mandarin is remembered more easily and for longer in society and is not easily lost.

But the question arises: why is it that Chinese characters have these quasi-mystical features? It may be by accident, by chance, or even by luck. But such an explanation disparages the characters and may be a failure of thought. This is not teleology, but we cannot rule out the possibility that these features of the characters and others yet to be discovered formed precisely so that the characters would continue to exist in the slow evolution of Chinese history (within an evolutionary framework we cannot say this was an advantage). These features and other characteristics of the Chinese linguistic and cultural community that came about reinforced each other. In other words, these were essential features that any language and script had to have in order to survive in the linguistic competition throughout the history of Chinese society. It was only thanks to these features of the language and script that it was possible to maintain the civilization of this large state. Thus, before any reliable evidence can disprove this supposition, it cannot be rejected solely on the grounds that it is a supposition.

It is necessary to bring evolutionary thought into reflection on the Chinese language and script, because simply looking at the language or the script itself is certainly insufficient for explaining the origins of Mandarin. The formation of Mandarin can certainly be related to the basic social conditions of life, social changes and disasters that affected the people who spoke it. Over the long course of history and the vast terrain of the country, many happy coincidences and even, or perhaps more, unhappy ones joined together to bring it about that the languages of each place in historical China developed or changed so that they became incommunicable dialects and even led to a forced linguistic amalgamation. The main pattern was the spread from north to south.

The first important social cause was the large-scale shift of population brought about by unrest in the course of history. Whether it was because of the invasions by the northern pastoral peoples or due to a change of dynasty or war in the central plain, a large number of northern people were left homeless and, leaving everything, took their lives and what was connected to life, namely the pronunciation of the central plain, and crossed mountains and rivers to settle in the south. Many even retired into remote mountain valleys. Each time a group of northerners moved south they brought their northern language, which took root and formed links with the local language and brought to the development of the local tongue the restraints imposed by the northern pronunciation, even forming its own linguistic family, such as the Hakka dialect.[32]

Second, in the interests of fulfilling various political, military, and economic works of construction, the state forced people to migrate either permanently or temporarily. This includes political migration, when people were forced to move so as to counter the localizing tendencies of the nobles in the subordinate states, or for engineering work such as to construct the Great Wall, palaces, tombs, roads, and waterways and undertake all kinds of forced labor, or conscription for the whole country so as to oppose and resist the northern pastoral peoples and set up permanent military posts on the borders and at militarily strategic locations.[33] All of these special cases brought it about that in a fairly large area the various dialects influenced one another, became amalgamated, and combined together and so helped people of different regions to communicate with one another, directly and indirectly influencing the linguistic ability of each place and of many people.[34]

However, one should not overestimate the influence of population migration on Mandarin. First, the linguistic influence of migration was greater at the level of society and mainly had a direct influence on ordinary people and influenced the political and cultural elite only indirectly. Second, we must also consider that migration at irregular intervals brought in foreign variables to the evolution and development of the language of each place, but the most basic motive for linguistic development must have been the social life of a given locale.

State politics is a factor that supports the argument made earlier, that the political and cultural elite of China, in order to unite and effectively carry out political governance, consistently used various means to take the Chinese characters and the northern (i.e., central plains) dialect as the basis for a common language (Mandarin) largely reserved for the political and cultural elite themselves.

In the early times one of the important institutions was the system of official schools that began to be established after the fall of the Western Zhou. In unifying pronunciation, the main factor was not what the teachers of these schools taught but that students from the whole country could, by various means, enter the court and receive the same education. This *process* certainly shaped general linguistic competence founded on a linguistic structure based on Chinese characters and the pronunciation of some given place, such as the capital city. It would also enable the scholars to become directly aware of, and sensitive to, the languages of the various places as they spoke with one another. This experience of the students would by various paths enter into the political and cultural integration of China and influence it.

In the reign of Emperor Wu of the Han dynasty, Dong Zhongshu's sugges-tion that "the hundred schools should be rejected and the Confucian school alone be accepted" was followed and the state actively guided culture and ed-ucation and selected scholars. In keeping with the injunction to accept only Confucianism, in the Southern Song dynasty, Zhu Xi selected the Four Books and Five Classics. Besides regulating the standard materials for the national examinations and thus restricting the scope of the answers and standard re-plies, his aim was to greatly restrict the divergences of pronunciation that could occur in reading the classics. By determining the books and Chinese characters of the core course and the important issues that state politics de-creed for the students to study, the scholars from every place could concentrate their attention on, recite, and commit to memory the characters and language of these books. The texts of the classics were read not just for their content. Indeed, these classical texts also bore the pronunciation of each Chinese char-acter in the text. We may suppose, for instance, that if the *Book of Odes* had not been included and thus not formed a community of many consumers over a long period of time and become a saleable commodity that scholars in the whole country were obliged to consume and willingly did so, then while the text of the first line, "'Guan! Guan!' the ospreys call, on the islet in the river," would never disappear, its *pronunciation* would have been obliterated owing to the lack of a covering note. Confirming the canon of the classics also had another role, even though it may easily be undervalued or even forgotten: to create a market for the script and language that was larger, more normative, and more stable and hence able to survive longer, such that the script of the classics was put in books and so the pronunciation of that script was delivered to a great many *readers*. It was enough for the readers to have entered the gate of this linguistic market, even if they were scattered in many places, to be able to gain long-term stability—which was yet a living force—formed by the market to be able to correct one's own pronunciation of Chinese characters.

Of course, this was the earliest standardization of the language for educa-tion and training reserved for those preparing to be officials and the intellectual elite. According to Qian Mu, in the time of Emperor Wu of the Han, profes-sorial chairs were founded for the Five Classics. The professors were assigned students, the number of which increased from an initial fifty to two hundred, a thousand, and even more. By the time of Emperor Huan toward the close of the Eastern Han, the number of pupils was even in excess of three hundred thousand. Once the course ended, the students took exams and the outstanding performers were chosen for public posts, while the weaker ones went back to their home provinces to serve as local government clerks.[35] Not only was this system important and very effective—it trained and standardized the speech and listening abilities of the students, leading the outstanding ones to be able to communicate in a highly standardized accent so that they could work as administrative officials outside their own provinces—but it also, even more importantly, meant that since students were sent home as clerks, they would help set up the conditions for the preparation of officials both from the outside and local, and as clerks they would communicate with the local people.[36]

In addition to helping with political governance, this system would also influence the culture and education of each place. When future students saw the distinction between officials, clerks, and the people, they would truly appreciate the importance of Mandarin for political governance and for realizing their own dreams. This simply linked Mandarin to the power of the state and strengthened the political and cultural attractiveness of Mandarin for the local candidates. In history, the Sui and the Tang soon after their inception sent out a decree to set up an examination system over the whole of this vast agricultural country. This is something that even in today's Central and Western Europe would be impossible, since there is no unity of languages or scripts. Yet the background to this one command under the Sui and Tang was the education in Mandarin that permeated and extended throughout China—since Emperor Wu of the Han's establishment of Confucianism as the orthodox, traditional primary education had already reshaped this agricultural society and laid the foundation for imperial examination.

There are also other social phenomena that made for the standardization of speech. The operas and songs that flourished in the Yuan dynasty made Pekinese (then called the speech of Khanbalik) popular among the people.[37] From this we may deduce that from the middle of the Tang there must have been a similar effect present. The Ming selected Nanjing as their capital, but the Emperor Zhu Yuanzhang, who was born in the south, decreed that the *Correct Pronunciation of the Hong Wu Era* should retain Pekinese as the standard form of speech, thus consolidating the foundations for the status of Pekinese as the common language. Faced with the problem of "a lack of communication between officials and the people," the Yong Zheng Emperor of the Qing dynasty issued a special decree requiring officials of all ranks to use Mandarin in official business and forbidding local dialects. As a result, there were even people who published books to help Cantonese speakers to learn Mandarin.[38]

Also to be taken into account in a consideration of the social environment of Mandarin is that after officials retired they would return home and open private schools.[39] Life goes on generation after generation. This meant that there were always officials coming from the source who could teach the recitation of the classics in an authoritative standard pronunciation and thus keep the local accent in communication with the Mandarin of the palace. This would all help to minimize any tendency toward local peculiarities of speech and ensure that such peculiarities were brought into the mainstream and within acceptable limits.

Finally, there were many microcultural institutions and measures. This required the political and cultural elite of each place to form a linguistic community and keep the local forms of speech in touch with one another and did not much require the interference of the central administration. On its own, this system could run itself, correct itself, and be productive of its own accord. Every scholar, having received the basic primary school training in writing and reading, would be able, by gleaning the information on pronunciation to be found attached to and stored in the characters, and by relying on the construction of writings and script, across space and time, to reconstruct the phonetics of unknown characters in Mandarin or something approximating to Mandarin.

Perhaps this helps to explain why poems and rhymed texts developed in China in time immemorial and why scholars were accustomed to reading poems and writing couplets. They also always stressed that essays should be elegant and sound harmonious and be good for reading aloud—for reciting. This demanded paired phonemes. For instance, the phonetic and tone of each adjoining character in every line of an essay normally should be clearly distinguished. In poetry, the phonetic and tone of each character must match the rhyme scheme. To obtain lines that rhymed, even changing the order of lines was permitted.[40] This could not merely be a common custom of scholars with no social effect, or only for the purpose of attaining an auditory aesthetic effect. Even though I have never seen anyone relate this feature of ancient Chines texts to unification of speech, from the point of view of its social effect, the two may well be related.

This kind of search, first, can help avoid texts becoming difficult to read because there are too many homophones, as in the extreme example by Zhao Yuanren: *The History of Mr Shi's Eating a Lion* (施氏食狮史, *Shīshí shì shī shǐ*). A phrase like that can be explained but not read. At any rate, it has become a purely literary form of expression that cannot be properly related to any ordinary form of speech. Even more important, having been through a training since youth in reading and reciting that provided a firm grasp of, and not just familiarity with, these rules of Chinese that are not easy to learn, a trained reader, in reading poetry or rhymed prose, encountering an unfamiliar character or characters in a fixed place would be able to make an informed guess not only at its meaning but even at its phonetic and tone. Just like "seeing the character and reading one half," this is concealed within the writing system and so does not require any other tool. In remote areas wholly cut off from the central plain, a former scholar would be able from the tonality of the text to grasp the phonetic of a given unknown character. This reading might then take root be spread by other scholars in the area when they used the character in poetry or prose.

Second, there is the creation by exegetes/phoneticists in the Han dynasty of the rule "to be read as. . . ." This took a character with a similar sound and allowed the reader to work out the precise sound of the unknown character. This is rather like the use of rhyme as a way of guessing the sound of an unfamiliar character. For instance, *kuangfa* uses a descriptive sound to state the special features of the phoneme; *zhiyinfa* (direct sound method) uses a character of the same sound to annotate the unknown character. These methods are ones that choose characters well-known to the reader to supply the phonetics for the unknown character. Given that the *Explanation of Words and Characters* used this method, at least by the Eastern Han the norm of "reading as" was a commonly used means by which readers could learn how to read unfamiliar characters.[41]

But the most important and most significant discovery was the *fan-qie* system, propagated and perhaps created by the classics scholar Sun Yan in the third century CE at the time of the Three Kingdoms. He wrote *Er Ya Yin Yi* and began to use the system to indicate the sound of unfamiliar characters. This system used two characters of known phonetics to give the sound of an unknown character. The initial consonant of the new sound was taken from the first character and the vowel and tone from the second. The new combination of consonant, vowel, and tone gave the phonetic and tone for the unfamiliar character. For instance, the character *kŏng* was glossed as *ku-lóng*. Before the adoption of a foreign alphabet and foreign phonetics to indicate sound and tone, this was the most important method to signify pronunciation, used for the longest period of time and discovered and developed on Chinese soil. It is a system of phonetics that is convenient and simple.

By the Sui dynasty, eight famous scholars discussed how to determine the principles for discerning the sounds, and in 601 CE they published the five volumes of *Qie Yun* [Spelling Rhymes], which became the earliest reliable guide to pronunciation that can still be used today. Phonologists often emphasize the great influence of this book on later phonology. This is quite correct. However, from the point of view of shaping the unified speech of the political and cultural elite, it represents a first effort and creation among the people that ultimately won recognition and support from officialdom as the standardized institution for the pronunciation of Chinese characters.

Cultural Constitution and the Emergence of the Scholar-Officials

At the beginning of this chapter, we noted that in the West states were formed on the basis of a preexisting common social body whereas historical China was a place of small agricultural villages with a rural economy and to establish a state based on the body of these innumerable scattered microlocations and at the same time to integrate land, people, and state into a country that was also a civilization was too difficult. A unified script and Mandarin Chinese were not themselves able to create or integrate such a large body. Yet, I have already pointed out that on the foundation of the common script, the scholars of the whole state may be seen as creating a common cultural elite body. The publication eight hundred years later of the *Qie Yun*, with its addition of a phonetic dimension, implies that this common body had been stabilized and strengthened. These two items composing the cultural foundation were such that the scholars of old became an independent class in Chinese society. The traditional division of "scholars, farmers, artisans, and merchants" testifies that the key class for the establishment, construction, and organization of the civilization of the state was the scholars.

Through the study of the officially prescribed Confucian classics, scholars from every place were connected not only to one another but also to past scholars—the main, but not sole, group of whom were Confucian intellectuals. On the cultural level, this created a "social contract" of many generations of scholars, tightly bound to one another along with their written and oral languages and phonetics. This was a lively cultural institution and tradition, a conservative cultural body transmitted from one to another like sparks of flame.

By relying on knowledge of this set of characters and their pronunciation, a scholar could communicate in writing with government officials anywhere, even without having studied at court, and enter into communication with intellectuals. Even if he did not know his interlocutors, thanks to Mandarin Chinese he could talk to them directly. Even if, as we noted earlier, by means of the script and especially by means of Mandarin the knowledge and categories of knowledge about which one could communicate and discuss—at least before secular works of literature began to be popular in the Yuan, Ming, and Qing—were very limited, knowledge of the classics, histories, masters, and collections that could be passed on in writing and discussed in Mandarin was very important for the political and cultural constitution and maintenance of historical China. Moreover, it was very important for a topic I shall address in the next chapter, the choice in the whole country of a political and cultural elite, especially from the Sui and Tang dynasties on.

The formation of this class—more properly, of a concrete person—was at least due to the thought, moral qualities, vision, and sense of mission of a group of persons among them. As was shown earlier, the issues that could be conversed about and discussed in writing or in Mandarin were a resource of thought, focused mainly on the household, state, and world. This implies that from the moment the scholars began to read and write, these issues and books, these questions and discussions, had already begun to infiltrate and silently shape the latent political and cultural elite by confirming them in the goal of their work. They did not study to make money for their households, nor did they write in order to record folk songs or legends. They studied, and the outstanding ones became scholar-officials, not (or at least, not only) to be officials but instead to participate in the politics of *the whole state*, to be officials of other districts, to loyally serve the state with gratitude, and even "to govern the state and bring peace to the world." The script and Mandarin Chinese, therefore, shaped scholars and then formed them into a community that became the elite that China's state politics could, and had to, rely on—even though later there would be a need for a more careful selection and training through the imperial exams and the bureaucracy.

When we add to this the feelings the scholars would have for the state and the world, and while communicating in spirit about their tasks conducted in the name of the emperor and the court, which would also be done through writing and speech, the two institutions of a unified script and Mandarin Chinese differentiated scholars from the local culture of their home districts and the ordinary people. It did indeed effectively unite government officials and scholars everywhere in a common cultural attitude.

Since it would be very difficult for the culture of the scholars' hometowns to spontaneously produce the use of writing and Mandarin Chinese, and since the scholars' elders and relatives would have great difficulty in sharing their new cultural concern, there would necessarily arise a feeling of communication between scholars and a new way of expressing it that would be conveyed in writing and Mandarin Chinese. This would include love for home and country, as in "The iron horse and frozen river enter into my dreams,"[42] and the "petty" emotion of "to compose a new poem I force myself to speak of sorrow."[43] You could "raise your glass to greet the bright moon"[44] or "take wine to ask the azure sky"[45] or even "make three persons with one's shadow."[46] These lines show a feeling for words and a sense of tone and rhyme. The expression and communication of feeling among the scholars, whether these arose from the ancients or from the scholars' own experience of sorrow, would consciously shape their sentiments, brotherly feeling, understanding, and appreciation and in imagination make persons who were scattered far and wide draw closer in culture and become a special, invisible community, unlike that of the rural villages, which they could see with their own eyes. Therefore, to a certain extent they were different from, and independent of, the elders of their own villages. This was a form of institutional separation and union such that from being individuals they gradually became a self-conscious and self-perpetuating class, with their own mutual self-recognition and pursuit of political and cultural goals. Hence, they were seen by ordinary people as an independent layer in society, a special group, even an independent social class, that of the scholar-officials.[47]

But the class of scholar-officials was not determined by a fixed identity. Rather, it was an intellectual group formed by Chinese culture from those who were familiar with it. In historical China, all males by dint of individual study could attain this mobile social identity. It was precisely because of this feature of the scholar-officials and because of the key role they as a whole played in China's politics, society, and culture, since they could not be completely cut off from their elders and relatives at home, that, even when the official and popular cultures were linked, they formed the link between China's highest political layer and the lowest layers of society. The connections among the scholars and their identity, to a very great extent, represented the connections and identity of all the various places in China. Thus, once this layer was created, the unified script and Mandarin Chinese strengthened the construction of China's politics and culture, although this was not on the foundation of the body of the ordinary people as a whole but on the foundations of this cultural (and political) elite community, constituting and integrating China's politics and civilization.

What should be made clear is that the integration of the scholars in the field of culture and contacts between them did not mean that they made the same profits or even that they made gains as a whole body. It does not imply that they lived and died as one. In fact, there was often conflict among the scholars, as among animals. But despite this, and maybe even because of these tensions, conflicts, and quarrels—"failure to hit implies a failure to communicate"— which shaped them in a particular way, and shaped China, the effect of their action was to bring about the unity of China's politics and culture.

Once this cultural community was formed, to perpetuate themselves the scholars established a space for their class that could provide a broader market of consumers for their literary and linguistic products, and while consuming this tradition they continued to produce it. While inheriting the tradition they further expanded it. One need only ask oneself how many people there have been over the years who have commented, analyzed, and explained the *Analects* and other important texts. Among them are many who have done this for later generations, including for us today. For these many reasons, perhaps history books may record where they were born, and indeed they do belong to the concrete agricultural community or place that reared them, but even more do they belong to this civilization, to this state that is founded on a civilization and not on a national group of people. This is why the saying "they first worry about what the world worries about and then rejoice in what brings joy to the world" is not only a normative demand laid on scholars, it may even be taken as what, in practice, at least a certain number of them take as their way of living each day.

A classic example is some of the poems of the Song dynasty. At that time, the territory of China was very limited and so the places referred to in the quotations below are ones that the authors could not have visited in person, since they were then under the rule of the pastoral peoples. However, in expressing their own ideas and feelings or resentments the authors do not see them as foreign places at all. Patriotism is a factor here, but the most important factor is perhaps that in the imagination of these politicians and poets, even if the state is split and rule is divided, they bear in their hearts the unity of a cultural China that goes beyond the politics of the time:

> "*Beyond the borders* Autumn brings a changed scene . . . at Yanran mountain I inscribed my coming but went back without having achieved my goal. *The Qiang flutes* are desolate and the night is full of hoarfrost." (Fan Zhongyan of the Northern Song)[48]

"Even though my moustache is turning white, what does that matter? When will the emperor send someone, like Emperor Wu of the Han sent Feng Tang to Yunzhong. I shall bend my bow like the full moon and look northwest and fire at the Dog Star [i.e., the Xixia Kingdom]." (Su Shi of the Northern Song)

"*The horse on the steppe* neighs in the morning, *the nomad's flute* sounds in the evening. I lift my head like snow." (Hu Shijiang of the Northern Song)

"Driving my horse chariot I reach and cross the *Helan Mountain* pass." (Yue Fei of the Southern Song)

"I still think of the country on the frontier guard at *Luntai*"; "I recall when I served *on the frontier at the Great Wall*; in the mirror I see my old whiskers are already flecked." "In this lifetime who could imagine it? My heart is in the *Tianshan mountains*, my body is growing old in Cangzhou." (Lu You of the Southern Song)

"Looking northwest toward *Chang'an*; how sad there are so many mountains in between." "Roasting beef under the colours scattered along the 800 *li* of the border; the sound of 50 stringed instruments echoes *beyond the border*." (Xin Qiji of the Southern Song)

The formation of this community of scholars, the spread of this market for writing and language, and the superior status of the scholars as a class in ancient China all contributed to increasing the attraction and binding force of the civilization that they supported and upheld for the latent political and cultural elite of the various people of this vast territory. Nor was it only a matter of speech and writing, or only of other abstract cultural factors. Rather, for China what mattered most was the political organization of this state of many peoples, its civilization. The local elite everywhere studied and practiced in some way or other—for instance, in poetry, painting, rhyme, and music—to enter into and make their own this common community, made efforts to acquire recognition and encouragement from the same community, and considered it a matter of pride to belong to the elite of this civilization. Through their familiarity with writing and Mandarin Chinese, the elite everywhere were able to look forward to participating in the governance of the whole state and to assuming the burden of administering places beyond the confines of their home districts and even to assuming the great political responsibility of the entire country. This option was something that only scholars had the realistic possibility of exercising. This option was also available only in times of peace. Therefore, from the very beginning it would expand and regulate the ambitions and vision concealed among the political and cultural elite with regard to the future of themselves as individuals, of their society, state, and the world, thereby shaping their sense of business, their political imagination and sense of responsibility, and their dream for China.

Along with the strengthening of the social and political environmental conditions that relied on writing and Mandarin Chinese, the market for writing and Mandarin would undoubtedly expand. The larger the community became, the more stable its tradition was, and so the market for speech and writing would expand further. Provided all other conditions remained stable, this community would all the more easily carry out its own self-production and self-expansion, relying less and less on interference or support from the state. A classic example of this is that after the demise of the First Emperor of Qin, there was no longer any official direct organized effort to unify the script. Another example is that it was only in the Sui and Tang period that the central government formally established a statewide mechanism for selecting talent and ensuring circulation in the bureaucracy based on Chinese characters and Mandarin Chinese, which was enough to cause regions to cease being content with their former isolation and also to cause scholars who were concerned with world issues to make an effort themselves to learn Mandarin Chinese.

Once this community of scholars that belonged not to any given region but to the whole of China was created on the cultural level—whether we call it a layer or a class—it would necessarily change the political administration of China. The central and local tiers of government to a considerable extent were able to diminish their reliance on the wealthy aristocracy and turn instead with confidence to the elite layer of persons who, through writing and Mandarin Chinese, had elected to leave their rural society. The force of the political and legal measures adopted by the court to penetrate society was strengthened thanks to the emergence of this community. Hence, the rule of warlords during the Wei-Jin period was not such as to be able to overthrow it.[49] Moreover, it implies that among the elite chosen in the whole state there would emerge a consideration of issues of local governance.[50]

Just four years after the publication of *Qie Yun*, the imperial examination system was set up. Perhaps this was coincidental. However, only a few decades later there appeared the great Tang dynasty, with its splendid ancient culture and civilization and its spirit of openness and tolerance, so the confluence of these developments could not have been wholly accidental.

Conclusion: Understanding China's Constitution

Trusting to the superior vision that historical distance grants to later generations, this chapter has analyzed the role and significance of a unified script and Mandarin Chinese for the political and cultural formation of ancient China. It has highlighted the particularity of the constitutional issue that ancient agricultural China had to respond to, and the particularity of ancient China's constitution formed in the historical process of responding to that issue. Understanding and grasping these particularities, I believe, will help in our understanding of more general constitutional problems and enable us to gain insights from China's ancient constitution for research into China's constitution today and its implementation.

Ancient China was the ancient agricultural China, a vast country with a complicated terrain. This determined that it could not adopt a democratic order.[51] But it also determined that China could not really be a monarchical autocracy. The historical, political, and cultural formation of this community over thousands of years had to, and could only, be founded on the integration of many peoples and nationalities. It was not like Athens in the time of ancient Greece or Rome or even like the many states of medieval Europe. The effective political governance of historical China is first, of course, shaped by the force of a political constitution, including its final unification through war and a central authority sustained by the military might of imperial authority, but there were also measures of economic constitution, such as the unification of the currency and of weights and measures. The gradual accumulation of this kind of economic constitution grew day by day just as dripping water can finally find a way through stone. Yet this chapter shows that for ancient rural China, the formative force of cultural constitution was at least as important. It not only supported the formation and effective functioning of political and economic constitution, it was also able to form a statewide political and cultural communication that at least did not systematically exclude anyone from participating in the administration of government and that was formed—the expression is perhaps contradictory—on the basis of a small agricultural economy. China's cultural constitution is a mechanism shaped by China's history, and it is also the process of the formation of this historical China. China was not "founded" on the basis of the approval of a constitutional law, or several. Like all great civilizations, it gradually flowered on the river of history like riding a boat without the need for a ticket.

It is only against the political and social background of this vast history that it is possible to understand how the unified script and speech were "co-opted" or "diverted" by politics to become the most important constitutional measure at the level of culture. For many scholars of the time and of today, these two institutions look like something cultural, or as being annexed to culture, and indeed they are only cultural, but when seen against the vast scope of the emergence of historical China, their chief and most fundamental role is in fact constitutional. And because of this, I describe them as ancient China's cultural constitution, and not simply the appurtenance of any particular dynasty or era. Even if this is vague, it is precise in meaning since what they constituted was historical China and never any particular dynasty.

This is particularly important for but not unique to China. The second quotation at the head of this chapter comes from the Bible and shows that in biblical times there were at least some people who had clearly realized the power of a common language in driving people to form a polity and transform society. In the West in modern times, a script and speech have also played an important role in the emergence of the nation-state. I am not yet talking about how many countries have constitutions with provisions governing language and script. The most notable perhaps is the political principle of a nation-state affirmed in 1789 during the French Revolution as "one state, one nation, one language." The revolutionaries made unity of language an important political and cultural measure for the political construction of the nation-state. The universalization of the French language was thus used to organize a new form of communal actor as well as a necessary means and political strategy for winning the people's support for the revolution. It even led to a movement to suppress dialects.[52]

But in a country of only one nationality, the language and script are usually seen as a factor of companionship in life for that nation, and the state comes later. Hence, language and script are definitely prepolitical or preconstitutional. Even when language and script are written into the constitution and even if they play a constitutive role in the nation-state, yet it may also be overlooked that it is very difficult to see them as one of the core institutions in the emergence and formation of the state in political terms. Except when dialects assume the mantle of rights and enter into the languages permitted to be used in the judiciary by the constitution, language and script as classical constitutional issues are introduced into the purview of constitutional research directed by Western scholars only with much difficulty. However, historical China provides us with a possible field of study, which is also a challenge to our knowledge and power of imagination.

Moreover, for historical China the cultural constitution was not merely a strengthening factor; it was formative. The word "formative" implies the adaptation of many social conditions in ancient China to this institution. In dealing with the political problem of uniting a large agricultural state, this one cultural constitution was not only applicable to ancient China—it was unique— but the search for it was also feasible only *on this soil* and only here could it be implemented as an effective institution. There could be nothing else like it in the world.

For instance, it never presupposed the exclusion of anyone from entering into the ranks of the scholars. Rather, it placed the burden of implementing the corresponding political and cultural responsibility in the world only on the shoulders of the scholars and did not entrust it to the people as a whole. By means of the scholars, it brought together high and low and joined all quarters of the land, bringing the world into one whole. It was an institutional arrangement and regulation of rights and duties that was duty-bearing, practical, and time-saving. Or again, this cultural constitution was not like the popular constitutional discourse that refers only to a cultural force that limits the government. On the contrary, it was a cultural force granted to, and expanding, the government. From the very beginning, unification of the script held a firm grip on education that would establish the state. Yet in what would seem to be a very autocratic cultural constitution, the government did, in fact, not interfere very much. It simply provided directives and set up basic institutions, helped in pushing it forward, relied on the cultural investment of individual effort and the autonomy of very scattered individuals and households, and then sat back and waited for time to act on many microinstitutions by helping them to grow, testing them, rejecting what was bad, accumulating what was good, and rubbing and polishing them.

Hence, it is necessary to clarify the terms "co-opting" and "diverting" used earlier to discuss the use of language and speech in the constitution and politics. Otherwise, it would be a classic form of essentialism, a type of teleology, a kind of dogmatism. For the better survival of humankind, there is in fact nothing that cannot be co-opted or diverted, even when it comes to God. God has not decreed that reading and writing must only be used for reading and writing as such and that they may not be co-opted or diverted, that they may not, or must not, contribute to the peace and stability of the state and a happier life for the people. In other words, co-opting and diverting are acts of creation, that is, in places where people generally think something must be done in a particular way, a different way of doing things can be created.

This chapter has in fact fully laid out the endogenous nature of historical China's cultural constitution. It did not come from the outside. It was imposed but not wholly so, whether by force or in the form of soft power, taking constitutional law as evidence, *relying on the executive and judicial powers that were forcefully supported by the state*. This cultural constitution emerged in a concrete historical China and, in the process of constantly molding China and being molded by China, it gradually became one with the China it molded, such that scholars of the Chinese constitution today have great difficulty becoming aware of it and recognizing that this once shaped China's cultural constitution. They have even greater difficulty in directly feeling and understanding the role and significance that reading and writing once had in molding this state and its civilization. The endogenous nature of the constitution, in fact, is not only a feature of ancient China's constitution; it is even more an important feature of most constitutions.

We need to awaken awareness of China's constitution. Even more, we need a scholarly sensitivity and awareness on the level of knowledge and feeling that can be gained only by entering into this tradition.

CHAPTER THREE

Scholar-Officials

Su Li

Only the benevolent ought to be in high stations.

—MENCIUS[1]

Until philosophers are kings of the city-state, or the so-called kings and princes of [this] the present world truly and fervently love [have the spirit and power of] philosophy, and political power [greatness] and wisdom blend into [meet in] one like water and milk, . . . cities will never have rest from their evils . . . and then only will this our [State] constitution have a real possibility of life and behold the light of day.

—PLATO[2]

Defining the Problem

I have already analyzed and discussed how the two most important cultural constitutional institutions of ancient China—a unified script and Mandarin Chinese—called forth, shaped, and constructed scholars from the countless village communities of historical China and turned them into a class of scholars (the scholar-officials) who belonged not only to their local villages and clans but also to China's political and cultural tradition, and thus can be said to be different from ordinary people. The cultural education and knowledge of the scholars from the whole country led them to form a statewide cultural community while still preserving sufficient local origins and roots. It was also a cultural community that traversed history, since it bound together scholars of the past, present, and future. They originally came from local areas, even from some nowheres that had been overlooked by people of this world, yet because

[98]

of their literacy, because they read books, because of their refined speech or Mandarin Chinese, and the ideals and pursuits of their political and cultural life, at the same time as they attained this sense of belonging to the entire world under heaven, they also belonged to the territory, politics, and culture of this China, both ancient and ever new. Indeed, it might be that they fell into such poverty that they could only save their own skin, but their thoughts and feelings would never fall away from the goal they had once embraced.[3]

However, for their lives to be truly part of the living structure of ancient China, for them to move from a conscious sense of belonging to China on the cultural level to becoming absorbed in China and building up China on the level of daily practice, constructing China by drawing together east and west, north and south, even high and low, an institution was necessary—which may seem to be cultural but was in fact mainly political. This institution would select them in a reasonable, equitable, and fairly accurate manner and allow them to participate in the various levels of administration in the state, and in this way it took them from a social level and transform them into a political and cultural elite that would function on the level of the body politic. This chapter focuses on this basic political or constitutional institution of their cultural, but also political, selection.

But is this a constitutional issue? Is it not only a matter of civil service exams? Administrative law or constitutional law should be enough then. Moreover, what society is there that is not governed by an elite? To tell the truth, without mincing words, what society is there in which "those who work with the mind rule over others and those who labour are ruled over by others"?[4] For the moment we will not discuss whether the yardstick for judging the elite is subjective or objective, whether it looks to individual talent or is influenced by relatives and acquaintances, or is due to the educational training a particular person has received, or even if it is selection by throwing dice, as in the ancient Athenian democracy, since history records that clearly the elite still had influence. We have heard, or know, about the names of Draco, Solon, Peisistratos, Cleisthenes, and Pericles and not "the great Greek people" or "the people of Athens." Does the addition of a high-sounding epithet such as universal values, justice, constitution, or truth raise someone up to be much closer to God, striding alone through the night and obviating the need to blow a whistle?

Therefore, this chapter must show why the way in which ancient China chose its political and cultural elite was different from, for example, ancient Greek society, such that it needed a special institutional framework even if this was subject to constant evolution. Moreover, why is that we can say that there was a form of constitutional institution founded in ancient China that had to do with a political elite, and what is the evidence for this way of speaking?

The basic premise, constraint, and condition is that ancient China was already a large state composed both of countless rural communities whose people never interacted with one another and of many different cultural groups. China was not like other ancient states that were small in comparison, such as the city-states of ancient Greece and Rome—and also including the later monarchical states or city-states of Europe such as Florence and Geneva—which naturally formed a political, economic, and social unit, nor like the larger monarchical states of medieval Europe in which a royal house shared rule with aristocrats of varying degrees, still less like the nation-states of today with their close political and economic links between places and their developed networks for transportation and communications. What makes historical China unique and explains why ancient China's elite political class was very different in practice from the elite politicians of ancient city-states in the West or modern Western nation-states is, first, a series of questions: Given the social conditions of ancient China, would it be possible to adopt a meritocracy among politicians? In what sense would this be a meritocracy? What standard should be used to measure the elite? Was the standard accurate? In many small-scale societies and small states, it would not seem too difficult to resolve these questions, but in the context of ancient China, they become huge issues that are beyond the power of the imagination to solve. To say that these questions were "big" implies that they were not simply invented; they were of the nature of basic presuppositions. For instance, a question may be described as belonging to historical *China* or to a local area. Even such a small issue requires a statewide consensus, based on the people's universal acceptance of and acquiescence in it.

China is a large country, and hence, whatever way of choosing and promoting officials is chosen in the context of the whole elite political institution the highest layer of politics must always keep many political considerations in mind and arrange for detailed and appropriate institutions, including the comprehensive restraints of a peaceful balance for political participation, by representatives of the interests of each place, national group, and nation. As society changed and in accordance with the special nature of some of the dynasties, such as the Yuan and Qing, in which minority peoples from the borders ruled the central plain, these considerations would show at the institutional level.

Also, since it was a large state, in historical China no planned design for an ideal institution for the selection of an elite could be simultaneously set up, and even if it were, it could never be used universally in all parts of the country. Hence, the institution for selecting the elite had to be ongoing, like a glacier that slowly but surely leaves a deep and implacable impression on even the hardest rock.

This is all something that civil service exams do not cover, nor is it something that the imperial exams discussed in this chapter necessarily covered. We must, and can only, take a constitutional view to review and understand the great constitutional significance of the institutional arrangements for ancient China.

This chapter addresses five questions:

First, how was the social consensus for historical China's meritocracy formed, and what are its foundations? Given that early China, at least the Western Zhou, laid a great emphasis on family relationships, and later Confucians continued to value these relations of consanguinity, how is it that in the sphere of China's ancient politics and constitution, family relationships were subordinate to the demand for the efficiency and efficacy of a rational political administration, such that the consideration of a meritocracy may be said to run through China's ancient constitution from beginning to end.

Second, there is the problem of the creation of ancient China's meritocracy, which is not the tale of Bo Le and the thousand-league horse, as many famous people have mistakenly believed and said.[5] Rather—and it has always been so—in a large state, how can you select an elite in an institutional way that is fair, accurate, and effective? Hence, it is a question of institutions and not of personal knowledge or moral standing.

Third, given the social importance of the political elite for historical China, any sites of influence or any levels of power in society would strive by all means possible, both formal and informal, to exert their political influence, and therefore, in establishing a statewide, uniform, standardized institution for selection, the central government represented by the monarchy would certainly have conflicts of interest of all kinds with other powers in society. The evolution and development of the means of selection in ancient China from selections (推舉, *tuiju*) to recommendations (察舉, *chaju*) and to examinations (科舉, *keju*) reflect the historical nature of the institution and its adaptation to the political, economic, social, and cultural conditions of each historical era.[6] They also reflect an inherent logic of political rationalization.

Fourth, for the standardization and comparative accuracy of the selection, historical China had no choice but to rely on a standardized written exam for the statewide selection of the elite. The ability measured by this method was not the practical rationality that was required for ancient China's political governance. Hence, alongside the institutions of the selections, recommendations, and examinations, there had to be other methods of testing, verifying, and allowing for practical assessment to reinforce the exams themselves. This must not be overlooked.

Fifth, given that China was a large country, with a complicated and vast natural terrain and many different nationalities and cultures, and for some issues had a pluralism of interests, the institution of selection had to also take into account factors of mobility between places and in society. Unlike the representative institutions that emerged in the post-medieval West and developed in modern times, the selection of the elite in ancient China to a certain extent was indeed a form of institutional engagement in society and politics and one that even brought an element of representation.

It is sufficient to raise all these questions to realize that ancient China's selection of a political elite and their participation in government can unashamedly be called "constitutional." It may be, or must be, those Chinese constitutional scholars who nowadays *only talk* about *Marbury v. Madison* or *Brown v. Board of Education* who feel ashamed before the great constitution of ancient China. "Great" here does not mean politically correct, but that, whether you agree or disagree with it, it transcends the issue of good or bad.

Meritocracy as Constitutional Consensus

The constitution of the Xia, Shang, and Zhou is said to be based on hereditary law. Yet the precise institutions of the Xia and Shang are not clear. Those of the Western Zhou are somewhat clearer and serve as a model. In principle the Western Zhou was a time when the Son of Heaven apportioned the world under heaven to princes of the royal blood. The Son of Heaven, feudal lords, ministers, and scholars had duties according to their place in the hierarchy and administered the state by hereditary succession: "hereditary succession and inherited incomes." In light of this, elsewhere I have discussed how reliance on family relationships arose from a rational, political, and constitutional consideration, in that it was an instrumental use of consanguinity and not simply a politics that sought consanguinity as its foundation, nor was it a matter of subordinating political rank to consanguinity or affinity. As soon as it was necessary and feasible politically, family relationships necessarily ceded place. Thus, in the Shang and Zhou, the daily political running of the state increasingly valued the talent of the rulers. After King Wuding of the Shang ascended the throne, he named a slave, who was clearly of a foreign race but was an outstanding politician, as prime minister.[7] King Zhou of the Shang "did not use the younger brothers of the king's father and mother."[8] Instead he employed criminals who had fled from all over the place.[9] The Western Zhou, which would seem to have set more store by blood relations, also tended toward a meritocracy. Guan Shu and Cai Shu were uncles of King Cheng, but the younger and worthier Duke of Zhou was appointed to assist in ruling. Jiang Ziya and other foreign members of the political elite also entered the ranks of the ruling class, participated, and shared in political governance.[10]

This shows that, whether or not one says one upholds some principle or however one labels oneself, the iron rule of politics is that, provided the final policy or decision maker has a sufficient number of options, competition within the ruling body or from outside the country will force the shape of the practical governance of a state to move in the direction of meritocracy. If not, then either this ruling clique or the political community it rules over will be made obsolete.[11]

Therefore, by the time of the Spring and Autumn and Warring States periods, fierce competition among the feudal states had already destroyed the ritual and administrative sensibility of the Western Zhou. Things went from "rites, music, expeditions, and punishments proceed from the Son of Heaven" to "they proceed from the feudal princes," to "from the prime minister," to "the accompanying ministers lay hold of the destiny of the state."[12] These events show clearly that only if hereditary succession was transformed into rule by persons who had the capacity to acquire, hold on to, and manage power could it be retained. As a result of some genetic factors, home education, possession of books, and the opportunity to take part earlier in high political posts (what may be termed the earliest form of a second generation of officials), in the Warring States and even in the Qin-Han period there were many generations of elite persons. In addition to the four great sons of dukes of the Warring States period, the most outstanding were several military families. For instance, in the state of Zhao there was Zhao She and his son Zhao Kuo; in Qin there was Wang Jian and his son Wang Fen and the family of Meng Ao, Meng Wu, Meng Tian, and Meng Yi. In Chu there was the Xiang family. From the Warring States period to the Han there was the Li family: Li Xin, Li Guang, Li Gan, and Li Ling, and in the Han dynasty there was Zhou Bo and his son Zhou Yafu. But overall, the days of hereditary ministers and salaries were beginning to pass. "The aura of a gentleman lasts five generations and then is snuffed out" had already become general social practice.[13] It was talent that was to become the norm of the future. In the Spring and Autumn and Warring States periods, a number of talented politicians had already sprung up, such as Guan Zhong, Bai Lixi, and Lan Xiangru.[14]

The norm of "valuing the worthy" in the sense of paying respect to an individual's ability may be said to have already become the political consensus of the society. But what is a worthy? What abilities were required to constitute a person as one of the elite? What terms, what language, would allow the higher level of politicians in the various states to understand and accept some standard of worth in an effective way? In differentiating between the talents of different individuals, what should be the norm and what would its social consequences be?

The worth that Confucius valued included a knowledge of books, practice of the rites, benevolence, wisdom and courage, filial piety, and fraternal love. It would seem that the stress here is on individual virtue. Yet through the generations, what Confucians valued was that which would enable a state to "have sufficient food and a sufficient army," and the political ability to "win the trust of the people."[15] They were not interested in individual virtues in the abstract. Hence, Confucius criticized Guan Zhong for "not knowing the rites" while praising him for his efforts on behalf of all of China and Chinese civilization.[16] The "worth and ability" esteemed by the Legalists were even more concrete, including rewards for farming, enriching the state, and strengthening the army, such that one could attack towns and seize land.[17]

This is not something that arose spontaneously out of Confucian or Legalist ideas. Rather, in the Spring and Autumn and Warring States periods, fierce political and military competition among the states led to them actively seeking, discovering, and appointing talented people to take part in the governance of their states and thus increasing their chances in the competition with other feudal states and political forces. Utilitarianism and pragmatism thus arose, and it is probably at that time that the saying "do not ask where a hero was born" emerged.[18] Furthermore, social class, experience, professional category, and even flaws in personality were not so important, because "the purest water would be without fish, the perfect person without followers."[19] Moreover, it was not only a concern for these abilities writ large. It was enough to be useful. "A rooster that crows and a dog that barks at a thief" aptly describes the kind of talent that at particular times entered into the scope of politicians in power and won favor.[20]

Political competition not only gave rise to a social consensus about meritocracy but also undid the sense of local belonging of the elite. Given the lure of interests, including political interests, and adding on the advantages of a relatively advanced system of communication in the central plain since the inception of the Western Zhou, the level of local loyalty among the political elite of the states had never been very high. Hence it was said, "The talent of Chu [the south] is used in Jin [the north]."[21] Confucius himself did not wait every day under the tree, in the hope that a hare would kill itself by crashing into a tree trunk.[22] Nor was he unwavering in his support for his home prefecture of Lu. Rather, he made himself into a commodity, put on the open market at the price of "if anyone uses me, can I not make an Eastern Zhou?"[23] By the time of the Warring States, this had become the general norm. The feudal lords openly competed to recruit people of elite ability. Su Qin, Zhang Yi, Sun Wu, Sun Bin, Pang Juan, Yue Yi, Wu Qi, Wu Zi Xu, Li Kui, Shang Yang, Lü Buwei, Li Si, Han Fei, and other elite persons went around the states looking for work. Among these famous elite persons, the one exception would seem to be Qu Yuan. Many people were thereby enabled to achieve something tangible, even something great, classic examples being Shang Yang and Li Si.

What all this implies is that, excluding other considerations, the state and world under heaven formed by the feudal states of the time rejected hereditary posts and salaries at all levels and accepted a meritocracy. All sought results, in either the long or the short term. This had already become the fairly fixed consensus of society. It was just that the world under heaven was not yet firmly defined and there were insufficient practical consequences to lead people to affirm what was useful, especially to determine what talents were required for the long-term governance of the state, what people could pass the test of history as a political and cultural elite that belonged to the whole of society.

Abstract elite governance was always the ideal form of governance in China, and something that had been achieved in political practice throughout Chinese history, though China at that time had not yet a united *norm* of recognition for being elite and even later it had difficulty in keeping a norm that was valid everywhere. Not only have empiricism and dogmatism been at war over this issue since time immemorial, but at any given period of history, apart from any formally systematized channels of communication, some varying ways of communication would remain, and people would accept these changes; as Gong Zizhen said, "don't get stuck on one way of evaluating talent." The basic principle is that you do not ask where a hero was born, or the very pragmatic and consequentialist saying, "the one who succeeds is a king; the one who fails a rebel." Although the second saying may seem a bit rough, it does accurately portray the ideal of the elite of secularism and populism. People do not believe in class, status, bloodlines, race, or distinctions in degrees of intelligence—though of course this does not imply that they do not take into consideration the political reliability that may accompany these traits. As a complement to the formal system, Chinese society has always had a certain tradition of anti-intellectualism.[24] In short, what mattered was practical use and not dogmatism or the influence of heredity. I will return to this issue in the fifth section of this chapter.

Indeed, even when the minority peoples of the frontiers entered into the central plain, they kept to a meritocracy, though with many limitations on the political participation of Han Chinese scholars, especially during the Yuan dynasty. But these forms of discrimination or restriction were even clearer in the assessment of political reliability, and so were not a matter of racism. Although China did experience a time in the past when powerful clans held political influence, it had never moved in the direction of classical aristocratic rule, or toward the type of caste system found in India, or even the widespread and grave implementation of racial segregation that lasted for several centuries in the southern United States up until the mid-twentieth century.

This form of social consensus was shaped by a whole series of concrete social and national responsibilities regarding personality, education, and the political elite. These included the idea that all people shared in many basic natural talents and potentialities, though to different degrees, and so individual preferences differed. These differences might emerge as society put them into practice: "people are alike in nature, but different in customs."[25] Genetic inheritance, home upbringing, social experience, and chance could all influence, and determine, the talents and achievements of people: "life and death are fixed; riches and standing are allotted by heaven."[26] Yet nobody was ever determined at birth. Theoretically, thanks to one's training at home and in society, everybody could become an important person. Important posts in society, including that of emperor, tended to be, and in fact were, open to all equally: "Are there really people such as kings, lords, generals and ministers born so?" "Anyone could seize their position and replace them."[27] A person's individual talent is that person's, but it also belongs to society. A person of lesser fortune could become an important human resource of exceptional value at the disposition of society: "one who has studied should try to be an official" (*Analects*); "only the benevolent are apt for high status" (*Mencius*);

"when poor one can make oneself good; when in a high position one can make the whole world good" (*Mencius*); "train yourself (修身), regulate your family (齐家), govern the state (治国), and bring peace to the world under heaven (平天下)" (*Great Learning*).[28] As a result, once one had become a member of the political elite, one's political duties to the state and society superseded moral obligations to the family and family clan: "let the prince be a prince, the minister a minister, the father a father, and the son a son" (*Analects*); "loyalty to the state and filial piety do not go together" (Yan Zhenqing); "in the first place let the concerns of the world be your concerns; secondly, let the joys of the world be your joys" (Fan Zhongyan); "even in a low position they did not dare to forget their concern for the state" (Lu You).[29] Education is the main conduit by which society and people themselves could develop and use these human resources effectively: "unless you study the rites, you do not have a foot to stand on."[30] The core of education is training received in the family, as can be seen in the stories *The Three Refusals of Mencius' Mother* and "to fail to educate one's son is a fault of the father."[31]

Given these basic presuppositions about natural talent, development of ability, and their significance for society, over the course of history, China was faced with various political considerations that always came together in the promotion of the worthy or in participation in political governance by a political and cultural elite. Viewed as a political ideal and seen as a social practice, it was always in contrast to the emperor, who treated the world as his family. Dynasties throughout history encouraged and recruited—which is a kind of forced request—the scholars of the empire to take part in government and stressed that the political elite should assume responsibility: "the responsibility is heavy and the road is long." Ordinary folk had responsibility for the rise and fall of the empire: "train yourself (修身), regulate your family (齐家), govern the state (治国), and bring peace to the world under heaven (平天下)"; "when promoted they made the whole world good."[32] If that were too much, then one should at least improve oneself. Or one could work for other social values that deserved to be valued, such as loyalty. New dynasties would allow members of the political elite who had served the previous dynasty to retire. In this way, ancient China transformed the individual talent hidden in society into a resource for society, something society could share in.

Bo Le? Individual Talent or Systematic Selection

Once this social consensus was agreed on, dynasties throughout China's history faced the issue of selecting an elite. But to implement this consensus, a number of difficulties had to be overcome, and this required a long period of slow development of a suitable system of selection.

The biggest difficulty was, in fact, not what Han Yu envisaged—something whose influence is still widespread today—namely, that "there are many horses which can run a thousand leagues but rarely is there a Bo Le."[33] The implicit logic of Han Yu's statement is that the key to the selection of a political elite lies in the love of talent or the capacity of the political leader himself to know a horse. It is a matter of his individual foresight and ability to choose a talented person from among the myriad persons on earth. This is illustrated in many stories taken from Chinese history that seem to prove the point, such as "Jiang Ziya went fishing by the river Wei; the fish that wanted to be caught jumped up to his hook," "Xiao He chased after Han Xin in the moonlight," and "Liu Bei went three times to the ruined cottage (where Zhuge Liang lived)." Hence, selection of talent was dependent on the personal virtue or wisdom of the political leader. As a result, over a long period of time people spoke as if the main means of implementing a selection of an elite was dependent on the morality of the ruler himself. He must thirst for worthy men, honoring such people with posts and choosing only talented persons, sparing nothing in his search. Second, his political judgment and insight required him to be able to discover rare persons of exceptional talent, choose, and employ them.

But this general understanding of the selection of the elite in China is wrong from the start in that it begins from the wrong point of view. Clearly, if politicians want to select talent and do so only from their own point of view, they will not only be able, but also will, tolerate some flaws or weak points in their chosen elite that would otherwise be unacceptable. Generally, they would also be able to recognize the elite—since these are virtually constructed by the politicians' own definition. The real problem, though, and one that is not easily overcome, is that of information. How could one discover talent or get a line on where talent lies, and how could one guarantee that talent? In particular, the greatest problem is how to decide whether one person is more talented than another. Without gathering sufficient reliable information, without a judgment based on a broad range of information, especially since one cannot make a judgment about the future on actual experience gained before the appointment, it would seem to be impossible. So from this point of view, the selection of an elite is a high-risk investment. If one lacks a uniform, reliable standard, then not only does an ardent desire to seek the worthy not resolve the problem, it rather becomes a problem in its own right, even a major one. If we think of the four great dukes of the Warring States period, we find they did not turn away any comers and each of them had several thousand aspirants knocking at his door. This is a perfect illustration of an ardent search for talent, but what great things were they able to carry out? Or if we think of the countless proverbs that circulated in the Warring States period, we can say that Han Yu's distant ancestor, Han Fei, saw the problem much more clearly.[34] That is, all of this can only, and must only, be supplementary to a system if it is to be effective.

The selection of an elite in a large agrarian state is exceptionally difficult. In a small community, such as in the Greek city-states, people meet and work together on a regular basis and thus can more easily find and identify talented individuals. It is also easier to win consensus on who belongs to the elite; the talent of individuals is less easily hidden away.[35] But in a large agrarian state, although there are certain to be elite persons, they may be scattered in rural communities that rarely communicate with one another and where communication and transportation are inconvenient such that people do not know one another and there is no common background or common standard of measurement. It is not possible to form a uniform standard in advance, and so no one can even talk of having an appropriate standard, and it is even harder to judge who is better than another. Indeed, even the so-called Bo Le comes from and belongs to a particular community or region, and he may not have seen much of the world and his judgment may not be much superior to another person's. "Beyond the mountain there are yet higher mountains; beyond this building yet taller buildings": "there is always someone of greater skill in a group of skilled persons." In a large agrarian state, it is very difficult for anyone to truly, reliably, and authoritatively compare others or make a judgment about them. Indeed, one cannot even do so for oneself. Or, even if someone had this ability and was able to judge dispassionately, yet it would be very difficult to get everyone everywhere to believe in his authority and fairness, since authority also requires a basis in social consensus.

It is essential to establish a uniform and effective means of gathering information and making comparisons before one can overcome the lack of a uniform standard in a large state with scattered sources of information. There must be a uniform standard by which to judge, one that is sufficiently comprehensive and accurate for effective assessments to be made. But there are also other problems to be faced. First, one must let all people who consider themselves to be the elite, whether their self-assessment is objective or not, participate and only subsequently discuss their willingness and ability and then they can either voluntarily, or based on a custom, or even actively participate under this uniform measure, recognizing and accepting the authority and evenhandedness of the standard of measurement. From a theoretical point of view, none of this was possible in early China.

Furthermore, in a large state with a complex topography there are bound to be inequalities in the level of economic, political, and cultural development. This implies that even naturally gifted persons are liable to have received different degrees of education depending on their place of birth. In today's language, we might say that from the start there was inequality of opportunity. In the past, however, inequality of opportunity was not to be seen as a matter of individual rights since people's outlook was limited and rarely went beyond one's own person and people like oneself, and so no one talked about equality with far-off strangers. But the inequality of opportunity was even more serious, since from the view of the structure of the state as a whole, without the participation of elite persons from all over the country or without balanced participation of all areas in the central government and in the politics of the whole state, imbalances of information and understanding about the regions on the part of the center might influence the unity of rule of that particular dynasty. Indeed, to a large extent they did so.

Moreover, we must ask what the concrete norm was. Howsoever the central government catered to the various interests, so long as there was one standard for the whole country, the factors that went into making that standard had to come from a certain place. Therefore, any uniform standard could be biased and any effort to achieve unity could lead to division rather than unity. But one could not, for this reason, either forsake the goal of establishing a uniform standard to measure what being elite meant or create a standard out of thin air. The only possibility was to take some existing local standard and try to ensure that it became the standard for the whole country. This change required sufficient time and effort to coordinate various mechanisms before the standard could silently permeate every place in the whole country and gain acceptance.

A further big problem is that of entanglement. What one wants to select is a political elite, but those who participate are military people in charge of affairs of state, war, and peace. So, it is not only a matter of assessing the wisdom and ability of the elite but also, and even more important, of examining their political affiliations and loyalty.

Political affiliation is not such a big problem for the political elite in independent city-states or small countries in ancient society, because the ideal community and the actual community in which one lives virtually coincide. But in a large state, there will arise the problem of a mismatch between the ideal and the real community and thus the demands placed on the political loyalty of the political elite will be much more complicated, and even entangled. On the one hand, the elite must be politically loyal to their employer. In the Warring States time, this was an issue.[36] On the other hand, the politics of a large state also required the political elite, to a great extent, to overcome local interests and think of themselves as belonging to a wider society and region, to make the affairs of the empire their own. Only then could they become persons the state could employ. They would not merely represent local interests; they needed to have professional ethics that their employer could rely on, political loyalty.

Unification under the Qin and Han did away with competition between employers and simplified the political and moral issues faced by the elite. But the problem became how elites from so many places could attach primary importance to the state, the people, public affairs, and the common interest. They had to understand who the people were, what a public issue was, what the state and the world under heaven were, and what important offices were. These were all major questions that elites from all over had to gradually respond to and resolve on the basis of their cultural education and political practice. They had to learn how to view things from the perspective of society as a whole rather than local or personal interests. They had to take this stance to understand the whole and judge what was important. Political ideas, political breeding, and political loyalty mattered, rather than political opportunism and egotism. The kind of demand laid on the political elite of historical China for a political and cultural community is something that could never be provided by a city-state or even a modern European nation-state. This demand required some special qualities. There had to be special political and cultural norms and corresponding systems such that a political elite with these qualities could be fostered and formed. To guarantee that they would be effective, these norms had to win acceptance from the people being formed by them.

Summarizing all these questions, we can say that all of them seek to provide the elite with a political ability to resolve the issues raised by the political, economic, and cultural aspects of a community in a large state, or we might say that they are an important aspect of China's constitution, for which China had to discover the preliminary systemic conditions. Because, without this basic political, economic, social, and cultural community, or if this community were unstable and liable to disappear, and there were no political or cultural boundaries imaginable, the selection of the political elite would certainly run into insuperable difficulties, such as how to set up a system for the selection or examination of the elite who were chosen or who presented themselves for examination. Without a sufficiently strong government body or reliable means of supervision, selection or examination would seem to be impossible. What interest could motivate the political and cultural elite of all places to actively move out of their home regions and cross, perhaps, a thousand mountains and ten thousand rivers, saying farewell to their relatives, setting out, and taking part in the selection process, "allowing the state to decide whom to choose"? If they did not cooperate or did not try to take part, then the selection of the elite would simply not get off the ground. Without a basic political and cultural identity, it would not seem possible to set up standards of knowledge and ability by which to undertake the selection or examination. Why use writing? Indeed, why use Chinese characters?

These questions suffice to show that the implementation of a meritocracy in historical China must have been directly related to the political framework established by the political and military measures put in place by previous dynasties and states, and that it could not have come from the political elite themselves. In other words, it was the success of unification by military conquest undertaken by the First Emperor of Qin that monopolized the market and ensured that the elite would no longer be able to turn to other rulers. Otherwise, their political ability would merely be like that of today, a commercial transaction. Their political loyalty would be reduced to a stable expectation of rewards. The unification of the script by the First Emperor of Qin, the rejection of the hundred schools and selection of the Confucians alone by Emperor Wu of the Han, and similar measures set out in this book and in the selection of the political elite in later China gained a significance that their then creators probably did not fully appreciate.

Unification of the script and preference for Confucianism alone and similar measures were very important for the selection of a political elite under subsequent dynasties. However, distant water does not slake a thirst. As a result of unification under the Qin, and even more under the Han, the problem of selecting a political elite for a large state was in fact exacerbated. The fall of the Qin thanks to the incompetence of the Second Emperor meant that no regular norms for selecting a political elite had yet emerged. In the early years of the Han, reliance was placed on the ministers who had helped to set up the state, such as Xiao He, Cao Can, Wang Ling, Chen Ping, Zhou Bo/Bei, Guan Ying, and others, and this was not a problem in the beginning. But forty-five years later, under Emperor Jing, there were no such capable ministers to be found and thus the problem of finding successors became all too apparent. The only thing to do was to employ the sons of the previous officials, such as Zhou Yafu and Liu She. By the time of Emperor Wu of the Han, the sparsity of talent had become pressing. Emperor Wu therefore sought a political elite among his distant relatives on a large scale, such that Sima Qian added a chapter for the biographies of distant relatives to his *Historical Records*. This use of distant relatives became an outstanding feature of politics under the two Han dynasties.[37] On his accession, Emperor Wu appointed Dou Ying, the nephew (*zhi-er*) of his father's empress Dou as prime minister and made his own uncle (*jiujiu*), Tian Fen, grand commandant and later prime minister. Some of the most important appointments under Emperor Wu were given to people of good repute and ability, but on close examination, even persons such as Wei Qing and Huo Qubing or the later Li Guangli all turned out to be his brothers-in-law (*xiaojiuzi*). Huo Guang, the minister appointed by Emperor Wu to assist his young son Emperor Zhao after his death, was also a brother-in-law.

These stories show that Emperor Wu tended to appoint relatives, but they may also show that his approach to choosing talented people did not stick to a fixed pattern.[38] Proof lies in the case of Wei Qing, who had once been a slave, and the genius Huo Qubing, who was very young when chosen. Moreover, before his death, Emperor Wu named Jin Midi as a high minister (*fuming dachen*). He was a Xiongnu who had been forced to surrender to the Han and been made a palace slave. Emperor Wu discovered him by accident and gradually formed him and shaped him into a politician for the Han dynasty.[39] But these few people were all close to the emperor himself and thus could be found and employed by him. Among persons who were not so close to him we could perhaps list Wei Qing or Huo Qubing, Huo Guang or Jin Midi.

But the legitimate expectations of a political leader such as Emperor Wu of the Han could not be satisfied by measures that did not go beyond their time or society at the time in identifying and choosing the most outstanding people in the whole country. Rather, in the conditions imposed on him, he could, and did, find and select the most outstanding persons possible. Thus, this demonstrates Emperor Wu's ability to spot talent, but it also demonstrates the paucity of political talent in his time. The Han had ruled for sixty years when he acceded to the throne, but the dynasty had not yet developed a system to select talent and was forced to rely on the personal acumen of the emperor himself. The Western Han desperately longed for the establishment of an effective system for attracting and selecting the elite from the whole country to take part in the political governance of the state.

Here is an issue that people today are apt to overlook: if the central government could not attract a sufficient number of gifted persons, this would imply not only that people would not be able to perform according to their talent but also that there would be an even greater danger, namely, that some of the political elite would be attracted by the feudal princes and form political forces that would rival or even oppose the central government. This would be a great disservice to the stability and unity of the state. The ability of Liu An, king of Huainan, to attract a cultural elite in the early years of the Han is something that later generations admired. In certain respects, the influence of Liu An's political and cultural thought eclipsed that of the central government of his time.[40] Even though the central government had a hold on the essentials and Emperor Wu himself had sufficient political clout, the problems are, first, that reliance on individual political clout alone cannot guarantee the regime will stand for long, and, second, there is no assurance that later emperors would have Emperor Wu's talent, clout, or authority. For these reasons, it was necessary to open up channels by which the political elite could take part in state politics and enable the state to use the human resources of the whole country more fully. Thus, in historical China, a meritocracy must be a constitutional issue.

Selections (tuiju), Recommendations (chaju), and Examinations (keju)

In this section, we will discover that it was in fact starting in the time of Emperor Wu that efforts for the selection of talent were for the first time systematized and placed on a long-term basis. We also will discuss how this system was implemented, what conditions—unalterable at the time—it was based on, what kind of measures were adopted, and to what concrete issues they corresponded. Only after a period of some 750 years as a result of the accumulation of scattered efforts was it possible for these efforts to crystalize in the great system of imperial examinations.

Before Emperor Wu, Emperor Wen had issued a decree calling for recommendations from the whole country of "worthy persons who could speak honestly as advisors."[41] But it was only under Emperor Wu that the most important institution, the appointment system, was set up to attract the elite to participate in politics. Emperor Wu, first, "ordered the provinces and command-eries to select officials who were exceptionally talented and might be made generals or sent as ambassadors."[42] This "opened wide the road for talented and worthy persons and welcomed scholars of all disciplines."[43] But Emperor Wu still accepted the advice of Dong Zhongshu to employ Confucians only and thus did not allow Legalists or Strategists to participate.[44]

There were largely two kinds of persons recommended to the court by different localities. The first was a percentage of the population of each commandery and "state" chosen from among virtuous persons who sought to implement Confucian morality. The second was outstanding persons of each region recommended by the high ministers and officials. The persons put forward included not only officials themselves but also virtuous persons from among the common people. The central government examined or employed the persons recommended on a trial basis. They were asked to suggest strategies for dealing with important political and social matters, and those who replied the best were chosen for service in the empire or were kept at the palace to work beside the emperor as *langguan* (staff officials). In addition, the Han dynasty also recruited specially skilled persons to be sent to work on the western frontier or to look after rivers and such technical matters. They could be recommended by others or could apply themselves.

The persons recommended had to finally undergo an examination by the emperor himself before their appointment. Perhaps legal philosophers today would say that this laid too much stress on the will of the officials and is a classic form of personal rule. But when it is compared to the previous unsystematized selection of talent, this form of recommendation was normalized and so was, in fact, rule by law. In particular, the selection of the Confucians took place once a year at a fixed time and in time came to replace other informal institutions that lacked such periodic timing. Furthermore, since Emperor Wu ordered that the high palace officials and local officials should recommend talented persons, the task of selection became the legal responsibility of government officials at all levels and entered into the agenda of government work. To a certain extent, this expanded the channels and opportunities by which persons of various talents could participate in politics and even more of the elite were able, as a result, to look forward to entering the government of the state. The final exam before the emperor was only one essential element in the selection process. It manifested the importance attached to selection by the highest authorities and their concern. It pertains to a necessary institutional measure that reinforced the central authority of the leaders and thus augmented the prestige of the center in the hearts of the people.

The choice of Confucianism must also be understood from the point of view of the institutional measures to select talent and at the level of the national constitution. This is, of course, because Confucian thought conforms to the essential social control and internal order of agrarian society itself.[45]

The ethical norms of Confucianism regarding personal morality, the family, the state, and the world as a whole are able to negotiate effectively between the family and the state and thus made a substantive contribution to the society and political governance. Hence, previous scholars are right to have understood Dong Zhongshu's suggestion as arising from his political concern to unite the state. But one leaf can blind the eye. This angle greatly underestimates this suggestion since the institutional significance and historic import of its implementation are much broader and deeper. If we start from the issues raised in this chapter, then we will discover that the adoption of Confucianism alone was, in fact, the first step in standardizing the state selection of a political elite. It unified the topics for the state exams and determined their scope and led to intellectual investment by the whole of society. From an objective point of view, cultural investment won out over the efforts of other schools. However, this does not mean that it sought to put down other schools of thought and culture.

Contention among different schools of thought is a standard mechanism that provokes human beings to think, but it is not a means for assessing and choosing talented persons. The two do not go together. Even in the most tolerant and accepting society, an examination cannot be tolerant and accepting: some people will pass and others fail. If examinations were created according to the Mohist school, then that would be unfair to other schools of thought. Even if the exams were all based on Daoism, if the topic was Zhuangzi, then that would be unfair to the disciples of Laozi, or an exam according to the *Mencius* would be unfair to the students of the *Xunzi*. If the exam was to be written in Chinese, then the native languages of non-Chinese students would be unacceptable. Although competition among the schools may be fair, in itself it cannot produce a uniform system of selection that could win the confidence of the public. Without any such system of selection, no one would willingly come forward to take part in the selection.

Therefore, the long-term historical contribution of the choice of Confucianism alone must be understood in terms of the long river of history. It is not only a matter of that time, or of the following few decades, but something that becomes obvious only some 750 years later, namely, the fundamental contribution that the choice of Confucianism alone made to the implementation of the institution of imperial examinations. In accordance with this cultural investment and its gradual permeation of every place in the country and at every level of society, the set texts for the whole country were slowly unified, and thus what the scholars studied was unified and standardized, as a result of which it was ultimately possible to establish a universally acceptable, statewide standardized test and system of evaluation for scholars in the whole country. Once this is understood it will be possible to appreciate that the choice of Confucianism alone, with the tradition of Confucius and Mencius as the mainstream—although since modern times this measure has generally been reckoned as unfavorable to the development of traditional Chinese thought and culture—was, in fact, a contribution of great and far-reaching significance to the cultural development of the Chinese people and their establishment of institutions.

Of course, some scholars might object that this measure could equally well be applied to other schools and encouraged them to develop too and thus increase cultural investment. Put like this, it seems that failure to do so is a price China had to pay, and hence it was a loss. But what is required here is not a simple judgment: was this a loss on the abstract level? That would be something everyone knows could be done. But this would be a complicated, delicate balance and, given that China then lacked the requisite personnel and was under the constraints imposed by the lack of other resources, whether historical China could have benefitted institutionally from other cultural institutions is a moot point. So this loss may be worthwhile.

The gains need to be viewed over the long term. Whatever the case, the Han dynasty was unable to reap the benefits. Emperor Wu was faced with a dire shortage of men and, leaving aside the long-term institutional view, he required an immediate solution. The measures he put in place were the countrywide recommendation procedure and the imperial academy, which was also founded in his time. According to Qian Mu, these two institutions were responsible for China's political turnaround. There were more than one hundred commanderies in the Han Empire, and each year more than two hundred worthy candidates were recommended. They entered the place to serve there as *langguan*. Soon, these scholars included people from all the commanderies of the empire and perhaps more than half of them attended the imperial academy. Some decades later, among those who passed the central government selection, the best were appointed officials of the central government while the rest were sent home to work as local officials. Gradually, officials of all ranks under the Han became either scholars themselves or at least people who had been educated. According to the uniform regulation of the laws and decrees issued by the central government, governance was thus made firm.[46]

At the time and for a considerable period afterward, the recommendation system was the most feasible system possible under the social conditions of the time and in this sense was the best way of choosing practical and able persons. Since at the time the scholars of the whole country could not possibly have been formed against a uniform intellectual background or scholarly tradition, there being no stable academic tradition or intellectual framework built on such a tradition, any other form of testing or examination of culture and knowledge could not have been implemented. Students, examiners, and those who put in recommendations could not have managed. Another important restraining factor is that, as is generally understood, the manufacture of paper began to develop only under the Eastern Han and so only from that moment on did the use of paper begin to become widespread. Hence, for this reason, universal written exams would have been basically impossible under the Western Han.

Given such social conditions, the opportunity to study would necessarily have been unevenly distributed in society. This inequality would certainly have nothing to do with people's natural intellectual capacity, but would be related to whether someone from a previous generation had studied, whether there were books at home, or even if they could be bought or copied. It would depend on whether one's family was well-off and, even more, on whether someone in one's family had been in politics and on one's relationship to dominant families (*menfa shizu*). Faced with such conditions, the choice of the elite by a written exam might well be even more unfair than the recommendation system. At least in the first stages, recommendation by local and central government officials would be a better institutional option. You might even say that the role of this institution was one of a division of power between the local and central governments and a way of choosing a political elite who would perform checks on each other.

The biggest disadvantage of the recommendation system—as was to be seen later—lay in that, since the power to choose whom to employ rested in the central government, although talented persons could be recommended by officials of all the commanderies and those in the highest posts, recommending persons naturally fell easily to the local clans and high officials, leading to local affiliations and dominant families. By the late Eastern Han, the recommendation system was played and used by the cliques who controlled popular opinion and brought about all kinds of corruption.[47] Political ethics and political logic clearly demanded a reform of the system. But what really made reform necessary was not political ethics or logic, but rather the rising of the Yellow Turbans in the closing years of the Eastern Han and the local separatism and years of war and chaos that followed. The population of the north declined considerably, and this meant that local districts were no longer able to recommend talented persons and the central government was unable to send persons to all parts of the country.

In these social circumstances, the state of Wei, in the Three Kingdoms period, created a central institution of nine grades of officials. This was in fact another version of the recommendation system, the difference being that it weakened the power exercised by local areas in selecting talent and strengthened the control and examination of the nominees by the center. The *chaju* system thus became the key institution for selecting officials during the Wei, Jin, and Southern and Northern dynasties. In practice, this system meant that the court chose worthy and competent officials for all posts at the local level in the prefectures, commanderies, and counties to inspect the scholars of their localities and assign ranks to them on the basis of their families—depending on the posts occupied by fathers or grandfathers and according to the rank held—personal virtue, and talent. These ranks were used as a reference by the

Ministry of Personnel (*Li bu*). Assignment of rank should mainly depend on virtue and talent, with family background being merely for reference. However, under the Wei and the Jin dynasties virtually all the central posts were held by dominant families who controlled the selection by the ministry. In assigning rank, talent and virtue gradually moved into second place while family background rose to the fore and even became the only criterion. By the Western Jin, it was said that "high-ranking persons never lacked visitors; low-ranking persons had no power."[48] The institution of nine grades by the center failed to effectively strengthen the control of the center over the choice of talent. Moreover, it sustained and reinforced the rule of the local dominant families and was itself an important part of the system of dominant families. The recommendation system that had once been a reform of the institution for selecting a political elite had itself become in need of reform.

When the Sui restored unity in the country, they sought to strengthen the central authority and reform politics. One measure that they used was to abolish recommendation and replace it with the institution of imperial examinations. In 587, Emperor Wen of the Sui decreed that each prefecture was to send three persons each year to take part in the *xiucai* exam, though artisans and traders were not to take part. In 605, Emperor Yang of the Sui began to use the *jinshi* exam to choose officials. This is generally reckoned to be the beginning of the *keju* (examination) system that was to last thirteen hundred years.[49]

Overall, it is accepted that there were two political measures that led to the historic transition from the recommendation system of selecting talent to the examination system. The first is that the Sui abolished the middle administrative level of the prefectures, commanderies, and counties and thus reduced the tiers of government. This measure cut the ground from under the system of recommendation of talent by the commanderies that had been in place since the Western Han. The second is that the Sui strengthened the central authority. Under the Sui, officials in the prefectures and counties were not permitted to name their subordinates themselves since this task was assigned to the Ministry of Personnel and thus coordinated by the center. This meant that the central government had to find another reliable and effective way of choosing even more officials. But aside from this, one important premise lay in the culture of society, namely, that the practice of central government from the Qin and Han onward included unification of the script and promotion of the refined language of the central plain. These measures had already accumulated cultural results at the institutional level in society. Moreover, the more than seven hundred years of institutional practice of the selection of officials by the selection and recommendation systems begun by Emperor Wu of the Han as well as the choice of Confucianism alone had already spread throughout the whole country and had gradually penetrated all levels of society. Taken together, this was an important institutional condition for the foundation of a system of selection of a political and cultural elite that was wholly dependent on writing, independent of other social interest groups, and completely under the central government. A statewide standard was also provided that ensured the social environment within which the imperial examinations could take place.

Compared to the selection system of the Han dynasty and the recommendation system of the Wei and Jin, a special characteristic of the imperial examination system is that scholars applied of their own free will and success or failure was largely decided by their score on the written exam. From a constitutional point of view, the main institutional change was that it strengthened the central government's control of the selection of talent, meaning that the various levels or groupings of power in society no longer had an *institutional influence* on social mobility and political selection of talent. Every scholar, wherever he was born, whether rich or poor, if he wanted to, could aspire, mainly by his own effort and relying on his own ability, to compete for a share in the political governance of the state. For ordinary people, this set out a clear, standardized direction for cultural capital investment equally beneficial for the family and the state and encouraged the creation and accumulation of the Chinese script as a form of capital for society. Thanks to institutional aggregation through the dynasties, including the affirmation of a central power for the political unity of the whole country, and also including a unified script, Mandarin Chinese, and Confucianism as the sole school of thought, the central government acquired in society a statewide source of talent of comparatively unified standardized virtue and one that would never run dry. The central government of the monarchy could begin to permeate society, resulting in its political legitimacy reaching to all levels of society, even to the bottom layer.

By means of the imperial examination system, and thanks to individual and family pursuit of secular renown and income, and the pursuit of the Confucian ideals for personal morality, the family (家), state (国), and the world under heaven (天下) as a whole, the political and cultural elite of each place were shaped into a statewide network and community that came from the localities but no longer simply belonged to them. They did not need to rely on the rich and powerful, nor did they need to rely very much on high officials or men of importance, but could directly look to the imperial power and be loyal to it. Even if they were far from the court in remote places, by means of the Confucian political and cultural norms built up over the years the scholars were able to see things as a whole. They were incapable of failing to love the state and would never fail to set their sights on the entire world under heaven. They were the product of the political and cultural unity of China and also the guarantee of that political and cultural unity. With them the culture was united and with them there was hope of maintaining political unity.

Thanks to the selection of scholars through the institution of the imperial examinations, which transformed the bureaucracy from the uppermost to the lowest levels of government, and to political governance by means of official documents, a government by writing (*wenzhi*) was implemented, which is Max Weber's sense of the rule of law. Even scholars who lay outside this bureaucracy—whether they had not yet or could not join, or had retired or even been dismissed—were still members of the local elite and hence of the political elite. This was the "power of the gentry" (*shenquan*) that helped ensure the cleanliness of local politics and the spread and unification of culture, and for this reason it later became an important force in local politics in China.[50]

Is it any surprise that in the first year of his reign, on seeing the students filing out of the examination hall, Emperor Taizong of the Tang sighed, "The heroes of the whole world have all fallen into my net!"[51]

Indeed, only after founding a statewide, unified institution for selection of the elite could the statements "talent alone is raised up" and "there is no exception in the matter of talent" be affirmed in a constitutional sense. It was but a form of auxiliary institution or reinforcement of the institution. Its significance did not lie in the norm by which only talent was selected, but rather in that by selection in a strict elite exam, an emergency door remained, creating room for maneuver so that in times of necessity there could be exceptions to the talent-only rule. This was not only because any institution has its loopholes and the institution was suited to selecting the elite but not talent, and the like, but, even more important, because it was not easy to standardize a test for the *selection of a political elite*. Written examinations tend to prioritize intelligence, cleverness, and a good memory, such that people with these abilities can more easily pass. These skills are very important, but people with such abilities are not necessarily the political elite or capable of becoming so, because the core requirement for a political elite is to be of use to the times.

To Be of Use to the Times

All forms of selection—the search for worthy people, the selections, recommendations, and examinations—were but steps in ancient China's meritocracy. In terms of politics, who is chosen and in whatever way, the ultimate problem to be faced is very practical: Okay, they are talented, but do they really have the ability to govern the state effectively? Can they truly solve and handle major political questions?

This has to do with the nature of politics. Politics demands wisdom and ability, but even more, practical reason rather than pure reason. One plus one equals two: that is pure reason. The answer is absolutely right. Practical reason, however, may be assessed orally or in writing, but any such assessment can never be accurate. A person who speaks well cannot necessarily act well. The best form of assessment is in doing and in practice.[52] Moreover, this action or practice cannot be like the assessment of martial arts carried out on the stage: Chinese people very early on realized that "writing does not come first." Thus, the various forms of selecting a political elite (the selection, recommendation, and examination systems)—although they may have been the best possible forms under the social conditions, such that one could not do without them—proved to be not very reliable.

Second, unlike other social practices that to a high degree rely on practical reason—such as driving, swimming, or athletics—political governance does not deal only with the self; even more important, it is always concerned with the lives and families of the broad mass of all the people. "One false step leads to a thousand ancient hatreds." Politics has a broad and profound influence and hence political governance brooks no failures. It does not accept the kind of logic exemplified in "failure is the mother of success" or "one fall is but a step in wisdom." This does not imply that one cannot go wrong or that an individual cannot gain lessons of experience from his practice. Rather, it means that in dealing with important questions in one's official capacity there is no second chance. Since it is political responsibility that is assumed, the demands for virtue laid on the political elite are always for prudence, confidentiality, *a sense of proportionality* (分寸感), and sometimes even conservativeness. In a large state, these issues are magnified because the sphere of interest of any political decision or the influence of any action is larger and the number of people affected greater.

In a large state with a vast territory, rather than in a little republic like a city-state, it is exceedingly troublesome to select a political elite with the practical ability to run a large state from an innumerable throng of strangers— and not from among very reduced minority groups such as the dominant families of the Wei-Jin period or from among the nobles in medieval Europe. Moreover, this had to be done by means of oral or written examinations. The problem is no longer whether the selected persons belong to the elite, but, insofar as it is possible to select potential talent from the whole country, one must use a standardized system of testing—including the selection and recommendation systems, and especially the imperial examinations with all their many constituent institutions and detailed systems, such as testing by the emperor or by the court, whether orally or by other methods. In all cases the emphasis is on wisdom and knowledge that depend on written texts, and even more on literary and oral expression. The tendency is to prefer elite persons who are good at reciting texts by heart, have a good memory, and are good at taking exams and using words. In other words, even though it was known that these forms of testing would not be able to assess the practical reasoning of the elite, for the sake of legitimacy and evenhandedness, it was necessary to adopt and hold firm to these systems that had proven to be biased. What was chosen was a cultural elite, among whom were undoubtedly a political elite, but as to who was politically talented and who was not, that could not be known, or at least not with any certainty. It was also very unclear how the ability that emerged from selection through exams and the practical reason required for running the state were related. At least we may suppose that, in general, since scholars who passed the exams were very attentive to the use of words, so too they might be more aware in other areas too. Intelligent people always have a greater chance of passing exams, and so it is reasonable to believe that those who had been through several levels of strict testing and exams would, generally speaking, have a higher level of ability and intelligence than those who failed or did not even sit for the exams. But this also implies that when the level of intelligence of those who passed was much the same, the persons who would shine in an examination system would be those who studied *hard*, those who held to the belief that "talent lay in effort," who were not lazy and hence might well be dogmatists (*benben zhuyi*), and less probably those who thought that "it is better to be without books than to have only books" or whose great ambition meant that they sought to read more than the set texts.

The ancient Chinese realized very soon that if the selection of talent was overly dependent on literary dogmatism, then this could have serious consequences, and so (as I noted earlier), as a rear guard or an antidote for the political elite, Chinese society always maintained a kind of anti-intellectual tradition. The classic example, which is still not forgotten today, is the tragic appointment in the Warring States period of Zhao Guo simply because he had only read books on war.[53] Later generations were always careful to avoid confusing knowledge with ability or intelligence with ability.[54] From the beginning the problem of practical reason may be said to have been involved in the selection and training of China's political elite. How could one set up, or according to what could one set up, objective, fair, and reliable systems of formulas to test, identify, and distinguish the political elite effectively? How could one guarantee that only the talented would be selected and only the worthy employed? "In choosing from outsiders one would not exclude one's enemies and from insiders one would not exclude one's sons."[55] This is a great difficulty. Let it not be forgotten that in the Warring States period, Prince Meng Chang, Prince Ping Yuan, Prince Xin Ling, and Prince Chun Shen all had thousands of hangers-on, which even numbered as many as 0.1 percent of the population of the whole state![56] This does not necessarily indicate that these princes longed for worthy retainers. Rather, it may show that they were unable to effectively identify and test for talent. All they could do was to turn no one away and accept all comers as their only method of response.

But acceptance of all comers is not a virtue. At best it is but a substitute for virtue. To put it another way, it is false. For example, when examining a topic based on strict reason there may be a margin of error permissible, but this margin should never be made public. One cannot say that "one plus one equals two" should also allow that "one plus one equals three." Accepting all comers will not necessarily improve politics. In fact, it is unable to guarantee that "each one will get a post according to his talent." There are also other bad consequences. A lowering of the criterion for talent will mean that genuinely talented persons will be even less likely to stand out. It was because of this that Mao Sui did not stand out and had to recommend himself.[57] Failing to turn away all comers and accepting all also leads to a vast waste of resources while truly talented people fail to earn a livelihood. Feng Huan complained that Prince Meng Chang gave too low a salary and said, "far better to go back home."[58] The saying "a gentleman-scholar will die for his close friend" was commonplace during the Warring States period perhaps because it reflects the sighs and sense of loss of some whose treatment was too paltry.[59] Even Han Fei's lament may not be such a bad outcome. Even worse was that at key moments they would get major things wrong. We need only think of Qin Wuyang, who frightened the people of Yan such that they "did not dare to look at him without trembling," as a result of which he was highly regarded by Crown Prince Dan, but when he himself had to deal with affairs he trembled all over and his face turned pale.[60]

It is in the light of this that the issue of names and realities is not a purely academic exercise. In fact, it is really a question of political practice, which was understood differently though equally well in actual practice by Confucians and Legalists. Confucians emphasized the family education and personal training of persons with practical talent, stressing their competence in managing themselves, their family, the state, and the world under heaven, highlighting "every day I examine myself three times," paying attention to overcoming the self and returning to the rites,[61] and training in political morality. Legalists, however, stressed rigorous testing and selection for the political elite. Guan Zhong stressed "weighing up ability before assigning posts."[62] Han Fei said that the prince should "assign posts on the basis of proven competence and assess results by looking at the title of the post assigned."[63] They were concerned with the practical ability of the political elite and their actual abilities rather than their reputation or certificates. This form of very practical thought continued to be used by later generations.[64] The key was to choose people who really had the talent to work in politics.

When implemented at the institutional level, this led to two basic systems or traditions. The first was to encourage *officials with practical experience in politics* to make recommendations of talented people to higher levels. For this reason, we can understand why Emperor Wu of the Han "ordered the heads of commanderies and prefectures to select elite persons from among the officials and ordinary people who could be sent to distant parts of the empire," why he called on higher officials, such as magistrates and feudal lords, to recommend outstanding persons. The nine degrees of mandarinate in the central system of the Wei and Jin, which later came under attack, was at least very reasonable at the time when it was first set up. One important reason for this was that high officials of virtue serving in the central government were also made inspectors and were responsible for examining the state of scholarship in their native regions. One advantage of the recommendation and *chaju* systems was that, generally speaking, the executive heads at each level of government not only normally had to be intelligent and capable, but also, owing to practical experience gained in long-term governance of one region or direction of some major central government department, tended to pay more attention to practical experience when faced with selecting the elite. They looked at the ability to form judgments and resolve issues. They stressed an ability for synthesis, fairness, and coordination. This was in preference to the tendency of the imperial examination system to overemphasize book knowledge and memory. Moreover, practice built up over a long time ensured that these officials frequently retained this insight and good judgment.

Like the ability in pure reasoning, an ability in practical reasoning may well be in part a natural gift and may not be something that can be either *acquired* or greatly improved by study or sheer effort. We are not simply Isaac Newtons who have read too little, or Mao Zedongs who have failed to put in enough effort, or Michael Jordans who have gone astray. Yet long-term, comprehensive, and varied political practice may give rise to, or even intensify, inherent practical reason in a person that originally could not be fully displayed in a written exam. It may help others to judge one's executive ability correctly. Sometimes this experience may also increase the self-confidence of persons who have a decided natural gift for practical reason. With rich experience and skill perfected in practice, their ability will be strengthened. Based on this point, since ancient times China has supported another even more important institution of a meritocracy, namely, to select persons who at the bottom level have been outstanding administrators in one department, to let them accumulate experience by working up through the grades until they can finally be entrusted with an important key political post. Thus, as far as possible, the selection of key officials from within the court is to be avoided—from what today we would describe as desk or secretarial posts. This idea is classically best exemplified in Han Fei's "in the bureaucracy of an enlightened ruler the prime minister has come up from the post of district magistrate and the renowned generals have risen from the ranks. For the officials of a clear-sighted lord, the prime minister should come from the post of district magistrate; the general of the army from among the foot-soldiers."[65]

Later Chinese experience shows that dynasties throughout history were careful to appoint outstanding local officials as prime minister. At the same time, they also often specially chose officials who were in charge of one post at court as the executive officials in the localities. "The renown of the two Han dynasties (East and West) was above all due to the importance attached to the head of a commandery."[66] In the Tang there was even a clear directive ordering an exchange between officials of the capital and of the localities. Talented persons selected from among the officials in the capital were sent to the localities as minor officials (*ce li*) and inspectors (*du du*), while minor officials and inspectors who had proved themselves in the localities were appointed to central government posts in each province (*sheng*), department (*bu*), *yuan*, and desk (*tai*). Furthermore, this system was institutionalized.[67] It was also decreed that when an important post fell vacant in the central government, the candidate to be chosen should have had experience as head of a commandery; a vacancy at the middle level was to be filled by a former county magistrate; and persons who had served as neither head of a commandery nor county magistrate were not to be appointed to important posts such as admonitor (*jianyi daifu*) or *zhongshu sheren*. These ideas and ways of acting were generally upheld in political practice from that time on.[68]

While upholding the system of statewide standardized imperial examinations as the basis, the purpose of these regulations was to pay attention to assessment and foster ability in practical reason and to take account of political experience at all levels, so that heads of the executive at all levels should all have basic work experience and capacity in at least one field, understand the lower echelons, realize where problems lay, appreciate the hopes of the ordinary people, and be familiar with all levels of the bureaucracy and their norms of working, and so be able to discover problems early on and have the capacity to solve them, to ensure that policies adhered more closely to realities at the lowest level and to the needs of society, thus being both apt and practical. In particular, it was necessary to avoid that under the power of the center—since the heads of the executive came from outside and their subordinates were generally local people—there should easily or frequently happen the phenomenon described in the phrase "the official is as pure as water; his subordinates are as thick as oil."[69]

Frequent assessment is not simply a matter of one test and verification or of allowing the political elite to show their ability and so provide an adequate foretaste of their ability to lead and guide the whole district and to enable them to gain prestige in the world, in the bureaucracy and among the people. In this sense, it can be seen as a replacement for elections. This form of selecting the *jinshi* guaranteed that China's political elite did not just become hangers-on, holders of paper documents, or merely academically qualified nobles. Hence, it is part of historical China's effective constitution.

It is very difficult to assess how far this practice was effective, but indirect evidence can be found in a political and cultural phenomenon: the political elite and the cultural elite after the Wei-Jin period began to take separate paths. Therefore, there was the saying "Wind and waves have their set time; one day I shall certainly hoist my sail and sail across the blue sea." And the sigh Li Bai applied to himself: "climbing up the mountains full of snow requires crossing the Yellow River and the frozen passes." There also appeared the determination of Du Fu, "Above Yao and Shun, the wind . . ." such that in the end one can but "know the dusty red world, flowers embroider the officials in the city." Also, although in later years some of the elite straddled politics and culture, they were few in number and, at least by the Tang, there began to emerge something close to the modern sense of a specialized or professional community of poets or cultural specialists. There were even disappointed groups of literati, which impelled the rise of the Song *huaben*, the Yuan mixed drama, and the novels of the Ming and Qing. This perhaps proves that the institution of the selection of China's political elite in later times had achieved adequate discriminatory ability.

The Politics beyond Meritocracy

In reflecting on meritocracy at the constitutional level, it is obviously necessary to discuss the political elite. But meritocracy is an institutional matter and may easily be read as—but it certainly should not be confused with or, even worse, treated as identical to—rule by a political elite. The latter is far more a case of individual members of the elite or at the most only a particular community of the elite.

For example, a meritocracy must rely on selection according to individual talent. This is very important, but it is not the whole story. Because the key issue for political governance may well be said to be to bring together a balance among the various groups in society whose interests have sufficient legitimacy and necessity to exist, and a balance between the interests of individual interest groups. From there it is possible to uphold and consolidate the unity of the country and social stability. For the vast agrarian society with its scattered communities that was historical China, the political, economic, and cultural links between the periphery and the center were not very close, nor could they easily be so. Hence, maintaining the unity of the country and political stability in society naturally had its own inherent particularity. The role of a meritocracy was to promote and constantly remain subordinate to this goal. The whole class of scholars was the political and cultural institutional product of the promotion of this goal. At the same time, they were also an important means for promoting and implementing this goal. These members of the elite belonged to China but also had deep roots in their own locality and had a profound influence on their place of birth. They were the nerves running from top to bottom of the state. Therefore, to implement this goal and develop a meritocracy, it was necessary—for the good of the whole state and keeping in mind the good of the periphery—and essential and also feasible to express local interests by means of the institutionalization of the political elite in each place by collecting and transmitting important information about every place, and thus promoting the political, economic, and cultural integration of the whole country.

This implies that meritocracy could not be simple. At certain times, if some specific ways of doing things in a meritocracy do not serve the implementation of this goal, then they might bring about misunderstanding between interest groups at the local, regional, or even higher levels, resulting in increased divisions and more intensive contradictions, such that the institution must be adjusted. At such times, the elite must move in the direction of political compromise, and they will do so. It would not be the case that politics would move toward a political compromise in favor of the elite. All this is latent as a subordinate theme running alongside the *language* of a meritocracy. Even more important, pragmatism both in China and in other countries must consider that in political *implementation* this must be the principal consideration. In other words, meritocracy never seeks to implement the rule of the philosopher kings.

In this section we will explore and highlight something that has for a long time been concealed in the constitution of historical China, but that at least since the selection of the political elite in the time of Emperor Wu of the Han has, indeed, always been patently obvious in the implementation of political integration for a large agrarian state, though subordinate to, or arising from, what has been said earlier about the selection system of ancient China's political elite. What it seeks, within the framework of the constitution of a united state, is to form the political structure of this country, to strive for balance and compromise and the creation of conditions sufficient for the political elite in each place to actively and actually participate in the central government and the political governance of the whole country, directly or indirectly expressing and transmitting information about local interests. This is very important for the effective running of a united country. It is, indeed, not based on representative democracy. Nor is it a matter of rubbing a touch of elitism into democratic rule. Rather, it is to add to meritocracy some elements of representation. Let it be noted: the aim here is not to try to seek some form of democracy in the political practice of ancient China. In my view, that way of proceeding is a waste of time and quite unreliable. What I say is that, in those times, this was the most reasonable and most necessary institution for the formation and integration of agrarian China. In fact, I do not care in the least if it is some kind of democracy or not!

Let us go back to those times in history. Emperor Wu of the Han sent out a decree ordering each commandery to recommend one person who was filial and one who was worthy.[70] When some commanderies failed to comply, he sent a further decree urging full compliance, at the risk of deviating from the center and/or indicating that the officials in the commandery were incompetent and should be dismissed.[71] Later on, the emperor also ruled that talented persons should be selected according to the population of each commandery, an initial and rather crude form of proportional representation.[72]

The question is why there was a call for distribution according to commanderies or, later, according to the size of population in each commandery. If the focus was solely on selecting a political elite, then surely *talent* should be the *only* criterion. Distributing the pool amounts to restricting numbers and thus is unreasonable. Or perhaps the commanderies should recommend all the elite persons they have, and the center should then make a choice. Or the center could fix a total number, pay no attention to which commandery they were from, and set some standardized way by which the requisite number could be uniformly employed. It is unreasonable to take the commandery as a unit and for it to put forward only one person. It is slightly more reasonable when later commanderies were divided into three sizes, large, medium, and small, and selection was according to the size of population. But this too supposes that talent is always evenly distributed among the population, yet an even distribution of talent in the population, especially educated talent, not only then but even today is not the norm.

Furthermore, when the commanderies failed to fulfill their duty, why did Emperor Wu think that the local officials were at variance with the center or that they were incompetent? Why did he not ask that local officials recommend talent based on the facts and ask them to be responsible for working strictly, rather than fabricating the numbers just to fill up the request of the central government? We have reason to think that political, economic, cultural, and educational development in each local jurisdiction was uneven and that the natural and social reserves of the political and cultural elite were certainly not the same everywhere. The facts prove that under pressure from the central government there came about what was popularly mocked as "recommending 'outstanding' persons who read no books; recommending 'worthy' persons whose fathers must leave home and live elsewhere." Surely, Emperor Wu understood the simple wisdom of "when the superior has a preference; inferiors will certainly go overboard in toadying to it."

He understood all right, but he did not care. This reveals Emperor Wu's unbending insistence on political pursuits and a greater political equilibrium, something that was founded solely on the basic premise behind the selection of elite and talented persons in politics and culture who came from every local area. What he sought was, first, that whether talent was distributed evenly or not, what passed for the political elite of *each place in the whole country* (even if they were not strictly of the political elite), could, in some way or other, take part in the political governance of the state. Second, he hoped, through the united hearts and minds of all local officials, and according to the political framework and channels of the state, to implement this political goal. The aim was to ensure that his dynasty truly brought together the political elite of the whole country and formed a political community that stretched from top to bottom, east to west, and north to south. At the same time, by means of this community and the mechanism of the state, he could train and shape a political elite that would be influential in each place, and thus comprehensively augment the political and cultural cohesiveness and esprit de corps of the court.

If this were merely the request of Emperor Wu of the Han, then perhaps it could be interpreted as merely accidental. If someone alleged that it was the emperor's personal preference, then that would be hard to challenge. But 750 years later, when the imperial examinations were set up, Emperor Wen of the Sui also asked each prefecture to present three people annually for the exams. This is to set the number of entrants by their place of origin. It was not a matter of accepting candidates according to the distribution of the prefecture or setting the exam and reemploying the graduates according to their distribution in the population as a whole. Yet, from the point of view of selection of a political elite, this was clearly not focused solely on *talent*. The three persons recommended by each prefecture were not necessarily comparable. How could you know that a potential fourth or even eighth person recommended by Xuzhou was not equal to the first person suggested by Suzhou? Or the other way around? But this form of recruitment according to locale was always insisted on in later years. It cannot be read as merely the personal preference of a given emperor. Even if wrong, it was the path taken. But is this not what we mean by the truth of institutional evolution?[73]

Necessities to repair this system did emerge. After some seven hundred years, there appeared the system of recruitment according to distribution in the north and south of China. In 1425, Emperor Ren Zong of the Ming dynasty decreed that the imperial examinations would take place according to equality of geographical provenance of candidates, that is, on the exam script itself the words "north," "south," and "center" were inscribed according to a proportion of 35 percent, 55 percent, and 10 percent.[74] The percentages were later changed and adjusted, but the system itself remained in place until the exams were finally abolished in the late Qing dynasty. Not only was this system in place for the *jinshi* exam, it was also repeated throughout the Ming-Qing era in every province, in that the central government decreed how many candidates from each province could take part in the exams and in the *jinshi* exam.[75]

Therefore, we can conclude only that whether it was a matter of equality of geographical provenance or percentage of population permitted to take the exam and be granted the post of *jinshi*, the focus was not on selecting the elite per se, nor on satisfying the distribution of the elite according to the goal of an ideal society thought up by the ruling groups, but purely for a political reason. So even though there was a meritocracy, even though it was a matter of only scholars, it was political and did not become something "cultural."

In the course of history, at least during the Northern Song dynasty, the imperial examinations did in fact take place without considering equality of geographical provenance. The result was that the economically and commercially developed capital city produced more *jinshi* than other areas, and proportionately more per capita than the whole country. This led to struggles among the scholars from north and south and their attempts to use this struggle to win influence and political clout in state politics and in the high levels of government. This brought the politician Sima Guang to suggest equality of geographical provenance for the exams.[76] During the Yuan, even though the Han Chinese were a majority, the rulers wanted a balance among the candidates for exams and among the *jinshi* according to the four regions of Mongolia, Semu (Turkic and Tibetan areas, etc.), the Han Chinese of the north, and the Han of the south.[77] The Mongols hoped that in this way they could guarantee that political governance and political equilibrium would be beneficial to them. Clearly, this was not fair, but unfair politics is not wholly devoid of common sense: selection of talent for a large state with both agrarian and pastoral communities and with many different ethnic groups could not solely be concerned with intelligence. It also needed to take account of political representation for regions and peoples.

This fact was soon to be proved by bloody means. After the Yuan dynasty was overthrown, during the imperial examinations held in 1397 in the early Ming, candidates were treated equally, which led to a conflict between north and south. When the results were declared, it was found that all forty-two *jinshi* who passed were from the south. Emperor Zhu Yuanzhang sent experts to check for irregularities, but this showed that the best script from a northern candidate was still far behind some of those from the south who had also failed. Such an imbalance is not unthinkable. The problem lay not in intelligence but in the social background. After the Eastern Jin, the economic center of China began to move south. From the Southern Song to the Yuan, the south was always more stable than the north. Its economy and culture were more developed. The Ming dynasty itself started off in the south and gradually spread its influence northward. This implies that the south had acquired peace and stability earlier and for longer. But although this makes good sense and in an abstract sense is perfectly fair, the results of the exam led to dissatisfaction among the political elite of the north. Even worse, although the emperor's family came from north of the Yangtze, they came under the jurisdiction of the south and so were reckoned as southerners. Even though he was emperor and it should not have touched him, he felt implicated. Therefore, he wrote a decree ordering the chief examiner to change the roster and enroll some northerners to counter the complaints. But in insisting on equality according to the marks gained, the rule of law, and a spirit of absolute rectitude, the chief examiner and the expert who undertook the review refused to countenance the emperor's demand and paid no attention to the political and social consequences of their practice of the law. When law pays no attention to political and social consequences, politics and society may well completely spurn the law. The emperor intervened in the political conflict and crisis between northern and southern scholars and ordered the execution of the chief examiner and the review expert and also of the candidate who won first place, albeit quite innocent in this affair, and then ordered a retaking of the exam. He then examined the scripts himself and selected sixty-one *jinshi*, who all happened to come from the north![78]

This is, of course, a tragedy for the law, but also for politics. It shows us that the elite were partially blind to reality and even more that politics can be very political. A meritocracy does not change political affiliation. In fact, meritocracy is even more sensitive to political interests and more ready to use politics to attain its interests. Not only is the inborn imagination of a community limited, being an agrarian society further limited the imagination of the ancients. Therefore, suspicions based on origins are very easily aroused and very easily used by others, and as soon as these suspicions enter into the higher levels of politics, in a large state like China, the consequences will be enormous, even—as this case shows—disastrous. It is essential to prevent ambitious persons using these suspicions from splitting the state and reigniting the spark of war. Therefore, in the early Ming, the reason it was decided to use equality of geographic provenance in running the exams and choosing those who passed was, first, to pacify the cultural elite's political ambitions and to maintain equilibrium of the political forces in each area. These are rules for examinations, but at the same time they touch on a constitutional issue of the selection of the members of the ruling political body.

This constitutional arrangement is something that politics throughout the dynasties had to face even during peacetime. If we look back into history, we can quite easily discover the rule: in the intense political and military conflict at the turn of a dynasty, there is historically a great crisis, a social revolution or a so-called restoration period, during which politics must overrule everything else. The top members of the political body virtually wholly ignore locality. Whether we look at the Pei County clique of Liu Bang, the Longxi group of Li Shimin, the Huaixi group of Zhu Yuanzhang, or the rule over China by minority peoples in the Yuan and Qing dynasties, at the foundation of the state, the key leaders paid no attention to geographical balance. But once an era of peace was inaugurated, the selection of the political elite, both among the high echelons and in the imperial examinations, could not fail to take into account provenance and ethnic origin.[79] This just goes to show that the *key* consideration in the way the political elite are chosen lies not in their being the elite but in politics. In other words, even without any awareness of representative democracy, the political elite in ancient China always bore an element of local representation.

Based on the evolution of the selection system from selection to recommendation and to the examinations, it can be seen that, while the power of the central government had in fact increased, thus weakening the influence of the nobles and dominant families in the selection process, yet from the way of recommending, examining, and selecting officials, in the large state that is China, where there was a high degree of centralization and an emperor who held himself to be above all, the strength of the power of the central government or of the emperor or its legitimacy and the degree to which it had a comprehensive grasp of the politics, economy, and culture of the whole country still had to take into account (or at least could not overlook) the scholars of the regions that relied on their participation in politics and interests to foster acknowledgment of that authority. Consideration of geographical provenance in selecting a person to take part in state politics influenced the local structures by which the elite actually participated in state politics. In each province of China, in the north, south, and other politically important regions—such as frontier areas—the question of provenance became an important matter that the political leaders had to seriously consider in peacetime and that they had to deal with to achieve equilibrium within the system.

This explains why, in 1426, one year after the Ming had divided candidates into north and south, a third category—the center—was erected. Although this was changed subsequently, the tripartite division of north, south and center continued even in the Qing. It is of special interest to look more closely at this central division set up by the Ming. It included the four southwestern provinces of Sichuan, Guangxi, Yunnan, and Guizhou but also the area around Zhu Yuanzhang's own family home of Hefei, Fengyang, Chuzhou, and Hexian. In other words, it combined four southwestern provinces and parts of Anhui near the Yangtze and Huai rivers. These two areas were not only not contiguous; they were several thousand *li* apart and the culture and customs of the people living there were very different. But it is precisely this strangely delineated central region that most clearly reveals the political considerations and goals of the central government of the Ming. It was not only a panacea by which the central government kept control over the scholars of the whole country. Rather, it was a means by which the central government let all scholars understand that it had this concern at heart.

The first thing was to affirm political legitimacy, so that the Ming emperors could free themselves from the struggle among the scholars that had been brought to a crisis in the dispute between north and south. In that dispute, what had led the emperor to use extreme methods to intervene was not his ruthlessness but rather the fact that his family home of Fengyang was ascribed to the south. In this political struggle among the literati, no one dared to openly criticize Zhu himself, but the emperor understood that if he failed to manage this battle correctly then it would certainly lead the northern scholars and other members of the political elite to question whether the politics of the dynasty was fair, to wonder whether the Ming could escape the ethnic and regional biases of the Yuan. The unbreakable flow of history and the important underlying consequences of cultural and political separatism made it such that Zhu had no choice but to use extreme measures and execute the chief examiner, the winning candidate, and the inspector to show that he himself showed no partiality to southern scholars and thereby gain the confidence and support of the northern political elite.

This act could assuage the suspicions of the northern political elite only for a time; it was more difficult to dissipate the clouds of suspicion entirely. The southern political elite may have thought that to win over the northerners he would not sacrifice them, while the northerners might have thought it was all just a show on the part of the emperor. This is hardly an explanation, since it would still be difficult to understand why Fengyang should be attributed to the north. Zhu's action in apportioning this small area, called Western Han, to the central region, which included the four southwestern provinces, and from which 10 percent of the *jinshi* were chosen, although it would not lead the northern and southern political elite to become suspicious, would help in the formation and reinforcement of the political and cultural community in the whole country. It was an option that could not be doubted.

But to appreciate the greater political interests Zhu Yuanzhang had in mind, we must wait until the end of the Qing dynasty. The establishment of the central area was to make clear to the scholars and latent political elite of the then politically and culturally underdeveloped regions of Yunnan and Guizhou, in particular, that the central government was determined to preserve a certain degree of participation for the southwest with its many ethnic groups and lower level of education, that it was determined to train scholars from that region to be able to participate in the government of the whole country. The bar for entry into politics for scholars from the four southwestern provinces was lowered. Possessing this real and predictable advantage, the scholars of the four provinces would strive even harder. This was a great advantage to the whole state in bringing about the political and cultural integration of the entire southwest. In particular, we should bear in mind that under the Yuan, this area had been classified as being barbarian, but from the Ming onward and throughout the Qing, it was brought under regular jurisdiction. This implies that the region had to furnish local people to work as the political and cultural elite, not only to participate in political governance of the whole country but also so that the local echelons of governance (or even the social elite) could take part in local political governance.

For this reason, we can confirm that the erection of the central district was carried out entirely for political reasons and not for elitist ones. Thanks to the special quota of *jinshi*, the central government in both dynasties was able to provide greater possibilities for the political elite of what was then more remote and underdeveloped regions to take part in politics. By affording various advantages in the central government to these districts, various channels of political representation and expression were set up. It created an important constitutional channel for the comprehensive integration of places and peoples within the whole county and for their cultural integration.

Is this not comparable to what, 550 years later, the constitutional political practice of the United States began to try, something that first emerged in higher education and then later in the fields of employment and professional promotion as affirmative action (for minorities)?[80] In ancient China, the imperial examinations were for high-level public officials and for their promotion. They were a necessary qualifying test for entering the higher echelons of politics, participating in high-level political policy making and planning. This measure was, for this reason, an effective means of opening up expression of local interests and transmission of information. This measure could not implement equal representation for local areas and ethnic groups in politics, but at least it could impress more effective channels of communication and some sense of representation of interests, such that in a large state covering a vast territory that was culturally backward and, for that reason, where local participation in politics at the state level was seriously inadequate, there were some basic channels and opportunities for the expression of local demands. By means of this quota system, officials from the remote southwest were able to enter the higher echelons of politics and, even if all they spoke about and all the issues they raised were matters of local interest, given that they had already accepted the political and cultural norms of China, they were not only representatives of the interests of their ethnic group or region but also members of the community of the political and cultural elite of the whole country. They came from the southwest but belonged to the political and cultural elite of the whole country and at least some of them spoke on political issues bearing in mind the long-term and fundamental interests of the whole state. For this reason, we may say that even though ancient China did not have a state-wide system of representation, the selection of the political and cultural elite itself always comprised elements of local elite representation that led toward the goal of political and cultural unity and stability in the state, giving rise to functions that allowed for the voicing of local interests and functions making for equilibrium among different areas within China's territory and among the interests of different ethnic groups and peoples.

Not only this. The imperial examinations also brought about social mobility. Ping-ti Ho studied 12,226 *jinshi* over a period of more than five centuries to look at social mobility in China. By analyzing their family backgrounds, he discovered that under the Qing, more than 30 percent of *jinshi* and more than 20 percent of *juren* and *gongsheng* came from among the commoners, defined as households that in the previous three generations had not given rise to any notable people. Moreover, his case studies also showed that there was downward social mobility, and one factor explaining this was rejection in the imperial examinations, which shows that the examinations were not monopolized by households that could not produce suitable candidates.[81] But this very social mobility was another form of political formation and integration for ancient China. Since, even though each scholar already belonged to the class of the scholar-officials, he could not escape his family background or his original social class, because he could not cut his ties of interest or feeling for them; therefore, when sociologists look at social mobility, from a political point of view, it is this representation of social class that matters.

These two elements of representation may seem to be trivial, but that is not certainly so.[82] Second, even if they are trivial this does not naturally create an effective basis for criticism, unless one thinks numbers are worth pursuing in themselves. A correct standard of criticism would be to ask whether, in a large agrarian state with many peoples, ethnic groups, and cultures and where transportation and communication are difficult, such a representative element is better than none, whether it is helpful in expanding peace and stability to the people who so much needed them. Furthermore, it should not be supposed that the greater the representation the better, because in agrarian China there were inevitably marked variations in the economic advantages enjoyed by each region, such that overrepresentation would be like throwing in a plate of shifting sand or a heap of potatoes and might lead to division or separatism rather than to affirming cultural identity or patriotism.

Given such social conditions, in a large agrarian state, what is required is meritocracy. Hence, whatever the case, intelligence alone cannot be the only criterion, elements of representation of localities and of class must be infused and included, to eliminate, as far as possible, any possible lack of confidence and maintain a balance in political power. In this sense, ancient China's choice of meritocracy was not because it superstitiously believed in elitism. Rather, it should be assessed and judged comprehensively in terms of many political factors at that given time and place and to satisfy a pragmatic, consequentialist approach to the relationship between these factors and the elite.

This analysis reveals the difficulty in ancient China's meritocracy. Behind attracting the elite to participate in politics, we can see that there must be deep and profound political considerations. Besides ensuring there are persons who are willing and able to participate in the process and running of the political governance of the state, and winning their unreserved political loyalty, it is also important to strive to reduce any possible suspicions arising in any place, class, ethnic group, or political faction. One must create a balance of forces among them and, thanks to the sense of security provided thereby, bring it about that they consciously rely on this institution to express and reconcile their demands, so that their individual talents mesh together and, when necessary, balance or cancel each other out.

Therefore, in evaluating naturally good persons or idealists, it is still necessary to point out that, in practice, among the political elite there will certainly be some who are not so outstanding. In China we call them "Thick Blacks," in the West "Machiavellian," but precisely for this reason they are truly political and constitutional factors. This is to take people who may have a certain share of ability and/or reputation, but who on the political level are not necessarily loyal, or not sufficiently so, or who are even downright opportunists, the pre-elite or even pseudo-elite, and "keep" them with the purpose of reaping the rewards of their intelligence and ability and doing so only to prevent them from being used by any major opposition force or faction, even if that is what they actually seek to do. In this sense, this "use" of them may well include, as a last resort, supporting them unemployed in order to preserve the effective unity and political governance of the whole state. Logically this is at least a feasible, even a necessary, part of the structure of an authentic meritocracy both in ancient China and even in any state at any time.

The uniform imperial examination did not just affirm the institution of one culture and education, nor was it a habitual way of selecting civil servants. Rather, it was an institutional framework that promoted participation in political representation and its realization. In every part of China and at every level, it encouraged and facilitated comparatively peaceful social, economic, cultural, and political development and strengthened political and cultural representation for every place in China, and thus reinforced the political and cultural constitution of ancient China. Even though people today see only the direct consequences of that institution—the selection of talent—what the institution was really concerned with and what it actually did was not merely to absorb the talent of the state, but to absorb it in a statewide, comprehensive, and balanced way, which had implications for representation and political participation of local places. This is a profound and far-thinking piece of constitutional intuition!

A Final Assessment

This chapter's argument is not just to explain why, in ancient agrarian China, the planning for the institution of meritocracy and the operation of that institution had to be at the constitutional level, had to be based on constitutional considerations, and had to have complex constitutional arrangements, but to go further to say that all the institutional considerations, concerns, and technical details relating to meritocracy cannot be perceived clearly, or even understood, if one uses only the framework and theory of some foreign constitutional order. It is enough to go into the society and linguistic history of ancient agrarian China not only to understand that it is possible to judge what is good or bad but even to understand the advantages and disadvantages of what was done. Most important, however you assess the matter, your outlook may suddenly broaden, and you will see that the ancients used their own strength and action to create the world of that constitutional practice and theory.

We must also note that for ancient China, meritocracy at another level had to be constitutional. This means that almost all of China's other basic institutions, such as the political framework by which the center and periphery were related, fiscal and taxation issues in the state's economic life, the peaceful livelihood of the ordinary people everywhere, the army that provided international and domestic security, and even the unified script and Mandarin Chinese in education, including the imperial examinations themselves, were all bound to these members of the political elite. There was not an independent institution bound to a concrete person that operated outside the system. All institutions were formed by concrete individuals who had accepted the institutional norms and customs and who naturally ran things according to the set norms, such that should anyone break the norms they would be checked by persons who held firmly to them. Without these people, the elite, there would be no institution; there would, at the most, be only a few texts.

This is why in a large state like China, the rule must be "the law alone does not suffice" and "there are governing people but no governing laws," and why the political line is drawn first while "the cadres are the deciding elements."[83] All this sounds rather like rule by man but in fact does not fit that description. Indeed, the opposite is true: it is rule by law and rule by law for a large state with all the concomitant issues. Since all posts are assumed by the elite and business is run by them, from Michel Foucault's perspective we can see that from what they say and do every day, there is a forceful constitutional life and institutional current at work.

But to say what institutions are constitutional is to simply point out that the issues they involve are very important for the state and in the long term, and it never means that they are closer to God or truth or ultimate truth or universal values. In no sense does it mean, either, that these concrete institutions lack faults or that their effects may not be disastrous. That is why they need to progress over time and not simply imitate the past without reform for the present. Under the selection system it was said that one could recommend an "outstanding" person who knew no books and "elevate" a worthy person who made his father move out of the house. The recommendation system ultimately led to the upper ranks never having an unvisited house while the lower ranks had no influential family members. The imperial examinations became ossified with the eight-legged essay and incidents such as the one mocked in the story "Fan Jin Passes the Exam."[84] But this was never the standard of assessment for the institution. The question was not whether the institution as such was wholly good or wholly bad but whether, overall, *in the social and historical conditions of the time*, it would have been better not to have had this institution or whether it was possible to imagine or create and run for a long time an institution that would achieve better results.

But also because of this, since time bears all away, it may be that what was once constitutional may no longer be of constitutional significance. With the needs set by modern China's economy, politics, and society and changes in knowledge, the imperial examinations were abolished in 1905 and replaced by modern schools. But an even more persuasive piece of evidence is to be found in the Taiwan region, which, following the Five-Powers Constitution of the Republic of China, has set up the *Yuan* examination that attempts to continue the system of ancient China, though in fact it has devolved into a Ministry of Human Resources.[85] "The autumn wind still sighs, but the world has changed."[86] Even though the authors of the Constitution *wrote it into the text of the Constitution and continued to use* what was once an important institution *by setting up a body for that purpose*, without the agrarian background of China in the past or the constitutional issues of that time, it lost its significance as something that could bind the whole country together and thus was no longer of constitutional significance. It is merely a piece of decoration.

It is precisely the change of the social background that has led many Chinese scholars today, either consciously or unconsciously, to equate the imperial examinations with the current civil service examinations, but they rarely understand this in terms of the constitutional significance that has, throughout history, shaped the politics and culture of China. But you can still feel the solemn weight of years!

Part II

CHAPTER FOUR

The Mixed Han-Tang-Song Structure and Its Moral Ideal

A REPLY TO PROFESSOR SU LI'S ACCOUNT OF THE CHINESE CONSTITUTION

Wang Hui

IN HIS DISCUSSION of the political order of ancient China, Su Li proposes an idea of the constitution that is different from the one usually referred to as the Constitution or constitutional law. According to his definition, a constitution is "a basic political-legal setup by which any state is formed and continues to run normally," responding to both the general questions of all mankind and to the state's natural geoclimatic conditions and resource constraints.[1] Su Li does not attempt to take the point of view of the Constitution or constitutional law. Rather the opposite, since he attempts to formulate an interpretation from the ante-constitutional or preconstitutional law point of view; that is, the constitutional question deals with how a state becomes a state, why it covers a particular territory or group of people, and how the persons or institutions that are later described as the lawgivers became the lawgivers.[2] Therefore the constitutional question is not something that divides China from the West, for it can be applied to the study of any political body. However, since this idea describes the political formation of a social community and any such social community is something that has developed under specific historical conditions, the constitutional question raises the historical question of the political formation of different communities or that of the difference in political formation between one such community and another.

Starting from here, Su Li proposes two fundamental arguments. The first lies on the surface; namely, in contrast to most legal scholars, who are more familiar with the Western model of a constitution, and academics who ground discussion of the constitution on a universalist basis, he holds that the constitution of each state has its own unique historical properties. The second argument is deeper and comes before the modern idea of a constitution. At this level, the constitution of ancient China is different from the constitutions of other civilized states since it had to deal with three core political issues. The first issue was how to get people from rural villages (which can be viewed as parallel to the Greek city-states) scattered over a large expanse to work together effectively and set up internal structures. The second issue was how to get the scattered rural villages to form one state, a royal dynasty—rather like the medieval monarchy in England—and to develop effective governance and a political identity. The third issue was how to deal with the relationship between the rural civilization of the central plain and the pastoral or montane civilizations of the frontiers—by opposing them? attacking them? creating alliances with them? offering tribute to them? or being absorbed into them?—so as to create a political culture centered on the civilization of the central plain by which "China" became China—comparable to the formation of the United States at the time the states adopted the U.S. Constitution or to the formation of the European Union. Of these three issues, it is the second that has priority since it involves overcoming the bonds of kinship and geography at the village level to create a large-scale political community.

To turn from the questions of the Constitution or constitutional law to that of the constitution amounts to taking the historical formation of the political body as the premise for the political order. This shift changes the standard teleological approach to the Chinese constitution using the European model of a written Constitution. It goes further in taking structural features of Chinese history that would seem to be at odds with the realization of a modern Constitution (such as clan-based feudalism and the imperial system) or which are considered irrelevant (such as the Chinese script, weights and measures, and transportation) as important for understanding the constitution. This is an important methodological change. However, the constitutional question that Su Li defines is also poststructural in nature, that is, it takes the historical formation of the constitution as the thread by which to examine the constitution of China and supposes the state that has actually been shaped by the Chinese dynasties or Chinese civilization, and thus in its analysis of the shaping of the Chinese constitution it bears the marks of a substantially structural-functionalist methodology. I am very much in favor of the first approach, the shift toward the historical formation of the political order, but am less happy with the second—the functionalist interpretation. That is not to say that rural society, a broad territory, a pluralist society, and the rest are not premises for understanding the material aspects of the political order of the Chinese dynasties, but rather that the shaping of a civilization is determined not only by its material aspects, its laws and language, and such functional features, but also by its beliefs, rituals, intellectual attitudes, and worldviews. Without the latter we would have great difficulty in understanding a civilization and its political order. If a constitution is "the political constitution of a state," then the conditions that allow for a state and its institutional arrangements to stand are not merely functional; they must at the same time be reasonable or legitimate. The scope of what is "reasonable" or "legitimate" is not purely a matter of modernity; rather, it is an anthropological dimension. For instance, it would be hard to understand the "constitution" of the Zhou dynasty without an appreciation of the relationship between divination and kingship. Without an understanding of the theories of *yin-yang* and the five elements (阴阳五行), the mutual interaction and differentiation of heaven and human beings, it would be impossible to understand the constitution of the Han dynasty; without an understanding of the Way of heaven (天道) and the principle of heaven (天理), it would not be easy to understand the special features of the political structure of the Song dynasty. Given that the constitutional question goes beyond the historical question of a legal document, if we are unable to discover the categories and concepts to interpret these institutions in the ancient institutions themselves and in relevant texts, then we would have difficulty in truly understanding China as a civilization and its political formation. With this belief as a foundation, my chapter takes the worldview of ancient China and its changes as the guiding thread and explains the political constitution and evolution of the pre-Qin, Han-Tang, and Song dynasties.

Religion or Science? Divination or Kingship?

As it developed, the School of Principle (理学) in the Song dynasty criticized and attempted to overcome three intellectual targets: Buddhism along with Daoism, textual criticism of the Han and Tang dynasties, and a utilitarian Confucianism centered on a discussion of institutions. Criticism of the classical studies of the Han and Tang find their roots in the later Tang with the reexamination of the relationship between heaven and human beings undertaken by Han Yu, Liu Zongyuan, Liu Yuxi, Li Ao, and others. They sought to provide a rational explanation for the Way of heaven, nature, and human affairs. This current of thought continued up to the School of Principle of the Song and Ming dynasties. Han Yu's affirmation that since the death of Mencius Confucian teachings were no longer transmitted amounted to a challenge to the legitimacy of the orthodox transmission of the classics from the Han dynasty. By leaping over Han and Tang scholarship and affirming a direct continuity with the Confucianism of Confucius and Mencius, Han Yu was denying that there was any other track by which the Confucian Way could be continued. In the moral discourse of the Song Confucians, the most prominent form of discourse was to reject the law of the Han and Tang dynasties based on affirming the legal system of the three pre-Qin dynasties (Xia, Shang, and Zhou), to criticize textual criticism in the light of the Way of Confucius and Mencius, and to clearly distinguish the institutions and ethical thought of the Han and Tang from the rituals and moral discourse of the three dynasties. In the language of the Song Confucians, this form of criticism of the Han-Tang institutions in the light of the rites of the Three Dynasties extended to the fields of politics (feudalism vs. commanderies and counties), agriculture (the well-field or double-taxation law), education (schools or examinations), and military matters. In the framework of the pre-Qin discourse on rites, this distinction between the Han institutions and the rites of the Three Dynasties could never have occurred. In this sense, the criticism of the institutions first arose from adopting a historical perspective that distinguished between rites and institutions. Therefore, we must go on to ask: Why is it that the Song Confucians thought that the institutions of the Han and Tang and their classical scholarship had turned their back on moral evaluation set up by the ritual community? What significance for the formation of the School of Principle does a historical approach that clearly differentiates between the ritual discourse of the Three Dynasties and the institutional discourse of the Han and Tang have?

The Han arose by succeeding the Qin. The central question for the political understanding of the Han was how to find a balance between the commanderies and counties (郡县制) of Qin and the earlier feudal system (封建制), between a central authority and feudal nobles, between the old part of "China" and the new "barbarian" areas absorbed into the state owing to imperial expansion. This is why the *Spring and Autumn Annals* and the *Rites of Zhou* were so important during the Han dynasty. The *Spring and Autumn Annals* were able to provide a hermeneutic for the law, institutions, and morality by employing categories of historical change. The *Rites of Zhou* could present the legitimacy and principles of the institutions based on a universal worldview. In Han times, the Way of heaven and nature were explained on the basis of the five elements theory of Zou Yan, the *yin-yang* theory of *Mr Lü's Spring and Autumn Annals*, and the scientific knowledge of the times.[3]

Later, according to the principles of the mutual correspondence of heaven and human affairs and the respective categories of heaven and human affairs, *yin-yang*, the five elements, and the four seasons, symbolic numbers were used to interpret the basic framework and ideas of the *Spring and Autumn Annals* and the *Rites of Zhou*. In his "Shamans and Confucians of the Qin and Han," Pei Wei developed the Han theory of *yin-yang* into a political theory encompassing three directions. The theory of the circle of the five virtues (五德终始说), which came originally from Zou Yan, and the very similar theory of the three ruling forces (三统说) and the Bright Hall theory (明堂说), which developed out of the directives for the months in *Mr Lü's Spring and Autumn Annals: 12 Records*, were combined to provide an inherent logic linking Han dynasty political theory to *yin-yang* and the five elements.[4] From the bibliography of the *Han History* we find that the Han Confucians reread the tradition of the shamans and developed a new basic model by combining the River Chart, Luo Book, eight trigrams, and the structural digits of fortune or misfortune, bad luck or good luck, the future, movement, and stillness from the *Book of Changes* and linked this to the Confucian account of history in the *Spring and Autumn Annals*. From this they extrapolated and developed political ideas appropriate for the time. Unlike for Confucius, the emphasis of the Han Confucians was no longer on human beings and implementation of the rites but rather on exploring the relationship between heaven and human affairs and the correspondences between political and natural order. If we were to describe the Confucian-Mencian view of the inner virtue of benevolence as a form of religious attitude—here the word "religion" is used only analogously—then the Han Confucian understanding of heaven was closer to a scientific attitude—that is, seeking to establish the principle of legitimacy based on knowledge of the relationship between heaven and human affairs. In this sense, what many people denounce as religious superstition or mysticism among the Han Confucians was, in fact, more in the nature of science.

Whether the description of heaven, the universe, and nature in Han naturalism should be described as religious and mystical or scientific, shamanic or kingly power-related, is a question that must be discussed through a consideration of the relationship between shamans and kingship. The ritual system of the Shang and Zhou dynasties embodied the kinship-based community centered on shamanic culture of the clans and villages and the early historical relationships among the states. The institutions and rites of the states developed from the coalescence, beliefs, and rituals of clan society. From shaman to prince, from clans to a state, from a community formed according to direct lineage to a state body constructed by ties of consanguinity, this process of the expansion of institutions achieved its apogee in the internal links of the ritual system. Anthropologists and historians of the Shang and Zhou have gradually come to the view that the tradition by which shaman and prince were united during the evolution of the Shang-Zhou institutions resulted in the ancient kingship and belief system being seen as two sides of the same coin. The presupposition of ritual kingship as heaven was that the king was the head shaman and that the shaman linked heaven and the human world.[5] In the oracle bone script, the same character is used for "shaman" (*wu* 巫) and for "dance" (*wu* 舞). The character depicts a shaman holding feathers or some other instrument in his or her hands and dancing.[6] "Dancing has always been a particularly important element in shamanic rites, but ventriloquy appears to have been used also, as well as juggling and tricks whereby the shaman releases himself from bonds."[7] Shamanic arts, medicine, pharmacology—including the use of poisons—and rainmaking are all related, such that shamanism includes an interpretation of the relationships between the human body, the universe, and the decree of heaven. The shaman prince can serve as a point of unity in the movement from clan society to an early state. As a mediator between human beings and the spirits, the shaman prince can communicate with the spirits through abnormal or even crazy behavior. Regarding the link between the shamanic arts and the culture of the early states, there is a very close relationship between the transformation of the shaman and the normalization of the organizational structure of the community. This process from the shaman to the historian and the installation of the ritual and musical order symbolizes the gradual shift of the early shamanic tradition into two elements of the state culture.

The process of moving from the shaman to the historian and the installation of the ritual and musical order are both inherently linked to the category of "number." According to the divination records on the Shang oracle bones, divination by oracle bones or by yarrow stalks comprised two factors. On the one hand, the evolving calculation of the numbers replaced the physical activity of the shaman's body, acting as a conduit between heaven and the human world and predicting good or bad fortune, disaster or blessings, movement or staying still. On the other hand, it used a means of examining heavenly phenomena to record royal affairs and predict the future and so became the origin of the role of the "historian."[8] Numbers could be converted into history because numbers embodied the internal link between the institutional order and heaven. Together they acted as an explanation and account of human activities. The *Record of Rites* says: "The turtle is for divination by cracking, the yarrow for divination by stalks. Cracking and stalks are the means by which the early sage kings brought the people to trust in the seasons and days, to respect ghosts and spirits, fear laws and commands. They are that by which the people decides matters of doubt and determines what is unclear. Therefore, it is said: In doubt divine the matter by the stalks and then it will not be so; on that day do something then it will certainly happen."[9] The *Record of Rites* says: "Honour the meaning which the rites determine as deserving respect. If you fail to grasp the meaning, then at least display its number: this is the business of the imprecator and the historian. Even if the number can be displayed, it is still difficult to know its meaning. Knowing the meaning and honouring it is the Way whereby the son of heaven regulates the world under heaven."[10] The orator and historian understand only the form of the number and are not able to interpret its inner meaning. Sun Xidan explains: "The numbers of the rites appear at the end of affairs whilst the meaning of the rites penetrates to the spirit of life."[11] Therefore, "number" alone is insufficient to lay out the decree of heaven. It requires an institution, the rites, a human input, and similar factors to fill it out. In the chapter *Confucius Quietly at Home* (仲尼燕居), the *Record of Rites* reads, "Institutions lie in the rites; writing and action also lie in the rites; carrying them out is a matter for human beings!" Again, "The rites are reason; music is restrained tempo. Without reason, the gentleman does not move nor does he act without restraint."[12] If divination by cracking or by yarrow stalks embodies the formalization or rationalization of shamanic culture, then Confucians put the emphasis on action according to real affairs, the not moving without a reason and not acting without restraint and the concern for human input. Numbers and the institution of the monarchy are intimately linked, and the Confucians are concerned about the actual process of implementation of the rites.

According to Zhang Xuecheng's theory that the six classics are all history books, the *Book of Changes* is to be seen as concrete evidence of the link between history and the symbolic numerical relationship of the early classics and the institutions, rites, and activities of the first kings. In his own words, "what makes [the *Book of Changes*] a political blueprint is that it is in the category of material for the historian."[13] In Zhang's view, the *Book of Changes* is both a book of divination and a book that is history in the form of using numbers. Gong Zizhen, who was greatly influenced by Zhang Xuecheng, concludes,

> Among the officials of the Zhou, the most important was the historian. Other than the historian, no one had the office of speaking or writing. Apart from the historian, there was no written script. Other than the historian, there was no human morality or assessment of moral value. So long as the historian was there, the Zhou existed; once his post was abolished, then the Zhou died. . . . The six classics are the epitome of the records of the Zhou historians. The *Book of Changes* is the divination of the historian; the *Book of History* is the record of the views of the historian; the *Spring and Autumn Annals* is the historian's record of actions. The *feng* Odes (*Lessons from the States*) are what the historian chose from among the people and edited on bamboo and silk and added tunes to. The *ya* and *song* Odes (*Royal Odes and Songs of Praise*) are what the historian chose from among the officials. The *Book of Rites* are the laws and commands for each generation . . . the degrees at capping and marriage, the distinctions at funerals and sacrifices to ancestors, and the regulations and etiquette for ministers and officials are all numbered in order. I do not believe you if you reject the number and only talk about the meaning.[14]

What constitutes a difference between the historian and the shaman is that the historian grasps the number but goes beyond divination and reliance on shamanic practices and dancing. The rationalization of the ritual order is the concrete embodiment of the form of the numbers.

Yin-Yang *and Five Elements Theory as Legitimation for a Unified Imperial Politics*

Gong Zizhen's "I do not believe you if you reject the number and only talk about the meaning" is particularly apt for explaining the way the Han Confucians brought together symbolic numbers, history, and a comprehensive sense. If we say that Confucius's use of benevolence to interpret the rites is a way of using an inner spirit to flesh out the content of the institution of monarchy, then what the Han Confucians sought was to search in the tradition of divination for the legitimacy of the unified communal institutions. Here we may take the *Luxuriant Gems of the Spring and Autumn Annals* of Dong Zhongshu (179–104 BC) as an example. Dong Zhongshu unites the scholarship surrounding the *yin-yang*, five elements theory with Confucian thought. There are two major tendencies in his *Luxuriant Gems of the Spring and Autumn Annals*. The first is to take the *Gongyang Commentary* as the measure by which to interpret the moral/political principles of the *Spring and Autumn Annals*. Second, he used the cosmology of *yin-yang*, five elements, four seasons, and omens that originated from Zou Yan and *Mr Lü's Spring and Autumn Annals* to provide a new reinterpretation of the moral/political principles drawn from the *Spring and Autumn Annals*. The combination of these two aspects resulted in a cosmological system that included everything and in which everything was interrelated. There are seventeen *juan* in the book. The transmitted book is divided into eighty-two *pian*, of which *pian* 39, 40, and 54 are missing. The book may be divided into two parts: the initial seventeen *pian*, which use the *Gongyang Commentary* to explain the *Spring and Autumn Annals*, which leads to the positing of a model of ideal morals/politics; and *pian* 18 to 82, which use the cosmology of *yin-yang*, five elements, four seasons, and omens to discuss how the principles and implementation of morality/politics are completely at one with the natural running of the universe, and on this basis draw up a cosmological system that includes all areas of moral, political, and social life within a framework based on the operation of the Way of heaven. This second part can be further divided into two types, one of which uses *yin-yang* and the five elements as its guiding thread and the other of which takes the five elements as the norm. Heaven and earth, *yin* and *yang*, embody a cosmology of corresponding hierarchical relationships. The relationship of prince to minister and that of prince to people are correspondences at one degree of difference. The five elements are natural categories within the cosmos. The specialized jobs, such as government offices, found in the distribution of tasks among human beings and the norms of human morality, such as the way of fidelity and filial piety, are direct correspondences within the same degree. The four seasons show the pattern of space, time, and order. Benevolence, justice, fidelity, and virtue are described as the four virtues of heaven. The changes of the cosmos and of history within this context of change develop naturally and teleologically. To bring out the absolute and supreme nature of heaven, Dong Zhongshu expounds rituals and sacrifices, especially the *xiao* sacrifice, thereby directly linking the ritual activity of the prince to the will of heaven.[15] The above, including the sacrifices that form part of ritual, is a path for communicating with heaven and a way of expressing the supreme status and awe of the emperor. There must be some premise by which concepts such as *yin-yang*, the five elements, and the four seasons can be linked to political, economic, and other social relationships in one natural process, namely, that there is some link and communication between heaven and the human world, which is the principle by which heaven and humans affect each other and are alike in kind. Taking the *tonglei xiangdong pian* of the *Luxuriant Gems of the Spring and Autumn Annals* as an example, we arrive at the following conclusions.

First, Dong's theory of correspondences between heaven and human beings is shamanic through and through, as can be seen by what Frazer says about sympathetic magic:

> If we analyse the principles of thought on which magic is based, they will probably be found to resolve themselves into two: first, that like produces like, or that an effect resembles its cause; and, second, that things which have once been in contact with each other continue to act on each other at a distance after the physical contact has been severed. The former principle may be called the Law of Similarity, the latter the Law of Contact or Contagion . . . Magic . . . [r]egarded as a system of natural law, that is, as a statement of the rules which determine the sequence of events throughout the world, it may be called Theoretical Magic: regarded as a set of precepts which human beings observe in order to compass their ends, it may be called Practical Magic.[16]

Second, Dong Zhongshu's theory of correspondence between heaven and human beings is also a form of science. He takes the example of acoustic resonance in music and the rise and fall of kings to explain the system of natural laws. This tendency shows a form of scientific viewpoint for looking at the relationship between heaven and human beings. Needham took Dong's use of phonology and the phenomenon of acoustic resonance as the basis for distinguishing five categories to prove that his thought was scientific. "To those who could know nothing of sound-waves it must have been very convincing, and it proved his point that things in the universe which belonged to the same classes . . . resonated with, or energised, each other. This was not mere primitive undifferentiatedness, in which anything could affect anything else; it was part of a very closely knit universe in which only things of certain classes would affect other things of the same class."[17] Needham uses an organic theory to explain a particular feature of Chinese thought, but here he does not explain the inner relationship between the phonological experiment and the ritual order. He lacks what the *Yi Shu* (佚书)[18] says about how music is formed and how virtue comes about in relation to the household, state, and world under heaven. When the *Record of Music* talks about "using rites to distinguish what is different and music to watch over harmony," isn't this going beyond "mere primitive undifferentiatedness" to incorporate the way rites and music include both pluralism and differentiation? Here within the magical viewpoint of correspondences between heaven and human beings, the scientific theory of similarity in type between heaven and human beings, and the ritual order there is an organic and generic link, such that the will of heaven can make itself apparent in all three realms.

Third, based on the premise of this organic link, Dong Zhongshu proposed the idea that things call forth other things according to type, and thus set conditions by which auspicious signs could explain the emergence of a king. "When things move each other without any visible form, it can be said to be natural. In fact, it is not natural; rather there is something that makes it so. Therefore, there is something which makes things so, that which does so is without visible form." The emergence of kings is a natural phenomenon, but it is not a purely natural phenomenon because in the back of this phenomenon lies "that which makes it so." Therefore, there is a relationship of mutual dependence that includes natural phenomena, the will of heaven, and the decree of heaven. By looking at natural phenomena it is possible to understand the will of heaven and the decree of heaven.

If it can be said that Confucius's "transmitting and not creating" takes the ritual and monarchical order as heaven, and "using benevolence to interpret the rites" places the ritual order in the practice of subject full of respect and awe, then Dong's theory of correspondence between heaven and the human world once more converts the sacred character of the ritual and monarchical order into a scientific recognition of natural phenomena and a magical experience with the supreme will that has a natural process as its background. For Confucius, the legacy of magic is largely embodied in an intrinsic value and its ritual implementation, whereas for Dong Zhongshu, the legacy of magic is transformed from the tradition of divination into the exposition of a formalization or scientization of heaven.[19] But it was precisely this form of scientization that led people to later place its key features under the rubric of religious mysticism. Frazer says that "magic is a spurious system of natural law as well as a fallacious guide of conduct; it is a false science as well as an abortive art" (chap. 3, sec. 1).[20] So long as humankind has not got a sufficiently strong grasp of the natural universe, then any knowledge about nature can be considered "a spurious system of natural law." Looking at the shift involving moral/political judgments by Confucians, we find that Dong Zhongshu clearly links them very closely to knowledge of nature and strives, by describing the natural heaven, to reveal moral/political norms. In this sense, Han Confucian thought can be described both as scientism and as mysticism, while it is also magic and monarchical.

Henri Hubert and Marcel Mauss forcefully argue that "magic has nourished science, and the earliest scientists were magicians. . . . Magic issues by a thousand fissures from the mystical life, from which it draws its strength, in order to mingle with the life of the laity and to serve them. It tends to the concrete, whereas religion tends to the abstract. It works in the same sense as techniques, industry, medicine, chemistry and so on. Magic was essentially an art of doing things."[21] Han dynasty calendrical astronomy, agriculture, medicine, and chemistry—geomancers' search for magic pills led them to discover the properties of mercury, lead, sulfur, and other minerals and the laws governing their changes—all developed considerably. Apart from the requirements for the development of agriculture, it is impossible to know today if these developments had any intrinsic link to the expansion of transportation under the Han, as in Zhang Qian's journey to the west. Study of the heavenly symbols was closely related to determination of the seasons for agriculture. Understanding of the structure of the heavenly bodies was very rich under the Han. Of the three cosmological theories, the Mysterious Night theory was no longer promulgated.[22] The *Zhou Bi Suan jing* and its Covered Heaven theory were already prevalent under Emperor Wu, whereas the more scientific Obscure Heaven theory gave rise to outstanding results during the two Han dynasties. Under Emperor Wu of the Han, Luo Xiahong, She Xing, Deng Ping, and Sima Qian revised the *Zhuanxu* calendar and composed the *Taichu* calendar, making the first month the beginning of the year and using the twenty-four calendrical periods that were good for agriculture. They also added a leap month to resolve the contradiction between the solar and lunar calendars, thus bringing it about that "on the first and last days of the lunar month the moon appears one quarter increasing, one quarter decreasing, full or empty."[23] The armillary sphere drawn up by Luo Xiahong and Geng Shouchang was the basis on which Zhang Heng, in the Eastern Han, built a new and better armillary sphere to observe the heavenly bodies. The section on Heavenly Offices in the *Records of the Historian* and the astronomical section of the *Han History* give a detailed list of the names of the twenty-eight heavenly mansions (*su*). Based on the movement of the stars, the Han people worked out the twenty-four divisions of the year. The names they chose and the order in which they occur are exactly the same as those used today. Along with developments in astronomy went new discoveries in mathematics. The *Zhoubi Suan jing* records how a pole was used to create the shadow of the sun and thereby calculate its height above the earth, and thus Pythagoras's theorem was discovered. Although the *Jiu zhang suanshu* assigns this to the reign of Emperor He of the Eastern Han, it must have been earlier to allow for the process of formation, modification, and refashioning. Many of the methods of calculation and mathematical ideas employed come from resolving the calculation of the size of agricultural fields, measurements of the land, proportional distribution, storage space in a barn, and tax collecting—all "practical arts" that involved "living among ordinary people and serving them."

In tandem with the developments in astronomy and the calendar, Han agricultural science had already become a professional subject. There are nine works of agricultural learning listed in the bibliography of the *Han History*, including Cui Shi's *Monthly Observances for the Four Ranks of People*, which came into being in the later Eastern Han. During the Western Han, however, the Monthly Observances of *Mr Lü's Spring and Autumn Annals* composed by Lu Buwei, prime minister of Qin, had already had a great influence on Dong Zhongshu and other Confucians.[24] *Mr Lü's Spring and Autumn Annals* is divided into three parts, named, respectively, *ji*, *lan*, and *lun*. The most noteworthy feature of the layout is the symbolic relationship of heaven and the human world reflected in the divisions of the text. The *ji* part is divided into twelve *juan*, matching the twelve seasons of the year. Each *juan* has five *pian*, thus making sixty in all, which matches the sexagenary cycle of the years. Every third *juan* of the *ji* corresponds to one season of the year, and each season has its own central theme, so spring is for fostering life, summer for music and education, autumn for war, and winter for death. The first *pian* of each *juan* is borrowed from the Monthly Observances chapter of the *Lost Book of Zhou*. These sections discuss what should be done during each season of the year to guarantee that the important affairs of state will progress smoothly. The following four *pian* discuss the ideas and actions that are appropriate for that season. The *lan* section has eight *juan* of eight *pian* each, making a total of sixty-four, thus the same as the eight trigrams and sixty-four hexagrams of the *Book of Changes*. The *lun* section has six *juan* of six *pian* each. The last four of these discuss agricultural issues, whereas the initial thirty-two *pian* are centered on the conduct of a prince who practices benevolence and justice. It cannot be known to what relationship in nature the six *juan* and total of thirty-six *pian* of the *lun* section correspond; however, given the whole structure of the book, it would seem that there must be some indication.[25] In addition to the use of the four seasons to structure the twelve months in the first *ji* of the twelve *ji*, there is, even more important, an attempt to place the two *qi* of *yin* and *yang* into the pattern of the four seasons, and to match up the five elements and the four seasons. In spring, the dominant virtue is wood; in summer, the dominant virtue is fire; in autumn, the dominant virtue is metal; in winter, the dominant virtue is water; and at the end of summer (the sixth month), there is added a section that reads: "In the center is earth; its day is *wu-ji* [the fifth and sixth of the heavenly trunks]; its emperor is the Yellow Emperor and its spirit is the god of earth."[26] This is used to bring the numbers "four" (the seasons) and "five" (the elements) into harmony. The heaven formed by the *yin-yang*, five elements theory is between a personal heaven and a heaven that is the natural order. It is not a personal god, but it has the ability to reward and punish and has a will.

Starting from here, we can reinterpret Dong Zhongshu's notion of the correspondence between heaven and the human world. Why is it that the Confucian ideal had to join together the *yin-yang* ideas of *Mr Lü's Spring and Autumn Annals* and the five elements theory of Zou Yan with the scientific discoveries related to the circular heaven and four seasons of the Han astronomers and school of agriculture? Why is it that numerology is accorded such a high place in Confucian learning, almost regaining the status that it had in the divination tradition? (The use of the five elements to interpret the fate of the state derives from the methods used by the *yin-yang* school. It corresponds clearly to the model of Confucian thought spoken of by Zi Chan: "the rites match heaven; this is the Way of heaven."[27] The method used by the *yin-yang* school can be said to come straight from the divination tradition.) Why is it that Dong Zhongshu's development and exposition of the meaning of the *Spring and Autumn Annals* had to be completed in the name of the natural law of heaven?

Let us begin our discussion by discussing the exposition and structure of the relationship between heaven and the human world in the *Luxuriant Gems of the Spring and Autumn Annals* and its relationship to *Mr Lü's Spring and Autumn Annals*. According to the structure of heaven and the human world in *Mr Lü's Spring and Autumn Annals*, the political rule of kings is wholly tied to the norms of heaven. Kings receive their office from heaven and therefore their conduct must aim to conform to the will of heaven, and on this basis political order and conduct must accord with the times for there to be success. Heaven and the things that express the will of heaven—*yin-yang*, the five elements, and the four seasons—construct the foundation for the legitimacy of the king's politics and the norms for his conduct. By following this logic, the *Luxuriant Gems of the Spring and Autumn Annals*, in its exposition of cases found in the *Spring and Autumn Annals*, expresses the basic principle according to which the will of heaven and its ordered sequence must never be infringed. This provides a cosmological basis for an imperially centered ideology. By drawing together the *Gongyang Commentary*, *yin-yang*, and the five elements, Dong Zhongshu is able to use theories about heaven to shape legitimacy for a unified rule. He adds the idea of the will of heaven to the *Spring and Autumn Annals* because heaven is the supreme measure of the cosmological system. The *Spring and Autumn Annals* gives the laws set up by Confucius for later kings so there is no other choice but to see Confucius as a "new king." To decide on the *Spring and Autumn Annals* as normative for the Han required the development of a special form of hermeneutics to reveal their real meaning. The *Gongyang Commentary* uses the idea of changes of power, and the *Luxuriant Gems of the Spring and Autumn Annals* builds on this, since only by introducing this idea was Dong Zhongshu able to develop a way of reading and interpreting the overall meaning in the details of the *Spring and Autumn Annals* and take the ritual order that existed under the feudal system and employ it as a unifying theory in the political system of commanderies and counties.[28]

The Han dynasty affirmed the central authority of the state around the power of the emperor, but "at the turn of the Chu and Han after each of the six states had established itself," the feudal system of the nobles continued to exist, so that the Han Empire can be described as a mixed system of a feudal (封建)/commandery system (郡县制) in which the commanderies (郡) and counties were dominant. During the Han, both commanderies (郡县)

and feudal states were set up side by side, resulting in severe tension between the centralization of the commanderies and counties and the feudal power of the lords. Early on, the Han set up eight feudal states, but later they were abolished. Later, the Han tried to imitate the feudal system of the Zhou and appointed relatives of the emperor as feudal lords, but this again provoked conflict between the central authority of the emperor and the feudal kings. Emperors Wen and Jing, respectively, accepted the advice of Jia Yi and Zhao Cuo and weakened the power of the feudal lords. Emperor Wu went one step further and granted marquisates as rewards for merit and set up relatives in the subordinate kingdoms to break up the feudal states.[29] The tenth chapter of the *Luxuriant Gems of the Spring and Autumn Annals* summarizes the main message of the *Spring and Autumn Annals* as follows: "The above is quite clear; therefore it is said that justice is set up to clarify the distinction between noble and base. The trunk is strengthened and the branches weakened to clarify what is important and what is not. It identifies devious conduct to clarify what is correct. It picks what is good and rejects what is bad to correct what falls short of correct procedure."[30] The strong trunk and weak branches refer to the absolute authority the central imperial power held over the feudal lords, and the distinction between noble and base, what is important and what is not, presumes this absolute sequence of power. This view of Dong Zhongshu changed the relationship of positions among the Son of Heaven, the feudal lords, and the great ministers in the *Spring and Autumn Annals* and created an idea of uniform rule that was quite distinct from feudalism. "Therefore, the way of the *Spring and Autumn Annals* takes the profundity of the origin to rectify the initial rulings of heaven and takes the rulings of heaven to determine the politics of the king and takes the politics of the king to put the feudal lords in their places and the status of the feudal lords to maintain order within the borders. When all five are correct then the transformation can proceed greatly."[31] The theory that Confucius had a mandate to change institutions set out in the *Luxuriant Gems of the Spring and Autumn Annals*, and the cycle based on *yin-yang*, the five elements, and five virtues of the three ruling colors of red, white, and black, must all be interpreted against the background of the theory of historical change and the new unity. The absolute character of heaven and the absolutism of imperial power are clearly linked.[32] Fu Sinian puts it this way: "Under the Western Zhou, feudalism was a means of founding a state and setting up rule over the people, so it was a special form of social organisation. The feudalism of the Western Han split up the commanderies and counties, so it was only feudalism in a geographic sense."[33] For Confucians, the difference between the feudalism of the Western Zhou and that of the Han can be expressed as a distinction between the rites and the institutions. The rites embody the values of feudalism whereas the institutions contain the idea of imperial power as the center. The bureaucratic governing body set up in the context of the commanderies and counties was at variance with the ritual relationships, such that the rites could no longer serve as the premise for the legitimacy of the political body.

In addition to the ideology of imperial power as the center, the idea of the grand unity also had an impact on the territorial expanse of the empire. The Han Empire expanded outward and achieved an extent that had never been seen before. The relationship of the inner to the outer circles constituted the main standard by which the empire understood itself. The empire expanded the area of pre-Qin China. The idea of the grand unity developed along with a contrast between the Chinese and the barbarians. Under these circumstances, it was necessary to change the relationship between feudalism and the rites found in the *Spring and Autumn Annals*. Dong Zhongshu's theory of a contrast between Chinese and barbarians greatly altered attitudes to the issues of domestic/foreign and barbarian/Chinese set out in the *Spring and Autumn Annals* and the *Gongyang Commentary*. The *Luxuriant Gems of the Spring and Autumn Annals* reads:

> The normal way of speaking in the *Spring and Autumn Annals* is for rites not to be ascribed to the barbarians but to China. Yet after the battle at Bi that was no longer the case. Why? I say, "The *Spring and Autumn Annals* has no fixed use of terms; it changes according to circumstances. Since the state of Jin had become barbarian and that of Chu was ruled by a prince, then the terms are changed to match the shift in realities. King Zhuang [of Chu] deliberately withdrew from his attack on Zheng. This is a virtue to be honoured. The people of Jin did not appreciate this goodness and went on to attack Chu, even though Chu had already raised the siege. To pick a war with Chu under these circumstances was not only to fail to treat good intentions well but also to treat the desire to save the people too lightly. This was to belittle Chu and brought it about that Jin could not be ranked among the good states that observed the rites."[34]

The dialectic of barbarians and Chinese is a key topic of the *Spring and Autumn Annals* and *Gongyang Commentary*, but with the expansion of the empire, there was clearly a great need to redraw the distinction between barbarians and Chinese to suit the new relations between domestic and foreign. In Dong Zhongshu's theory of the comparative levels of rites and the natural theory popular in the Han, especially the rise of the views of Zou Yan, we can find that the *yin-yang*, five elements theory can encompass the comparison of what is domestic with what is foreign. *Juan* 74 of the *Records of the Historian* is named *Biographies of Mencius and Xun Qing*, but Zou Yan and his school occupy an important position in the text:

> Zou Yan saw that the rulers were becoming increasingly dissolute and extravagant, unable to rectify themselves and then spread their virtue

among the common people. . . . Thereupon he delved deep into the interplay of the *yin* and the *yang* and wrote more than a hundred thousand words about their strange transmutations. . . . Using wild and magniloquent language he went on from a study of some minor object to extend his deductions to infinity. Going back from modern times to the Yellow Emperor and the common origin of all teachings, he covered the rise and fall of different ages, the good and bad omens, and the various institutions, tracing these to the remote past before Earth and Heaven were created, and to the mysterious and unknown origin of things. He began by tabulating the famous mountains, mighty rivers and valleys of China, its birds and beasts, products of water and land and precious objects, going on from these to things hidden from men's eyes beyond the Four Seas. He claimed that since the separation of Heaven and Earth all things must change according to the specific laws of the Five Elements and show definite manifestations. He maintained that what Confucians called the "Central States" were only one of eighty-one regions of the world. The Middle Kingdom, known as the Red Divine land, comprised the nine "continents" of which Great Yu spoke, but these were not real continents. Outside the Middle Kingdom there were nine regions as large as the Red Divine Land, and these were the true Nine Continents. These were each surrounded by "small seas" separating the people and beasts on one from those on others and formed one region which made up one continent. There were nine such continents, surrounded by a "great ocean" at the boundary of Earth and Heaven.

Zou Yan's theories were all of this sort. Yet these were the premises for his conclusions about humanity, justice, frugality, and the relationships between ruler and ruled, high and low, and kinsmen. Princes and nobles were impressed and influenced by their first acquaintance with his teachings.[35]

Zou Yan was aware of the chaos of the ritual order and turned instead to observing the natural world, and applied his study of nature to the relationship between politics and rites, both past and present, in the center and across the borders. He brought to the theory of the size of the nine states a natural foundation for ritual governance and not a form of China-centralism. Based on Zou Yan's geographical theory of the size of the nine states and redefinition of China, Dong Zhongshu changed the traditional view of the *Spring and Autumn Annals* and the *Gongyang Commentary*, and, guided by the idea of the grand unity, he added to the theory a comparison between the barbarians and the Chinese.[36]

The third feature of the idea of the grand unity was the correspondence between the natural divisions established by heaven and public offices. The unity of the Han was closely connected to the institution of commanderies and counties. Unlike the feudal system, which was wholly based on a network of relationships of kinship, the institution of commanderies and counties relied on imperial power and formalized the model of rule jointly set up by the bureaucratic government bodies. Qin destroyed six states and set up one unified rule. The nobles of the six states became commoners. As a result, the Zhou institutions of feudalism, the well-field system, and the schools fell apart. Under these circumstances, the power of the moral value system of the ritual theory that formed the cornerstone of clan law and relations of kinship inevitably faced radical alteration. The bureaucratic administrative system and the peculiarity of its impersonal functionalism were objects of reflection, discussion, and interpretation for the Han Confucians. The rites that were still functioning no longer had the same import as they did within the context of the Zhou institutions. In the linguistic field in which rites and institutions were divided, if the functionalist systems of the bureaucracy and the law were to be understood as a moral spectrum, then one must look outside the institutions for resources that can make them legitimate and reasonable. The absolute nature of heaven and its intrinsic link to what lay within the institutions or the law was discovered as a solution to a moral difficulty. Dong Zhongshu listed 232 examples of legal judgments in the *Spring and Autumn Annals*, that is, he used the words of the sage and their meaning as a basis for resolving cases. This is a mark of development for Legalist thought in the unified empire. To provide the Han with theories of a moral ideal and moral standard for their institutions, Dong Zhongshu used numerology to link heaven to official posts:

The king institutes his officials such that there are three ministers, nine lower ministers, twenty-seven great officials, and eighty-one scholar-officials, 120 persons in all, and that way the hierarchy of ministers is complete. I have heard that the standard that the sage-kings adopted is the great circuit of heaven, which has three [monthly] starting points to make [one season], and four [seasonal] revolutions to complete [one year]. Is not this the model for the similar arrangement of the officials? That three men constitute the first selection [of officials] is modeled on the fact that three months constitute one season. And that four such selections are made, and no more, is modeled on the fact that with the four seasons [the year] is brought to its conclusion. The three highest ministers are the men by whom the king supports himself. Heaven completes itself by three, and the king supports himself by three. When this complete number is established and [the process of selection] is multiplied four times, there can be no error. Therefore, the Son of Heaven himself chooses the three ministers; the three ministers themselves choose the nine lower ministers; the nine lower ministers themselves each choose three great officials, each of whom in turn chooses three scholar-officials. There is a fourfold selection of three persons. This is to take the way of three to govern the world under heaven [天下], just as heaven works by a multiple of four and with three months in each quarter it completes the year. Does not the fact that there is one *yang* [for spring], but three spring [months covered by it], derive from the appropriateness of three? Heaven then multiplies this by four [the number of the seasons], the number [of months] being identical [for each season]. Heaven has its four seasons and the seasons have their three months. Likewise, the king has his four selections [of officials, in each of which] three ministers are selected. . . . It is only the sage who can [similarly] give complete expression to the changes of man and harmonize them with those of Heaven. This is why it is he who institutes kingly affairs. . . . Thus, according to their variations, men were classed so as to constitute the four selected groups, in each of which there were established [subsidiary groups of] three ministers [each]. This is similar to the way in which Heaven divides the year according to its variations, thus forming the four seasons, in each of which there are three [monthly] divisions.[37]

The four selections refer to the selection made for the four ranks: the three dukes, the ministers, great officials, and scholar-officials. The text then refers to using the number three as the basic number. The four selections are then calculated as follows. The three dukes are the first group selected, the nine ministers the second group, and the twenty-seven great officials the third group. The eighty-one scholar-officials compose the fourth selection. The numbers associated with all these posts are linked to the changes of the four seasons and serve as mediators so that the legitimacy of the posts is referred back to the working of heaven. In the twenty-eighth *juan* of the *Luxuriant Gems of the Spring and Autumn Annals*, Dong Zhongshu adds a remark about the numbers starting from the three dukes and nine ministers: "The Son of Heaven separates into left and right of five ranks, 363 persons, imitating heaven and the number of days in the year." This highlights the number 360,[38] which imitates the 360 degrees of the circular heaven and so symbolizes heaven.

The mixture of unity and feudal regimes brought it about that feudalism was subordinate to the unity of the empire, but rites and institutions were not thereby separated. For example, with regard to the tendency toward severe punishments of the Qin-Han era, he proposed "to establish the Academy to teach the state, erect *yangxu* to transform the cities, soak the people with benevolence, mould the people with friendship, temper the people with the rites, then even if punishments are light the people will not dare do wrong. You can educate their conduct, and their customs and habits will become good."[39] This is to bring together the unity of commanderies and counties with the learning of the rites of the three dynasties. Again, Dong Zhongshu criticizes the Qin for "using the law of Shang Yang and changing the institutions of the kings. By abolishing the well-field system, the people were able to buy and sell; the rich had thousands of acres of land, whilst the poor had no place to put a stake." Dong proposes using one institution of the three dynasties, that of the well-field. He makes a comparison: "In the past, the tax on the people did not exceed 10 percent; they found it easy to pay on demand. Within the space of three days' work, the people could easily supply what was required." But now that "there are taxes on fields and on exports, salt and iron now cost twenty times the old rate. The poor have to farm the fields of the rich and give half of the produce to the landlord." This leads the rich to become corrupt, dissolute, and violent, while the poor grow poorer, flee, and turn into brigands and robbers. He looked into the idea of the well-field but did not take "return to the well-field system" as a slogan. Rather, he used the idea of change to say, "Whilst it would be difficult to suddenly restore the well-field system, yet at least one should get closer to the old system by allowing people to have their own defined land and so allow the poor to have sufficient to live on and stop their lands being expropriated. Salt and iron should all go to the people. The killing of slaves and terror of despotic executions must be abolished. By reducing taxes and cutting down on demands for forced labour, the strength of the people will be safeguarded and then there will be good governance."[40]

The cosmology of the *Luxuriant Gems of the Spring and Autumn Annals* provides a moral/political norm and also an epistemology for understanding that norm. The sacralized description of the relationship between heaven and the human world clearly altered the structure and way in which the rites had been explained in the time of the Zhou dynasty and Confucius. This shows a tendency toward a new moral/political philosophy. *Juan* 29 of the *Luxuriant Gems of the Spring and Autumn Annals* sets out the basic principle of Dong's moral/political thinking, which took benevolence and justice as its center:

> Therefore, the *Spring and Autumn Annals* relies on benevolence and justice as its norms. The norm of benevolence lies in loving others and not in loving oneself. The norm of justice lies in correcting oneself and not in correcting others. If I fail to correct myself, then even if I am in a position to correct others yet I cannot be considered as acting justly. If others are not loved by me, then even if I love myself deeply, yet I cannot be considered to be benevolent. . . . Therefore, kings love even the four barbarian nations; hegemons love as far as the feudal lords. Someone who is secure loves within the borders of his territory; someone who is insecure loves only as far as those beside him, whilst one who is lost only loves himself. Even if a selfish person is made Son of Heaven or a lord, yet he is simply one common fellow and cannot make use of any of his ministers or the people. In this way, though nobody causes him to die, yet he causes himself to die. . . . Therefore I say: the

benevolent loves others and does not place his love in himself: this is the norm. Justice means not that one corrects others but that one corrects oneself. Even in times of chaos and turmoil, nobody does not want to correct others, but how can this be said to be just? . . . Therefore I say, justice lies in correcting oneself and not in correcting others: this is the norm. . . . The gentleman seeks to distinguish between benevolence and justice so as to discriminate between others and the self, and then judge what is internal and what is external, and pay attention to what will run smoothly and what is against the tide. Therefore, internally one regulates affairs by going back to principle and correcting oneself, and one accords with the rites so as to bring about prosperity; externally one regulates by promoting grace to extend one's good influence and by enacting lenient administration so as to hold all people in one.[41]

The moral ideal propounded here by Dong is close to Confucius's understanding of morality. There is a difference in the framework given to the theory of rites, however. Confucius sees the rites themselves as an institution of mutual relationships, which provide the basic norms for moral/political conduct. In Dong's framework of the complementary interaction of heaven and the human world, the institutional relationship must be subordinate to the will of heaven and the way the decree of heaven arranges things if it is to gain legitimacy. The former relies on an intrinsic relationship with heaven (the rites are heaven-oriented); the latter is a symbolic counterpoint relationship, in which the will of heaven becomes a testable thing. Rites such as sacrifices to ancestors are ways of discovering the path for what heaven wants. Therefore, the principles that govern Dong Zhongshu's exposition are utterly different from the institutions of the sage kings expounded by Confucius. Dong seeks to remold institutions and rites according to changing historical relationships and to use heaven's name as a vehicle for exposing the legitimacy of these institutions and rites. Under the guidance of this leading interpretation, "to transmit and not create" and "interpreting the rites in terms of benevolence" no longer constitute an appropriate method for theory.

Numerology and Offices

The use of symbolic numerology to set out the relationships between government posts and the universe was later systematized and expressed more fully than in the old-text version of the classic *Rites of Zhou*. The links between heaven, formalization of the institutions, and the law were formed on the common moral/political scaffolding of the rites. Unlike the rites, the institutions and the law needed an external source of legitimacy. In the Western and Eastern Han, there was a distinction between new-text and old-text scholarship, but there was one thread handed down in the theory of the monarchy within the study of the classics. When the Eastern Han was founded, the rulers cut back the power of the feudal lords and kings by reissuing the law against forming cliques promulgated under Emperor Wu. This restricted the activities of the lords and kings by requiring them to keep to a system of norms, such as that they must not use the rites of the Son of Heaven and, in appointing ministers, they had to use Han institutions. They had to pay a regular tribute tax to the court. Without a tiger tally they could not send out troops. They were not permitted to pan for salt or smelt iron within their states for their own use. They were not to form private cliques within the state or form private links with their in-laws, and so on.[42] In this sense, the absolute nature of heaven in Eastern Han thought and its power to decide things still affected relationships between the Son of Heaven and the feudal lords and officials.[43] The original title of the *Rites of Zhou* was the *Officialdom of Zhou*, and it is this name that is first recorded in the *Records of the Historian*. Later in the bibliography of the *Han History*, a *Classic of the Officialdom of Zhou* in six *pian* is recorded, showing that the book already was considered a classic in the Han dynasty. Tradition holds that the *Rites of Zhou* dates from the mid-second century BC, but it was known only in Han times and now contains many ideas from Liu Xin and Wang Mang.[44] Proof of this comes from an attempt by Liu Xin (46 BC–23 CE) to gain the post of a scholar-official for the *Rites of Zhou*.[45]

The main characteristic of the *Rites of Zhou* is its use of numbers to regulate the system of offices and thereby express its political ideals. As was noted earlier, the importance of numbers in the ritual order can be traced back to the tradition of divination in the Shang and Zhou dynasties and attained its apogee in the writings of the *yin-yang* school. With the prominence accorded to natural science in the Han dynasty, "number" increased in importance as an expression of knowledge of nature whereby the will of heaven in relation to human affairs could be thought of, something that we might well call a form of proto-science. The *Rites of Zhou* uses the number of years and months to match the categories of *yin-yang*, the five elements, and the four seasons, and on this basis constructs a complete system of government offices. What is worth noting is that in the time of Emperor Cheng, Liu Xin produced the *san-tong* calendar based on the *tai-chu* calendar, determining that there were 365.25 days to the year and 29.53 days to the month, which is very close to our present usage. This was the most accurate calendar in the whole world at the time. Liu understood the relationship of numbers in the *Rites of Zhou* in relation to the numbers of the circular heaven. The *Rites of Zhou* takes the structure and organization of the posts of the offices as its focus and divides them into six ministries: (1) Celestial Offices: Prime Minister (in charge of state governance and matters of general administration), (2) Terrestrial Offices: Overseer of Public Affairs (in charge of state instruction, i.e., education), (3) Spring Offices: Patriarch of Ancestral Affairs (in charge of state rituals, i.e., sacrifices and rites), (4) Summer Offices: Overseer of Military Affairs (in charge of affairs of the state, i.e., military matters), (5) Autumn Offices: Overseer of Penal Affairs (in charge of state punishments, i.e., punishments and fines), and (6) Winter Offices: Records of the Scrutiny of Crafts (in charge of state affairs, i.e., the records of approval and inspection of works and crafts). Under each office there were 60 officials, making 360 in all, such that the 360 degrees of the circular heaven perfectly matched the four seasons and both heaven and earth and thus formed a complete system for the relationship between heaven and the human world. In a note to the first section on the celestial offices, Zheng Xuan (127–200) writes: "this post resembles the office set up by heaven. The term *zhong* (elevated mound) means 'big'; '*zai*' means 'official.' Heaven rules over the myriad things; the Son of Heaven sets up the Prime Minister (*zhongzai*) to be in charge of state governance and coordinate the work of all the other officials so that no one fails to do his job. It is not said that he is an overseer since the Prime Minister coordinates all the officials and is not the master of any one post alone."[46] According to this account, this post is set up in imitation of heaven. That there is no specific task to oversee for the celestial office implies that there is a rigid hierarchy among the celestial bodies and that the various posts are distinguished according to the affairs assigned to each. The running of the political community as a whole demands a system of posts and distribution of tasks, which is like what is found in ritual society. However, the new development here is that it expresses the ideal for society.[47] The tradition of shamans and historians used names to show what was right. The *Rites of Zhou* brings together government posts and numbers such that the government posts themselves are the way in which what is right is expressed. There is a formal similarity between the use of government posts to express an ideal and Confucius's narrative of the royal institutions. Both methods adopt a certain organization as the recipient of determining moral ideals. However, in the category of ritual theory, the institutions of the sage kings form the body of the ritual system as a whole. Rites and institutions are unified such that the whole system constructs an objective support by which a moral evaluation can be made. Furthermore, under a centralized system of power, official posts are a formalized functional system that is distinct from ritual, such that the official posts themselves no longer have moral significance. By restoring, reshaping, and developing the relationship of being like heaven that was part of the tradition of shamans and historians, and providing the government posts with moral legitimacy, the process of constructing a moral ideal was carried out on the premise of separating the rites from the institutions.

Heaven and the system of symbolic relationships that derive from it refer not to the imperial power itself but to the structure of commanderies and/or feudal holdings that are centered around that imperial power. For the central government, that structure is embodied in the three dukes and nine ministers, the *chengxiang* and similar posts are the center of the administrative body. At the bottom level, the basic units are the county, district, *ting*, and neighborhood. The distribution of offices at each level of government is largely similar to that found in the central government, that is, a united structure of administration, justice, military, and economic affairs. Since there is only one center of power, a tendency for local government to drift away from the central government may easily arise, resulting in a conflictual tension between authoritarianism and dispersion. The running of the commanderies and counties relied on the norms of the executive and the *zhao*, *ling*, *zhi*, and *su* of the imperial court. Under these circumstances, administration and the law devolved into a functional structure. The feudal posts under the commanderies and counties lost the real sense that they held under the Zhou so that the family relationships that had served Shang and Zhou feudalism could no longer be used in the politics of a centralized state. Continued use of the moral/ political principles of the ritual theory would be unable to provide legitimacy to the new institutions of commanderies and counties centered on imperial power. This is the premise against which the Han Confucians sought to give political legitimacy to the imperial authoritarianism of the idea of divine rule for the prince. Therefore, the theory of correspondence between heaven and the human world is a theory of legitimacy for an imperial political community centered on imperial power.

However, the use of a rigid system of numbers to set out the system of offices also shows the rigidity of the official posts themselves, such that it included a certain degree of restriction of the power of the emperor. Under the system of centralized authority, formalized law and administration could not operate autonomously for three main reasons. First, the emperor reserved the final power of decision to himself. Second, the legal system was neither perfect nor formally enforced. Third, policies were arbitrary.[48] Under Emperor Wu, the chancery placed within the court, consisting of commander in chief (大将军), *shizhong* (侍中), *Shangshu* (尚书) and so on, all vested with additional titles of duties, became the major policy-making bodies of the center while the post of *chengxiang* (丞相, prime minister), as a position outside the court, was weakened. Under Emperor Guang Wu, "although the posts of the three dukes were present, their affairs were referred back to *the chancery of Shangshu*."[49] The chancery of Shangshu was more important than the three dukes. Under these circumstances, the use of numerology to determine the respective relations between the will of heaven and administrative posts, by strengthening the sacred character of the administrative system, clearly included respect for the central administrative system and limited any arbitrary change to the official posts or any interference in the administrative process.

The increased authority accorded to the emperor and the policy of centralized authority in the Western Han led to many economic and political consequences, such as—because merchants were allowed to buy official posts— encouraging landowners to simultaneously run businesses, such that officials, merchants, and landowners became three in one, leading to a buying up of land and bankruptcy of farmers. With this as a background, Wang Mang took patriarchal landlord as the mainstay of society and revived the institutions of the three dynasties, restoring the hereditary system of the nobles and the patriarchal system. This was referred to as the New Administration (9–23 CE). The New Administration revised administrative boundaries and institutions, revived the five ranks of duke, lord, earl, viscount, and baron, returned to the well-field system of agriculture, and in the field of commerce reverted to the ideal by which workers and merchants fed the officials, putting into practice the five *jun* (均) and six *guan* (管), an early form of planned economy. It used the *Rites of Zhou* and its structure that resembled heaven to complement the realization of the political setup described earlier. Between the *Luxuriant Gems of the Spring and Autumn Annals* (which would later be seen as a classic by the new-text school) and the *Rites of Zhou* (which was the classic of the old-text school), we can see some similarities in the way things are described. One reason for this is that they both seek, under the aegis of a relationship between heaven and numerology, and via a strict account of the institutions themselves, to provide some form of limitation on the way imperial power functioned.

A Shift of Cosmologies, Authority Centered on the Emperor, and Separation of Powers

There is a historical link between the Daoist learning of the Northern Song and the Confucian learning of the later Tang inasmuch as both relate to the relationship between heaven and the human world. Discussion of this topic in the late Tang was directly focused on the theory of correspondence between heaven and the human world of Han politics and Confucianism. From different viewpoints, Han Yu (768–824), Liu Zongyuan (733–819), and Liu Yuxi (772–842) were all critical of the phenomena of flattering the Buddha and making charms that flourished in Tang politics and the tradition of textual annotation centered on the *Correct Meaning of the Five Classics*. Criticism of the Han study of the classics was, in fact, an extension of this current of thought. The most valuable text for breaking down the theory of a correspondence between heaven and the human world is Liu Zongyuan's *Discourse on Seasonal Commands*. He presents a direct and cutting criticism of the theories of *yin-yang* and the five elements as they had been prevalent from the Han dynasty onward.

> Observing the *Monthly Ordinances*, we note that they bring together five areas of business, match the five elements and bring it about that their administrative decrees do not depart too far from the way of the sages. In the working of any political decree there are those things

which must wait for their time before being carried out and those which do not have to do so. Therefore, in early spring you level the soil and repair the paths by the fields and check to see what kind of grain the soil will support. You do not need to do a lot of work. In late spring repair the dykes, clean out the ditches, and stop hunting. Prepare the tools for raising silk worms, feed cattle and horses. No task, no undertaking may be out of time. In early summer you should not undertake any building or expend a lot of energy. You should encourage the people to get on with their farm work. In midsummer publish the regulations for rearing horses and collect all kinds of medicinal herbs. In late summer dig ditches for irrigation, remove weeds from the crops, fertilise the fields, and set the land in order. Do not undertake any building or military expeditions. In early autumn collect timber and reeds. In mid-autumn encourage the people to sow wheat. In late autumn stop all the work of the craftsmen, let everyone go home and prepare clothes for winter. . . . [I]n early winter repair the city wall and moat, dig an earthen kiln. . . . [T]hese things must all be done on time, as it is said, "tell the people what to do in each season." There are also sacrifices to heaven and earth and to the ancestors which are all ceremonies handed on from the past that may not be abolished. In the past rulers always did as follows: except in spring they did not practise a life-giving rule, nor relax commands, grant rewards, bestow dignities, look after children, visit prisoners, help the poor, or give preferential treatment to worthy persons; except in summer they did not select the worthy and elite, nor bestow ranks or grant emoluments, examine and deal with minor criminal cases, or cut back on desires so that the officials would be at ease; except in autumn they did not select generals, prepare weapons nor employ useful persons, nor punish the violent and recalcitrant, nor distinguish good and bad, nor revise laws and regulations . . . ; except in winter they did not honour those who gave their life for the country, have compassion on orphans and widows, examine persons who formed into cliques, reduce taxes on the market, look for merchants, survey each district and household, correct bad habits in the family, get rid of indolent officials nor throw out anything useless. In all this there was much else to think about that dealt with governing. These other things did not need to wait for a particular time to be carried out.[50]

In addition to breaking up the politics, sundering the links between institutions and the decree of heaven, the *Discourse on Seasonal Commands* leaves room for change so that human affairs can develop of their own accord.

In defending political institutions centered on imperial authority, why is it that Dong Zhongshu had to appeal to the theory of correspondence between heaven and the human world, whereas Liu Zongyuan sought to undo the relationship between *yin-yang*, the five elements, the four seasons, disasters, good luck and politics, the law, and morality? First, for Dong Zhongshu imperial authority stands for the feudal lords, nobles, and bureaucracy. Direct links between heaven and imperial authority reflected the important lingering influence of the feudal system, whereas for Liu Zongyuan, assertion of imperial authority was a way of breaking down a society that was built on the institutions of the aristocracy. In the early Tang there was conflict between feudalism and commanderies and counties with the result that both systems existed together. From the middle of Emperor Gaozong's reign onward, since the military institution by which the center directly controlled military power was destroyed, the sixteen southern garrisons were only nominal such that the court could rely on only the northern garrisons to prevent invasion. To accommodate the needs of the military, the Tang set up military governors, and the destruction of the militia directly led to a rapid expansion of the power of military men under these governors. After the suppression of the An Lushan Revolt, the court had no choice but to accept the ministers who had helped in suppressing the revolt and sending demoted ministers to barbarian towns as governors with military responsibilities, such that the institution of military governors expanded over the whole country. Against this background, after three autonomous provinces of Hebei refused to pay any taxes to the center, other barbarian towns also opposed the court and the Tang dynasty gradually sank into decline. Liu Zongyuan's criticism of the theory of correspondence between heaven and human affairs was formulated within this linguistic environment. He sought to escape from the meshes of the decree of heaven and turn attention toward the impulses and process of historical development.

In his *Discourse on Feudalism*, Liu Zongyuan starts out from what he calls "force." He treats the institutions of feudalism and of commanderies and counties as the result of the inner shift of history and so denies that any given political institution has absolute legitimacy. In his view, making princes responsible for penal and administrative affairs is the result of conflicts among people at a very early date. The ranks of the feudal lords are the product of competition among different clans. Conflict among the lords led to the ranks of leaders such as district chiefs (*fangbo* 方伯), leaders of groupings (*lianshuai* 连帅), and the like.[51] The centralization of commanderies and counties was the product of this slow historical process. Here Liu Zongyuan creates a historical philosophy in which the shape of politics lies at the heart. His central task is to prove that a central authority centered on imperial authority has historical and moral legitimacy.

> Now the conflict between these leaders increased. The chiefs and leaders (*fangbo* and *lianshuai*) went to listen to those persons of great virtue to pacify their subjects. Then the world under heaven (天下) could be united . . . from the Son of Heaven down to the head of the

neighbourhood, the offspring of anyone who had treated others vir-
tuously would be invited on the death of his father and enfeoffed, so
the feudal system was not what the sages wanted; it was the result of
force. . . . Under the ancient sage kings—Yao, Shun, Yu, Tang, Wen, and
Wu—feudalism was not abolished, not because they did not want to
abolish it, but because force did not allow it.[52]

As an institution of hereditary aristocracy, feudalism easily leads to separation and war and impedes the employment of worthy persons. Via effective
grading, the institution of commanderies and townships can guarantee that
the worthy are promoted and the unworthy demoted. Here "power" is not the
decree of heaven but the force and movement of the inner working of history.
Precisely because he began with "force," Liu Zongyuan believed that the replacement of feudalism by the institution of commanderies and townships
was a natural and reasonable process of history.

One reason Liu Zongyuan wanted to do away with the direct relationship
between heaven and the human world was that, in Tang politics, portents
and luck had already become sources of useless corruption. Another, more
important reason was that within the structure of Tang politics lay a heavy
component of feudalism, a feudalism that was often purported to come from
the *Rites of Zhou* and to be the actual rites of the Zhou era. As has been noted
earlier, a feature of the *Rites of Zhou* is that it brings heaven and the human
world together by means of numerology. Hence, a criticism and denial of the
hereditary aristocracy of Zhou feudalism and of the power of barbarian towns
was at the same time a repudiation of the construct of heaven and the human
world in the eternalization of feudalism in the Han dynasty. However, the appeal to "power" as the category that could provide a new legitimacy for society
meant that "power" had to face an insurmountable difficulty. First, there is no
constancy in changes of power, for a social order produced by power will also
be subject to the threat and structure of a power that is constantly changing.
Second, to argue that the institution of commanderies and counties is better
adapted to sort out the ranks of worthy and unworthy is to use a functional
argument. In short, abolition of the theory of correspondences between
heaven and the human world brought back into the foreground the following
fact: a functional institution suffers gravely from a lack of moral resources.

Han Yu conceded more to the theory of a relationship between heaven
and human affairs, partly in response to the separation between the institutions described earlier and the issue of moral rationality. In *On the Source of
Humanity*, Han Yu used the notions of "what is above form," "what is below
form," and "the decree is in between the two" to describe the way of heaven,
the way of earth, and the way of human beings, respectively, still distinguishing the way of human beings from that of heaven.[53] Han Yu clearly understands the order of society and ritual relationships as things that are created

by human beings, but he still retains a belief in heaven and the decree of heaven. "Though the historian does not suffer ills from men, yet he must wait for heaven's punishment: how much then should he hold it in awe and not treat it lightly!"[54] "The fate of these three gentlemen hangs on heaven. . . . Therefore, I have set out how their fate is linked to heaven and explained this."[55] Han Yu's theory of three grades of nature also includes the idea of the decree of heaven: "The birth of Lord Millet (*Hou Ji*) was not a disaster for his mother. At first, he crawled on both hands and feet. Then he was able to stand upright. When King Wen was still in his mother's womb, she was not alarmed. When he was born, his nurse did not have to work too much. When he studied, his teacher was not over-taxed."[56] Seen in terms of the decree of heaven, Han Yu's understanding of the Way and his efforts to establish the correct Way have all been ascribed to this category of the decree of heaven: "The ruler knows what to keep and what to discard in his teaching. He suppresses strange doctrines and keeps to the great way of the mean, puts down showy ceremonies and selects worthy and straightforward people. How vast is the path of heaven; it penetrates minute changes; the course of the Way is indeed unique!"[57] If the Way requires the support of the decree of heaven, then how can moral discourse itself truly escape from the influence of the theory of the relationship between heaven and the human world of the Han dynasty?

In constructing their own cosmologies, Zhou Dunyi, Shao Yong, Zhang Zai, Cheng Hao, and Zhu Xi, to varying degrees, remained marked by the Han theory of heaven and the human world. In this area they came up against the same difficulty that faced Han Yu. The chief supporters of the discourse on the celestial Way in the Northern Song—Zhou Dunyi, Shao Yong, and Zhang Zai—developed their own particular paths and key terms, but they all used the same overall sequence as their focus, finding the norm for morality and values in an extension of cosmology. Zhou Dunyi (1017–73) has been hailed as the "ancestor of the study of the Way." His *Explanation of the Diagram of the Supreme Ultimate* and his *Penetrating the Book of Changes* both explain the *Book of Changes* and take this to establish a system of thought that is both metaphysical and cosmological. The *Explanation* ascribes the cosmology of the "ultimate of non-being and the supreme ultimate" to the human dimension, whereas the second work starts from the discourse on the celestial Way and the moral heart, and from the moral heart expands to a discussion of the rites and so sets up the way of thinking of the Northern Song School of the Way in which cosmology, metaphysics, ethics, and discourse on rites are all combined into one body of thought. The *Explanation* understands the ultimate of nonbeing, the supreme ultimate, *yin-yang*, and the five elements as belonging to the celestial level, while the relationship of the five elements and the myriad things is on the second level. The human world is on the third level, while the sages and the human ultimate are on the fourth level. The celestial Way, terrestrial Way, and human Way cover all the above levels and so shape a cosmology in which heaven and the human world are one. This cosmological ontology of the ultimate of nonbeing and the supreme ultimate provides a dynamic cosmology from the ultimate of nonbeing to the supreme ultimate to *yin-yang* and the five elements and joins into one principle the celestial, terrestrial, and human ways. From this cosmological framework he constructs a comprehensive sequence. Zhou Dunyi opened a cosmological type of description through his study of the *Changes*. In this he clearly drew on the successful study of the *Changes* of the Han Daoist philosophers, religious Daoists, and *yin-yang* scholars.[58] "Heaven generates the myriad things by means of *yang* and perfects the myriad things by *yin*. To generate is benevolence; to perfect is justice. Therefore, when the sage is in charge he uses benevolence to foster the myriad things and justice to correct the myriad things. When the celestial way runs then the myriad things flow with the current; when the virtue of the sage is cultivated then the myriad peoples are all transformed."[59] According to this cosmology based on the *Changes*, benevolence and justice are the standard principles by which the celestial Way runs and also the basis for the virtue of the sage.

Shao Yong (1011–77) was particularly into numerology such that he attempted to use numbers to explain the growth and development of the cosmos and of history. From this he revealed that what he was concerned about was concealed behind the appearances of things in the cosmos and that this governed the whole cosmic order. In his *Supreme Principles Governing the World*, he says: "The circle is the stars which give the numbers for the calendar. Here it has its beginning! The square is the earth. The way of marking the regions and fields imitates this. The circle gives the number of the *River Chart*; the square gives the text of the *Luo Writing*, therefore Fu Xi and King Wen used them to create the *Changes*, Yu and Ji expanded on them and wrote the *Great Norm*."[60] Later Zhu Xi commented on this passage as follows: "'The circle is the stars; the circle gives the number of the *River Chart*.' This refers to the fact that there are no four corners because its shape is circular."[61] He also says, "The *River Chart* does not have four corners and so compared to the *Luo Writing* it is circular. . . . The square is the earth; the square gives the text of the *Luo Writing*. This refers to what is relied on to mark out regions and fields." He similarly uses numbers to link together the cosmos, marking out regions and the well-fields, believing that the institution of the well-field "is modelled on the figure 'nine' of the *Luo Writing*."[62] This shows that the theories of Shao Yong and Zhu Xi retained certain key elements of Han cosmology. There has been much discussion throughout history on the relationship between Shao Yong's *Supreme Principles Governing the World* and Chen Tuan's *Diagram Which Antedates Heaven*,[63] but one thing worth pointing out is that while the *Diagram* discusses the order of the eight trigrams and the sixty-four hexagrams, using numerology to relate heaven, earth, and the human world, it ascribes the myriad things of the cosmos to a common ontology of the mind. If we compare Shao Yong's numerology with the *Rites of Zhou* or with Dong

Zhongshu's *Luxuriant Gems of the Spring and Autumn Annals*, we can clearly see the difference between the two. Based on perfect institutional structure, Dong Zhongshu constructs a reciprocity between heaven and human beings, whereas Shao Yong's numerology lacks such a clear reciprocity with institutions. Shao Yong says, "What is referred to as principle is the principle inherent in things; what is referred to as nature is the nature imparted by heaven; what is referred to as destiny lies in principle and in nature. That by which it lies in principle and nature is surely the Way, is it not? This is to know that the Way is the root of heaven and earth, and heaven and earth are the root of the myriad things. By observing the myriad things from heaven and earth, you will see the myriad things as things; by observing heaven and earth by the Way, then heaven and earth will also be seen as part of the myriad things."[64]

An important feature of Shao Yong's antedating heaven theory is to see mind as the source of the myriad things, not only directly linking the Way and the mind, but also placing the order of the cosmos in the category of mind. In this sense, this order is first closely connected to the intrinsic vision of a sequence of observing or letting things appear. Only by completely reverting to the mind is it possible to have any knowledge of the reality of the cosmos because the mind itself is the origin of the cosmos. "Heaven is generated from the Way; earth is perfected by the Way; things are formed by the Way; human beings walk by the Way."[65] "Heaven separates and gives rise to the earth; earth separates and gives rise to the myriad things, but the Way cannot be divided. At the end, the myriad things return to the earth, earth returns to heaven, and heaven returns to the Way."[66] Heaven, earth, human beings, and the myriad things can all be separated out, but the Way is one, an absolute indivisible order, the original substance and root. The source of the absolute and objective nature of the Way lies in the mind, which people generally classify as subjective. "The mind imitates the study of what is prior to heaven. Therefore, in the diagram everything proceeds from the centre. The myriad transformations and myriad affairs are generated in the mind."[67] If the universe and the myriad things in it are generated in the mind, and the pattern of the universe is that everything proceeds from the center, then the order of the cosmos is generated and perfected internally, and this process cannot be divided, nor is it influenced by the myriad things or feelings. It is the most objective order possible. Starting from this objective and internal order, Shao Yong says that the Way is the supreme ultimate and that the mind is the supreme ultimate and, based on the supreme ultimate, he unites the Way and the mind.[68] The Way, the supreme ultimate, and the cosmic order are interpreted here as a design for the unveiling and discovery of something within the mind.

Shao Yong's mind and the unique, subjective nature of each person or the particularity of people's feelings have no relationship to each other. To say that the myriad things are the mind does not mean that ultimate stuff of the cosmos and its myriad things are the mind. To say that "the mind is the great ultimate" and "the only mind of the myriad things" implies that the root of the universe and the myriad things lies in an intrinsic order. Perhaps we could ascribe it to an order of existence or an existing vision. Cheng Hao assesses it as follows: "The learning of Yao Fu (i.e., Shao Yong) first derives meaning from principle, speaks about symbolic numbers, speaks about how the principles in the world under heaven must come from 'four.' In extrapolating back to where principle is, he says: 'when I obtain this great one, then the myriad affairs come from me and there is then nothing which is not fixed.' Then there must be a method."[69] Here, concepts such as the Way, the supreme ultimate, the mind, and principle are interrelated, such that the mind is not our subjective mind of flesh or our mind/heart that is unceasingly touched by feelings or closely related to our capacity to judge. Rather, on the presupposition of the unity of the mind and things, it is an order or reality that appears. Shao Yong's learning has a quality of contradiction about it and yet is in fact coherent. On the one hand, it is marked by a profound determinism, while on the other hand, it is focused on the subject and its ability to know. The reason these two aspects can be combined into one description of cosmic order is that Shao Yong deems the Way, the supreme ultimate, the mind, and the One to be all one thing. Therefore, in knowing things human beings cannot only not restrict themselves to limited individual experience; they should rather not see things from a human point of view at all. This is what he means by "do not make things mine but make things things." We should look on things as they are in the natural order or according to the principle in the world under heaven, and this perspective is itself objective.[70] Qian Mu describes Shao Yong's standpoint as one "which takes the path of Daoism to arrive at the ultimate goal of Confucianism," which he says is "a new objective humanism" or an "objective idealism."[71] However, objective concepts would still not seem able to cut to the heart of Shao Yong's thought, because his mind includes an existential way of understanding knowledge, so it is better described as an existential theory. The idea of a "vision or view of an intrinsic, natural order of existence" may perhaps reveal what Shao Yong means by making things things. Here, the "vision or view of an intrinsic, natural order of existence" differs in an important way from what today we describe as the self's inner depth. The two stand for two different views of order and methodologies of understanding order, but at the level of terminology these two different types of views of order and methodologies both have a tendency to turn inward.

The learning of Zhang Zai (1020–77) "honoured the rites and valued virtue, rejoiced in heaven and was at peace with destiny, taking the *Changes* as the starting point, the *harmony and mean* as the body, and Confucius and Mencius as the method. Doing away with strange and foolish things, discriminating between negative and positive spiritual forces," he took as a foundation for the Guan Learning (关学).[72] In this sense, he had a profound link to pre-Qin ritual theory. However, in Zhang Zai's thought world, ritual theory was already placed in a new vision of cosmology or natural order. The *Western In-scription* states that the myriad things are one body, that there is one principle and many manifestations, which first affirms that heaven, earth, the myriad things, and human beings all form one body and then ascribes what is proper to heaven and earth to human beings or the myriad things as well. The saying "all people are my brothers and sisters and all things are my companions" truly reveals the heart of Zhang Zai's thought.[73] In *Correcting Youthful Igno-rance* he uses the term "great harmony" to describe the collectivity in which the myriad things are generated and changed, but he also is not satisfied with using only this one term and proposes the great vacuity as the substance of the universe. "The great vacuity is without form; it is the substance of qi. Its com-ing together and falling apart are merely objectifications of change. The real source of human nature is utterly still and unchangeable; there is awareness and knowledge when it encounters external things."[74] This is the monism of qi or the ontology of qi that many scholars have spoken about in Zhang Zai's view of the cosmos. This is a dialectical structure whereby unity shows itself as qi, and the great vacuity comes together as things and falls apart back into pure qi. The ontology of qi broke through the cosmology of Daoism based on an ontology of nonaction, such that it has been seen as "the highest achievement of natural science of its time, combining with traditional studies based on the Appendices to the *Book of Changes* into one path and radically cutting through the duality of *qian wang* and being/nonbeing of Zhuangzi and Laozi, creating a simple materialist, dialectical ontology of qi."[75] Because he acknowledged the externality and materiality of things and qi, Zhang Zai's ontology of qi and its study including its emphasis on getting to know the activity of nature provided some degree of help.[76] With his influence, the tradition of the Guan Learning "largely took what was practical as what it valued and crossing over vacuity as its mechanism"[77] and tended toward a practical interpretation of the Way.[78] For example, Li Fu and Li Yeming affirmed the concepts of the prin-ciple of nature and the number/sum of nature and even saw heaven as a thing that was in movement, which is quite some way removed from the categories of study of the *Changes* of Zhou Dunyi and Shao Yong.[79]

The ontology of qi leads us to understand the substance and origin of the cosmos from within the world, and from here to move outward making a clear distinction with the Buddhist and Daoist tendency toward what is concealed within. The ontology of qi and the attempt to study nature can be seen as a logical corollary of the Northern Song School of the Way, because as soon as the search for a moral norm is linked to a cosmological model, there will be a demand for an epistemological model that can relate to the natural order. Within this epistemological model, every level of knowledge can be accorded a place in an evolving hierarchical system, at the top of which is the celes-tial Way itself.[80] However much Zhang Zai's views are peculiar to himself, a more fundamental feature that led him to construct his ontology of qi is the idea of cosmological order and so we should not exaggerate the difference between Zhang Zai's ontology of *qi* and the *Diagram of the Supreme Ultimate* and the *prior-heaven* numerology of Zhou Dunyi and Shao Yong. All three—Zhou, Shao, and Zhang—sought to construct a cosmological ontology to find a place for morality and ethics and a theory of mind and human nature, based on which they could construct a logic that brought together heaven, the Way, human nature, and the mind. The central concern of Zhang Zai was not to discuss questions of natural philosophy but, as Wang Fuzhi said, "to set up the rites as the root."[81] Hence, the ontology of *qi* should be seen as providing a support for "correcting the mind" and "exerting the mind."[82] In other words, Zhang Zai's "setting up the rites as the root" had also to derive the norms for daily ethical practice from the natural order. This is why the seventeen chapters of *Correcting the Unenlightened* follow an internal logical structure or comprehensive order. Chapter 1, "Great Harmony," speaks of the myriad things all together as one body. Chapters 2 ("Sharing in the Two") to 5 ("Moving Things") speak about the process of transformation of *qi* in heaven, earth, human beings, and things. The eleven chapters from 6 to 16 take the way of human beings as the focus and form an anthropology, epistemology, morality, and politics. Finally, chapter 17 coordinates the human way with the celestial Way and reiterates the ontology of all things as having one root and one *qi* for heaven and human beings. The dualism of the nature of heaven and earth and the nature of *qi* and stuff opened out what was to become a constant topic of discussion in the School of Principle of the Song and Ming dynasties, but without the inner substance or intrinsic order contained in the idea of supreme vacuity, the above dualism would have lacked theoretical support.[83] In this sense, Zhang Zai's ontology of *qi* provided the idea of a comprehensive intrinsic order.

The above rough outline of the discourse on heaven from Han to Song times shows the significance of the history of thought sustained by the worldview based on the principle of heaven.

First, the study of the Way inherited certain elements of Han cosmology, such as the way of linking heaven and human affairs by numerology. It continued discussion of the *River Chart* and *Luo Writing* and the scientific tendency that arose from cosmology. But while these things were continued, we also find that there is a marked distinction and difference. The ontology of the study of the Way was established between a description of the reality of the cosmos and a description of metaphysics, with the latter becoming more and more the center of attention. In following this direction provided by the Northern Song School of the Way, the Cheng Brothers and Zhu Xi developed theories of one principle for all things in the universe and of different manifestations of the one principle, or of each thing having its own principle and of each thing having its own specific identity. From within moral theory they posed the requirement to know things. Within the framework of the School of Principle, even if things are external objects they are also human conduct. In reply to the question, "In the investigation of things, are the things external objects or are they objects within our nature and identity?" Cheng Yi says, "It does not matter. Anything in front of eyes is never not a thing. All things have principle, as that by which fire is hot and that by which water is cold, even up to the relations of prince and minister, father and son; all are principle."[84] What "all things have principle" presupposes is to get to know each concrete thing and not to see them by a numerological extrapolation undertaken according to the theory of correspondence between heaven and the human world, by which things are internalized.[85] Clearly, in the metaphysical world of the principle of heaven, the relationship between heaven and human beings no longer had the same concrete and clear relationship it did in the Han theory of correspondence. The absolute nature of heaven was gradually replaced by a view of order based on principle.

Second, following the tendency set out earlier and found in early study of the Way, the Cheng brothers posited the categories of the principle of heaven or principle *tout court*. Principle or the principle of heaven retained the inner relationship of heaven and the human world, but rejected the tendency to found that relationship based on naturalism. Rather, it changed "heaven" into a category of metaphysics. Cheng Hao said, "Heaven is principle. 'Spirit' is said of the mystery of the myriad things. The Lord gets his name from being the master of affairs."[86] Here, the idea of the decree of heaven is retained, but there is now a clear distinction between "heaven," "spirit," and the "Lord." With this as a presupposition, the Song Confucians transformed the decree of heaven into nature and principle, that is, a principle of nature, and there was no longer any whiff of the correspondence between heaven and the human world that was found in the Han idea of the decree of heaven.[87]

Third, therefore, principle and the principle of heaven are not to be seen as absolute orders given from above, but as immanent in the cosmos, in all things, and in human beings themselves as having a real substantive nature. So, to obey the principle of heaven is to obey our inner nature. From the topic of the supreme ultimate and the ultimate of nonbeing to that of each thing having its own principle, the idea of the principle of heaven shaped a forceful challenge in favor of a cosmology with only one center. Seen from the point of view of the principle of heaven, the material order of the real world was in tension with principle/the principle of heaven. It made it such that obedience to principle or the principle of heaven was a form of immanent moral conduct but also one that retained a support for autonomy in the material order.[88] Starting from here, the Song Confucians affirmed the cosmological dualism of principle and *qi*, the epistemological dualism of principle and things, the two distinctions in nature as the nature of heaven and earth and the nature of *qi* and stuff, and the distinction of principle and desire in morality, so as to resolve the contradiction between ought and is, value and fact. In this framework of principle and qi, the use of numerological relationships to directly connect heaven and human affairs no longer had any hold.

Fourth, the epistemology of investigating things and seeking their principles even if it did presuppose self-cultivation and realization of the self was yet also the path for the self-perfection of the whole political community. "The extension of knowledge is in investigating things, and is spoken of as the root, the beginning. Governing the world under heaven and the state are spoken of as the branches, the end. Governing the world under heaven and the state must be rooted in the self. There has never been a case where the self was not correct and it was possible to govern the world under heaven and the state. 'Investigation' is like going to the utmost. 'Things' are like principles, as if one were to say: go to the utmost in the principle; that is all. Going to the utmost in the principle is enough to make you know a thing; if you do not go to the utmost you cannot extend your knowledge."[89] Government of states and the empire is entrusted to the cultivation and epistemological practice of scholar-gentlemen. This shift marks a weakening of the direct relationship between Confucianism and royal politics. The School of Principle was developed by the new class of scholar-gentlemen and sought to maintain a tension between the institution of imperial power and moral judgment.

Finally, from Han cosmology to the establishment of the Northern Song Way of heaven, there was a shift. The latter no longer concentrated on the mutual influence of heaven and human beings or the numerology of heaven and human affairs. Instead attention was focused on the inner moral quality and moral conduct of human beings. The evolutionary shift from a view based on the Way of heaven to a worldview with the principle of heaven or what is called a discourse of root nature is indeed an important shift. As a result, the standard for the moral/political practice of Confucianism and what was based on it underwent a profound change. This change can be summarized as follows: cosmology shifted to an immanentology; moral/political practice that followed the master of heaven or commands changed into a following of immanent nature. The epistemological relation between human beings and the world shifted from a structure built on relations between the number of things toward a concrete awareness of affairs and things. In these two senses, we can see the seeming moral/political distinction between the School of Principle of the Song and Ming dynasties and the Way of Confucius and Mencius, but the political institutions that responded to this had already undergone change. The idea of the principle of heaven was affirmed at a time that was directly related to maturity of the institutions of commanderies and counties centered around imperial power, an undermining of the institution of the nobility, the reconstruction of ritual within the context of centralized administration, an examination system that had become normative, and the hierarchical system of scholar-officials and government representatives. Therefore, we must understand how Song Confucianism looked back to Confucius and Mencius in the context of the historical change from the political institutions of the Han and Tang to those of the Song.

In concluding this essay, I note that an ancient constitution is not only functional relationships such as the material structures of means of production, structures of law and power, language and writing, ways of bringing together, or preventing dispersion. It is at the same time also a cosmology, a system of belief and knowledge. Ancient constitution cannot be the same, or have the same structure as, modern scientific ways of looking at the center and the periphery, family and the state, individuals and the group. It cannot be a merely functional relationship. Rather, it can be understood only on the basis of a complex relationship of a meaningful system of institutions and their operation. In fact, cosmology, belief, or the epistemological system are potential forces shaped by participation in the forms of daily life. It is enough to grasp the expressed method and content to be able to truly understand particular principles formed by given eras of political governance.

CHAPTER FIVE

The Symbolic and the Functional

SU LI ON THE CONSTITUTION OF ANCIENT CHINA

Liu Han

A PROMINENT LEGAL thinker in China, Su Li often makes mainstream Chinese legal scholars uncomfortable. Trained in the United States, he seems to be a gadfly who annoys people committed to the modern Western idea of the rule of law. Writing about law, he criticizes the dominant legal imagination, at the center of which are the ideas of constitutionalism, legal transplant, judicial independence, and the like. Constructing his own theory, he deconstructs a lot of systems of ideas, sometimes in an ironic fashion. For many contemporary Chinese legal scholars, as well as intellectuals in general, he thinks and writes from a postmodern perspective in the context of China's modernizing process. As the former dean of Peking University Law School, his theory, in the eyes of many of his colleagues or peers, is useless for, or even detrimental to, China's long march toward the rule of law.

Su Li, on the other hand, forces Chinese legal scholars as well as other readers to ponder what they fail to notice or tend to evade. He pushes the reader, sometimes in a polemical fashion, to grapple with troubling issues that underlie popular, unexamined discourse on legal issues or law-related sociopolitical topics. In the 1990s, for example, when legal transplant gained ground in China's legal theory as well as legal practice, Su Li advocated China's "indigenous resources" of law, understood as social norms separated from, and sometimes in conflict with, the state-made law.[1] That voice, in fact, was a discordant one in the popular concert of legal transplant at the time. In 2003, when the dominant legal academia vehemently criticized the *Yanan Huangdie Case* ("Yanan Pornography Watching Case," in which policemen entered a clinic to arrest a couple who were watching pornography) from a liberal standpoint (the right to privacy, for example), he argued for the right to preserve basic community order from a communitarian perspective.[2] In 2007, he argued that the Chinese Communist Party's rule has a positive impact on China's judiciary, in contradistinction to what Chinese and Western observers commonly believe.[3] Trained in the United States, he talks about American constitutional law in a way contrary to the popular perception and even reverence for it prevalent in China.

Su Li's new target is Chinese constitutional law. With a set of essays, he begins to treat the topic of constitutionalism from a historical point of view. Indeed, discussion about constitutionalism has been fermenting in both China's legal discourse and public discussion from the beginning of the twenty-first century. The trend culminated in a recent polemic on the question of whether socialism is compatible with constitutionalism, starting from mid-2013. Actually, Su Li spoke out when most jurists urged the adoption of judicial review into the Chinese constitutional framework after the famous *Qiyuling Case* in 2001, which was considered China's first constitutional case or even its *Marbury v. Madison*.[4] Judicial review, for Su Li, was an accidental development of American constitutional law, a contingent matter in the American political experience; it was neither an original design of the U.S. Constitution nor an application of any preexisting political theory. A constitutional institution like judicial review was formed and established by chance. But this time, he takes up constitutional law in a more systematic fashion. More than that, he sets out to treat China's ancient constitution both in itself and as an example of his conception of the constitution.

It would be helpful to describe the popular ideas about constitutional law and constitutionalism in contemporary China before delving into Su Li's arguments in detail. For many Chinese legal scholars as well as public intellectuals, China was, and still is, notorious for its lack of constitutionalism. China has a written Constitution, now the 1982 Constitution, but no constitutionalism. Constitutionalism, as the idea that a written document should be created and enforced to check government power and protect citizens' basic rights, is a modern Western achievement that China should learn. In other words, it embodies universal values in the legal domain. China lacked such an idea and the accompanying institutions in both its ancient and revolutionary times. Ancient China was a despotic regime: no rights were protected; no powers constrained. In a word, ancient China had no "Constitution" in the common sense. Since the late Qing dynasty when the West intervened, the task before China has been to transform a premodern political regime into a modern constitutional government. Today, that task remains unfinished. A bit oversimplified, these accounts basically constitute the constitutional ethos among many legal scholars. For people who share that ethos, Su Li's discussion of the ancient Chinese constitution seems to be talking about something that hasn't existed at all—a fairy tale.

Su Li, again, dissents. He has argued recently that ancient China did have a constitution, and it worked very well: it ensured basic order; it created a unified country/civilization out of multiple groups and multifarious regions. No doubt, Su Li uses the word "constitution" in a different sense from the one commonly held. With this, he urges Chinese legal scholars to rethink the meaning of the "constitution" not as a modern, liberal, normative conception, but in its original, constitutive, descriptive sense. Su Li's in-depth study of ancient China's constitution, therefore, serves as an example of constitutional rethinking.

Redefining the "Constitution": The Small-c Constitution, the Big-C Constitution, and Constitutional Law

To discuss a topic, one needs primary, proper definitions of the words that constitute it. In Chinese, the word *xianfa* (宪法), like the word "constitution" in English, has multiple connotations. To clarify his thought, Su Li sets out to distinguish between the constitution, the Constitution, and constitutional law—these concepts are all called *xianfa* in contemporary Chinese. He calls these three things, respectively, *xian zhi* (宪制), *xian zhang* (宪章), and *xian fa* (宪法). A constitution (*xian zhi*), according to Su Li, is what constitutes a polity; it defines, in ancient, political-philosophical terms, a regime. Here, things that constituted a polity did not necessarily need words or legal documents to describe or record themselves. And words even could not express things fully. For Su Li, this is the original, descriptive, fundamental meaning of the word "constitution." Every polity, ancient or modern, big or small, has its constitution.

The Constitution, however, is usually a written document made by a special representative political entity. It lays down the basic laws of a state, especially defining the structure and limits of government power and enumerating citizens' fundamental rights. The Constitution usually serves as a basic law and a higher law. This concept of the Constitution began its life only in modern history as an invention of the Enlightenment. Unlike the original, descriptive counterpart, it is a purposefully contrived, unitary juridical codification of the major rules governing the state and predetermining the whole legal system. The U.S. Constitution, for example, is usually thought to be the first significant written Constitution in the world. In addition, the modern written Constitution usually has a normative dimension: a Constitution must bear the basic liberal values of individual rights and the rule of law. By contrast, the original concept of "constitution" is merely descriptive.

Constitutional law is the narrowest and most professionalized of the three concepts. It is a legalized, judicial, lawyerly constitution. American constitutional law is a typical example: the U.S. Supreme Court interprets the U.S.

Constitution to resolve concrete cases or controversies. Constitutional law, in this sense, comprises the procedural rules of constitutional litigation and substantive constitutional rules developed by judicial decisions or precedents, as well as the basic rules set out in the written Constitution and fundamental legislation or statutes that bear constitutional significance.

In addition to making these distinctions, Su Li sees a conceptual hierarchy among the three senses of the word "constitution." For Su Li, the constitution is the most important. For him, "A constitution is not a natural law full of moral warmth, nor is it human effort constantly progressing toward some ultimate moral goal. At least at times, or perhaps it is always so, it is a law of necessity that upholds the state in the long term or for a special period of time."[5] Modern Westerners think about the constitution more as a normative document or a branch of law, rather than the fundamental composition of a polity. The normative concept of the Constitution therefore bears a reformative, transformative orientation; it always points to the destination a particular polity should go to, that is, a limited government with a relatively independent judiciary to protect human rights. Su Li, however, thinks that this is not the case. The upshot is, before a written Constitution can limit the power of the state, there must be a state, however constituted or organized.

All regimes, ancient or modern, Chinese or foreign, according to Su Li, have their constitutions, although they may not have Constitutions or a normative, lawyerly constitutional law. Su Li discusses Greek, Roman, English, and American constitutions. Each bore, or bears, a constitution in the original, fundamental sense. Here, I consider the example of the United States of America, the one most familiar to me. The United States is commonly taken to be the first modern constitutional project with a written Constitution, a bill of rights, and an institution of judicial review. But for Su Li, what is at stake in the American constitutional experiment is very much the question of the constitution, more than that of the Constitution or constitutional law. Throughout its history, the fundamental, vital issue of the United States has been how to create a unified political authority among diverse and diversified political entities like states or ethnic groups—*e pluribus unum*. This is what the Constitutional Convention of 1787 was about. This is what the bloody Civil War was about. This is what a set of landmark Supreme Court decisions were about. Almost all important constitutional law issues pertain to federal-state relations.

What was at stake was how to found a unified, national regime in part of North America. Federalism, therefore, was the single most important theme in U.S. constitutional design. Without a strong central government, it was meaningless to talk about separation of powers, judicial review, or protection of individual rights, which constitute the major pillars of a contemporary, normative constitutional framework. Here, Su Li's point is similar to Hannah Arendt's observation about the foundation of the United States: the primary task for the framers was not to limit the government, but to create a government at the national level.[6] The original U.S. Constitution, therefore, had no bill of rights. It mostly laid out the basic structure of the state. In short, even in the early period of the modern "Constitution," the question of the original "constitution" was equally vital.

With the distinction between the constitution and the Constitution, Su Li tries to argue, the question of the constitution has been perennial and universal. He sets out to propose an "effective conception of the constitution"—a set of working, fundamental rules that govern a polity over a relatively long time. The question of the "constitution," rather than that of the "Constitution," haunts every relatively big country, ancient or modern, Occidental or Oriental. It came into existence as soon as man formed society. It never went away from human history. Especially, he emphasizes that we cannot bind democracy and constitution together without reflection, as contemporary constitutionalists would tend to assume. At least, neither the Magna Carta nor the U.S. Constitution was a product of democracy. The proposition that the constitution/Constitution is a product of modern democracy cannot be upheld. Distinguishing between the constitution and the Constitution, the phrase the "ancient Chinese constitution" is no longer a misnomer or an oxymoron. In this way, Su Li clears the way to discuss the ancient Chinese constitution. That is what we turn to now.

Reimagining Ancient China's Constitution

Ancient China was a big country as well as a civilization—an empire indeed. Su Li sets out to discuss the fundamental institutions that constitute the ancient Chinese polity and hold together multiple peoples and regions. How to "constitute" such a huge polity was the very question that haunted the lawgivers of China, understood as both a country and a civilization. And the unified Chinese empire was a huge accomplishment. Its longevity deserves respect and in-depth study. As Su Li observes, ancient China, in terms of geographical extent, was much bigger than the United States in its founding era. The question is how to build up a unified political framework to ensure domestic order and ensure peace on the frontiers, with only discrete small rural communities and without metropolises that could attract political, economic, and cultural power. Put more simply, how is it possible to build up the big political-cultural community called "China"? What was the institutional constitution of China? Su Li calls these questions "the question of constitution." No doubt this question haunted the Founding Fathers of the United States and still haunts the elite of the European Union, too.

Political unity captures the whole point of the constitution of historical China. China united multiple small communities, peoples with divergent tongues, and elites of different origins. The constitution put them together into a political community and then held them together. Thousands of years later, the unity of China has become a moral-political intuition that effects social-political actions. But in the original phase, the unity must be constructed and the concept of "grand unity" (大一统) must be exalted.

Su Li, in this volume, puts forward three factors that forged the unification of historical China that contemporary constitutional scholarship seldom visits. First, he discusses the geopolitical constitution of ancient China: how its territorial borders were formed. Second, he considers what he calls the "cultural constitution" that undergirds the centralized bureaucratic system: "unified script" and "Mandarin Chinese," as well as educated elites who used them. Third, he stresses the "political and cultural elite" serving as officials, selected through examinations. These are the links that held China together.

The key to these links was the position of emperor. All these constitutional elements served as the skeleton and muscles of the political body of historical China. The head was the emperor, which Su Li has discussed at length elsewhere but not in this volume.[7] The body of the emperor linked multiple territories and peoples. He presided over the ecumenical community of scholar-officials connected by unified script, common language, and cultural life. He was, to use Western terms, the *unum* that tied up the *pluribus*. He served as the focal point of the huge polity.

The emperor, for Su Li, was an indispensable constitutional institution in ancient China. Conventional wisdom in modern China, tinged with republican ideology, takes the emperor as a single despot who held arbitrary, unbridled power for himself or for his family's private interests. Su Li, by contrast, takes the emperor as a constitutional institution. In other words, the emperor was a position, not just a person. It was a legal persona, rather than a private man who exerts despotic, arbitrary power. As an institutional position or a legal person, it sits in a web of norms and is subject to institutional control.

To Su Li, the emperor, as a constitutional institution, therefore, was indispensable to the ancient Chinese regime. He exerted the crucial social function of preserving basic order. Without the emperor, man was in a Hobbesian state of nature, in which there exists no common power to dominate all men, and all men live in continual fear and danger of violent death, a "solitary, poor, nasty, brutish, and short" life.[8] Chinese thinkers, in Su Li's eyes, knew this much earlier, before Hobbes. As Master Lü put it: "There is no more severe disorder than the lack of an emperor."[9] Without the emperor, the polity would collapse. Ancient Chinese people had no choice but to accept imperialism.

Recent studies in the history of politics confirm this point. Francis Fukuyama, for example, argues that China constructed the first state in human history, much earlier than Western Europe, which only did so in the early modern era. He writes,

> The state that emerged in China was far more modern in Max Weber's
> sense than any of its counterparts elsewhere. The Chinese created a
> uniform, multilevel administrative bureaucracy, something that never

happened in Greece or Rome. The Chinese developed an explicit anti-familistic political doctrine, and its early rulers sought to undermine the power of entrenched families and kinship groups in favor of impersonal administration. This state engaged in a nation-building project that created a powerful and uniform culture, a culture powerful enough to withstand two millennia of political breakdown and external invasion. The Chinese political and cultural space extended over a far larger population than that of the Romans. . . . Even though the Chinese monarch called himself an emperor rather than a king, he ruled over something that looked much more like a kingdom or even a state in its uniformity.[10]

Moreover, the existence of an emperor was a prerequisite for meritocracy, which largely characterizes the historical Chinese regime. Without him, as Su Li writes, the elite intellectuals or scholar-officials would be in a constant state of factional division and conflict. Factional politics would endanger the basic order. Ancient Chinese intellectuals, like modern intellectuals at home and abroad, valued themselves more than their peers. Academic debates, differences of opinion, and even intellectual polemics were transformed easily into political struggles among intellectual camps, as intellectuals became, and were supposed to become, statesmen or bureaucrats.[11] Absent the final decision of the emperor, constant debates among intellectual bureaucrats would encumber the normal operation of social governance, and even divide the country. For effective governance of the large empire, intellectuals had to cooperate. For intellectuals to cooperate, an emperor was indispensable.

With the central example of the emperor, Su Li urges constitutional scholars to think deeply about the truthfulness of modern constitutional imagery: a written document is thought to construct and constrain the political power in a polity. It definitely cannot do that. Success requires more than that. A polity must first exist. That polity must lump together diverse, conflicting groups into a unified whole. There must then be stable and effective political power. Fundamental rules must be laid down to ensure stability. None of these things can be achieved by merely drafting a constitutional document.

Stressing the original constitution, rather than the written Constitution, of a state can be of great relevance to the contemporary development of constitutionalism. Ever since 1945, the Western model of constitutional engineering has engulfed newly established and reformed regimes, especially in third world and postcommunist countries. Many would think the crucial issue in these states is the drafting of a new Constitution with liberal-democratic values, rights, and a mechanism to protect them. The trinity of a written Constitution, a bill of rights, and constitutional review has become the standard. Many American constitutional scholars have been sent, or invited, to help draft a constitutional document or establish a constitutional court.

Indeed, what is first and foremost at stake in constitutional engineering and constitutional understanding is effective governance, rather than the Constitution or constitutional law. A state must have order, before it has a constitutional order in the normative, liberal-democratic sense. In other words, state-building prioritizes Constitution drafting and constitutional review. A bill of rights with a constitutional court is ineffective without a unified, stable political order. Merely removing a dictatorship does not automatically lead to liberty. It can more likely lead to chaos: secession, civil war, and inflation. Think about the situation of Eastern Europe after 1989. Think about the Arab Spring. The drafting process of a liberal, written Constitution does not help settle the fierce postrevolutionary political battle; rather, it aggravates the situation, because every political force tends to shape the new Constitution according to its interest and outlook. In this sense, Su Li revives the original sense of the constitution before the rise of the global trend of constitutionalism. He gives the original sense of the constitution its due.

The Functional and the Symbolic

Throughout his analysis, Su Li adopts a functionalist approach to ancient China's constitution. In other words, Su Li's approach is a legal-sociological one. He, for example, takes a functional point of view toward the Chinese emperor. The emperor was a glue to hold together a far-flung, multicultural polity.

Su Li's functionalism, however, cannot fully appreciate the meaning and significance of ancient China's constitution, especially the position of the emperor. He claims at the outset of his work that he tries to "applaud" the wisdom of ancient China's constitution. But his analysis turns out to be insufficient to achieve that goal.

Su Li tends to downplay the political-cultural meaning of certain institutions. It looks as if the emperor was necessary just because of his practical use, rather than the sentiments attached to him. Practical use, after all, cannot warrant loyalty; it cannot directly produce legitimacy. To fully appreciate the ancient Chinese constitution, we must revisit ancient China's political theology (if I may use this word) in which the emperor occupied a cardinal position in the political imagination and invokes a whole set of meanings.

Take the emperor for example again. The emperor was not only a functional institution. He was, first and foremost, a political symbol, or even a political-theological figure. Behind him was an entire worldview and set of beliefs. As Yuri Pines put it,

> His exaltedness was, above all, symbolic: by the mere fact of his singularity, the emperor personified the supreme principle of the realm's unity, while in his capacity as the "Son of Heaven," he acted as the sole mediator with and representative of the highest deity, Heaven. The

emperor presided over the elaborate system of state rituals and per-
formed (personally or through substitutes) manifold sacrifices through
which he supposedly ensured his subjects' well-being. His sacredness
was conceived of as "matching" (*pei*) Heaven itself; hence he could promote or demote any deity or abolish any cult. He was venerated as the
supreme regulator of time and space: years were counted according
to his reign titles, and the annual ritual calendar was invalid without
his approval. Elaborate rites elevated him to superhuman heights; his
body and his paraphernalia were considered sacrosanct and any harm
to them regarded as the gravest crime; even his personal name was
tabooed. The emperor's august presence was disseminated throughout
society down to its lowest levels through a variety of ceremonies, legends, and even proverbs. The institution of emperorship was the ritual pivot of the Chinese polity from 221 BCE until the early twentieth
century; during that lengthy period China without an emperor was as
inconceivable as the Catholic Church without a pope.[12]

A constitution cannot succeed without a public belief in it. Beliefs sustain institutions. Legitimacy comes from something other than function. The longevity of Chinese imperialism cannot be explained only by the social functions of
the emperor. Su Li's functionalism can answer only the question "Why did we
need the emperor?" It cannot answer the question "Why should we obey the
emperor?" In other words, the question of function cannot be a surrogate for
the question of legitimation. Here, Su Li might have spent some ink on Confucian ideas about the nature of political order and its natural legitimation. The
emperor's identity as "Son of Heaven" (*tian zi*) needs a separate treatment in
Su Li's account. The people obey the emperor because his rule is granted by
Heaven. Despite several slight differences, this is the Chinese counterpart of
the theory of the divine right of kings, which was popular from medieval to
early modern times in Europe.[13]

Su Li's functionalist, historical-materialist account of the emperor turns
out to be anticlimactic for readers whose intellectual inspirations are stim-
ulated by his novel analysis. On second thought, to approve of the emperor
just because he is useful rather suggests modern sentiments. It implies that
an emperor who was less useful would warrant the abolition of imperialism.
If we can find some modern surrogate for the post of the emperor—a president as the figurehead of the state, a Machiavellian-Leninist socialist political party, or even a national flag or emblem—the emperor himself becomes
useless. Trying to articulate the logic—yes, logic, not absurdities—of ancient
Chinese imperialism, Su Li demeans it. The position of the emperor, in this
light, is supportable just because it functioned well according to the measure
set by modern social sciences, for example, by institutional economics as Su
Li employs it. If we say something old is good according to a modern scale,

we are actually testifying to the validity of the latter rather than to that of the former. After all, the old thing was judged by its own scale. Efficiency does not warrant legitimacy.

Even from a practical point of view, the symbolic character of the emperor is still indispensable. Here I turn for help to the English author Walter Bagehot, whose work Su Li cites several times. Any successful constitution, Bagehot maintains in his masterpiece, *The English Constitution*, consists of two essential parts: "First, those which excite and preserve the reverence of the population—the *dignified* parts, if I may so call them; and next, the *efficient* parts—those by which it, in fact, works and rules" (italics in the original). The English monarch (he wrote during Queen Victoria's reign) took up the former position, the cabinet the latter. "The use of the Queen, in a dignified capacity, is incalculable. Without her in England, the present English government would fail and pass away." Monarchy, Bagehot explains, is an "intelligible government." The queen is easily seen and understood; she captures the imagination and stimulates the feelings of ordinary people. She is not only the visible head of state, but also the visible head of society, of religion, and of morality. Her personality holds together a large empire.

As a practical, pragmatic man, Su Li tends to ignore or even do away with the dignified part of the constitution. In his work, he does not treat the dignified dimension of the Chinese emperor, namely, that which inspires political belief in the people and therefore serves to maintain meaningful political practice. He looks only to means and results in the constitution of a huge polity and maintaining effective governance over it. In that equation, the dignified appears to be useless and therefore meaningless. But even as a practical matter, to ignore the dignified part is mistaken. The reason is clear. It is the dignified part that gives "force" to the government of ancient China. The efficient only utilizes that force and employs that power. The dignified, in Bagehot's terms, "raise the army, though they do not win the battle." Absent the army, however, battle would be impossible.

By imagining the ancient, we recognize that we are modern. Su Li is no exception. Perhaps modern observers can take only a functional approach to the ancient Chinese emperor, however they intend to applaud his position. After all, Chinese imperialism is lost, politically and historically, if not culturally. People could still analogize the general secretary or the president to the emperor; they cannot treat him as a real emperor in politics and law. At least the general secretary or the president is chosen rather than born. He is subject to a limited term in office. To make full sense of ancient Chinese imperialism, one must recall the faith in the emperor. That is difficult if not impossible. At least, we must rearticulate or re-present the imaginary structure of that belief. In other words, we need a cultural anthropology of the ancient Chinese polity.

In a larger sense, perhaps man can have a practical nostalgia only for a past political regime. At the time of its publication, Bagehot's *The English*

Constitution was outmoded in some respects. It was written in the two years before the passage of the 1867 Reform Act, which fundamentally advanced democracy in England. Likewise, Su Li's appreciation of ancient China's constitution, especially the emperor, takes place more than a century after the emperorship passed away. Perhaps only when a great political concept is in the past can we begin to expose the myth that underlay and sustained it. When it still holds sway, talking of it aloud would show neither tact nor prudence. It might even seem an outrage against the normal operation of that politics. Yet after its fall, we are doomed to appreciate only its usefulness while trying to praise it. Exposed, a myth ceases to be a myth. Disenchanted, a sacred institution is subject, or at least susceptible, to somber social-scientific analysis.

On the other hand, even a modern republic needs such a cultural symbol. In the United States, the Constitution, as a whole, serves as the source of reverence and dignity. Su Li tends to take the U.S. Constitution purely as a normative document. But it is more than that. It is the equivalent of the English king or queen. In America, paraphrasing Thomas Paine, the Constitution is the king. The Constitution, George Washington reminded his "friends and fellow citizens," must be obeyed by all because it is "sacredly obligatory upon all"—"sacredly," more than "dignified." Almost a half century later, the young Abraham Lincoln, speaking to the Lyceum, a young men's society in Springfield, Illinois, on the subject of "the perpetuation of our political institutions," echoed that sentiment: "Let reverence for the laws . . . become the *political religion*. . . . Let those materials [founded in reason] be molded into *general intelligence, sound morality* and, in particular, *a reverence for the constitution and laws*" (italics in the original).[14] Again, "reverence"—not for a person but for a Constitution that transcends persons, as it also transcends parties, politics, and all other divisive tendencies.

To further Su Li's depiction of the ancient Chinese constitutional world, we should say not only that institutions, like the emperor, were *useful*. We should also point out that they were *meaningful*. Properly interpreted, the ancient Chinese constitutional narrative could contribute to the formation and entrenchment of the modern, even contemporary, Chinese constitutional identity. Yet Su Li does not touch on this dimension while trying to rearticulate the ancient Chinese constitution. He might have done this. Even if we take a functionalist point of view, culture is still important. Consider the U.S. Constitution. Throughout the past two hundred years, it has become a beacon of American identity. It is not only a normative document, what Su Li calls a Constitution. It also serves as the political-cultural symbol of the American nation, like the emperor for the ancient Chinese or the queen for the British. Losing sight of this, and describing only the functional part of the constitution fails to fully capture the ancient Chinese constitutional picture. For any constitution to succeed, both the functional part and the symbolic part must act. Pragmatism alone cannot get to the whole point.

The Problem of Legitimacy Continuity
and Constitutional Discontinuity

Since 1911, the idea of a new beginning has been a dominant theme in the Chinese constitutional mind. To welcome a new constitutional beginning, the Chinese constitutional mind tended to deny its past, not only politically but also culturally. It seemed that China's past was in total darkness, awaiting the coming of light, a constitutional genesis. Republican China undertook multiple constitutional experiments by importing Western, republican, constitutional systems, American or French. Then the People's Republic adopted socialist Constitutions. Post-1978, many intellectuals embraced a Western, liberal-democratic Constitution and called for a constitutional remaking. That attempt is still vibrant among contemporary Chinese intellectuals, especially legal scholars.

In a larger sense, a modern Constitution is often taken as a symbol of the break, total or partial, with a nation's past. The U.S. Constitution was a product of the American Revolution, a break with British rule. The German Basic Law serves as a total denial of Germany's Nazi past and the brand-new beginning of a liberal-democratic order founded on human dignity. Postcolonial states adopted written Constitutions to initiate new phases of political history. To this rule, modern China is no exception. It underwent a great transformation, an uprooted reconstitution. Its multiple experiences of constitution making are a history of replacing old regimes with new ones: from imperialism to republic, from capitalism to socialism. Revolution by revolution, reform by reform, China has been in a constant state of change. Nothing seems stable.

In recent years, a shift in the constitutional-historical narrative has been going on. Instead of the story of discontinuity, some efforts are now being put into constructing continuity. Su Li's account of the ancient Chinese constitution is the first significant one in Chinese constitutional scholarship. He points out that the fundamental constitution remains largely unchanged. He argues, for example, that in spite of the abolition of imperialism, the question of unity in such a huge country and civilization continued and continues to haunt the statesmen and intellectuals of modern China. Moreover, the ancient solutions are still relevant today, if not directly applicable. Remarkably, China largely retained its territorial extent throughout the post–World War I revolutions and post–Cold War upheavals. By contrast, Eastern European countries, for example, collapsed into smaller states (think of the breakup of the Austro-Hungarian Empire and the collapse of the Soviet Union). No doubt the emperor is dead in China, and perhaps forever. Yet the Chinese "empire" remains, both in the land and in the hearts of the Chinese people. To think about its reconstitution, we must know its constitution—in a traditional Confucian phrase, "an old country, a new mission" (旧邦新命).

Su Li tries to link China's present constitution to its past by constructing their functional continuity. Elsewhere he makes an important distinction between the ideational and the institutional understandings of Confucianism.[15] Here, he uses such a distinction to analyze the history of China's constitution. For Su Li, neither 1911 nor 1949 makes a decisive, total break with the institutional past of law and governance in China. He seems to admit the break in legitimacy in China's modern transition—from monarchical sovereignty to popular sovereignty. But he responds that, despite this ideological shift, the fundamental, practical problems of effective governance in a large country remain unchanged. And there is a remarkable continuity between the ancient solutions to these problems and the modern ones. In its institutional aspects, the transition from empire to nation-state and from imperialism to republicanism seems to be of little importance.

I do not disagree with his distinction between the ideational and the institutional. I appreciate his effort to detect institutional continuity in China's modern constitutional transformation. To me, however, it seems that a more crucial task is to make a connection between the past and the present in the issue of legitimation. There remains to be answered an ideational question in addition to the institutional question. Besides the emperor, there is Confucius. In other words, to make the story complete, the continuity of the "dignified" or "symbolic" part of China's constitution, not only that of the "functional" or "efficient" part, must be established. One must at least, for example, link the emperor to the party in the political imagination to ground the legitimacy of the rule. Otherwise, the ancient Chinese constitution is like a foreign county to contemporary China. Contemporary China can learn from its own institutions just as it can learn from the United States. I do not think Su Li would approve of this.

Such a constitutional continuity can be constructed in two ways. One can do intellectual-historical studies to reconcile Confucianism, socialism, and perhaps liberalism. That would be a task for intellectual historians or philosophers. Or one can do a cultural-anthropological study to map out the political imagination of the ordinary people who take the general secretary of the party as an emperor with a limited term of office.[16] That would be a task for social scientists. Either way, the point is clear: China's constitution is not legitimate just because it works well. For a country/civilization freighted with ideology like China, the ideational question cannot be evaded by simply highlighting institutional efficacy. The constitution must also be "our constitution" for the Chinese as a historical-cultural community.

A legal scholar may contribute to the task of constructing political-imaginary continuity. One can read the first paragraph of the Preamble of the Constitution of the People's Republic of China (1982) for insights: "China is one of the countries with the longest histories in the world. The people of all nationalities in China have jointly created a splendid culture and have a glorious revolutionary tradition."[17] Taken seriously, the first paragraph of the

1982 Chinese Constitution needs proper interpretation: Why does a socialist-republican Constitution begin with an imperial past? What constituted the historical China? Su Li's work provides an effort of constitutional interpretation, although it needs to be deepened, as I have argued. Su Li's account of the constitution of historical China, in my eyes, can serve as a commentary on not only a past regime, but also the current Chinese Constitution. Here, Su Li's historical-sociological study can be integrated into an exegesis of the constitutional text. Proclaiming a new beginning, the Constitution invokes the past. The 1982 Constitution actually offers a possibility of continuity by introducing an oxymoron: "revolutionary tradition." Students of China's Constitution, therefore, are invited to build on Su Li's work by trying to account for that *continuity of discontinuity* in Chinese constitutional history as a continuous line from antiquity to modernity.

That project has its contemporary relevance. It first and foremost touches on the legitimation of the Chinese regime. Traditionally, the Chinese Communist Party claims a charismatic legitimacy. The Chinese Revolution endowed the Party with a strong legitimacy to rule through telling narratives of defending the nation against enemies, foreign and domestic, and the awe that emerges from the memories of revolutionary sacrifice. Today, this charismatic, revolutionary legitimacy is losing its force to charm. We see a visible continuity between the concept of legitimacy that grounded the emperor and that which grounded the Party.[18] Confucianism has become a valuable resource to ground legitimacy. China's past is now thought of as a living presence for ordinary people as well as for some intellectuals, rather than a huge burden that must be thrown into the dustbin of history in the course of modernization. Ever since the beginning of the twenty-first century, and especially with China's rise, both official and unofficial opinion seems to valorize continuity over discontinuity. Many have come to believe that China has remained "China" over millennia in its essential constitution, both functionally and symbolically. The sediment of Confucianism can provide resources for imagining political discourse and even political action. It can be reactivated in contemporary Chinese thought and society. It is being reactivated.

Against this backdrop, Su Li does primary, pathbreaking work to rearticulate the functional past of the constitution and construct constitutional continuity in its functional part, adopting a pragmatic approach to the business of ruling a large country. The more difficult, yet necessary, task is to do similar work for the symbolic part of China's historical constitution. That would require a different approach.

CHAPTER SIX

The Ideal of Civilization and Formation of Institutions in Ancient China

A REPLY TO SU LI

Wu Fei

MY FIRST REACTION on reading Su Li's writings on China's constitution was delight. The current trend in discussion of the constitution and constitutional issues is to follow traditional Western theories taking no account whatsoever of the inherent rationale of China's own political tradition or oversimplifying ancient China's pattern of governance by relegating it to the category of backward authoritarianism, and making no effort to investigate the matter in any greater depth. In this sense, Su Li's revisionist account, which starts from ancient China's own institutional tradition, is, of course, of immense significance.

Su Li's research is first of all based on a thorough understanding of Western constitutions and constitutionalism. This is made clear in his chapter defining constitutional issues. He shows that the constitutional question arises in the constitution/formation of a state, in an unwritten text. To appreciate how we are to understand this formation, though, may require a little further reflection. Su Li's understanding can be traced back to Aristotle. In his discussion of the formation of a state, Aristotle adopts two approaches. The first sees the boundaries assigned to the population of a state and military affairs as being shaped in tandem. The second looks at the level of political philosophy. In other words, there is both form and matter. In book 7 of the *Politics*, Aristotle presents the borders, population, and other such factors as the matter of the city-state while the form of the state is its political shape as a monarchy, aristocracy, or democracy.

More in-depth, postmodern discussions of constitutional issues can in fact be assigned to one or other of these two levels. The formation of the city-state is not purely a matter of arranging or managing borders and population. Rather, it involves an ideal of civilization or a comprehensive idea of the good life. Since the emergence of Christianity, the understanding of what constitutes the good life is very different since, in the context of the whole of life, political life is no longer what is most important. The formation of an ideal of civilization is basically turned over to God and the Church. The formation of secular politics is what modern constitutionalism is about. But seen from the angle of civilization and nation-states, the constitution of the modern West is not only a matter of nation-states. It is also an ideal of civilization.

In comparison, there is also an ideal of civilization present in the formation of China's actual institutions, which transcends constitutionalism at its most basic level. Concrete political institutions rest on the base of a political ideal. We recognize that the idea of China today is one that forces a great civilization into the tiny space of a nation-state. To understand ancient China, however, we must still go back to its civilization as such and only then examine the formation of its actual institutions. Should we impose the framework of modern structures on our understanding of civilization, then we will transfer questions that were originally ones of civilization into institutional questions and run the risk of oversimplification. Su Li's approach does, in fact, tend in this direction, in that he understands the past in terms of the present. Such an approach may give rise to problems, which will be outlined in more detail below.

First, the ideal of civilization articulated in China's ancient tradition is to be found in the institution of the rites. Many political institutions were determined by ritual norms. We cannot simply refer to "regulating the household (齐家), governing the state (治国) and bringing peace to the world under heaven (平天下)" without first appreciating the hierarchical relationships of feudal clan law. According to this, distinctions of rank were very clear with three levels: the *daifu* (大夫), feudal princes, and the Son of Heaven. The "household" referred to then is not the same as that of today. The household is the area under the *daifu*. A *daifu* with a household could become a prince. Thus, these levels set out in the text of the *Great Learning* just quoted refer to the levels in the hierarchy. The *daifu* can regulate his household, the feudal princes their states, while the work of bringing peace to the world under heaven (平天下) is assigned to the Son of Heaven. The *Rites of Zhou* opens by stating that "only the king may establish a state." The state here is a walled town. The royal domain administered by the Son of Heaven and the states under the authority of the feudal princes are similar. All were city-states. Although the Son of Heaven governs his royal domain, this is not what is meant by "bringing peace to the world under heaven (平天下)." The relationship between the Son of Heaven and the feudal princes was not simply one of the center to the periphery, but rather one of distribution of tasks. The feudal princes were responsible for actual political governance whereas the Son of Heaven operates more at the level of culture and civilization. Bringing peace to the world under heaven (平天下) is an ideal of civilization and not part of the concrete political structures. "Making one's bright virtue shine in the world under heaven" is not equivalent to international relations, nor to dealing with ethnic groups on the border. All of these concrete issues are at the level of governing the state, whereas the Son of Heaven is at the level of the ideals of the civilization.

Second, I do not completely agree with Su Li's understanding of the transition from feudal clan law. Su Li clearly states that ancient China was opportunist in its treatment of family relationships. This way of putting things leans too heavily toward pragmatism. Though it does have a grain of truth in it, yet it is still inadequate. I have already noted that whether we are talking of the Duke of Zhou or someone else, in determining the feudal clan law—considering it not only from the angle of political stability but also as the embodiment of an ideal of civilization—within human relationships taken as a whole the ideal of loving those who merit love (parents) and respecting those worthy of respect was an ideal for civilization. In understanding this concrete institution, we must distinguish between the ideal of civilization and the political structure. If we wholly accept Su Li's actual reading I still think that above it there is something higher that he has tended to neglect.

Third, in his writings, Su Li has dealt with the change from the Zhou to the Qin, but I do not think that this shift is purely a matter of history since it also touches on more important theoretical questions. Su Li has also discussed the imperial system, the unified script, and the bureaucracy, but by simply relying only on grasping the "constitution of the state" the Qin Empire in fact collapsed very rapidly and the reason why the Han did not suffer the same fate was not purely due to its adoption of a constitutional model that opted for Confucianism alone as a tool. Rather, it was because the Han refounded the ritual order and made an effort to develop study of the classics and so remade the core sense of the values inherent in the clan law. At a time when the clan-based legal order no longer existed, the Han were able to develop and use the role of the Three Constants. The work of the Han was not limited to furthering the institutions of the Qin. Of greater importance was its providing a theoretical and cultural format. We can ask ourselves how the efforts of the Han should be understood. I think that one important point here is the formation of the tradition of study of the classics. The slow and gradual work of the professors in the capital city under the Han dynasty led to a culmination in the collected commentaries of Zheng Kangcheng. Seen in this light, Dong Zhongshu is only a beginning and not the completion. For instance, the Qin emperors and Zhou Sons of Heaven were very different from one another. Many of the functions assumed by the feudal lords in the clan law of the Zhou were assumed by the emperors. But even so, besides its reinforcement of the authority of the emperor under the Han, the renewal of the ritual status of the emperor through the classics was such that he virtually attained the same status as the Son of Heaven had once held—though in fact there was a big difference. The texts of the classics we see today were collated and commented on in the Han dynasty. After the Qin-Han period, efforts developed in two directions. One direction was at the level of the institution of commanderies and counties and the institutional constitution of a large state that is indeed more a matter of the constitution. The other direction was the work of the scholars in the Han dynasty, who, at a time when the clan law of the Zhou no longer existed, were able to reconstitute the significance of the Zhou institutions through the classics and join these to the Han institutions. This work of the Han Confucians is fully deserving of our attention. Therefore, in the post-Han period, although it may seem as if there was a state machinery formed by the bureaucracy with the emperor at its head, in fact its core spirit always lay in that it was bound to the spirit of the ritual order of the clan law and served to integrate the whole. Su Li reduces this spirit almost only to the constitution of the formation of the machinery of state and thinks that all of this effort was solely geared toward forming a large state and ensuring that the empire could develop effective governance. This would seem to be to use Western logic to understand the formation of ancient China's monarchy and to fail to follow through on the inherent logic of the Chinese institutions themselves.

Fourth, let me briefly discuss the question of the sovereign and the citizens because this is also a matter to which Su Li pays particular attention in his discussion of China's ancient constitution. The question of the sovereign is not unique to China. I think that unless we understand the Western monarchical system properly we cannot understand the formation of democracy. If we look at the classical exposition in book 1 of Aristotle's *Politics*, we see that, owing to purely natural needs, mankind first forms the family and this then grows into the village. The most natural village is simply the clan that forms from the gradual expansion of one family. Aristotle goes on to say that the earliest form of the city-state is, therefore, always a monarchy since these early monarchs are simply the heads of the clan. Among uncivilized barbarians it was also the same and so it was among the early Greeks. But these early monarchical city-states were not truly city-states in the sense of civilization. A civilized city-state must be the result of a union between villages and not simply a village writ large. Monarchy is not a true city-state. This is related to the definition of the citizens in book 3 of the *Politics* as people who can participate in political governance. A monarchy cannot have citizens because governance is wholly in the hands of one person only. Yet toward the end of book 3, Aristotle also recognizes that in fact an absolute monarchy may be the best form of political body since it is the rule of a father. Of course, this supposes that the virtue of the monarch exceeds the sum of all other people. He does not believe that monarchy is always bad. He also holds that the governance of the monarch is very similar to that of the head of a household but such a monarchy has its own inherent problems. Monarchy may be one form of the city-state, but it is not the rule of law and is very different from a state that has a constitution. This understanding of monarchy is very close to that of China but there are some basic differences.

In his *City-States under the Zhou Dynasty*, the Taiwanese scholar Tu Cheng-sheng tries to show that the city-states of the Zhou were very similar to those of ancient Greece. If so, we may ask why it was that the Zhou was unable to practice democracy. I think that this involves an ideal of civilization. For ancient Chinese people, the world under heaven under the Son of Heaven was the unlimited expansion of the sphere of the head of household; the Son of Heaven was simply the head of a big household. Therefore the *Four Institutions of Mourning* and the *Classic of Filial Piety* both emphasize that "the nature of respect shown in serving one's father and serving one's prince is the same." Zhang Zai also says, "The great prince is my father, mother, and ancestor." The Three Constants is the framework for the feudal clan law. The prince is the norm for the minister, the father for the son, and the husband for his wife. In each relationship, the structure of obligation and responsibility is the same. In the matter of mourning, mourning clothes are to be worn for three years by the minister at the demise of the prince, by the son for his father, and by the widow for her husband. They do not think that there is any theoretical issue here. Aristotle's conundrum simply does not exist even though the succession to the monarch will still give rise to some concrete problems. The source of this difference between Greece and China is one that, I think, deserves far more study.

Fifth, the issue of how to talk about the constitution in a Chinese linguistic field is one that has been debated many times since the late Qing dynasty. Toward the end of the Qing, a Constitution was set up and there was then a lot of discussion about it: how the Constitution should enter into the traditional structure. Or how could one understand the Constitution within the framework of Chinese thought? The way of thinking proposed by Su Li is one that scarcely existed at that time. For instance, Kang Youwei used the three eras of the *Gongyang Commentary* to discuss the change in law and did not see any particular problem in following a traditional Chinese system by a Western one, even though there were many big problems in practice. He said,

A glance at what makes countries in both the East and West strong shows that it comes from setting up a Constitution and opening a national assembly. In a national assembly, the prince and the citizens discuss the politics of the state together. We may set this out according to the tripartite division of powers: the national assembly establishes the law, the judges implement it and the government executes it, whilst the lord of men draws all into one. By establishing a constitution everything is governed equally. If the lord of men is exalted as a god he is beyond responsibility and the government stands in for him. The various states of East and West all employ this form of politics, therefore the prince and the millions of citizens are united as one body. How then can the state not be strong?[1]

Sun Yirang (1848–1908) wrote a book titled *The Essentials of Zhou Officialdom*, in which he claimed that many constitutional questions could be resolved by taking the *Zhou Officialdom* as a blueprint. Later, in the preparation for drawing up the Constitution, the court set up three offices: a constitutional office, a law office, and an office for study of the rites. The three had to work together such that in the writing of a new Constitution and new laws, it was necessary to consult the *Rites of the Great Qing Empire*. Cao Yuanzhong of the Office of Rites said, "The word 'constitution' comes from English and French and refers to politics and the law. The term *xianfa* is adopted from Japan and combined with an expression from the *Rites of Zhou*. It is little realised that in the *Rites of Zhou* the term *xianfa* is restricted to punishments of the criminal law." Although the expressions *xianfa* or *xianzhi* both come from Japanese translations of Western terms (constitution and constitutionalism, respectively), the word *xian* does have a sense in ancient Chinese institutional theory. Cao quotes the *Autumn Offices* section of the *Rites of Zhou*: "Displaying (*bu-xian*) and manifesting (*zhang-xian*) the criminal punishments of the state is auspicious in the first month. One takes the banner and tally to display them in all four quarters." Zheng Kangcheng comments, "*xian* is to display; it is 'to hang something up.' Punishments are what the five laws of the state decree to accompany the judicial officials. The Minister of Justice declares the punishments in the first month for the world under heaven and for the whole year the text is hung on the city gate-towers." Again in the *pian* on setting up government in the *Guanzi*, we read, "On New Year's Day, the officials are all at court; the officials are all at court. The prince issues his decrees and displays (*bu-xian*) them to the state. The teachers of the five districts and the *daifu* of the five *shu* take their cue (*shou-xian*) from the Grand Historiographer. On the day of the great court meeting the teachers of the five districts and *daifu* of the five *shu* show (*xian*) before the prince that they have put them into practice. The Grand Historiographer displays the truth by entering it into the government archives and showing it to the prince." In his commentary on the *Rites of Zhou*, Zheng Kangcheng had already made it plain that the meaning of *xian* was to display. Cao Yuanzhong says, "Any law that is hung up on display is called a *xian*." In other words, *xian* means to hang up laws for all to see. In part 1, Celestial Offices, of the *Rites of Zhou*, we read "display the laws of governance" and in another passage "display the laws of education," again "display the laws of administration" and "display the laws of punishment." Hanging up the law is done so that everybody can read it and refers in particular to the punishments of criminal law. It does not refer to the basic principles for ruling the state. Of course, Cao Yuanzhong also recognizes that "what is called *xianfa* today is not what the *Rites of Zhou* meant by *xianfa*."[2] But what is the constitution today? Cao's criticism of the view advocated by Chen Zhuo would seem to be correct because the latter held that the constitution and the book of rites should be combined and that today's constitution and the rites were the same thing. The ancient rites of China, especially the *Rites of Zhou*, and the Western Constitution have similar functions but their places and roles in the culture are very different. Roughly speaking, we may perhaps say that the ritual system can be treated as China's ancient constitution, but on a finer analysis we must acknowledge that this way of speaking is not very appropriate. The crux of the matter is that the law and rites are of dissimilar status, the law being under the rites. Rites are the framework of Chinese civilization. The constitution is lower than the ideal provided by civilization. If today we want to discuss the constitutional issue, we must take full account of these matters.

Su Li also says that many institutions of today's China are the legacy of Chinese traditions. Now this seems to lead to the conclusion that we have at the moment no problem since the ancient constitution has been perfectly preserved. But China today does in fact have many problems, the biggest of which is that morality is not shaped by any concrete social form or institution and this is a loss at the level of the ideals of civilization. Even though what constitutionalists discuss are concrete institutions, behind these are questions about the ideals of our civilization and the many issues that come from the nonrecognition of China's ancient ideals. If these ideals of civilization cannot be established, then all clever institutions will be in vain.

CHAPTER SEVEN

History, Culture, Revolution, and Chinese Constitutionalism

Zhao Xiaoli

WHY IS IT NECESSARY to discuss the constitution of ancient China? This is the first question we must ask on reading Professor Su Li's chapters in this book. There are many books on the topics of politics in ancient China or the constitution in modern China, enough to fill a house. The former is a subject for historians, the latter for legal scholars. Why is it that a legal scholar like Su Li would want to discuss the constitution of ancient China? Could it be that he is not afraid of the question put to scholars who discuss ancient China's civil law: "Given that the term 'civil law' comes from the Western, continental system of law, why is it necessary to look for traces of civil law in ancient Chinese law? Could it be because of the childish attitude expressed in the adages 'if you have it I too want it' or 'our family is more ancient' and such like expressions of a nationalist self-respect?"

In this chapter I attempt to reply to this question on behalf of Su Li. I hold that a discussion of the constitution of ancient China proves that since Shang and Zhou times ancient China has had a constitution, affirmed in the Qin-Han era, and that this is not simply the expression of childish pique, nor does it arise from a historian's penchant for the antique; rather it is an inherent demand of the rationality of the Constitution of the People's Republic of China.

Revolution, Constitution, and History

The first line of the Preamble to China's 1982 Constitution reads: "China is one of the countries with the longest histories in the world. The people of all nationalities in China have jointly created a splendid culture and have a glorious revolutionary tradition." In this passage there are three key terms: history, culture, and revolution. Written Western Constitutions are generally promulgated after the success of a revolution and serve to make a clean break with the past and make a new start in time. Hence, they obviously do not refer to history or culture. For instance, the American Declaration of Independence of 4 July 1776 reads:

> When in the course of human events, it becomes necessary for one people to dissolve the political bands which have connected them with another, and to assume among the powers of the earth, the separate and equal station to which the laws of nature and of nature's God entitle them, a decent respect to the opinions of mankind requires that they should declare the causes which impel them to the separation.

However, in his *Summary View of the Rights of British America* of 1774, Jefferson argued that the Anglo-Saxons brought these rights with them when they moved to Britain and the American colonists brought them from their British ancestors to North America. Why is it that two years later, in the declaration, he made no reference to rights as coming from ancestors or from history, ascribing them instead to God and nature?

The fact is that in 1774, Jefferson claimed that

> the emigrants thought proper to adopt that system of laws under which they had hitherto lived in the mother country, and to continue their union with her by submitting themselves to the same common sovereign, who was thereby made the central link connecting the several parts of the empire thus newly multiplied.

At the time, the British North Americans still sought political union and so stressed the historical rights they held in common. But in 1776, when they were seeking to be free from this political union, the colonists wanted to break their historical link and place the American and British nations on a completely natural footing based on "natural law and the God of nature."[1]

The wording of the 1787 U.S. Constitution reads: "We the people of the United States, . . . do ordain and establish this Constitution for the United States of America." This opening indicates that the Constitution is a cutoff point from the past and one from which the future unfolds. The final section reads: "Done in convention by the unanimous consent of the states present the seventeenth day of September in the year of our Lord one thousand seven hundred and eighty-seven and of the independence of the United States of America the twelfth." This section links the independence of America to the birth of Jesus and also affirms a break with the history and culture of Britain, alleging obedience only to natural law and the God of nature.[2]

A reference to history is something confined to the 1949 Constitution of the People's Republic of China and the Constitutions of only a few other states. In the various Constitutions of the Republic of China drawn up since the Revolution of 1911, which overthrew the emperor, there is either no preamble or, if there is, at least no mention of history.[3] For instance, the Preamble to the 1947 Constitution is similar to the U.S. Constitution of 1787 in stating, "The National Assembly of the Republic of China, by virtue of the mandate received from the whole body of citizens . . . does hereby establish this Constitution."

However, starting with the Common Program of the Chinese People's Political Consultative Conference of 1949 and in the Constitutions of 1954, 1975, 1978, and 1982, there is always a preamble and it begins with a reference to history.The opening line of the 1949 text reads:

> The great victories of the Chinese people's war of liberation and of the people's revolution have put an end to the era of the rule of imperialism, feudalism and bureaucratic capitalism in China.

The opening line of the Preamble of 1954 reads:

> In the year 1949, after more than a century of heroic struggle, the Chinese people, led by the Communist Party of China, finally won their great victory in the people's revolution against imperialism, feudalism and bureaucrat-capitalism, and thereby brought to an end the history of the oppression and enslavement they had undergone for so long and founded the People's Republic of China—a people's democratic dictatorship.

The opening line of the Preamble of 1975 reads:

> The founding of the People's Republic of China marked the great victory of the new democratic revolution and the beginning of the new historical period of socialist revolution and the dictatorship of the proletariat, a victory gained only after the Chinese people had waged a heroic struggle for more than a century and, finally, under the leadership of the Communist Party of China, overthrown the reactionary rule of imperialism, feudalism, and bureaucratic capitalism by a people's revolutionary war.

The opening line of the Preamble of 1978 reads:

> After more than a century of heroic struggle, the Chinese people, led by the Communist Party of China headed by our great leader and teacher Chairman Mao Zedong, finally overthrew the reactionary rule of imperialism, feudalism, and bureaucratic capitalism by means of people's revolutionary war, winning complete victory in the new democratic revolution, and in 1949 founded the People's Republic of China.

The shortest text is that of 1949, which refers to revolutionary history starting from the war of liberation in 1946. The three subsequent texts of 1954, 1975, and 1978 take this revolutionary history as beginning more than a hundred years earlier, in 1840, at the outbreak of the Opium War. But the best exposition of this revolutionary history is to be found not in the preambles to these three versions of the Constitution but in the inscription Mao Zedong wrote on the Monument to the People's Heroes on 30 September 1949:

> Eternal glory to the heroes of the people who laid down their lives in the people's war of liberation and the people's revolution in the past three years!

> Eternal glory to the heroes of the people who laid down their lives in the people's war of liberation and the people's revolution in the past thirty years!

> Eternal glory to the heroes of the people who from 1840 laid down their lives in the many struggles against domestic and foreign enemies and for national independence and the freedom and well-being of the people![4]

The narration of the revolutionary past in the Preamble to the 1982 Constitution is based on Mao Zedong's inscription, though it changes his poetic text into that of a historian. The account in the preambles to the 1954, 1975, and 1978 Constitutions is abstract and lacking in detail, whereas the 1982 Preamble makes explicit mention of the historical moments of 1840, 1911, and 1949 and of both Sun Yat-sen and Mao Zedong.[5]

> After 1840, feudal China was gradually turned into a semi-colonial and semi-feudal country. The Chinese people waged many successive heroic struggles for national independence and liberation and for democracy and freedom.
>
> Great and earthshaking historical changes have taken place in China in the 20th century.
>
> The Revolution of 1911, led by Dr Sun Yat-sen, abolished the feudal monarchy and gave birth to the Republic of China. But the historic mission of the Chinese people to overthrow imperialism and feudalism remained unaccomplished.
>
> After waging protracted and arduous struggles, armed and otherwise, along a zigzag course, the Chinese people of all nationalities led by the Communist Party of China with Chairman Mao Zedong as its leader ultimately, in 1949, overthrew the rule of imperialism, feudalism and bureaucrat-capitalism, won a great victory in the New-Democratic Revolution and founded the People's Republic of China. Since then the

Chinese people have taken control of state power and become masters of the country.[6]

With the death of Mao Zedong, that section of China's century or more of revolutionary history came to an end and China's modern revolution entered into an even larger history, the whole history of Chinese history. Before the account of revolutionary history in the 1982 Preamble, the text opens with another line: "China is one of the countries with the longest histories in the world. The people of all nationalities in China have jointly created a splendid culture and have a glorious revolutionary tradition."

By comparing this first line of the Chinese Constitution with the last line of the 1787 U.S. Constitution, we find that the revolution, that is, American independence, in the United States had the sense of marking a new creation and the only historical fact with which it could be compared was the birth of Jesus. By contrast, in the 1982 Chinese Constitution and its account of revolutionary history since 1840, neither the revolution led by Sun Yat-sen nor that led by Mao Zedong has such significance, since the post-1840 revolutions are in continuity with China's previous, glorious revolutionary history. But, in comparison with previous revolutions, and although those in China in the twentieth century are not new creations, they are earth-shattering events since previous revolutions were merely a case of changing dynasties, one small group of leaders replacing another, but now what has been effected is the people's own self-rule. The past history of China, in which a small group of persons ruled over the many, has been utterly overthrown. According to Professor Qiang Shigong, this is as if heaven and earth had been reversed and thus it can be described as "earth-shattering."[7]

The 1982 Constitution goes on to say that the glorious revolutionary tradition of China exercises the role of creating a splendid culture, and therein lies its glory. Of course, culture is not only created by revolution. The phrase "the glorious revolutionary tradition" is prefaced by the statement that "the people of all nationalities in China have jointly created a splendid culture" to indicate that revolution is only one way of creating culture and not the only way.

Latent in the 1982 text is the idea that Chinese culture is constantly renewing itself and that revolution should be seen as part of this inherent dynamic and so prevent a fixed view of culture according to which revolution would create a break in history or obliteration of the past. This, then, makes it possible to read China as being one of the countries with the longest histories in the world. The same idea can be put more succinctly in the statement, "Although Zhou is an old state, yet its mandate is new."[8]

Time in the Constitution

The view of time set out in the phrase, "Although Zhou is an old state, yet its mandate is new," and in the Constitution of 1982 differs from that of a modern written Constitution exemplified in the opening and closing lines of the Constitution of the United States of 1787. The former is set out in three stages, past, present, and future; the latter in only two, present and future.

The two-phase notion of time is that of God creating the world. The opening line of the U.S. Constitution—"We the people of the United States, ... do ordain and establish this Constitution for the United States of America"—resembles the first words of God in the Book of Genesis: "let there be light." This is a decision in the present that simply looks to the future. It is what Carl Schmitt said about creating a new state: "Such a constitution is a conscious decision, which the political unity reaches *for itself* and provides *itself* through the bearer of the constitution-making power."[9]

Now the people can imitate God, but as human beings they are not God. The bodies of the persons in that generation that draws up the Constitution will turn to dust. At that time, where should one then look for the will of the people? A two-phase view of time in a Constitution usually brings one to Jefferson's dilemma, namely, that the "we the people" of that time determine the future and are subject to the limits of the human lifespan incumbent on this "we the people." For future generations, "we" are not "they" and "they" are not "we." The living cannot accept the rule of the dead and so the Constitution should be renewed every nineteen years and constitutional history becomes a revolutionary history.[10]

Countries use different ways of coping with Jefferson's dilemma. After the revolution, France issued new Constitutions or constitutional laws in 1791, 1793, 1795, 1799, 1802, 1804, 1814, 1815, 1830, 1848, 1852, 1875, 1940, 1945, 1946, and 1958. Sometimes more than one are drawn up in the span of a single generation.

Since 1787, the United States has accepted twenty-seven articles of amendment, of which the first ten of 1791 and the three post–Civil War articles, the Thirteenth, Fourteenth, and Fifteenth Amendments, are, according to French and Chinese standards, completely sufficient to be rewritings of the Constitution and are not merely amendments as such. There are also new constitutional norms implicit in the interpretations of the Constitution made by the U.S. Supreme Court. For instance, the 2008 ruling of the Supreme Court on the Second Amendment presents itself as an interpretation of the amendment, but it might better be described as a remaking of the Second Amendment two centuries later.[11] Justice Antonin Scalia applied the hermeneutical method of "original intent" to this case.[12] Use of the notion of original intent implies a two-phase theory of constitutional time: the present and the future. On the surface, it would seem as if a reference is being made to the past and the idea is to search for the intent of the makers of the Constitution or the meaning implicit in the wording of the text so as to determine a present issue. But whatever sleight of hand is employed, the common feature of this approach is as set out below:

To take the present as the future envisaged by the Constitution; to take the past as the present of the Constitution.

In fact, the truth of the matter is that the "we the people" faced with a present constitutional problem are taken to be the "we the people" of two hundred years ago, and the justice imagines how the present-day "we the people" would rewrite the Constitution to see how they would decide a constitutional rule that may or may not have existed two hundred years earlier. Using this act of imagination, the original intent turns a matter of constitutional interpretation into a constitutional question. Under the cover of interpretation, a judge can effect a revolution and set up a Constitution. In this way Jefferson's dilemma can be temporarily resolved by the trick of constitutional interpretation.

Any such act is only a temporary resolution because the decision made cannot bind the American people of the future because they, like those of today, can also perform the same act of time travel and create any number of constitutional times, putting the past to naught and writing off all previous makers of the Constitution and creating a new decision for the future.

The question then arises as to whether there is only one or many constitutional times for the People's Republic of China. Have there been five Constitutions between the Common Program of 1949 and the Constitution of 1982 and so five constitutional times? Professor Chen Ruihong holds not. There is only one constitutional time for the People's Republic of China, namely, the time when the Common Program was drawn up in 1949: "the time from 21 September to 1 October 1949."[13] The makers of the Constitution "were not a dynasty, or nobles, but the people. But 'the people' is not be understood here as an abstract idea but as a class. It has the proletariat as its core and is a mixed body formed from representatives of various classes."[14] This people was constituted by a form of unelected proportional representation of the 510 official delegates to the first political consultative conference.[15]

The proof for the constitutional text justifying this theory is that in the text of the fifth Constitution of the People's Republic of China, the only maker of the Constitution is the Common Program. The Preamble to the Common Program reads:

> The Chinese People's Political Consultative Conference unanimously agrees that New Democracy, or the People's Democracy, shall be the political foundation for the national construction of the People's Republic of China. It has also *adopted* the following Common Program which should be jointly observed by all units participating in the Conference, by the people's government of all levels, and by the people of the whole country.

The subsequent Constitutions, from 1954 to 1982, simply state below the title the date on which the document was passed by whichever session of the

National People's Congress and not the date on which it was *adopted*. For instance, the 1982 Constitution was "passed on 4 December 1982 at the fifth session of the Fifth National People's Congress." This shows that, according to the sense of a relative concept of the Constitution and constitutional laws, the People's Republic of China has issued five constitutional laws, but according to the absolute sense, which declares that a Constitution is the concrete political existence of a polity, there is only one Constitution for the People's Republic of China.[16] This one Constitution shares one view of time.

Unlike the U.S. Constitution of 1787 or the Republic of China Constitution of 1947, the Constitution of the People's Republic of China employs a three-phase view of time. It does not take a two-phase structure of present and future or of God creating, but sees itself as a historical entity with the three phases of past, present, and future. This view of time does not amount to a denial of revolution. However, the revolutions of King Tang and King Wu and the revolutionaries of modern times are not imitations of God. A revolution can be earth-shattering without being an act of original creation. A revolution does not cut history in two or destroy the whole of the past culture. Rather, it simply removes the decayed parts of past history and culture. The success of the revolution forms a new element in the culture. This notion of constitutional time recognizes that the present is the continuation of the past and does not set up the present and the past in opposition. Viewed in the light of this form of constitutional time, the constitutional time that seeks to make a clean break with the past can be seen as a form of historical nihilism.

The draft text for the Preamble to the 1954 Constitution did indeed proclaim the text as China's first Constitution, but this statement was removed from the final version. In discussing the draft Constitution on 14 June 1954, Mao Zedong said,

> Up to the present China has had nine Constitutions, not including draft texts: the Nineteen Constitutional Articles of the Qing dynasty, the Provisional Constitution of the Republic of China of Sun Yat-sen, the Constitution of the Republic of China of Yuan Shikai, the Constitution of Cao Kun, the Constitution of the Republic of China for the Political Tutelage Era, the Constitution of Chiang Kai-shek, the Ruijin Constitution promulgated by the Workers, Peasants Democratic Central Government and the Common Program of the Chinese People's Political Consultative Conference. To say that the present Constitution is the first is incorrect. To say that it is the Constitution of the People's Republic of China is correct.[17]

From the 1949 Common Program to the 1982 Constitution, the history appealed to by China's Constitution is ever larger and more distant. It was the 1982 Constitution that finally placed the whole of Chinese history in its narrative. China's modern revolutionary history became part of China's revolutionary history; modern China became part of historical China. In this sense, the Constitution of modern China has been subsumed into the Chinese constitution that runs continuously from the Shang and Zhou, Qin and Han dynasties up to the present. To understand modern China's Constitution, it is necessary to begin from the constitution of ancient China.

The Sense of Writing about Ancient China's Constitution

Therefore, I believe that Su Li's writing about ancient China's constitution is not due to some form of nationalist self-respect or from a historian's love of past ills. Thirty-two years have gone by since the three key terms—history, culture, and revolution—were written into the first line of the Preamble to the 1982 Constitution, and it is only now that Chinese scholars have realized the connection between history, culture, and revolution and modern China's constitution. However you put it, that day has come too late.

In Su Li's introduction in this book, he identifies three constitutional issues facing ancient China. The first is how to get effective cooperation among people from rural villages scattered over the whole territory of China both in the north and south and how to provide them with an internal order and ensure the long-term maintenance of that order. The second is how to ensure the integration of countless rural villages that would not naturally meet and could be formed into a common polity only with great difficulty, and construct a state, found a dynasty, provide basic peace for the people, and implement effective governance and so gain widespread acceptance among the people and win their allegiance. Third, how, with the central plain as the base, can one effectively repel, oppose, and even actively attack the pastoral peoples to the north, or should one use other "lower-cost" means, such as marriages, paying tribute, or even ceding territory, to make peace with them? How can one actively expand southward and gradually bring the small numbers of people in the tiny states there into the political and cultural tradition centered on the agricultural civilization of the central plain, such that, in many different ways, they can become elements in the constitution of China?[18]

These three issues correspond to the three phrases of the *Great Learning*: to run one's household, govern the state, and bring peace to the world under heaven. Of these, the second, governing the state, is the most important. This most vital constitutional problem that ancient China faced continues to exist down to the present, as Su Li says:

> The reason that the traditional issue of "managing the household" (i.e., rural order) has disappeared is that in new China, state authority has stretched downward. Rural governance has become part of governing the state. . . . Toward the end of the twentieth century, as state power

withdrew from the villages, the issue of managing the family reappeared in "village governance" (the academic term) or "basic political construction in rural villages" (the official term).[19]

It was revolution, and in particular the revolution led by Mao Zedong in the twentieth century, that made the question of regulating the household become that of governing the state, a constitutional issue for modern China. As the influence of Mao's revolution of the twentieth century fades away, so the issue of regulating the household present in ancient China has come back to the surface again, to become something that the constitution of modern China cannot avoid facing. In this sense, the Organic Law of the Villagers' Committees (enacted on a provisional basis in 1987 and amended in 1998 and 2010) should be seen as a law that is constitutive of modern China's Chinese Constitution and we should study its constitutional significance.[20]

We simply mention this one example to indicate how important it is that Su Li has opened this historical and cultural space for us to understand China's constitution. There are many other similar examples. For instance, in attempting to understand the constitution of the People's Republic of China, it has always been difficult to know how to understand the relationship between the Chinese Communist Party and China's constitution. In his article "The Emperor as an Institution" ("Zuowei zhidu de huangdi"), Su Li has begun to explore the role of the position of the emperor in the constitution of ancient China. It is my hope that his ideas will also provide insight and inspiration for understanding the significance of the Chinese Communist Party in the constitution of modern China.

Part III

CHAPTER EIGHT

Response to My Critics

Su Li

I WOULD LIKE to thank the critics and the blind reviewer, less for your specific critical opinions, queries, and suggestions than because you oblige me to look at things from your point of view. Many of your comments may well be those of readers coming from other disciplines. You help me to look at, and reflect on, my own research and a few specific issues. Some of these issues may well be ones that I have perhaps thought about but considered unimportant and therefore left them out or failed to analyze sufficiently, whereas other issues are ones I had not thought about and so they require more thought and a response. Or it may be that I simply took them for granted and did not really grasp them or develop them. But it may also be that what I said here was only a part of my research, a part that was already set out in a complete text, limited by the themes and constraints of that particular text. I cannot develop every point that I have thought about. For organizational reasons, I had to leave some questions for further chapters. But because of this you have both obliged me to reply and given me the chance to respond to some of your questions. My response is still selective. I cannot deal with many particular issues here, but taking your comments and queries as a whole, I will selectively set out my own view and way of thinking. I cannot actually reply to, or resolve, the doubts raised by my critics and reviewers. Some, indeed, are simply highlighting the way in which I judge.

Let me first define my research. This is practical theoretical research about historical China's constitution. My core concern is under what natural constraints and by means of what basic institutions this historical China was formed. This response will focus on setting out the three common issues that run right through the text I have presented. First, this is research into practical theory and not into history. Second, this research seeks to work from an explanation of institutions and not from culture or ideas to clarify the particularity of the constitution (composition and institution) of Chinese history. Third, this research takes constitution as its core concern. How does this differ from the stress on constitutional law that, owing to American influence, has been prevalent from the mid-twentieth century on? Why is it necessary and why should we make this distinction? Finally, I end by reflecting on myself, both as a form of summarizing conclusion and as a self-appraisal.

{≈≈≈≈≈}

Since the presupposition underlying this research is a historical China, it is natural that critics and reviewers will discuss some definite historical facts and institutions and provide relevant information about these. Yet within these questions there lies an important issue that boils down to the question of how one can speak of "one" China in the face of disparate facts and institutions scattered through the long history of dynasties and regimes and found in disparate places. How can one affirm that there is really one China lasting through time and of the same basic nature?

This query is without a doubt well placed. I myself acknowledge that, in fact, there is one such China, existing as basically one entity through the millennia in the approximate geographical area of the present China.[1] And my research does indeed require there to be one China; there must be one such abstract idea of China. If there were not, then it would be necessary to choose some characteristic facts, cut out a lot of other facts, and construct one historical China.

This is because this research is focused on a theoretical problem and is not historical research per se. The core question that runs through my research is how this historical China was formed. Looking back and making a comparison with the various states that have emerged from the past to the present, the most striking features of historical China are that it is a big country with agriculture on the central plain. It has many peoples and tribes. It has been historically divided, yet in terms of civilization it is continuous. Now, what are the most important institutions that have made it so that a historical China has come into existence? What fundamental constraints gave rise to these institutions and enabled them to continue to exist? This basic question means that I cannot limit myself to any one dynasty but rather focus on a historical China that has undergone many developments and revolutions, including having its central plain occupied by northern peoples. I must find in the twists and turns of a complicated history some important institutional threads that, in my view, run through the whole from beginning to end and that have had an influence on the entire area that is China.

Even though many scholars from different fields raise doubts, I still have good reason to set things out this way. In fact, since ancient times traditional

Chinese scholars, and not only historians, all have to some extent spoken of China at some level of abstraction (as, indeed, they must). For instance, historians are accustomed to speaking of the First Emperor of Qin as "abolishing feudalism and instituting commanderies," or again, to saying that "the Han adopted the institutions of Qin." But history was not so simple. The early Han did revive a form of feudalism; Zhu Yuanzhang (Emperor Taizu, 1368–98) of the Ming dynasty also set up a feudal rule. But there is no doubt that later generations all said that "the hundred dynasties all used the administrative laws of the Qin."[2] This is certainly a form of abstraction, a summary view. Indeed, you can even say that it is an exaggeration. In fact, what dynasty or period is there that to some extent does not create or do what later people will describe as a regression, even though contemporaries thought of it as a new creation? For instance, when at the beginning of the Han dynasty Liu Bang (Emperor Gao, 206–195 BC) made princes of the ruling Liu family feudal kings, this was not the same as the feudalism of the Western Zhou. It was also not the same as the commanderies of the Qin. So later persons could say that this move by Liu Bang was a regression from the Qin, but as a politician Liu Bang at the time of the founding of the Han probably could not have had such a view of historical trends or any so-called historical view, and even if he did, he was not concerned with questions of the philosophy of history and whether there was progress or regress. The issue he faced was, above all, a concrete, practical one. He cared for results, and perhaps even immediate and temporary results. He needed to use a pragmatic approach to deal with the problem of "getting warriors to hold down the four quarters."[3]

If we examine many other such institutions, we will find that indeed they certainly went through many changes and variations. For instance, later generations all say that the First Emperor of Qin united the currency, but the order to unify the currency was issued only in the final year of his reign and so we have reason to believe that the Qin did not unify the currency, and this point has been proven by later discoveries of Qin coins.[4] The First Emperor is also credited with unifying Chinese script, but other important dynasties are credited with comparable undertakings.

But these are all concrete questions for historical research, and not my concern. I want to glean from the twists and turns of institutional changes those institutions that I deem to be most important for the constitution/formation of China. To do this I must make choices and engage in abstraction and summarizing. Not only must I leave some things out, but this work of abstraction and summarizing, even if it is only making certain connections, may indeed be a form of creation, or what some scholars may see as editing or even distorting. For instance, in chapter 3, I argue that the elements of a representative system are contained in the criteria by which candidates were selected from different regions in the old systems of civil service exams. This is a case in point. Without a clear and precise description, it is very difficult to make an accurate summary. Yet the success of my research lies not in whether it has lacunae, omissions, errors, or even distortions, but rather in whether, in spite of these, it is reasonable, justifiable, and inspirational overall, can avoid misunderstanding, and is in some way "better" than current analytical theories.

Yet one can still ask if it is right to abstract and summarize in this way, running straight through three thousand years of history across a vast land mass and explaining it all in terms of constitution. In general, people are used to describing and discussing political order by dynasty or even under one reigning emperor. The issue is much bigger than the short span of one person's life and even too large for traditional history and study of institutional change divided into dynasties. But, if the constitution (formation) of historical China over a period of three thousand years does indeed have some foundational institutions, there is indeed an institutional thread and perhaps my theory can stand, for then the allotted time and space are not so enormous. To be honest, there have been other such works.[5] In the context of the three million years of human existence or the half million years since Peking Man, three thousand years seems to be a relatively short period of time. Placed in the wider context of time, the changes in human society that have taken place in this small piece of land are not of such great consequence. Perhaps they are rather like the changes of one month in a person's life. Therefore, it is right to fail to be precise, and indeed one cannot but fail to do so. Concepts and theories ought to be used as tools to help us understand the world and not the other way around. Wittgenstein pointed out that there are some details and accuracies that do in fact make people confused.[6] The same reasoning applies to a discussion of the institutions that have been established in the land of China.

As I see it, given that there are many differences, the question as to how historical China could be integrated is the basic question that constitution must reply to. Within the broad vista I have taken, at least up until modern times, there has been no fundamental change. The key issue has always been how to bring together scattered villages where the sounds of chickens and dogs carry but the people never meet one another. That is how an agrarian society can become one political, economic, and cultural entity, guaranteeing security of life from cradle to grave, with peace now and prosperity for future generations, while also guaranteeing an expansion of territory such that agrarian and pastoral peoples, as well as other peoples, can find some way of living together and what the possible conditions for coming together are. Put simply, this is the Confucian ideal of managing one's household, administering the state, and bringing peace to the world under heaven. These three (household, state, and world under heaven) run right through China's history—at least from an early emergence in the Western Zhou—and have played out in the historical dynasties of China in many different ways. The institutions erected on this land have constantly and repeatedly responded to these problems, in many ways, both positive and negative. In this process, this historical China has been formed and has expanded to become the only continuously existing ancient civilization in human history.

That statement should not be read as a peon of praise, even though as Chinese people we can be proud of our civilization. As a researcher, I know that I must be on my guard against such biases and prejudices, and prevent them from creating blind spots in my work or, even worse, hidden traps. The unique phenomenon of the great continuity of historical China within the context of other ancient civilizations needs to be explained and can be explained. To explain this point, it is possible to see the rise and fall of dynasties throughout this long time and space of historical China as a constantly repeating natural experiment, to varying degrees and within the constraints imposed by natural geography and climate, imperceptibly, individually, and deliberately, or blindly and collectively, following a process of trial and error, replying to the question of China's constitution/formation. On this vast chessboard of time and space, the pieces have been put in place one by one, ultimately giving rise to some basic institutions to administer this land, even if there are many slight variations visible. Yet it is still possible to abstract from them common institutional principles. This is what the aforesaid "unique civilization that has existed continuously up till now" means to my work. It is not merely a cultural prejudice or a show of pride.

It may be that my quest falls into error because, as I have said, the question is one that I have formulated. But even if it is wrong, it is still something that others have sought, too. In the *Records of the Historian*, Sima Qian set himself to look precisely for this: "the word that forms one family throughout heaven and the human world and throughout the changes from past to present."[7] In other words, what he sought was not history but the words of one family, that is, theory. He grounded this search for theory in collating records and organizing the vast corpus of history on a foundation. Later generations would honor him as a historian, but history may not necessarily have been what he himself sought.

My search is not for history, but for theory. But this theory is not historical philosophy or abstract political-social theory. My research is better *classified as* experimental sociology, even if the chapters here do not look very experimental in terms of today's experimental sociology, since they lack systematic data and have no strict statistical analysis. Yet experimental research is not only a matter of data or statistical analysis. Research worth its salt cannot be without the guidance of theory. "Without theory . . . there is nothing that can be handed down, except a vast mass of descriptive material either waiting for a theory or waiting to be burnt."[8] The road I take is broadly that of Coase's new institutional economics.[9] The question that concerns me can even be translated into the type of question raised by Coase. If historical China can be seen as a vast business enterprise, we can ask how the enterprise has come about and what its institutional conditions are. What institutions have been employed, and how has historical China realized its inner constitutive capital? I have simply discussed this institutional question in a broader framework of time and space.

Therefore, I must pay attention to experimental phenomena, namely, the history of China, historical persons and their activities, and historical events. But I cannot list them all one by one, nor am I able to summarize them all. Rather, I have chosen classic people and events as evidence, both for raising questions and for replying to questions. These choices are not because I want to talk about such and such a person or about the event in itself, but so as to highlight some abstract questions that must arise and are therefore genuine. For instance, from among the persons Emperor Wu of the Han gathered about him, Wei Qing, Huo Qubing, Li Guangli, and Huo Guang, the question that I have abstracted is how, for a large state lacking institutions, the central government had great difficulty fairly and effectively choosing a political elite from the whole country to share in the administration of the state. I could have not used these people or this fact to prove my point and simply extrapolated from theory and arrived at the same question. But for Chinese readers, these pieces of evidence are more immediate. At the same time, within the background to these concrete examples implicitly lies an issue of the point in time at which the constitutional question surfaced in historical China. The question did not arise in the Western Zhou because they used feudalism. In the Spring and Autumn and Warring States periods, because the size of the princely states was relatively small and because talented scholars moved freely from one state to another, this question also was not in evidence. The death of the Second Emperor of Qin and the break-up of Qin meant that there was no chance of the question surfacing, and even in the early years of the Han before the accession of Emperor Wu, that is, in the sixty years from 202 to 141 BC, this question was not particularly remarkable or urgent. It was only after the politicians who set up the Han state had all died, and Zhou Yafu (d. 143 BC) had put down the Rebellion of the Seven States and Emperor Wu had actually established uniform rule, that this question began to surface and become ever more urgent in the face of his increasing centralization of power.

Even though this is a discussion of the abstract and theoretical question of the formation of China's constitution, the theoretical model must be able to attract experimental factors that have great explanatory power. For instance, a theoretical model itself is synchronic, but the use of a theory does not exclude time as a constituent factor of theory. Indeed, the time axis is a factor in the formation of an abstract Chinese constitution, because time is empirical and the sequence of time is empirical. For this reason, an effective theory can transcend time in expounding historical experience. Therefore, in my writings I have used examples drawn from later periods or from abroad (for instance, the history of the United States from the formation of the country to the Civil War) to support what I say about the conflict of interests between the early

Han court and the princely states, in order to clarify that even the broadest discussion of constitutional theory cannot resolve immense issues of conflict of interests.[10] However, when looking at the sequence of the empirical facts of relevant historical events, this sequence must be interpreted. For instance, I do not place the feudalism of the Western Zhou in opposition to the commanderies of the Qin and Han, but rather I read the divisions and feudalism of the Western Zhou as the first emergence of a centralized power structure. It was the best possible such structure under the given historical conditions.[11] In the same way, I see the three forms of selecting officials—selection (*tuiju*), recommendation (*chajue*), and examination (*keju*)—as institutional progress under the historical conditions pertaining at each time, and not as the unfolding of some form of idea or a political or moral truth.[12]

{⟨≈≈⟩ɯᶜ≈≈⟩}

Following the guidance of sociological theory, and drawing on the empirical facts found in historical personages and events, I interpret the formation of historical China's institutions. This is what determines my research and differentiates it from historical research and also from political social theory in general. The latter type of research frequently displays a marked teleological goal in its search for universal historical norms or historical trends. It stresses universality or universal applicability, whereas what I am concerned about is the exact opposite, namely, the historical particularity of the formation of China's constitution/formation.

It is just that this particularity is not something that cannot be understood at all, or can be understood only in the context of the Confucian tradition or so-called Chinese culture. In fact, my research shows that I do not support many ideas and methods of research touted by New Confucianism, even though I do support a sympathetic understanding of Chinese history and Confucian thought. My basic search is, within the sphere of historical language, to restore the pragmatic flavor of engaged Confucianism and its real place in administering historical China as shown by empirical research. I am not concerned, like the New Confucians, to restore its status in historical China or to divinize it. The reason I adopt this position is that, as a scholar of jurisprudence and sociology, I acknowledge that there are believers and practitioners who are inner sages and outer kings, and who even to some extent will gain followers and, in this sense, be successful. But I do not really think that society as a whole or a large state or a civilization can rely on individuals becoming inner sages and outer kings, using an idealistic method to achieve this goal by progressing through the stages of "investigating things, extending knowledge, making the will sincere, rectifying the heart/mind, cultivating oneself, managing one's household, administering the state and bringing peace to the world under heaven."[13] Maybe my academic training and academic tradition have already changed me into a materialist and institutionalist. Institutions already imply moral and ethical customs and habits that in modern society have become unofficial institutions that correspond to legal institutions reinforced by the power of the state.

According to my research, some important institutions are indeed rooted in Confucian thought and have led historical China to grow, progress, and form, such as "When the Way runs in the world under heaven . . . rites and music, and military expeditions proceed from the Son of Heaven."[14] This stresses centralized authority. Yet without strong institutionalized restraints, there is nothing else that can be done against those who infringe them except to lament, "If this is acceptable, what is there that is not acceptable?"[15] Hence, what matters is not thought or aspirations alone. What matters is how to put a valuable way of thinking into practice, how to transform it into norms governing institutions, and how to implement those institutions. In fact, if we confine ourselves to thought alone: "Under the wide heaven there is no land which is not the king's; within the land's sea-coasts, there is no-one who is not the king's subject."[16] This is much more explicit as a norm with respect to the centralization of power than the passage from the *Analects* quoted at the beginning of this paragraph. It is also more reasonable, because the notion of king's minister implies both political centralization and local delegation of power as well as a sequence of relationships under very tight conditions. But this aspiration of the Western Zhou had to wait until the Han before it could be implemented and realized in the course of historical institutions before the institutions were complete such that they could integrate historical China into one.

I do not mean to completely debunk the institutional contribution to historical China of Confucianism, but inasmuch as it is institutional, this contribution may be far more restricted to the level of village society, to rural areas that the imperial power did not touch or to places where it may be said "heaven is high and the emperor is far away." By means of institutions such as Confucian moral teaching, family education, and popular customs, the individuality of Chinese people and the villages that relied on the family and to which they belonged were shaped. This was the everyday real world for the common people. But this kind of Confucianism is not that found in the *Rites of Zhou* or that of the Song-Ming School of Principle. Rather, it is a much more local kind of Confucianism. For many reasons and based on much evidence, I am led to say that Confucian teaching could not have shaped the organization and ordering of historical agricultural villages. Rather, it is more probable that the many problems faced by agricultural villages persuaded the villagers there through a process of trial and error to adopt many measures, principles, and institutions to cope. Confucianism simply expressed these norms in a solidified way.[17]

There is still one other way in which the Confucian contribution to historical China's institutions can be expounded. It was only in the many rural villages that an order was possible that did not require the law. This in itself was an advantage to the creation of the political governance of historical China. It not only greatly reduced the need for the political authority of the state and a formal legal system in rural society; it also provided a powerful extrinsic corrective force of regulations and education for rural households and society and the whole of society, because "there are few who are respectful of parents and elder siblings who are keen to offend their superiors; there has never been anyone who, not wanting to offend their superiors, has been keen to cause chaos."[18] Later interpretation building on the original terms and principles led Confucianism to attempt to extend the relationship of father and son in the family to become the model for that between the prince and the minister in political affairs ("at home one practices filial piety; in the state one practices loyalty").[19] Thus, all this can be counted as a contribution from Confucianism to institutions. But I believe that all these ways of speaking require evidence and not merely words. For instance, the expression "at home one practices filial piety; in the state one practices loyalty" is definitely a folk saying and not the result of the implementation of a widespread, long-term political institution, because this expression oversimplifies politics, even ridicules it, as if all one required were loyal ministers. In practice, the experience of historical China shows that it is much more important to have a political elite.

If it is really necessary to stress the point, then, perhaps we can say that Confucian thought provided historical China with a theoretical model for a constitution/politics/law that lasted for twenty-five hundred years. This was a sacred discourse on constitutional theory, of cultivating oneself, managing one's household, administering the state, and bringing peace to the world under heaven. Even if it was not actually put into practice, according to the saying "if you believe, then the spirit is there," Confucianism did indeed uphold the symbolic political role of recognition of a political and cultural elite.

But all in all, the contribution of Confucianism was not that great. For this reason, in the preceding chapters I have not paid much attention to Confucianism. This is not because I have overlooked it. Rather, it is the result of my research. In previous research and in this current research I have paid sufficient attention to Confucian thought and its institutional implementation.[20] I am unable to believe that the constitution of historical China was provided by Confucianism. I also do not believe that Confucianism will have, or should have, any great influence on the constitutional setup of China in the future, even though I believe it will attract, and is worthy of attracting, the attention of some scholars, just as in the West there are scholars who are attentive to Plato and Aristotle. But I do not believe that anyone imagines that Plato and Aristotle have some secret knowledge that can help govern the West or the whole world in the future.

In rejecting a significant contribution by Confucianism to historical China, I use the method of general theoretical abstraction and empirical research, but my research still shows and strives to underline the uniqueness of the formation of China. This uniqueness does not come from an abstract culture, "Chineseness," or a Confucian tradition that has already become a sign for China itself, or from the thought of any other school. It also does not come from any Asian values, or from a necessary response to concrete problems evolved by the people on the land that we now call China. These concrete problems are linked to the fact that the continental mass of East Asia must first deal with the natural geographic and climatic conditions of the middle and lower reaches of the Yellow River and must then go on to the possible ways of adapting to these conditions. Overall, this area is suitable for small-scale agricultural villages, but to manage the frequent flooding of the Yellow River and to prevent the incursion of pastoral peoples from the north, it is necessary that the scattered self-sufficient agricultural villages group together. A common interest in survival led to the appearance of civil authority, then its expansion, extension, and integration, and finally it acquired borders, peoples, and a political state. It became a country or a nation/culture or a state and not only one state among many. It was the lasting product of all the people who took this whole piece of land as their lived environment.

It is impossible that there could be any other large landmass on the globe that has exactly, or even largely, the same geographical and climatic environment. Hence, the problems of existence to which the people of each large area must respond are definitely unique. Thus, consciously or unconsciously, in response to the geographical features they encounter, they will form groups, economic and cultural units, and political groups. Even though today we can call all of these states, they are all different, depending on the various natural geographical and climatic environments they face. In this respect, the constitution/formation of historical China is unique.

This does not mean that we need to develop an ad hoc theory to tackle historical China, or that we require some mystical belief. A diamond is unique, but not because the materials that compose it are unique; its uniqueness simply comes from the unique structure formed by its atoms under particular conditions.

My work does not then stress the uniqueness of China. Still less do I take any uniqueness it might have as a reason for indulging in praise or criticism. I do not even ask the reader to respect Chinese civilization or culture. That form of cultural pluralism betrays an attitude or even political correctness that may be an expression of strong power, a looking down from on high. Likewise, I do not ask that one should treat this uniqueness based on curiosity, superstition, or humility regarding a foreign culture. I simply want to use what I consider to be adapted to the sense of what a normal person can generally understand and the empirical methods used in the social sciences, to *show* how the unique formation/constitution of China came about, under what conditions, and for what reasons. Whether the reader will accept it, or agree with me, has nothing to do with me. I do not mind if I am seen by the reader as being in conflict with an immemorial cultural tradition or its ideas.

Moreover, to emphasize the uniqueness of the constitutional question of historical China does not deny that at other abstract dimensions or levels there may still be comparable or similar points in the constitutional question of other countries. For instance, any large state is bound to come up against some form of the relationship between the center and the periphery. It may naturally encounter conflict between nations, races, or ethnic or other groupings of people. Again, from an abstract point of view, whether large or small, ancient or modern, the political setup of any state may have a strong or weak government, and procedural issues of permission and exercise of power, as well as a functional division of labor. Yet when studying the constitutional questions of other countries and the constitutional measures by which they respond, without at the same time studying purely abstract academic questions such as the types of constitution, I do not think that reflecting on the common problems at the abstract level makes any particular practical sense. Indeed, at times *it may not have any significance even as a point of reference*. There is no sense whatsoever in common knowledge at this abstract level. The only genuine knowledge is that which comes from responding to specific issues. This does not mean that I have a love for exceptions, but rather that the only things that really need to be considered or challenged and that can, finally, increase our reflection and knowledge are what originally seem to be oddities or exceptions. We must certainly avoid cutting them into shape or parceling them up and so forcing them into the mold of what is normal. Perhaps that task does call for much effort, but it has nothing to do with thinking; it is absurd. Everyone faces the issues of food and drink, male-female relationships, life and death, old age and sickness. For instance, does the death of Socrates or his drinking hemlock or his homosexual behavior have referential significance *for me*? Or can I choose to assume that it has none?

My research does not deny that under generally similar natural geographic and climatic conditions, the institutions of neighboring regions (even independent "countries") may be formed in a similar way, for example, the city-states of ancient Greece, the various states of Western Europe, the colonies of North America. As a result, the institutions of these states, including their constitutions, may be copied or transferred from one to another. But this does not mean that the same is possible in all places. In reality, I am not emphasizing this, just pointing it out. Even on our one planet at the same time, the constitutional questions of at least some countries are very dissimilar, and one cannot simply use a universal measure or method to reply to them. Sometimes there is no means of consulting the experience of other countries, nor is there a need to do so. This is especially important for the constitutions of those civilizations or countries in which the responses are to common questions that have occurred or developed only in those unique civilizations and in which one can write only their own history and cannot copy some other country's history. At the same time, because it just so happens that the questions that originally arose in a given country are internal to it, it must create its own response. It would seem to be a case of doing one's own thing. This is a basic feature by which something can be said to be great or unprecedented.

{⸻⸻}

From what has been said above, one could skip the next section on constitutionalism, constitutional law, and the constitution (i.e., formation) that I am stressing here. Yet it would seem that I cannot do so. This is because the constitution that is the formation of the political setup and the constitutional law of the United States are both translated by the same Chinese word, *xianfa* (宪法). Constitutionalism bears the sense of the implementation of a constitutional legal order, but in today's exclusivist definition it tends to refer only to the political setup of nation-states. It has three core characteristics. First, the power of the state comes from a basic law that is called the Constitution and is always exercised under its restraint. Second, the Constitution protects the fundamental rights of each citizen, especially life, property, and liberty, and it also implies that there must be, third, a democratic polity. According to this definition, the written Constitution has become some kind of sacred idea. Many scholars and readers want you, in some way or other, to express an opinion. Even though this is of no help toward understanding my argument, it does help readers to judge the author according to this ideology and to use this evidence to decide whether or not to read my text. They have a right to choose authors and works in this way; authors, however, have great difficulty choosing their readers.

I must state clearly, however, that this idea of a sanctified Constitution is the product of the political facts of Western nation-states, and that it mainly comes from the judicial review system of the United States and a political system in other countries that is not of long duration, having largely begun only after the Second World War. After that war, the influence of the politics, economy, and civilization of the United States was such as to persuade quite a number of countries to adopt a similar political practice. *It would seem* that the results of this have been quite successful in some countries, so much so that today many scholars, political pundits, and political groups in various countries of the world want to promote it throughout the whole world and often use this understanding of a Constitution to judge the Constitutions of other countries and their corresponding political and legal standards.

I do not reject this idea of the Constitution, or the corresponding constitutional practice, or the way in which some people insist on this idea of a Constitution. I am a pragmatist and consequentialist. If there are lasting, good consequences for society, I have no reason to reject them. In the long run I do not think anybody would.

Yet for myself, I think this idea of a Constitution is simply an idea suited to one locality. To adopt it universally would be to give rise to a whole series of practical and theoretical problems. Therefore, it may seem to be a fine idea, but based on my research it is of no practical use.

First, many countries do not hold that the Constitution is a law subject to the judiciary, and therefore there is no meaningful judicial review. The United Kingdom does not even have a written Constitution; the British constitution is made up of laws and, importantly, precedents that are described as constitutional. For a long time, British scholars discussed only the British constitution, and not constitutional law, as in the classic work by Bagehot.[21] Even though there are scholars, such as Dicey, who do discuss British constitutional law, since it is not possible to separate out any strictly constitutional law, it would be very difficult for the United Kingdom to have any judicial review in the strict sense of the word.[22] Furthermore, even when there is a text that bears the name "Constitution," some of these explicitly state that the judges cannot use it to review legislation or treaties, for example, the Constitution of the Netherlands.[23]

Second, even though many states after the Second World War tried to introduce American-style judicial review, the results are dubious to say the least.[24] I say "dubious," and earlier I said that it may seem to be a fine idea, because even if there are exceptions, as in Western Europe, where the political, legal, economic, and social developments would seem to be not bad and worthy of emulation by other states, we do not really know how, or even if at all, this success is related to this form of constitutional practice because there are also examples that prove the opposite. At least there are some states that have borrowed the U.S. Constitution wholesale and on many counts are not particularly good, or are even pretty bad.

Third, from an academic point of view, if we simply acknowledge the modern practice of written Constitutions and their subordination to the judiciary, then it would not only be unfair to the United Kingdom; it would even leave us at a loss in talking about the constitution of ancient Greece. If we go back to the history of the term "constitution," I acknowledge that it implies the constitution of a state or a commonwealth. When a group of people have, by and large, formed a collective body in terms of cultural and social life, as in the city-states or villages of ancient Greece, then this structure is chiefly one of political integration. However, should the political body surpass its traditional community, incorporating a few or several historical links while not yet putting great store on mutual recognition, then this structure will not only require political support, it will also require other forms of support: economic, cultural, social, even linguistic. From a theoretical perspective this structure is a structural framework, but from a chronological perspective it must be a process.

Surely the United Kingdom is just such a society, which is why there is the Magna Carta and a whole series of later texts and many legal precedents. In fact, the same holds true for the United States. The country would seem to have been created by the U.S. Constitution, and according to the same Constitution, but from the American colonies to the Continental Congress, from the

Articles of Confederation to the Federal Constitution, and, even more important, from the Civil War and the Reconstruction of the South, at least to European eyes, it was only after this war that the United States began to be *one*
country. Only then did the U.S. Supreme Court declare that the United States
is *one* indissoluble state composed of indissoluble states.[25] If we talk about
protecting civil rights, then the U.S. Constitution of 1787 deliberately makes
no reference to them.[26] Only in the latter half of the twentieth century did the
American judiciary begin to pay more attention to the question of the citizens'
constitutional rights, largely on the basis of the 1791 Bill of Rights and three
amendments passed during the Civil War. That similar documents were not
created in Africa or Asia may, I am afraid, be due to a few countries in the past,
whose names I will, if you forgive me, avoid mentioning. People forget what
they want to forget and remember what they think worth remembering. In
fact, it was not the text of the U.S. Constitution that created the great United
States of America, but rather the course of American history brought a sacred
luster to the U.S. Constitution. In the course of American history, even though
the U.S. Constitution was an important instrument in protecting civil rights,
yet at least before the Civil War, it would be difficult to say that it was the most
important means of implementation. In fact, it was not. The chief instrument
of a constitutional legal nature that strengthened the bond between the states
and the federal government was the acts governing interstate commerce.[27]
Although they later declined in economic importance at the time of the New
Deal,[28] even into the 1960s the antisegregation movement was still appealing
to the acts governing interstate commerce.[29]

As I have said, the constitution of China happened on the basis of an agrarian civilization by forming a large state that was adequate to regulate the Yellow River and respond to the conflict between a pastoral civilization and an
agrarian one. This was not only a matter of a political constitution, but also
one that established a civilized body, which would join the lands separated by
valleys and mountains into one country. What had to be linked and given at
least a basic degree of assimilation was a large group of people divided into
villages that never communicated with one another and where there was no
knowledge of the Han dynasty let alone the Wei and Jin, so that they would
become one people whom later generations would call the Chinese people. On
this foundation a basic, yet necessary, sociopolitical governance set forth by
the various dynasties, a state, would be established. This process was quite different from what took place with the city-states formed by the ancient Greek
cities working together, or the political consolidation of European feudal states
in the Middle Ages, or the political consolidation of modern nation-states in
Europe, or even the political consolidation of many American colonies into
one federal republican state. In the course of this history and faced with this
geographical space, how can we use today's idea of European-American idea
of constitutionalism as an analytical tool and produce even a basic concordance?

In fact, the idea of constitutionalism faces major challenges in Europe today in the sense of whether the European Union needs to, should, or could constitute a United States of Europe. This has, indeed, been the dream of some Europeans in modern times, starting with Napoleon.[30] If we count from the Coal and Steel agreements of 1951, which inaugurated the European Community, sixty-seven years have passed, but, at least at present, the prospect of greater unity is not bright. Furthermore, what this unity clearly needs goes far beyond a mere written Constitution. It is not only a matter of upholding the rights of the citizens, or simply an issue of judicial review or such political, legal practices. In fact, the Eurozone and the Schengen Agreement are both important institutions and have constitutional importance for the European Union and for the potential United States of Europe, but they cannot be described as constitutional for the member states themselves. Rather, they would be better termed deconstitutional or reconstitutional, since they remove the citizens and the countries from the ambit of nation-states and place them under the aegis of an American-style United States of Europe.

But precisely for this reason, in my view, an overly sacralized concept of constitutionalism that is limited to a given locality is one that is of no use in empirical research. This is especially so for the subject of my research: the constitution/formation of historical China. To attempt to limit the power of the government in a democratic way by a text in an agricultural society of two or three thousand years ago, covering a vast terrain, and to protect the fundamental rights of all the people on this land is just one massive myth. The magic of it all is a bit like saying, "Let there be light! And there was light." A large state can implement only monarchy. This is not something that Chinese people alone say. This is what Montesquieu and Jean-Jacques Rousseau both say, and to a certain extent it is also the consensus of the American Federalist Party.[31]

Moreover, a monarchy does not have to have unlimited powers. The distinction between orthodox and deviant polities/constitutions of both Plato and Aristotle plays a normative role.[32] In China, however, the stress has always been laid on "serving heaven with virtue." If there is no one else, then you must turn to the prince, and all depends on whether or not the people accept him.[33] Therefore, revolution is permissible according to China's history. The term "revolution" is a meaningful one in Chinese and is the greatest restraint placed on the power of the monarch.[34] Centralization of power should not be construed as despotism. The inherited monarchical power of Chinese history and the corresponding power of the secular world have always been in tension with each other and hold each other in check. At the level of local government there has also always been a kind of separation of three powers: the executive (including financial administration), the military, and the supervisory. Of course, the judiciary was not independent, since it was placed under the executive, but is that not also the case with Locke's theory of separation of three powers?[35] This was but a description of the actual relationship of the judiciary and executive in England at the time. Of even greater importance is that the judicial function was virtually the most important role of executive officials in ancient China—the other role being that of collecting taxes—and so, in reality, if one were to give a correct empirical description, then it would be wholly true to say that the executive was normally subordinate to the judiciary at the local level in ancient China.

Given that the bureaucratic structure of historical China was both monarchical and centralized, it was not only composed of an elite, but composed of one that was drawn from all levels of society with a very high social mobility.[36] Furthermore, given the emphasis on recruitment from all localities throughout the country (so much so that from remote areas lacking economic, social, or cultural development there was a form of affirmative action in the choice of officials), the choice of officials in China's elections or examinations always took into account fair representation or had the practical effect of increasing political participation. The aim was to have a political elite that took the *whole world under heaven* as its concern. In fact, in the then conditions of such a large state, it was a way of ensuring that information was conveyed and the state governed effectively by those who enjoyed the greatest level of popular support.

Indeed, there was no Constitution to hold the power of the government in check. The rights of the citizens did not enjoy protection. But this question is vacuous. It is one put by someone who lives in a modern nation-state, or someone who can imagine such a state. Only such a person could ask such a foolish question. It is rather like a peasant imagining that an emperor uses a golden yoke to carry water for his household to use. In traditional agrarian China were there workers or citizens? There were only the people of the state, and the people of those times were not like the people of today. Today the people are citizens. In premodern times, the difference between the people and the citizens lay in that their personal relationship with the state government was different. Early citizens were, by and large, citizens of the same town or had some particular relationship with a city-state. They were members of an urban community and may even have been obliged to take part in the politics of the city-state, with no possibility of exemption.[37] The ordinary people of historical agrarian China, however, passed their lives solely in their native locality, in their own village community, unless they became officials or gentry and joined the political and cultural elite. A well-worn saying in China is that "heaven is high and the emperor far off." It should be recalled that previously I noted that there were still some people "who had no knowledge of the Han dynasty, let alone the Wei and Jin." This means that there were many people who knew nothing of what went on beyond their villages, even that the dynasty had changed hands up to six hundred years previously.

They did not know, not because they did not want to know, but rather because they were confined to a natural and cultural environment in which this was so. Hence, even if state power sought to touch these people, it could hardly do so. There was no way for state power, even in the absence of the restraining force of a Constitution, to assault the rights to life, property, and freedom of the people. The very idea lacks any real basis in fact. The people of historical China were an agrarian people. Beside the issue of war and peace, their rights were *basically* confined to the produce of their own agricultural community, and any increase or decrease was determined by that community.

This is how we can explain why we said that in ancient China the most important task of the lowest tier of executive officials was indeed judicial. They all sat in court apart from when they accepted the grain or labor offered to the emperor by the country gentlemen. Things could not be regulated unless one first made an accusation in court. This role corresponds more closely to the ideal judge of today. Indeed, they were even more cautious and passive than English or American judges in the past. At least there were circuit courts or tribunals in England and the United States, with judges riding their horses all over the place to adjudicate cases.

I have already said that the rights of the people in historical China were *basically* a product of the agricultural communities to which they belonged. This does not imply that the state failed to provide any form of public benefit for the people, even though it was always the case that the ordinary people questioned whether the emperor had any concern whatsoever for their lives. Especially when we judge by modern standards, the state, as represented by the emperor, did indeed provide very little for the people. However, even a little is important. The most important thing was peace in the world: "there is no greater disaster than to have no emperor."[38] The emperor stands for the political order, which is the all-important premise that ordinary people in agricultural communities need in order to have the security within which they can get on with their own lives. There are also other public benefits, such as a unified currency, a unified system of measurements, and the importance of linking the economic life of the different places. Also the smooth running of the political and military center of the state and world peace are very important. But these are qualities that self-sufficient peasant societies are not easily aware of. A unified script and unified code of law also matter for the scholars from among their families in that they afford the possibility of participating in government and make a bureaucracy possible, including allowing for lawsuits to settle major rivalries or cases. Yet none of this is very important to ordinary people, since in rural society there is no writing and disputes are rare.

Hence, in one sense we might say that the people of historical China did enjoy a form of negative freedom with respect to the state. But this was only relative to the state. Even so, I do not intend to paint too rosy a picture of this negative freedom since they still belonged to rural, agricultural communities. I am not a romantic communitarian. I do not believe that rural, agricultural communities are necessarily better. To lie at a distance from the domination and violence of a centralizing and centralized government does not mean that one is far removed from other forms of domination or violence. Any seemingly wonderful society always has its less wonderful side, not only as in Sparta, but also in democratic Athens, where Socrates was condemned to death. But even if we take note of this, where do we go from there? In an agricultural era, who can go far from a community? Going away is a form of self-exile, and that is a kind of punishment and not a form of liberty. Moreover, is freedom something that each person seeks at every moment of the day? Do not free persons in today's society who enjoy a high level of freedom often wonder in their dreams if they are victims of confusion or tragedy?

It is just that I cannot discuss constitutionalism according to the tradition of today's political-legal scholars; I cannot boast of constitutions to the same degree. This is not because I oppose universality on the grounds of upholding China's particularity, but rather because the constitutions and constitutionalism spoken of come from a particular context that is not itself universal. These concepts and the norms they entail are of no use to my empirical research. I am a pragmatist. Theory is my tool. I am sincere but humbly so. I do not believe in the law. Still less do I pretend to seek to implement some kind of theory or other, whether it takes as its tools truth or constitutionalism or democracy.

⟨━━━━⟩

I have responded very selectively to what I think are important questions, that is, I have explained why I use a contemporary way of grappling with the questions that I have studied. At the same time, I have avoided a number of questions I am not able to answer. Hence, my response is not intended to be persuasive. Scholarship is dialogue and exchange of ideas; it does not necessarily lead to communication.

But in conclusion I would like to set out some of the things I have thought about and that are indeed notable weak points in this research.

First, the concrete questions that come up in my research are all ones that my predecessors have already studied and written about in great detail and systematically. I have no original contribution to make, except perhaps in the case of the use of Mandarin Chinese as an official language. My role has been to integrate the scholarship of various disciplines into one from the angle of constitution and illustrate the constitutional significance of the findings of others, alive or dead.

This research is perhaps geared toward the field of constitutional studies in China. The political changes in China in modern and recent times and the fact that China's constitutional studies are wholly imported from the West and lifted out of time and space mean that for more than a hundred years, constitutional studies in China has indeed been lacking any root in historical

China's scholarship. The concerns of China's constitution through the ages cannot be transformed into the language of modern constitutional studies. Many constitutional scholars would seem to discuss many constitutional issues, or criticize social phenomena from a normative standpoint, but they fail to see the constitutional problems of contemporary China and are unable to resolve these problems at a practical level on the basis of the political system. The joke of China's constitutional studies is that for any given question, the Chinese government or any other government has infringed section X of article X of the U.S. Constitution or precedent X. I hope by my research to change that situation. I hope that by following the lines of historical China I can present the constitutional questions, constitutional practices, and constitutional wisdom and teaching of historical China. Even if I fail, my task is still necessary and urgent.

Second, although I am engaged in empirical research and strive to explain the constitution of historical China's political institutions, and make an effort to avoid surreptitiously introducing things only to rely on them as "explanations," I must acknowledge that my research is confined to the tradition of empirical social science and is not strict social science empirical research.

By providing a macrohistorical explanation, I am fully aware that my view of constitution integrates some data and research and even provides new possibilities for understanding and explaining history or historical data. But I also know that all of my explanation is simply in accord in a general sense with current historical sources. Furthermore, I know that "we certainly cannot suppose that even when a general theory satisfies all the observations, it may be taken as proven true."[39] Hence, I cannot be satisfied even if what I say seems to be quite good.

Third, as a pragmatist, I certainly look forward. The reason I have taken the empirical path of social science and sought theory and not the path of history as such is that I am concerned about the constitution of historical China, not entirely out of an academic interest but rather because I want to strive to avoid other concerns that have a negative influence on the possibility of research.

The constitution of historical China is already a fact, a basic political institution. Whether or not it is written into the text of China's current Constitution is not important, since people generally, and consciously, put it into practice in daily life, and so it has become part of China's constitution, as, for instance, in the unification of the script and the spread of *Putonghua* (Mandarin Chinese), even if they do not seem quite so important as they did at first. Similarly, the conflicts between the Protestant Churches and the Catholic Church are not as important today as they were in the past, such that some articles of the Law of Succession, which was once so important in England, have been changed.[40] Or again, the acts governing interstate commerce in the United States rarely give rise to disputes today.

Other questions related to the constitution of historical China and questions about the political constitution of contemporary China may now become important, however, thanks to what began in the nineteenth century (which Li Hongzhang described as "the greatest revolution in millennia") and the contemporary context of far-reaching and fierce international competition. Thus, there are still major disputes over the replacement measures to be taken to deal with issues of a constitutional nature. For instance, the function of the now-abolished state exams has been taken over by university exams and civil service exams, but the inherent factors of political representation have not been addressed. Although contemporary China has reached consensus on using a democratic way of producing a political elite, whether or not this is the best way and how to implement it in daily practice are still matters to be decided. Since the twentieth century, generation after generation of Chinese people have propelled great constitutional revolutions, but some important constitutional issues remain unresolved, including constitutional learning, which was mentioned in the preceding section as something that most Chinese legal scholars take as a universal, but which I hold to be local in nature. I have always said that local knowledge or local products may possibly be of universal significance.[41] However, this general proposition cannot be used to reply to this question: Can a written Constitution, based on democracy and aimed at upholding the rights of citizens, thereby limiting the power of the government—along with judicial review—respond to the problems of contemporary China? Therefore, at the most my research can simply ask us to reconsider the road taken so far, but perhaps more important, it can tell us how we arrived where we are today and how we should go forward into the future.

Bright Hall theory (明堂说): This theory developed out of directives for the months in *Mr Lü's Spring and Autumn Annals*: twelve records. The Bright Hall is the architecture in which the king worships his ancestors and heaven, and transforms the will of heaven into his teaching and governance. Therefore, the theory emphasizes that the construction of the hall should observe certain rules of the interaction between heaven and humankind.

circle of the five virtues (五德终始说): This vision of history derives from Zou Yan, a representative of the *yin-yang* school in the Warring States period. The five virtues refer to those represented by metal, wood, water, fire, and earth. The five elements and their virtues revolve, constituting a circle. A dynasty corresponds to a certain element and the corresponding virtue. Therefore, the vicissitudes of history can be explained by the revolving of the circle.

commandery system (郡县制): Antithetical to the feudal system, this concept refers to the direct rule that a centralized empire established between the central government and local governments. It was named after many kingdoms' practice of dividing territories into prefectures (commanderies) and counties in the Warring States period. The system was promulgated by the unified Qin Empire and consolidated during the Han dynasty. Since it highlights the direct rule of the central government rather than self-governance by local aristocrats, this term was still used after the Yuan dynasty when the provincial system was promulgated.

constitution: In contrast to the formalistic understanding of constitution as constitutional law regulating political life from above, Su Li uses this term to refer both to the action of constituting a political community and to the fundamental institutions that play a constituting role. Some of these functioning institutions may take the form of law, but most of them work in a less explicit way. Constitution in this sense is synonymous with the concept of "effective constitution."

Gongyang school (公羊学): Based on the written version of the oral commentary on the *Spring and Autumn Annals* by Gongyang Gao (a legendary author in the Warring States period), this school of Confucianism prospered during the Han dynasty, and culminated in Dong Zhongshu's theory. Compared to the other two schools of commentary on the *Spring and Autumn Annals*, the Gongyang school highlights the role of Confucius as a lawgiver, and tends to decipher his intentions between the lines. This school created many new theories to legitimate the new empire, including the theory of the grand unity (大一统), the theory of bridging three traditions (通三统), the theory of distinguishing the interior and the exterior (异内外), and others. During the Han dynasty, this school also highlighted the use of divination as a form of interaction between heaven and humans. The Gongyang school declined after the Han dynasty but revived in the mid-Qing period, achieving new heights in Liao Ping and Kang Youwei's Confucian theories.

grand unity (大一统): This concept derives from the interpretation of the *Spring and Autumn Annals* by the Gongyang school scholars. Literally, it means "respect the great unity." The unity refers to the emperor's authority to integrate the land into a whole. As a theory cherishing and legitimating the new centralized empire vis-à-vis the previous feudal order, it was adopted as the official doctrine of the Han dynasty beginning with Emperor Wu.

imperial examination system (科举): Starting from the Sui dynasty, this institution of official personnel recruitment became widely utilized as an important path to office in the mid-Tang dynasty. Beginning with the Song dynasty, the system was regularized and developed into a roughly three-tiered ladder (*xiucai, juren, jinshi*) from local to provincial and then court exams. The core of the institution was the written examination based on knowledge of the Confucian classics and literary style. Open to the majority of the population, the examination helped to create a common elite culture and the ideal of achievement by merit to legitimate imperial rule. The abolition of this system in 1905 led to the alienation of many members of the local gentry from their Manchu rulers.

political meritocracy (贤能政治): The idea that the political system aims to select and promote public officials with superior intelligence and virtue by means such as examinations, recommendations, and performance evaluations at lower levels of government.

principle of heaven (天理): This is a core concept of Neo-Confucianism. Since the Song dynasty, in a state now unambiguously based on bureaucratic instruction rather than aristocratic fealty, leading literati, troubled by the gulf between factual arrangements and moral substance and influenced by the philosophies of Buddhism and Daoism, responded by developing a worldview based on the concept of Tianli, the principle of heaven as the final criterion of truth, beauty, and goodness. Tianli was universal and intrinsic in the order and movement of things. The rise of this concept made it possible to develop an abstract Confucian philosophy, and also led to a relative decline in textual learning (经学), the philological study of Confucian classics.

recommendations (察举): An institution of official personnel recruitment prevailing during the Han and Sui dynasties. Local magistrates selected capable and virtuous persons from their jurisdiction and recommended them to higher authorities, but there was some form of investigation and examination before appointment. Compared to the previous institution of selections (推举), it has an element of examination; compared to the later imperial examination system, it still has the residue of recommendation and is less open to the general public.

the Guan Learning (关学): This was a sect of the Confucian School of Principle (理学) in the Northern Song period. Originating from Shen Yan and Hou Ke, the sect was formally founded by Zhang Zai and acquired its name from Zhang Zai's hometown, Guanzhong (关中, the central Shaanxi plain).

theory of the three traditions (三统说): This concept also derives from the interpretation of the *Spring and Autumn Annals* by Gongyang school scholars. According to the theory, history revolves through three traditions dominated by three ruling forces. Each dynasty receives legitimacy from the mandate of heaven and corresponds to a certain ruling force; therefore, the founding emperor of a new dynasty should reset chronology and official uniforms, but maintain cardinal social relations and the way of life. The theory of bridging the three traditions (通三统) is a part of this doctrine. It emphasizes that the current emperor should build historical continuity with the previous two dynasties. Some intellectuals in mainland China use this theory analogously, emphasizing that the Chinese Communist Party should establish a historical continuity between the classical tradition, Mao's tradition, and Deng's tradition.

tributary system (朝贡体系): This was the mutually beneficial network of trade and foreign relations between China and its tributaries, premised on the belief that China was the cultural center of the world and that foreigners were "less civilized" or "barbarians." Although the interstate relationships were symbolically unequal under this system compared to the Westphalian system in Europe, the imperial court usually offered more extravagant gifts in return to its tributaries and did not interfere with their internal affairs, in sharp contrast to modern colonialism and imperialism. This system dissolved after the invasion of Western powers in the nineteenth century. In this book, Su Li connects the tributary system with *Ping Tianxia*, bringing peace to the world under heaven.

Editors' Introduction

1. See Yanfu, "Xianfa dayi" [The Essence of Constitution], in *Yan Fu Ji* [The Collected Works of Yan Fu], ed. Wang Shi (Beijing: Zhonghua Book Company, 1986), 239.

2. For a discussion of Politeia in the ancient Greek contexts, see A. H. J. Greenidge, *A Handbook of Greek Constitutional History* (London: Macmillan, 1914), 4–6.

3. See Walter Bagehot, *The English Constitution* (Cambridge: Cambridge University Press, 2001).

4. See Carl Schmitt, *Constitutional Theory*, trans. Jeffrey Seitzer (1928; repr., Durham, N.C.: Duke University Press, 2008), 59–66.

5. See Su Li, "Zaoqi rujia de renxingguan" [The Early Confucian View of Human Nature], *Law and Social Development* 5 (2010): 3–14; Su Li, "Dangdai Zhongguo de zhongyang yu difang fenquan: chongdu Mao Zedong 'Lun shida guanxi' diwujie" [Contemporary China's Separation of Power between Central and Local Governments: Rereading Section 5 of Mao Zedong's "On the Ten Major Relationships"], *Chinese Social Sciences* 2 (2004): 42–55.

6. Su Li, *Fazhi jiqi bentu ziyuan* [Rule of Law and Its Indigenous Resources] (Beijing: China University of Political Science and Law Press, 2004). This book was translated into Vietnamese in 2016, but no English translation is available yet.

7. Fei Xiaotong, Gary G. Hamilton, and Wang Zheng, trans., *From the Soil: The Foundations of Chinese Society* (Berkeley: University of California Press, 1992).

8. See Su Li, *Song Fa Xia Xiang* [Sending Law to the Countryside] (Beijing: China University of Law and Political Science Press, 2000). For a discussion in the Anglophone world, see Frank K. Upham, "Who Will Find the Defendant if He Stays with His Sheep? Justice in Rural China," *Yale Law Journal* 114 (2005): 1675.

9. See Su Li, *Daolu Tongxiang Chengshi* [The Road to the City] (Beijing: Law Press, 2004).

10. For the distinction between etic and emic, see Thomas N. Headland, Kenneth Pike, and Marvin Harris, eds., *Emics and Etics: The Insider/Outsider Debate* (Newbury Park, Calif.: Sage, 1990).

11. Su Li, "Zuowei zhidu de huangdi" [The Emperor as an Institution], *Law and Social Sciences* 13 (2013): 153–92.

12. Su Li, "Xianzheng de Junshi Suzao" [How the Military Shapes the Constitution], *Faxue Pinglun* [Law Review] 1 (2010): 1–16.

13. Su Li, "Qi Jia: Fucizixiao yu Zhangyouyouxu" [Governing the Family: Let the Father Be Affectionate and the Son Be Dutiful and Let Elders and Juniors Each in Their Places], *Fazhi yu Shehui Fazhan* [Law and Social Development] 2 (2016): 100–113.

14. Su Li, "A Response to My Critics," 224.

15. Samuel P. Huntington, *The Clash of Civilizations and the Remaking of World Order* (New York: Simon & Schuster, 1996), 56–80.

Introduction

1. Adam Ferguson, *An Essay on the History of Civil Society* (Cambridge: Cambridge University Press, 1995), 119.

2. Cf. Richard A. Posner, "The Homeric Version of the Minimal State," in *The Economics of Justice* (Cambridge, Mass.: Harvard University Press, 1983), 119–45; and William Ian

Miller, *Bloodtaking and Peacemaking: Feud, Law, and Society in Saga Iceland* (Chicago: University of Chicago Press, 1990).

3. Perhaps the earliest example of such an assemblage is that of Bolingbroke: "By a constitution we mean . . . that assemblage of laws, institutions and customs derived from certain fixed principles of reason, directed to certain fixed objects of public good, that compose the general system, according to which the community has agreed to be governed." Henry St. John Bolingbroke, "Dissertation upon Parties, Letter X," in *Political Writings*, ed. David Armitage (Cambridge: Cambridge University Press, 1997), 88.

4. U.S. Supreme Court Justice Robert H. Jackson pointedly noted, in *Terminiello v. City of Chicago*, 337 U.S. 1 (1949), that if the U.S. Constitution is interpreted literally without any practical wisdom, it becomes a suicide pact. With regard to the terrorist attacks of 11 September 2001, see Ronald Dworkin, "The Threat to Patriotism," *New York Review of Books*, 28 February 2002; Alan M. Dershowitz, "Wiretaps and National Security Surveillance" and "Torture of Terrorists: Is It Necessary to Do and to Lie about It?," in *Shouting Fire: Civil Liberties in a Turbulent Age* (Boston: Little, Brown, 2002); and Richard A. Posner, *Not a Suicide Pact: The Constitution in a Time of National Emergency* (Oxford: Oxford University Press, 2006).

5. According to Mencius, there were three factors that led to the formation of feudal states in the Spring and Autumn period: land, people, and politics (*Mencius* 7B 28, Legge 2:492). These three elements are basically those that constitute a state today, with the addition of sovereignty.

6. Cf. Ingo Müller, *Hitler's Justice: The Courts of the Third Reich*, trans. Deborah Lucas Schneider (Cambridge, Mass.: Harvard University Press, 1991); Richard A. Posner, "Review of Ingo Müller, *Hitler's Justice: The Courts of the Third Reich*," *New Republic* 36 (17 June 1991).

7. Jill Lepore, "The Rule of History, *Magna Carta*, the Bill of Rights, and the Hold of Time," *New Yorker*, 20 April 2015.

8. Therefore, the study of constitutional law in the United States cannot but trace the Constitution back to preindependence times. See Paul Brest, Sanford Levinson, J. M. Balkin, Akhil Reed Amar, and Reva B. Siegel, *Processes of Constitutional Decision Making: Cases and Materials*, 5th ed. (New York: Aspen, 2006). Even though this book is about constitutional law, it includes pre-Constitution American society and the Declaration of Independence within its purview. The first disputed point at the constitutional level that it discusses is the legitimacy of the Bank of North America, set up by the Continental Congress held before the Constitution was promulgated.

9. "The Union existed before the Constitution," *United States v. Curtiss-Wright Export Corp.*, 299 U.S. 304 (1936).

10. Common Program of the Chinese People's Political Consultative Conference, adopted by the first plenary session of the Chinese People's Political Consultative Conference on 29 September 1949.

11. "A hundred generations all followed the politics and law of Qin" (Mao Zedong, "Qilui: du 'fengjianlun' cheng Guo-lao" [Seven-Character Poem: On Reading "A Discourse on Feudalism" for Guo Moruo], in *Mao Zedong's Writings after 1949*, vol. 13 [Beijing: Central Party Literature Press, 1998], 361). Also Qian Mu, *Qin-Han shi* [A History of the Qin and Han] (Hong Kong: Joint Publishing Company, 2004). In discussing the "political setup" of Han times, he discusses the relationship between the center and the localities—feudalism against commanderies and counties, the formation of the organizations at the central and local levels—central officialdom and local officialdom, and ranks in the feudal hierarchy. Other scholars, including myself, used to hold similar views. See Feng Xiang, *Zhengfa biji* [Notes on Politics and Law] (Nanjing: Jiangsu People's Press, 2004; rev. ed., Beijing: Peking University Press, 2012); Su Li, "Dangdai Zhongguo de zhongyang yu di-

fang fenquan"; and Qiang Shigong, "Zhongguo xianfa zhong de buchengwen xianfa: lijie zhongguo xianfa de xinshijiao" [The Unwritten Constitution in China's Constitution: A New Way of Understanding China's Constitution], *Open Times* 12 (2009): 10–39.

12. For a discussion of what law is, see Richard A. Posner, "What Is Law, and Why Ask?," in *The Problems of Jurisprudence* (Cambridge, Mass.: Harvard University Press, 1990), 220–44.

13. "At sunrise we go to work; at sunset we take our rest. We dig wells and drink; plough fields and eat. What has the Lord's power to do with us?" *Song of the "Bowls" Players*, available at http://ctext.org/wiki.pl?if=gb&chapter=286074. This poem is alleged to date from the time of Yao, in the twenty-fifth century BC, four centuries before China's earliest dynasty, Xia. Although this date of composition is unreliable, we can still appreciate it as an expression of the people's attitude.

14. Wang Yumin says, "according to documentary evidence, in the three millennia from the pre-Qin era until Liberation in 1949, the banks of the lower Yellow River were breached 1,593 times, an average of twice every three years. The river changed course drastically 26 times." Wang Yumin, *Zhongguo lishi dili gailun* [An Introduction to the Historical Geography of China] (Beijing: People's Education Press, 1987), 50.

15. For the influence of hydraulic management on the state institutions of ancient China, see Karl A. Wittfogel, *Oriental Despotism: A Comparative Study of Total Power* (New Haven, Conn.: Yale University Press, 1967).

16. In the Spring and Autumn era, Guan Zhong (管仲) has pointed out, "One who is good at running a state should first do away with the five harms. . . . Of these five harms water is the gravest. Once the five harms have been eliminated the people can be governed" (*Guanzi* 57 Managing the Land, http://ctext.org/guanzi/du-di#2). Following a plan proposed by Guan Zhong, the first of the five hegemons of the Spring and Autumn era, Duke Huan of Qi, undertook a great task, namely, to get the feudal princes to draw up a contract to regulate the waters and prevent flooding and to forbid "dykes to be turned into ditches" (ibid.).

17. The earliest documentary record is from the Western Zhou, when the northwestern pastoral peoples invaded Xianyang (咸阳) and killed King You of Zhou (周幽王), forcing King Ping (平王) to move the capital east, giving rise to the Eastern Zhou dynasty. According to the *Records of the Historian* (149), under Guan Zhong's direction, Duke Huan of Qi (齐桓公) "respected the king and repelled the Yi barbarians." He worked with the other feudal princes to attack the northern nomadic peoples, something that won Guan Zhong praise from Confucius (*Analects* 14:17, Legge 1:282). But from this praise we can see that the threat was already very serious. In the Warring States period, in order to stand up militarily to the northern nomadic peoples (胡人, the Hu) effectively, King Wuling of Zhao (赵武灵王) undertook perhaps the first recorded military revolution in Chinese history, which was, in fact, also an important political and social revolution, "the wearing of barbarian costume (i.e., trousers) by mounted archers." Sima Qian, *Records of the Historian* 43 *The Hereditary Family of Zhao* 65 (http://ctext.org/shiji/zhao-shi-jia).

18. On the decisive role played by mounted soldiers in conflicts between pastoral peoples and rural peoples as it refers to Chinese history, see Yan Gengwang, *Zhishi sanshu* [Three Books on the Study of History], vol. 2 (Shanghai: Shanghai People's Press, 2011), 11; for Western history, see Jared Diamond, *Guns, Germs, and Steel: The Fates of Human Societies* (New York: Norton, 1997), 76–77.

19. Lucian W. Pye, "China: Erratic State, Frustrated Society," *Foreign Affairs*, Fall 1990, 58.

20. If we measure by the standard of its time, China was the third largest state in the world. The borders of today's China are nowhere near as great as they were under the Yuan and Qing dynasties or even when the Republic of China was founded in 1912.

21. Here we refer to the territory we call China, where "times of partition and division are the longest whilst times of unity are very short. Once there was a monarchy in the

central plain periods of unity were just slightly less than those of partition. However before the Yuan dynasty partition was more common, whilst afterwards the country remained basically united." Ge Jianxiong, *Tongyi yu fenlie: Zhongguo lishi de qishi* [Unity and Division: Lessons from Chinese History] (Hong Kong: Commercial Press, 2013), 83.

22. Cai Yan, "Resentment," in *Gushiyuan* [The Origin of Ancient Poetry], ed. Shen Deqian (Beijing: Zhonghua Book Company, 1963), 63.

23. Apart from vague ideas such as "great harmony under heaven" or "all under heaven is for everyone" or "treat the elders in your own family with the reverence due to age so that the elders in the families of others shall be similarly treated; treat the young in your own family with the kindness due to youth so that the young in the families of others shall be similarly treated" (*Mencius* 1A 7: 12, Legge 2:143), pre-Qin Confucianism didn't make significant contributions to drawing a practical scheme and proposing feasible institutional measures for a large-scale unified political community. However, post-Qin Confucians gradually accepted the end of feudal society and began to conceive of the unity of the empire.

24. Early China had no metropolis (都市), but there was no lack of cities (城市). As long as some rudimentary political bodies emerged, there would be political centers or *cheng* (城, walled towns). Military conflict between early Chinese states or the need to resist invasions from the northern pastoral peoples led to the emergence of many walled towns or garrisons (镇, *zhen*). They did indeed seem much like cities because the large number of inhabitants attracted much trade and commerce. However, in fact, these walled towns and garrisons were political and military centers placed over a vast agricultural area. As their name suggests, their major role was as military garrisons and as moated and walled towns. On walled towns, market towns, and garrisons, see Fei Xiaotong, "Xiangtu chongjian" [Rural Reconstruction], in *Xiangtu Zhongguo* [Rural China] (Shanghai: Shanghai Century, 2007), 253–67.

25. This does not mean that these constitutional issues for historical China have completely changed in modern times. Even if they are refashioned, they continue in one way or another and remain important. In 1950 Mao Zedong said, "The unification of our country, the unity of our people and the unity of our various nationalities—these are the basic guarantees for the sure triumph of our cause." Mao Zedong, "On the Correct Handling of Contradictions among the People," *People's Daily*, 19 June 1957, reproduced at https://www.marxists.org /reference/archive/mao/selected-works/volume-5/mswv5_58.htm. This is simply to express the matter in today's vernacular Chinese. In the body of the modern nation-state, even in a China with united sovereignty, the problems of governing the state and bringing peace to the world under heaven still exist. The reason that the traditional issue of "managing the household" (i.e., rural order) has disappeared is that in new China, state authority has stretched downward. Rural governance has become part of governing the state (see Huang Renyu, *Zhongguo da lishi* [China: A Macro History] [Beijing: Joint Publishing, 1997]). Toward the end of the twentieth century, as state power withdrew from the villages, the issue of managing the family reappeared in "village governance" (the academic term) or "basic political construction in rural villages" (the official term). There are quite a few studies on this topic; see He Xuefeng, *Xin xiangtu Zhongguo: zhuanxingqi xiangcun shehui diaocha biji* [New Rural China: Notes from a Survey of Rural China at a Time of Transition] (Guilin: Guangxi Normal University Press, 2003) and *Cunzhi moshi: ruogan anli yanjiu* [The Village Model: A Study of Some Key Cases] (Jinan: Shandong People's Press, 2009).

26. Editors' note: Wang Mang (46 BC–23 CE) began as a minister of the Western Han dynasty, usurped imperial power, and established a new dynasty, Xin, which lasted for only fifteen years. He was a Confucian idealist who attempted to restore many ancient institutions of the Zhou dynasty but failed miserably.

27. Cf. Zhu Yongjia, *Shang Yang bianfa yu Wang Mang gaizhi: Zhongguo lishishang de liangci zhuming gaige* [Shang Yang's Reforms and Wang Mang's Regime Change: Two

Famous Revolutions in Chinese History] (Beijing: China Chang'an Press, 2013). But this expression comes from American scholars discussing the U.S. Constitution; see William N. Eskridge, Jr. and Sanford Levinson, eds., *Constitutional Stupidities, Constitutional Tragedies* (New York: New York University Press, 1998).

28. On the law of necessity, see Richard A. Posner, *Law, Pragmatism, and Democracy* (Cambridge, Mass.: Harvard University Press, 2003), chap. 8, and Posner, *Not a Suicide Pact.*

Chapter One: The Constitution of the Territory and Politics of a Large State

1. *Book of Poetry* II.6.1 "North Mountain," Legge 4:360.

2. *Sayings of the States* 1 *Sayings of Zhou* A10, http://ctext.org/guo-yu/zhou-yu-shang/zh.

3. *Song of the "Bowls" Players*, http://ctext.org/wiki.pl?if=gb&chapter=286074.

4. *Daodejing*, chap. 80.

5. Tao Yuanming, "Peach Blossom Spring," in *Anthology of Chinese Literature*, vol. 1: *From Early Times to the Fourteenth Century*, edited by Cyril Birch (New York: Grove Press, 1965), 167–68, http://afe.easia.columbia.edu/ps/china/taoqian_peachblossom.pdf.

6. Editors' note: In his "Peach Blossom Spring" mentioned earlier, Tao describes a Peach Blossom Land free from poverty, war, and anxiety, which is often seen as the Chinese equivalent of Thomas More's Utopia.

7. Cf. Su Li, "Introduction," 22.

8. According to the *Huainanzi*: *Attending to Duties* and on archaeological evidence provided by research into the Erlitou site, Song Zhenhao has estimated the population of the Xia to be between 2.4 million and 2.7 million (Song Zhenhao, *Xia-Shang shehui shenghuo shi* [A History of Social Life under the Xia and Shang Dynasties] [Beijing: Chinese Academy of Social Sciences, 1994], 100, 107). For the Western Zhou, Shen Changyun has estimated a figure of more than 7 million, whereas Pang Zhuoheng has given the figure of 10 million at its height. See Shen Changyun, "Xi Zhou renkou lice" [A Rough Estimate of the Population of the Western Zhou], *Journal of Chinese Social and Economic History* 1 (1987): 100, and Pang Zhuoheng, "Guanyu xi Zhoude laodong shengchan fangshi, shengchanlü he renkou guce" [Methods of Production, Productivity and an Estimate of the Population of the Western Zhou], *Journal of Tianjin Normal University (Social Sciences)* 5 (1998): 41–50, 48.

9. Alexander Hamilton, James Madison, and John Jay, *The Federalist Papers* (1788; repr., Watertown, Wis.: Tribeca Books, 2010), esp. docs. 9 and 10.

10. There were three forms of constitution for the ancient Greek city-states: monarchy, oligarchy, and majority rule, each of which could be healthy or unhealthy. These ideas were quite widespread later. See Plato, *Statesman*, ed. Julia Annas and Robin Waterfield (Cambridge: Cambridge University Press, 1995), 54; Aristotle, *The Politics*, rev. ed., trans. T. A. Sinclair, revised by Trevor J. Saunders (Harmondsworth: Penguin, 1981), 186–90.

11. "Scottish Referendum: Scotland Votes 'No' to Independence," *BBC News*, 19 September 2014, http://www.bbc.com/news/uk-scotland-29270441.

12. There are scholars who, with good reason, repudiate the idea of using the relation of the center to the localities to talk about Western Zhou feudalism; see Zhou Zhenhe, *Zhongguo difang xingzheng zhidushi* [A History of Local Administration in China] (Shanghai: Shanghai People's Press, 2005), 9–14.

13. Cf. Xu Zhuoyun, *Xizhou shi* [A History of the Western Zhou], rev. ed. (Hong Kong: Joint Publishing Company, 1993), chap. 5.

14. Ibid., 165.

15. Cf. Ge Jianhong, *Zhongguo lidai jiangyude bianqian* [Border Shifts in the Course of Chinese History] (Hong Kong: Commercial Press, 1997); Gu Jiegang and Shi Nianhai,

Zhongguo jiangyu yangeshi [A History of the Evolution of China's Borders] (Hong Kong: Commercial Press, 2000). Translator's note: the four tribal names refer to the barbarians of the west, north, south, and east, respectively.

16. Zhou Zhenhe, *Zhongguo difang xingzheng zhidushi*, 226–28.

17. Ban Gu, *Han History*, treatise 10, literature 349, http://ctext.org/han-shu/yi-wen -zhi/zh.

18. Zhou Zhenhe, *Zhongguo difang xingzheng zhidushi*, 228.

19. It is said of the Western Zhou that "seventy-one states were established, out of which fifty-three were given to princes surnamed Ji" (*Xunzi* 5 *Ru Xiao* 1, http://ctext .org/xunzi/ru-xiao/zh). *Zuo's Commentary*, however, says "fifteen of his brothers received states and forty princes surnamed Ji also did so" (*Zuo's Commentary* 10 Duke Zhao year 28, Legge 5:727).

20. "Care for your parents when they are at the end of their lives and continue to rever-ence them by sacrifices when they are gone, and the virtue of the people will be restored to wholeness" (*Analects* 1.9, Legge 1:141).

21. Friedrich Nietzsche, *The Will to Power*, ed. Walter Kaufmann, trans. Walter Kauf-mann and R. J. Hollingdale (New York: Vintage, 1967), 387n732.

22. "In the *Spring and Autumn Annals*, there are thirty-six cases of regicide and fifty-two cases of the extinction of a state, while the cases of feudal lords who fled without being able to protect their altars of grain and soil are innumerable." Sima Qian, *Records of the Historian* 130 *Postface by the Grand Astrologer*.

23. *Analects* 16 *Ji Shi* 2, Legge 1:310.

24. *Hanfeizi* 8 *Wielding Power* 1, http://ctext.org/hanfeizi/zh (cf. Burton Watson, trans., *Han Feizi: Basic Writings* [New York: Columbia University Press, 2003], 35).

25. Su Li, "Jingying zhengzhi yu zhengzhi canyu" [Elite Politics and Participation in Politics], *Chinese Journal of Law* 5 (2013): 77–92.

26. *Mr Lü's Spring and Autumn Annals*, chaps. 66, 100, and 99, http://ctext.org/lv -shi-chun-qiu/zh.

27. Zhao Dingxin, "Warfare in the Eastern Zhou and the Rise of the Confucian-Legalist State" (presentation at the University of California, Los Angeles, 10 October 2006), http:// web.international.ucla.edu/institute/event/5207.

28. Sima Qian, *Records of the Historian* 6 *Annals of the First Emperor of Qin*, Yang and Yang, *Selections from "Records of the Historian,"* 168. See also Hou Xiaorong, *Qindai zhengqu dili* [Administrative Division in the Qin Dynasty] (Beijing: Social Sciences Aca-demic Press, 2009).

29. Sima Qian, *Records of the Historian* 8 *Annals of Emperor Gaozu*, 55 *The Hereditary Family of Marquis Liu*, 87 *Biography of Li Si*.

30. Sima Qian, *Records of the Historian* 9 *Annals of Empress Lü* 7, Watson, *Records of the Grand Historian: Han Dynasty I*, 271, http://ctext.org/shiji/lv-tai-hou-ben-ji/zh.

31. *Han History: Biographies* 18 *Jia Yi* 10, http://ctext.org/han-shu/jia-yi-zhuan/zh.

32. Sima Qian, *Records of the Historian* 11 *Annals of Li Jing* 11. The text was subse-quently altered to "taking away barbarians lands."

33. Sima Qian, *Records of the Historian* 112 *Biography of the Marquis of Ping Jin and Zhufu*. Translator's note: Emperor Wu of the Han allowed sons of the feudal lords to revert to the titles their fathers had been deprived of.

34. On the pre–Civil War constitutional debate between Lincoln and Douglas, see Harry V. Jaffa, *Crisis of the House Divided: An Interpretation of the Issues in the Lincoln–Douglas Debates*, 50th anniversary ed. (Chicago: University of Chicago Press, 2009); see also Don E. Fehrenbacher, "The Dred Scott Case," in *Quarrels That Have Shaped the Con-stitution*, rev. ed., ed. John A. Garraty (New York: Harper & Row, 1987).

35. For example, the purpose of the institution of military inspectors inaugurated by the Western Han was to use lower officials to supervise high-ranking local officials, but toward the end of the Eastern Han the military inspectors became regional commissioners, the first rank of administration in the commanderies and counties, with power over the army, administration, and supervision of the whole region. This ultimately brought about the military breakup of the Han and the subsequent wars and chaos. In the time of the Xuanzong Emperor in the Tang dynasty, the post of military governor was established to give unilateral command over military affairs on the vast frontiers so as to fight incursions by the northern pastoral peoples. But later, as military direction and preparedness were sorted out, the military governor's powers expanded to include power over the military and administrative, financial, and supervisory functions. Since many tasks were interrelated, the Tang also often allowed one person to be in charge of several garrisons. Clashes at court also led to low-status barbarians being commissioned as military governors, which ultimately led to the chaos of the An Lushan Rebellion.

36. Mao Zedong, "Qilui: du 'fengjianlun' cheng Guo-lao," 361.

37. Mao Zedong, "Zhongguode hongse zhengquan weishenme nenggou cunzai?" [Why Is It That Red Political Power Can Exist in China?] (5 October 1928), https://www.marx ists.org/reference/archive/mao/selected-works/volume-1/mswv1_3.htm; "Jinggangshan de douzheng" [The Struggle in the Jinggang Mountains] (25 November 1928), https://www .marxists.org/reference/archive/mao/selected-works/volume-1/mswv1_4.htm; "Xingxing-zhihuo keyi Liaoyuan" [A Single Spark Can Start a Prairie Fire] (5 January 1930), https:// www.marxists.org/reference/archive/mao/selected-works/volume-1/mswv1_6.htm.

38. Gu Zuyu, *Dushi fangyu jiyao* [Important Notes on Reading the Geography Treatises in the Histories], ed. He Cijun and Shi Hejin (Beijing: Zhonghua Book Company, 2005), 2.

39. Gu Zuyu, *Dushi fangyu jiyao*, 2449, 2500. Also Zhao Dingxin, "Warfare in the Eastern Zhou," 142.

40. The most prominent geopolitical effect of Meng Kuo's restoration of the Great Wall was that "the Xiongnu withdrew over 700 *li*; the barbarians no longer dared come south to pasture their horses" (Jia Yi, *New Book* 1A, available at http://ctext.org/xin-shu/guo-qin -shang/zh).

41. Gu Zuyu, *Dushi fangyu jiyao*, "Preface 3," 18.

42. "The strategic geography of the empire lies in mountains and rivers; the key to mountains and rivers lies in cities and towns"; "*Mountains and rivers should be made secure and prefectures and frontier districts be separated*, geopolitical power arises between them." Gu Zuyu, *Dushi fangyu jiyao*, "Overview," 1 (emphasis added).

43. Sima Qian, *Records of the Historian* 55 *The Hereditary Family of Marquis of Liu* 20. Cf. Watson, *Records of the Grand Historian: Han Dynasty I*, 108–9.

44. Chen Shou, *San Guo Zhi* [Records of the Three Kingdoms] (Beijing: Zhonghua Book Company, 2006), 912–13.

45. For the administration of a large state it is necessary to have both central and local authorities. See Mao Zedong, "Lun shida guanxi" [On the Ten Major Relationships], https://www.marxists.org/reference/archive/mao/selected-works/volume-5/mswv5_51.htm. This is also a key advantage of federalism.

46. Zhou Zhenhe, *Zhongguo difang xingzheng zhidushi*, chap. 7.

47. Ibid., 236–38.

48. Ibid., 241.

49. Having united the six states of China into one, the First Emperor of Qin began to move south into the Lingnan area occupied by the Yue (Việt) peoples. In 219 BC, the emperor sent a large army, numbering five hundred thousand troops, and by 214 BC he

had pacified Lingnan (mostly present-day Guangdong and Guangxi). He established the three commanderies of Nanhai, Guilin, and Xiang there. In 221 BC, the emperor also sent the army to Fujian, and in 220, he set up the Minzhong Commandery there. However, although Minzhong was counted among the forty commanderies of the empire, yet since it was far from the central plain, the mountains were steep, the roads were difficult, and the Yue were strong, its administration was unique. The central government did not send a military governor to Minzhong. It merely removed the title of king from the king of the Min-Yue while allowing him to continue to rule the area. The central government exercised no effective rule over Min-Yue.

50. The earliest evidence of double appointments is in the *Record of Rites*: "In a great state there were three high ministers, all appointed by the Son of Heaven. . . . In a state of the second class there were three high ministers, two appointed by the Son of Heaven and one by the prince. . . . In a small state there were two high ministers, both appointed by the prince" (*Record of Rites* 3 *Royal Regulations* 8 [trans. Legge], http://ctext.org/liji /wang-zhi).

51. Zhou Zhenhe, *Zhongguo difang xingzheng zhidushi*, chap. 10.

52. Institute of Chinese Administrative Divisions, *Woguo xingzhengqu gaigeshexiang* [A Reform Plan for China's Administrative Divisions] (Beijing: Chinese Society Press, 1991).

53. Anthony Giddens, *The Nation-State and Violence: Volume Two of a Contemporary Critique of Historical Materialism* (Oxford: Polity, 1985), 85.

54. Su Li, "Xianzhi de junshi suzao" [The Constitution Shaped by Military Affairs], *Law Review* 1 (2015): 1–16.

55. John K. Fairbank, *The Chinese World Order: Traditional China's Foreign Relations* (Cambridge, Mass.: Harvard University Press, 1968), 2, 9. In his discussion of the Chinese world order, Fairbank points out that it was composed of three levels: the Chinese cultural circle, the tributary tribes or political authorities of the pastoral peoples of continental Asia, and the outer barbarians. He further divides the barbarians into inner and outer. Under certain conditions the outer barbarians could become inner barbarians. Also see the chapter by Yang Lien-sheng, "Historical Notes on the Chinese World Order," in Fairbank, *Chinese World Order*, 20–33. Yang distinguishes between the Chinese central state and all under Heaven, and between the inner, royal domain and areas of the outer lords.

56. For instance, Zhou Zhenhe divides the administrative areas on the frontiers into two kinds: one was military, directly under the central government; the other was a special form of civilian prefecture under military authority (slack-rein prefectures) for minority areas. See Zhou Zhenhe, *Zhongguo difang xingzheng zhidushi*, chaps. 12–13. Li Dalong holds that there were three or four levels of administration in the border areas under the Han and Tang dynasties. See Li Dalong, *Han-Tang fanshu tizhi yanjiu* [A Study of Barbarian Administrative Areas under the Han and Tang] (Beijing: China Social Science Press, 2006).

57. Zhou Zhenhe, *Zhongguo difang xingzheng zhidushi*, chaps. 12–13.

58. Li Dalong, *Han-Tang fanshu tizhi yanjiu*.

59. Yang Lien-sheng, "Historical Notes on the Chinese World Order," 18; Li Dalong, *Han-Tang fanshu tizhi yanjiu*, 329–33.

60. Editors' note: Many translate "Xiongnu" and "Tujue" as Huns and Turks; however, the relationship between the two nomadic peoples in ancient China and the two peoples invading the Western Roman Empire and the Byzantine Empire is still to be explored. Therefore, we prefer using a phonetic transliteration of the Chinese characters.

61. Cf. Zhou Zhenhe, *Zhongguo difang xingzheng zhidushi*, chaps. 12–13.

62. Yang Lien-sheng, "Historical Notes on the Chinese World Order," 28–31; see also Fang Tie, "Lun jimi zhice xiang tuguan tusi zhidu de yanbian" [A Discussion of the Shift from the Slack-Rein Prefectures to Native Administrative and Military Rule], *China's Borderland History and Geography Studies* 2 (2011): 68–80.

63. *Record of Rites 3 Royal Regulations* 35, http://ctext.org/liji/wang-zhi.

64. At its foundation, the Tang did not rule over the barbarians. After Emperor Tai-zong had pacified the Tujue, the barbarians of the northwest and the south were gradually brought under central rule and their villages were made prefectures and counties. The larg-est town in each was made the seat of government and the tribal leader was appointed in-spector, a post that was hereditary. See Ouyang Xiu and Song Qi, *Xin Tang Shu* [New Tang History] (Beijing: Zhonghua Book Company, 1975), 1119. Also see Tan Qixiang, "Tangdai jimizhou shulun" [A Description of the Slack-rein Prefectures in the Tang Dynasty], in *Changshui cuipian* [Selections from Changshui Collections] (Shijiazhuang: Hebei Educa-tional Press, 2000).

65. See also Zhang Zhongkui, *Gaitu guiliu yu miao jiang zaizao* [Reforming the Bar-barians and Remaking the Miao Region] (Beijing: China Social Science Press, 2012), 57–59.

66. Ibid., 56.

67. A study of the Ganzi Tibetan district of Sichuan carried out in 1956 demonstrated that "the common feature of the 'improved areas' was that the means of production in farming and handicraft was better there than in newly recovered areas. . . . Feudal owner-ship (*lingzhu*) had been abolished; in name at least the land belonged to the state; the rela-tion of dependency among the farmers had been weakened; the farmers were already half serfs and half free. Only a few were still full serfs. Relationships of renting had increased; pawning (典当), mortgaging (抵押) and buying and selling of land were already common. Land had gradually become concentrated such that there were a few landowners. There were the beginnings of a richer peasant economy. These areas did not have dual governance, but the lowest level of administration was provided by the temples, nobles, and high lamas." See Sichuan Province Editorial Group, "Zhongguo shaoshu minzu shehui lishi diaocha zi-liao congkan," in Editorial Revision Committee, *Sichuan sheng ganzi zhou zangzu shehui lishi diaocha* [A Survey of Social History in Ganzi Tibetan Region, Sichuan Province] (Bei-jing: Nationalities Publishing House, 2009), 12.

68. Gong Yin et al., eds., *Zhongguo tusi zhidu* [China's Headman System] (Kunming: Nationalities Publishing House of Yunnan, 1992); also Zhang Zhongkui, *Gaitu guiliu yu miao jiang zaizao*, esp. chap. 4.

69. Zhao Erxuan, in the *Draft Qing History Juan 512 Biography 299 Headmen* A, has a note about this in the chapter on the headman system: "Beyond the river the headman sys-tem is appropriate; circulation of posts is not. On this side of the river circulation of posts is appropriate; the headman system is not." The river is the Lancang, the upper reaches of the Mekong. Zhao Erxuan, *Qing Shi Gao* [Draft Qing History] (Beijing: Zhonghua Book Company, 1977), 14205.

70. See Li Shu, "Sun Zhongshan shangshu Li Hongzhang shiji kaobian" [A Study of the Account of Sun Yat-sen's Letter to Li Hongzhang], *Historical Research* 3 (1988): 75–83.

71. For the Ryukyu Islands, see Wang Hui, "Liuqiu: zhanzheng jiyi, shehui yundong yu lishi jieshi" [Ryukyu: War Memories, Social Movements and Historical Interpretation], in *Yazhou shiye: Zhongguo lishi de xushu* [An Asian View: An Account of Chinese History] (Beijing: Oxford University Press, 2010); Wang Hui, "Liuqiu yu quyu zhixu de liangci ju-bian" [The Ryukyu and Two Major Shifts in Regional Order], in *Dongxi zhijian de "Xi-zang wenti"* [The Tibetan Question between East and West (with 2 Additional Chapters)] (Hong Kong: Joint Publishing Company, 2011).

72. In my view the most systematic treatment of this among ancient authors is that of Gu Zuyu, *Dushi fangyu jiyao*. Among contemporary scholars, see the studies by Tan Qix-iang, "Tangdai jimizhou shulun"; and Zhou Zhenhe, *Zhongguo difang xingzheng zhidushi*.

73. The earliest Western accounts discussing the influence of geography on the consti-tution of a state are to be found scattered in Plato, Aristotle, Cicero, and Montesquieu. In the *Laws*, Plato treated geography as a key consideration for the constitution of a city-state

(Plato, *Laws*, trans. Wang Xiaochao [Beijing: People's Press, 2003], 460–63, 496). In founding a city-state and choosing a location, one should consider various conditions for the purpose of the legislator. The city should be in the center of its territory, not too close to the sea. The surroundings should be large enough to provide for the livelihood of the people. The population should be such that it can defend itself, and it should have neighbors that can assist in times of invasion. Aristotle also pointed out that the location of the city should be such as to make entry by enemies difficult and yet allow the inhabitants to travel out easily. The central city of the state should be its military center, from which troops can easily be sent to the frontiers. It should also be a commercial center to permit the transportation and storage of grain and other foodstuffs. Aristotle, *Politics*, 405–8. Cicero (*On the State*, trans. Shen Shuping [Beijing: Commerce Press, 1999], 58–59) also mentions that, although a maritime setting permits military expeditions by sea, the foresight of the founders of Rome was that if one wanted to stay in a place securely for a long time and rule over a broad territory, it would be better not to build by the sea, because a maritime city faces too many unpredictable dangers. Sea-based enemies might arrive unannounced, making defense difficult. Maritime cities also easily become corrupt; they fall under the influence of foreign languages and foreign customs and ways of living, increasing the difficulty of upholding order.

Chapter Two: Ancient China's Cultural Constitution

1. *Zuo's Commentary* 9 Duke Xiang year 25, Legge 4:517.

2. Max Weber, *Economy and Society: An Outline of Interpretive Sociology*, 2 vols. (Berkeley: University of California Press, 1978), 1:217–23, 2:954–56, 973–78.

3. For example, Aristotle believes that man is naturally a political animal that is adapted to the city-state. See Aristotle, *Politics*, 60. Therefore he overlooks the question of the emergence and constitution of the community that is the city-state. In recent times, the classic model is that of the social contract. Both Hobbes and Locke presuppose the existence of a basic social body. Not only do people live within the confined space of a city where they cannot avoid meeting others, they are also able to use a language that all understand to communicate with one another and so draw up a social contract and establish a state. This is possible only because of the preexisting community, which at most can be only a small-scale community. In a contemporary version of the social contract, Rawls writes about the "circumstances of justice" (John Rawls, *A Theory of Justice* [Cambridge, Mass.: Harvard University Press, 1971], 126). He would seem to presume a particular Western society as his model. In defense of his views, Rawls holds that the only condition for justice as fairness is to determine the basic obvious ideas *including the tradition of interpretation of the political institutions of a democratic society* (John Rawls, "Kantian Constructivism in Moral Theory," *Journal of Philosophy* 77 [1980]; "Justice as Fairness: Political not Metaphysical," *Philosophy and Public Affairs* 14 [1985]). There are also authors who emphasize that research into the constitution should include a sense of history, taking preconstitutional political practice and its relevant documents into account. For example, see Paul Brest, Sanford Levinson, J. M. Balkin, Akhil Reed Amar, and Reva B. Siegel, *Processes of Constitutional Decision Making: Cases and Materials*, 5th ed. (New York: Aspen, 2006), especially the foreword.

4. "The earliest forms of writing were used in the temple and up until now were not something ordinary people used." Fei Xiaotong, "Zailun wenzi xiaxiang" [A Fresh Look at How Writing Moved into the Countryside], *Xiangtu Zhongguo* [Rural China] (2007): 22. See also Arthur Sigismund Diamond, *Primitive Law, Past and Present* (London: Methuen, 1971), 39; Jack Goody, ed., *Literacy in Traditional Societies* (Cambridge: Cambridge University Press, 1975), 1–2, 27–36; and Giddens, *Nation-State and Violence*, 41–42.

5. Since at the time there were no state borders, there is much discussion as to what constitutes the national territory and over what area the state had authority, but the records of the fiefs granted to feudal lords in the Western Zhou show that the kingdom extended to the sea in the east and crossed the Yangtze in the south. The territory under control was at least a million square kilometers. See Ge Jianhong, *Zhongguo lidai jiangyude bianqian* and Xu Zhuoyun, *Xizhou shi*, 14–16. This was already larger than modern Germany, Great Britain, and France and larger than the combined territory of the thirteen colonies of British North America.

6. A well-known instance comes from 536 BC, when the state of Zheng recorded its laws on bronze *ding* (see *Zuo's Commentary* 10 Duke Zhao year 6, Legge 4:609). This is generally reckoned to be the earliest formal announcement in writing. In 513 BC, Zhao Yang of Jin had the laws previously promulgated by Fan Xuanzi inscribed on a *ding* and made public for all (*Zuo's Commentary* 10 Duke Zhao year 29, Legge 4:732). Editors' note: *Ding* was originally an ancient Chinese cooking vessel with two loop handles and three or four legs, used by political elites as a symbol of legitimate power.

7. According to Guo Moruo, the official script of the Western and Eastern Zhou, the bronze script, was much the same everywhere. However, the popular scripts developed in the late Eastern Zhou showed regional differences. Guo Moruo, "Gudai wenzi zhi bianzheng de fazhan" [The Dialectic Development of Ancient Characters], *Acta Archaeologica Sinica* 1 (1972): 9–10.

8. More than twenty-one hundred years after the founding of the Qin dynasty, Weber wrote about the importance of an official script for a legal system developed by a professional bureaucracy. Weber, *Economy and Society*, 2:957.

9. The later political-legal setup shows that, provided the case was important, the petitioner would exercise this "natural right." Cf. Jonathan K. Ocko, "I'll Take It All the Way to Beijing: Capital Appeals in the Qing," *Journal of Asian Studies* 47, no. 2 (1988): 291–315.

10. "The greatest contribution the First Emperor of Qin made to the reform of the characters was the adoption of the scribal script." Guo Moruo, "Gudai wenzi zhi bianzheng de fazhan," 10. "In the Qin dynasty, the scribal script had, in fact, already replaced the small seal-script. . . . The Qin unified the script by means of the scribal script." Qiu Xikui, *Wenzixue gaiyao* [An Introduction to Chinese Characters] (Shanghai: Commercial Press, 1988), 72.

11. Fei Xiaotong, "Lun zhishi jieji" [On the Intelligentsia], in *Huangquan yu shenquan* [Imperial Power and the Power of the Gentry], ed. Wu Han, Fei Xiaotong, et al. (Shanghai: Shanghai Guanchashe, 1948).

12. "If you want people to study the laws and decrees, make the minister the teacher." Sima Qian, *Records of the Historian* 6 *Annals of the First Emperor of Qin*, Yang and Yang, *Selections from the "Records of the Historian,"* 177.

13. Cf. Su Li, "Xiucixue de zhengfa jiamen" [Rhetorics in Its Legal Branch], *Open Era* 2 (2011): 38–53, sec. 2.

14. "An imperial decree ordered that candidates were to be examined in four subjects and also to add one poem to each. The custom of adding poetry to the exams began from this." Liu Xu, *Jiu Tang Shu* [Old Tang History] (Beijing: Zhonghua Book Company, 1975), 1:229; and Zang Jinshu, *Yuanqu xuan* [An Anthology of Yuan Poetry] (Beijing: Zhonghua Book Company, 1958), 3.

15. *Analects* 7:18: "The topics of the Master's refined speech were the *Book of Odes*, the *Book of Documents*, and upholding the rites. All of these were part of his refined speech."

16. Cf. Xin delin, *Ladingyu he xilayu* [Latin and Greek] (Beijing: Foreign Language Teaching and Research Press, 2007).

17. Cf. Fei Xiaotong, "Wenzi xiaxiang" [How Writing Moved into the Countryside], *Xiangtu Zhongguo* [Rural China] (2007): 18; Fei Xiaotong, "Zailun wenzi xiaxiang."

18. Both in the past and in the present, in China and abroad, the first and most committed cultural and political separatists are not illiterate. Rather, they are the scholars of their locale or native people. The ultimate success of cultural separatism must also rely on scholars. The classic example of this is the case of pastor Martin Luther, who had a good grasp of Latin and split away from the Roman Catholic Church. He used the local dialect of German to translate the Bible. He unified and in some senses created the German language and script. The unification of the German language led to the flourishing of German politics and social culture and provided an indispensable condition for the later unification of Germany. Cf. Hou Suqin, "Mading-Lude yu xiandai deyu" [Martin Luther and Modern German], *Shanghai Technical University Journal (Social Sciences)* 2 (2006): 53–55.

19. Please note that although the term "Mandarin Chinese" used here comes from the official speech of the Yuan, Ming, and Qing dynasties, it is an academic term referring to the oral speech shared by the Chinese political-cultural elite. It includes the refined speech and common speech of the Spring and Autumn period that took the phonetics of the central plain as its standard or foundation. It also includes the various later forms of "Mandarin."

20. Li Rong, "Guanhua fangyan de fenqu" [The Area in Which the Mandarin Dialect Is Spoken], *Dialect* 1 (1985): 2–5.

21. The earliest authority for this is given by the *Analects* (7:18), which says that Confucius used refined speech to talk about the *Odes*, *Documents*, and rites. Consider also this: "every time you see the people of this place learn Mandarin, their pronunciation is very clear and the accent good, but for the names of things and in popular speech they still keep to their local dialect, which is very hard to understand." Gao Jingting, *Zhengyin cuoyao* [The Essence of Standard Pronunciation], vol. 2: *Guanhua biesu* [Uncommon Customs of Mandarin] (1834), cited by Li Dandan, "Guanhua de xingzhi" [The Nature of Mandarin Chinese], *Xinjiang Social Sciences* 5 (2011): 106; Zhang Yulai, "Ming-Qing shidai hanyu guanhua de shehui shiyong zhuangkuang" [The Social Use of Mandarin in the Ming and Qing Dynasties], *Language Teaching and Linguistic Studies* 1 (2010): 90–93 ("'Mandarin' is simply an administrative and commercial use of the word").

22. Zhang Yulai, "Ming-Qing shidai," 93, notes that "there was no absolute standard for Mandarin in the Ming and Qing dynasties." Moreover, "the Mandarin spoken in society was hardly ever correct."

23. At least for the pre-Ming-Qing era, this can explain why scholars very rarely wrote much about novels or opera scripts and other such "literature." Even if they did mention them, it was only as an afterthought. Those who did pay more attention to such works are basically excluded from the scholars of the political and cultural elite and are persons who are not considered to be part of the elite, such as Guan Hanqing and Shi Naiyan.

24. I am not clear about the situation in other countries, but in the United States recitation is not used in early reading classes.

25. According to the *Veritable Records of the Qing Dynasty* (Beijing: Zhonghua Book Company, 1985), 7:1072–74), in the time of the Yongzheng Emperor, Mandarin was not widely understood in Fujian and Guangdong: "The languages of officials and the people are mutually unintelligible." This influenced the implementation of government orders. In the sixth year of his reign, in 1728, Yongzheng ordered that within eight years Mandarin should be used in Fujian and Guangdong. To begin with, official Correct Pronunciation Academies were to be set up in each town in Fujian Province to teach Mandarin to the people. Officials were enjoined to ensure that "everybody understood the same language." He also decreed that after eight years, no one who did not speak Mandarin could be a candidate for the exams (*ju ren, xiu cai, gong sheng*, or *tong sheng*). Despite its strictness, however, this decree could not be fully enforced. Seventeen years later, it was noted that "after many years of teaching, local dialects were the same as ever." In the tenth year of the Qianlong Emperor, the Correct Pronunciation Academies in Fujian were abolished. Candidates who were *ju*

ren or *xiu cai* were not refused admittance to the exams even though they did not speak Mandarin. See Suerna et al., *Xuezheng Quanshu* [Collection of Administration of Schools and Examinations], vol. 65 (1793), in *Lidai keju wenxian zhengli yu yanjiu congkan. Qinding Xuezheng Quanshu Jiaozhu* [A Series of Editions and Study of Literature on Imperial Examinations in All Dynasties: Notes on the "Collection of Administration of Schools and Examinations" Made by Imperial Order] (Wuhan: Wuhan University Press, 2009).

26. It is said of the Western Zhou that "seventy-one states were established, out of which fifty-three were given to princes surnamed Ji" (*Xunzi* 5 *Ru Xiao* 1). *Zuo's Commentary*, however, says "fifteen of his brothers received states and forty princes surnamed Ji also did so" (*Zuo's Commentary*10 Duke Zhao year 28, Legge 4:727).

27. Cf. Lin Tao, "Cong guanhua, guoyu dao putonghua" [From Mandarin, the National Language to Putonghua], *Language Planning*, October 1998, 6.

28. On refined speech, the common speech, or Mandarin, there are many different studies, including Li Shiyu, *Tianjin de fangyan liyu* [Slang in the Tianjin Dialect] (Tianjin: Tianjin Classics Publishing House, 2004); Xu Tongqiang, *Lishi yuyanxue* [Historical Linguistics] (Hong Kong: Commercial Press, 1991), esp. chaps. 10 and 11; Geng Zhensheng, ed., *Jindai guanhua yuyin yanjiu* [A Linguistic Study of Modern Mandarin] (Beijing: Languages & Culture Press, 2005); Qian Zengyi, ed., *Hanyu guanhua fangyan yanjiu* [A Study of the Mandarin Dialects of Chinese] (Jinan: Qilu Press, 2010). However, too many studies focus on the differences between dialects and their interrelated influences. At least in my own limited reading, I have not found any scholar who has directly addressed the mechanism by which Mandarin was formed. Yet many studies still show that there were many factors, many social, political, and cultural institutions in ancient China, that consciously or unconsciously led to the formation of Mandarin and guaranteed and upheld a minimum standard of oral intelligibility among the political and cultural elite spread throughout the whole of China.

Can the scattered, functionally related social, political, and cultural institutions that created and formed Mandarin be described as an institution? There is nothing to show that the ancients in China did anything similar for speech as for the uniform script with its evident constitutional significance. However, from the points of view of sociology and of political science, whether a series of social institutions and practices are sufficient to form an institution is not to be decided by looking at the explicit idea of the subjective creator or actor himself or the group as a whole. Even if what the creator or actor seeks is different, if objectively it establishes a pattern that has a lasting effect on society, people can describe it as an institution. A classic example of this is a market. A market is not created by anyone's subjective desire, nor from any longing or dreaming for liberty, equality, and efficacy. People simply exchange goods, including money, but unconsciously they give rise to the great institution of the market.

29. If there is no great work of literature composed in a particular script, the script will have difficulty in having any genuine cultural attraction or consolidation. This is why, although many peoples had their own scripts and languages early on and failed to have any great authors, they could not become scripts or languages with any cultural attraction. Such great authors are Shakespeare for English, Martin Luther for German, Pushkin for Russian, and Lu Xun, Mao Zedong, and others for modern Chinese. Also because of this, although the Taiwan independence circles have created a special Taiwanese culture and history, that there is no great text in "Taiwanese" has led to disappointment and cultural shame. The inborn psychology of humans always implies the hope that one can belong to or at least share in a great tradition. This can explain not only the popular drawing up of genealogies but also the deconstructionism of the intellectual genealogy of Nietzsche and Foucault.

30. A counterexample is that, apart from political and economic causes in the twentieth century, one reason that North and South Korea left the Chinese cultural circle may

be that, by the end of the nineteenth century, the Hangul phonetic script composed in the fifteenth century began to be written along with Chinese characters. The mixture of Chinese characters and Hangul became the main way of writing Korean. After the Second World War, for various political reasons, North and South Korea both began to use Hangul without Chinese characters, that is, a de-sinicized version of the script.

31. Zhang Shilu and Yang Jianqiao, *Yinyunxue rumen* [Introduction to Phonetics] (Shanghai: Fudan University Press, 2009), 7.

32. For the influence of social unrest in northern China on Hakka, see Luo Xianglin, *Kejia yanjiudaolun* [A Guide to Research in Hakka] (1933; repr., Shanghai: Shanghai Literature and Art Publishing House, 1992), esp. chap. 2.

33. For example, research has shown that the Tianjin speech of today is the result of Zhu Li, King of Yan, who brought many members of his family to the border area of Beijing and Tianjin in the early Ming dynasty. They became the largest and most influential group living in Tianjin, and the dialect they brought from the Yangtze, Huai River basin, became predominant. See Li Shiyu, *Tianjin de fangyan liyu*.

34. Cf. Bao Jiang, "Yunnan de guanhua fangyan cong he erlai?" [Where Did the Mandarin Dialect of Yunnan Come From?], *Wenshi Monthly*, February 2011, 79–80.

35. Qian Mu, *Guoshi xinlun* [A New Account of Chinese History] (Hong Kong: Joint Publishing Company, 2001), 145–46, 243–45.

36. On the selection and appointment of local officials in the Qin and Han, see Yan Gengwang, *Zhongguo zhengzhi zhidu shigang* [A Historical Outline of Chinese Political Institutions] (Shanghai: Shanghai Classics Publishing House, 2013), 83: "The head of the commandery and of the county was always from outside, but the officials under him were always local people."

37. Research by Liu Jinqin shows that "the common terms found in Yuan dynasty operas are still very much alive in the northern Mandarin-speaking area." Liu Jinqin, "Yuanqu ciyu fangyan jinzheng" [A Modern Study of the Dialect Terms in Yuan Operas], *Chinese Knowledge* 4 (2012): 41ff.

38. Hou Jingyi, "Bainianqian de Guangdong renxue 'guanming' shouce 'zhengyinjuhua'" [*Correct Pronunciation* as a Handbook for Cantonese People a Hundred Years Ago Studying Mandarin], *Wenzi gaige*, December 1962.

39. Cf. Fei Xiaotong, "Sunshi chongxi xia de xiangtu" [Native Soil under Erosion], in *Xiangtu Zhongguo* [Rural China] (Shanghai: Shanghai Century, 2007).

40. Classic examples are the *Book of Odes* 191 *Jie Nan Shan* (where "wudai xiaoren" [not endanger: small men] is changed to "wu xiaoren dai" [not small men endanger], i.e., Small men would not be endangering [the commonweal]) (Legge 4:312); and *Mozi* 32 *Against Music A* (where "yinshi yuye" [drinking and eating in the fields] is changed to "ye yu yinshi" [fields: in: drinking and eating]) (see Watson 116). In both cases, the changes are made to form a rhyme with the preceding or following lines. See Guo Zaiyi, *Xunguxue* [Phonetics] (Beijing: Zhonghua Book Company, 2005), 11–12.

41. Xu Shen, *Shuowen Jiezi* [Explanation of Words and Characters] (Beijing: Zhonghua Book Company, 2004).

42. Poet: Lu You (1125–?), written 1192. The poet is dreaming of the army defending China's northern border.

43. Poet: Xin Qiji (Southern Song). The poet describes how he forced himself to write poems about grief when he was young and as yet knew no grief.

44. Poet: Li Bai. The quotation about the shadow (at the end of the sentence) is the second half of the line.

45. Poet: Su Shi. Poem: "When Will There Be a Bright Moon?"

46. It is unclear who the three persons are: the moon, the poet, and his shadow, or the poet, his reflection in his wineglass, and his shadow on the ground.

47. Fei Xiaotong thinks that the script created the class. See "Lun zhishi jieji" [On the Intelligentsia], in *Huangquan yu shenquan* [Imperial Power and the Power of the Gentry], ed. Wu Han, Fei Xiaotong, et al. (Shanghai: Shanghai Guanchashe, 1948), 16.

48. Translator's note: This poem and those that follow refer to attacks by the Xixia Kingdom on the Song empire around 1038–40. Yanran is the name of a mountain in modern-day Mongolia. Here and in the quotations that follow, italics are added to emphasize references to places beyond what the poets could have known personally.

49. Tian Yuqing, *Dongjin menge zhengzhi* [Noble-Family Politics in the Eastern Jin], 5th ed. (Beijing: Peking University Press, 2012); and *Qin-Han-Wei-Jin Shi tanwei* [A Study of the Qin, Han, Wei, and Jin Histories], rev. 3rd ed. (Beijing: Zhonghua Book Company, 2011).

50. Su Li, "Jingying zhengzhi yu zhengzhi canyu."

51. "In general, democratic government suits small states; aristocratic government suits middle-sized states; monarchy suits large states" (Jean-Jacques Rousseau, *The Social Contract*, trans. Willmoore Kendall [Washington, D.C.: Henry Regnery, 1954], bk. 3, chap. 3); "If the natural property of small states is to be governed as republics, that of medium-sized ones, to be subject to a monarch, and that of large empires to be dominated by a despot" (Montesquieu, *The Spirit of the Laws*, trans. and ed. Anne M. Cohler, Basia C. Millers, and Harold S. Stone [Cambridge: Cambridge University Press, 1989], pt. 1, bk. 8, chap. 20, 126).

52. At the time of the French Revolution, in 1794, Henri Grégoire proclaimed in the National Assembly a report on the necessity for the abolition of dialects and the means to spread the use of French. He held that the variety of languages was a key impediment to the unification of the French people and therefore French should be learned and dialects outlawed. See Alyssa Goldstein Sepinwall, *The Abbé Grégoire and the French Revolution: The Making of Modern Universalism* (Berkeley: University of California Press, 2005), chap. 4, esp. 96–97. The French government of the time adopted a monolingual policy, decreeing that only French could be used in public places and in schools. Further legislation followed, especially the 1881 Education Act, which made primary education compulsory and decreed that this could be done only in French. The ministry of education and the teachers had to ensure that other languages were kept out of school. See http://en.wikipedia.org/wiki /Language_policy_in_France; also see R. Anthony Lodge, *French: From Dialect to Standard* (London: Routledge, 1993).

Chapter Three: Scholar-Officials

1. *Mencius* 4A1, Legge 2:290.

2. Plato, *The Republic*, bk. V, 473c–e, trans. Benjamin Jowett, https://www.gutenberg .org/files/1497/1497-h/1497-h.htm.

3. Su Li, "Wenhua zhidu yu guojia goucheng: yi 'shu tongwen' he 'guanhua' wei shijiao" [Cultural Institution and Structure of State: In the Light of Unified Script and Mandarin Chinese], *Chinese Social Sciences* 12 (2013): 78–95.

4. *Mencius* 3A4, Legge 2:249–50.

5. Editors' note: Bo Le, a superior horse selector living in the Spring and Autumn period, was able to choose swift horses from a huge herd. He is a symbol of acute leaders who are able to promote the most talented person from the multitude.

6. Translator's note: See Rui Wang, *The Chinese Imperial Examination System: An Annotated Bibliography* (Plymouth: Scarecrow, 2013).

7. Sima Qian, *Records of the Historian 3 Annals of the Yin* 23: "Wuding dreamed one night that he had found a holy man named Yue. . . . He then made all his officers search for

him in the wilds, and Yue was discovered at the crag of Fu. . . . Having talked with him, and finding that he really was a holy man, Wuding promoted him to be his prime minister. The kingdom of Yin was well governed in consequence."

8. Sima Qian, *Records of the Historian* 4 *Annals of the Zhou* 14; *Book of Documents* 5 *Books of Zhou* 2 *Speech at Mu* criticizes King Zhou of the Shang: "In his blindness he has also cast off his paternal and maternal relations, not treating them properly. They are only the vagabonds from all quarters, loaded with crimes, whom he honours and exalts, whom he employs and trusts, making them great officers and high nobles" (Legge 3:303).

9. Sima Qian, *Records of the Historian* 5 *Annals of Qin* 3: "Fei Lian bore E-Lai. E-Lai was very strong; Fei Lian was good at running. Father and son used their talents to serve King Zhou of the Yin." However, he also describes the evil of King Zhou of the Shang as due to E-Lai being keen to vilify others. Sima Qian, *Records of the Historian* 3 *Annals of Yin* 31 (English translation of ctext.org).

10. "71 states were established, out of which 53 were given to princes surnamed Ji" (*Xunzi* 5 *Ru Xiao* 1).

11. Confucianism stressed the authority of the husband, the father, and men over the household. These three forms of authority were founded on permanent norms for the governance of the household. However, a brief glance suffices to show that they never became dogma and when there were major accidents or happenings, they could be changed. Normally, the father made decisions for the family because he was older, had more experience, had greater physical strength, and was better placed to manage the internal business of the household. But when his eldest son grew up and became more intelligent and stronger than his father, the ultimate decision-making power would gradually shift into his hands. This shift was not indicated simply by the father's death. If the elder son was an imbecile or had some other major impediment, authority did not have to transfer to him. If, in the family, the wife was more capable than her husband, she would control the household either explicitly or implicitly, even if, to save face, she would do so only in her husband's name.

12. *Analects* 16 *Ji Shi* 2, Legge 1:310.

13. *Mencius* 4B 50, Legge 2:327. The real state of affairs was probably even more marked, likely a case of lasting for only three generations. The famous case of Chu Zhe speaking to the Dowager of Zhao is proof of this. *Sayings of the States* 6 *Zhao* 4.1. "Chu Zhe said, 'Counting back three generations from now, only the Zhaos ruled Zhao. Are there now any children or grandchildren of King Zhao you have inherited?' She replied, 'No.' He said, 'Is there even one of the family still around?' She said, 'This old lady has not heard of any.' "

14. In his time, Guan Zhong was misrepresented as a mere merchant. Moreover, he made mistakes in politics and was arrested and put in prison. Thanks to the backing of his friend Bao Shuya, he was made prime minister of Qi, and enabled Duke Huan of Qi to become a hegemon (Sima Qian, *Records of the Historian* 62 *Biography of Guan Zhong and Yan Ying* 1). Knowing Bai Lixi to be a talented person, Duke Mu of Qin bought him from Chu for five sheepskins. After speaking to him for three days, he invited him to become a high official and put all political and military power in his hands. This laid the foundations for Qin's subsequent growth in power (Sima Qian, *Records of the Historian* 5 *Annals of Qin* 19). Lin Xiangru was the steward of Mu Xian, chief eunuch in Zhao. History records that he twice led the army to victory and defended the interests and dignity of Zhao. For this he was immediately made a high councilor and then later chief minister, with a post above that of the famous general Lian Po (Sima Qian, *Records of the Historian* 81 *Biography of Lian Po and Lin Xiangru*, Yang and Yang, *Selections from the "Records of the Historian,"* 142–43).

15. *Analects* 133. Confucius also thought that in governing a state, the first task was to make the people rich and only afterward to educate them: "If good men were to govern a country in succession for a hundred years, they would be able to transform the violently bad, and dispense with capital punishments" (*Analects* 13 *Zi Lu* 11, Legge 1:267).

16. "If Guan knew the rules of propriety, who does not know them?" (*Analects* 3 *Ba Yi* 22, Legge 1:163). "Duke Huan assembled all the princes together, and that not with weapons of war and chariots—it was all through the influence of Guan Zhong. Whose beneficence was like his? Whose beneficence was like his?" (*Analects* 14 *Xian Wen* 17, Legge 1:282). And "Guan Zhong acted as prime minister to Duke Huan, made him leader of all the princes, and united and rectified the whole kingdom. Down to the present day, the people enjoy the gifts that he conferred. But for Guan Zhong, we should now be wearing our hair unbound, and the lappets of our coats buttoned on the left side. Will you require from him the small fidelity of common men and common women, who would commit suicide in a stream or ditch, no one knowing anything about them?" (*Analects* 14 *Xian Wen* 18, Legge 1:282).

17. For instance, "What makes the state flourish is agriculture and war." "The state attains security through agriculture and war; the Lord gains respect through agriculture and war." "Therefore, when a sage is in the state, in domestic affairs he ensures the people are involved in agriculture and in external affairs that they plan for war." "To defeat the enemy and not wear out one's amour [alternatively, fields do not lie fallow], the result will be strength and power, without even having to move." *The Book of Lord Shang* 3 *Agriculture and War* 1, 4; 6 *Calculation of Land* 7, available at http://ctext.org/shang-jun-shu (trans. J.J.L. Duyvendak). Also, "to hope to enrich the nation through agriculture and ward off the enemy with trained soldiers" (*Hanfeizi* 49 *Five Vermin*, Watson 107). And again:

> Therefore an enlightened ruler will make use of men's strength but will not heed their words, will reward their accomplishments but will prohibit useless activities. Then the people will be willing to exert themselves to the point of death in the service of their sovereign. Farming requires a lot of hard work but people will do it because they say, "This way we can get rich." War is a dangerous activity but people will take part in it because they say, "This way we can become eminent." Now, if men who devote themselves to literature or study the art of persuasive speaking are able to get the fruits of wealth without the hard work of the farmer, and can gain the advantages of eminence without the danger of battle, then who will not take up such pursuits? So for every man who works with his hands there will be a hundred devoting themselves to the pursuit of wisdom. If those who pursue wisdom are numerous, the laws will be defeated, and if those who labour with their hands are few, the state will grow poor. Hence, the age will become disordered. Therefore, in the state of an enlightened ruler there are no books written on bamboo slips; law supplies the only instruction. There are no sermons on the former kings; the officials serve as the only teachers. There are no fierce feuds of private swordsmen; cutting off the heads of the enemy is the only deed of valour. Hence, when the people of such a state make a speech, they say nothing that is in contradiction to the law; when they act, it is in some way that will bring useful results; and when they do brave deeds, they do them in the army. Therefore, in times of peace the state is rich, and in times of trouble its armies are strong. These are what are called the resources of the ruler. . . . [H]e who would surpass the Five Emperors of antiquity and rival the Three Kings must proceed by this method. (*Hanfeizi* 49 *Five Vermin*, Watson 110–11)

18. Cho-yun Hsu made a statistical analysis of the persons who were active in the Spring and Autumn and Warring States period and found that there were twice as many persons of humble origin active in the Warring States era compared to the earlier Spring and Autumn era. Cho-yun Hsu, *Ancient China in Transition: An Analysis of Social Mobility, 722–222 B.C.* (Stanford: Stanford University Press, 1965), 39.

19. *Record of Rites of the Elder Dai*, 141. Also see the story of Lord Mengchang in *Strategies of the Warring States* (Shanghai: Classic Publishing House, 1985), 384, http://ctext .org/zhan-guo-ce/meng-chang-jun-you-she-ren/zh.

20. Sima Qian, *Records of the Historian* 75 *Biography of Lord Mengchang*, Yang and Yang, *Selections from the "Records of the Historian,"* 79–80.

21. "The ministers of Jin are not the equal of those of Chu, but the great officials are more worthy, with the quality of a minister. Like the wood of the trees and the leather skins they are exported from Chu to Jin, so while Chu has the raw materials, they are all used by Jin." *Zuo's Commentary* 9 Duke Xiang year 26, Legge 4:526a.

22. Editors' note: This phrase, rendered from *Shou Zhu Dai Tu* (守株待兔), is a fable in *Hanfeizi* 49 *Five Vermin*, http://ctext.org/hanfeizi/wu-du/zh. The Legalist Han Fei uses it to mock those Confucians committed to the outdated way of ancient sage kings.

23. *Analects* 17 *Yang Huo* 5, Legge 1:320; and "Zi Gong said, 'There is a beautiful gem here. Should I lay it up in a case and keep it? or should I seek a good price and sell it?' The Master said, 'Sell it! Sell it! But I would wait for one to offer the price'" (*Analects* 9 *Zi Han* 13, Legge 1:221).

24. The earliest instance is perhaps that in the *Laozi*: "When the great way is left aside, there is benevolence and justice; when wisdom emerges there is great pretense; when the six relationships are not in harmony, there is filial piety and brotherly affection" (*Daodejing* chap. 18); "Banish sageliness, do away with wisdom; the people are a hundred times better off; banish benevolence, do away with justice; the people revert to filial piety and brotherly affection; banish clever trickery and do away with profit; there will be no robbers or thieves" (*Daodejing* chap. 19); "The flesh-eaters are poor creatures, and cannot form any far-reaching plans" (*Zuo's Commentary* 3 *Duke Zhuang* 10, Legge 4:86a). In later times there was a widespread popular saying: "Those who act justly are mostly dog-meat butchers; those who act against their conscience are mostly scholars!" (Cao Xuequan, 1574–1646). A contemporary example is found in Mao Zedong, "Zai bada erci huiyi daibiaotuan tuanzhang huiyi shangde jianghua" [Speech at the Conference of Heads of Delegations to the Second Session of the 8th Party Congress: The Elites Are the Most Ignorant and the Lowly the Most Intelligent] (18 May 1958), https://www.marxists.org/reference/archive/mao /selected-works/volume-8/mswv8_11.htm. Also the novelist and screenwriter Wang Shuo admits candidly his own social history "led him to have no trust in any intellectual; rather, he disliked them and even hated them. . . . Should an intellectual lead him to drop his prejudice, he would immediately encounter another, whose speech would lead him [Wang Shuo] to revert to his original view" (Wang Shuo, *Wuzhizhe wusi* [The Ignorant Is the Brave] [Liaoning: Chunfeng Wenyi Press, 2000], 107–8). Wang describes Chinese society thus: "The roots of the hypocrisy lie among the intellectuals" (ibid., 141).

25. *Analects* 17 *Yang Huo* 2, Legge 1:318.

26. *Analects* 12 *Yan Yuan* 5, Legge 1:253.

27. Sima Qian, *Records of the Historian* 48 *Hereditary Family of Chen She*, Yang and Yang, *Selections from the "Records of the Historian,"* 198; Sima Qian, *Records of the Historian* 7 *Annals of Xiang Yu*, Yang and Yang, *Selections from the "Records of the Historian,"* 205.

28. *Analects*, 19 *Zi Zhang* 13, Legge 1:344; *Mencius* 4A 1, Legge 2:290, *Mencius* 7A 9, Legge 2:453; *Great Learning*, Legge 1:357.

29. *Analects* 12 *Yan Yuan* 11, Legge 1:256. "Loyalty to the state and filial piety do not go together" is from Yan Zhenqing (709–85): "Things out in the world are different; loyalty and filial piety are not the same. A filial son cannot be a loyal minister, nor a loyal minister a filial son. So to seek for loyalty among those who are filial, you will only find people who serve their parents first and the prince second. If you replace filial piety with loyalty, then such people will only serve their lord from the moment of birth." Feng Yan [Tang dynasty], *Fengshi wenjianji xiaozhu* [Annotated Edition of the Memoirs of Feng Yan] (Beijing: Zhonghua Book Company, 2005), 44; Fan Zhongyan, "Yueyanglou ji," in *Fan Zhongyan quanji* [Collected Works of Fan Zhongyan], vol. 1 (Chengdu: Sichuan University Press,

2007), 195; Lu You, "Bingqi shuhuai," in *Lu You Shi Xuan* [Selected Poems of Lu You], selected and annotated by You Guo'En and Li Yi (Beijing: People's Literature Publishing House, 1997), 41.

30. *Analects* 16 *Ji Shi* 13, Legge 1:316.

31. See *Lienü Zhuan*, http://www2.iath.virginia.edu:8080/exist/cocoon/xwomen/texts /lienuzhuan/d2.11/1/0/bilingual, and *Three Character Classic*, http://www.yellowbridge .com/onlinelit/sanzijing.php.

32. *Mencius* 7A 9, Legge 2:453.

33. Han Yu, "Four Poems on Various Subjects," in *Han Changli wenji jiaozhu* [The Annotated Collection of Han Yu], annotated by Qu Shouyuan and Chang Sichun (Chengdu: Sichuan University Press, 1986), 2709.

34. *Hanfeizi* 6 *On Having Standards*, Watson 24.

35. Therefore, early proponents of democracy, such as Rousseau, believed that the number of people should not exceed the scope of what they could reach, the area in which they could normally travel and in which they could know one another. This would set the size of the ideal democracy. See Rousseau, "Dedication to the Republic of Geneva," in *What Is the Origin of Inequality among Men, and Is It Authorised by Natural Law?*, http://www .gutenberg.org/files/46333/46333-h/46333-h.htm.

36. For instance, General Tian Dan of Qi used trickery to get the King of Yan to send Qi Jie as general to replace Yue Yi. Yue Yi fled to Zhao, while Tian Dan defeated the Yan army led by Qi Jie (Sima Qian, *Records of the Historian* 80 *Biography of Yue Yi* 4). In the Warring States era, Qin bribed Guo Kai, favorite of the king of Zhao, to slander Li Mu, the general of the Zhao army, and have him killed (Sima Qian, *Records of the Historian* 81 *Biography of Lian Po and Lin Xiangru*, Yang and Yang, *Selections from the "Records of the Historian,"* 151). There is also the tragedy of Han Fei (Sima Qian, *Records of the Historian* 63 *Biography of Laozi and Han Fei*).

37. Zhao Yi, *Nianershi zhaoji* [Notes on the 22 Dynastic Histories], ed. Cao Guangfu (Nanjing: Phoenix Publishing House, 2008), 44.

38. "The three great generals of Emperor Wu were all borne by the emperor's female favourites." Ibid., 35.

39. *Han History* 9:2959.

40. "In the early Han . . . kings of the royal surname attracted wandering scholars in great numbers, especially in the south with King Liu An of Huainan and in the north with King Liu De of Hejian. The scholars crowded to them rather than to the central government." Qian Mu, "Zailun zhongguo shehui yanbian" [A Second Discussion of the Evolution of Chinese Society], in *Guoshi xinlu* [A New Discussion of Chinese History] (Hong Kong: Joint Publishing Company, 2001), 45.

41. Sima Qian, *Records of the Historian* 10 *Annals of Li Wen* 13.

42. *Han History* 6 *Annals of Emperor Xiao Wu*, Dubs, *The History of the Former Han Dynasty* 2:97.

43. Sima Qian, *Records of the Historian* 128 *Story of Divination* 3.

44. "In appointing good and worthy officials, anyone who upsets the politics of the state by propounding the views of Shen Buhai, Shang Yang, Han Fei, Su Qin or Zhang Yi is to be dismissed" (*Han History: Annals of Emperor Wu*, Dubs, *The History of the Former Han Dynasty* 2:28).

45. Su Li, "Gangchang, liyi, chenghu yu shehui guifan: zhuiqiu dui rujiade zhiduxing lijie" [Morality, Rites, Titles and Social Norms: In Search of an Institutional Understanding of Confucianism], *Chinese Journal of Law* 5 (2007): 39–51.

46. Qian Mu, "*Zhongguo lidai zhengzhi deshi* [The Experiences and Lessons of China's Politics throughout the Centuries] (Hong Kong: Joint Publishing Company, 2001), 14–20.

47. A children's rhyme from the Eastern Han said: "Raise up *xiucai* who cannot read; raise up filial sons who chuck their fathers out." Shen Deqian, ed., *Gushi yuan* [The Origin of Ancient Poems] (Beijing: Zhonghua Book Company, 1963), 101.

48. Fang Xuanling et al., *Jin History*, vol. 4 (Beijing: Zhonghua Press, 1974), 1274. On pp. 1273–77 there is a detailed analysis of the eight major shortcomings of the *chaju* system.

49. Cf. Liu Haifeng and Li Bing, *Zhongguo keju shi* [A History of China's Civil Service Examinations] (Shanghai: Orient Publishing Centre, 2004), 57–65; Lin Bai and Zhu Mei-fang, *Zhongguo keju shihua* [A Brief History of China's Civil Service Examinations] (Nanchang: Jiangxi People's Press, 2002); and Miyazaki Ichisada, *A Study of the Law of the Nine Ranks of Officials: Before the Imperial Examinations*, trans. Han Sheng and Liu Jianying (Beijing: Zhonghua Book Company, 2008). For a view that it was only in the Tang dynasty that the imperial exams were actually established, see Jin Zheng, *Keju zhidu yu Zhongguo wenhua* [The Imperial Examinations and Chinese Culture] (Shanghai: Shanghai People's Publishing House, 1990), 46–49.

50. Wu Han and Fei Xiaotong, *Lun shenquan, Zailun shenquan, lun shi daifu* [On the Power of the Gentry, A Second Look at the Power of the Gentry, On Officials, and Imperial Power and the Power of the Gentry] (Shanghai: Shanghai Guanchashe, 1948), 48–74.

51. "Emperor Wen cultivated the arts and put aside warfare. Heaven approved and the spirits blessed him, favouring his action and bringing blessings to his doorway. He saw the new *jinshi* pouring out and said joyfully, 'The heroes of the empire have fallen under my sway!'" Wang Dingbao, *Tang Zhiyan* [Collected Sayings of the Tang] (Beijing: Zhonghua Book Company, 1959), 3.

52. Posner, *Problems of Jurisprudence*, chap. 2.

53. Sima Qian, *Records of the Historian* 81 *Biography of Lian Po and Lin Xiangru*, Yang and Yang, *Selections from the "Records of the Historian,"* 147.

54. Similar in meaning but contrary in presentation to the story of the discussion of war on paper of Zhao Guo is the story from the Spring and Autumn period about horses: "A good horse can be judged by his shape, muscles, and bones. A perfect horse has something invisible in it, which defies description. It kicks up no dust and leaves no hoof prints. My sons are all of mediocre talent; they can recognize a good horse, but not a perfect horse. To judge the latter, one must look at the inner spirit and not the outer form, see what he [the horse expert] sees and not look at what he does not see; observe what he observes and forget what he does not observe." *Liezi* 8 *Shuo Fu* 16, http://ctext.org/liezi/shuo-fu/zh.

55. *Master Lü's Spring and Autumn Annals*, chap. 5, http://ctext.org/lv-shi-chun-qiu /qu-si/zh.

56. According to Fan Wenlan, *Zhongguo tongshi jianbian* [A Simple Edition of the General History of China] (Shijiazhuang: Hebei Educational Press, 2000), 1:71–72, and Guo Moruo, *Zhongguoshi gao* [A Draft History of China] (Beijing: People's Publishing House, 1979), 2A:24, in the Warring States era, the population of Chu was about 5 million; Qi and Wei each had around 3.5 to 4 million; Qin and Zhao each had about 3 million; and Han and Yan each had around 1.5 to 2 million.

57. Sima Qian, *Records of the Historian* 76 *Biography of Lord Pingyuan and Yu Qing* 4, Yang and Yang, *Selections from the "Records of the Historian,"* 129.

58. Sima Qian, *Records of the Historian* 75 *Biography of Lord Mengchang*, Yang and Yang, *Selections from the "Records of the Historian,"* 83–88; also see *Strategies of the Warring States*, 395–400.

59. *Strategies of the Warring States*, 597.

60. Sima Qian, *Records of the Historian* 86 *Biography of the Assassin-Retainers* 32; Burton Watson, *Records of the Grand Historian: Qin Dynasty* (Hong Kong: Columbia University Press, 1993), 173–75.

61. *Analects* 1 *Xue Er* 4, Legge 1:139.

62. *Guanzi* 566.

63. *Hanfeizi* 49 *Five Vermin*.

64. For instance, Chen Shou praises Zhuge Liang: "He is familiar with all the everyday work; he can grasp the essence of affairs and assign duty according to everyone's position; he disdains hypocrisy." *Records of the Three Kingdoms* II Books of Shu 5 Biography of Zhuge Liang 31.

65. *Hanfeizi* 50 *Eminence in Learning*, Watson 124.

66. Gu Yanwu, *Rizhilu Jishi* [Explanations Collected by Huang Rucheng], vol. 1 (Shanghai: Shanghai Classics Publishing House, 2006), 545.

67. "Promote military governors and prefecture governor from prominent officials in the capital, promote prominent military governors and prefecture governors to the magistrates of the capital, and maintain the constant balance between the inward and outward transference." Sima Guang, *Zi Zhi Tongjian* [Comprehensive Mirror to Aid in Government] (Beijing: Zhonghua Book Company, 1956), 14:6694.

68. Cf. Zhang Xiaozheng, "Gudai zhouxian zhuguan de xuanren" [The Selection of Heads of the Prefectures and Counties in Ancient Times], *Study Times*, 15 October 2012, 9.

69. Li Site, "Qingdai difang falü shijian zhong de xiandai luoji : weirao 'fanjian' zhankai" [The Modern Logic of the Implementation of Local Laws in the Qing Dynasty: Revolving around Adultery], *Peking University Law Review* 14, no. 1 (2014): 212–13.

70. *Han History* 6 *Annals of Emperor Xiao Wu*, Dubs, *The History of the Former Han Dynasty* 2:34–35. Note that this text can be also read as implying only one person in all is to be sent from each jurisdiction.

71. The high officials submitted a memorial saying, "Those who do not promote filially pious persons do not respect the imperial edict and should be sentenced as being disrespectful; those who do not seek worthy persons fail in their duty and should be dismissed." *Han History* 6 *Annals of Emperor Xiao Wu*, Dubs, *The History of the Former Han Dynasty* 2:47.

72. "One person from commanderies of 250,000 people, two from those of 450,000, three from those of 600,000, four from those of 800,000, five from those of one million, six from those of 1,200,000. Commanderies under 250,000 should send one person every other year and those under 100,000 one every three years." Du You, *Tongdian*, vol. 1, ed. Wang Wenjin et al. (Beijing: Zhonghua Book Company, 1988), 311.

73. Friedrich Nietzsche, *The Gay Science*, ed. Bernard Williams, trans. Josefine Nauckhoff (Cambridge: Cambridge University Press, 2001), 110–12, 151, 110, 265. See also Nietzsche, *Beyond Good and Evil: Prelude to a Philosophy of the Future*, trans. Judith Norman (Cambridge: Cambridge University Press, 2002), 5–6.

74. Xie Qing and Tang Deyong, eds., *Zhongguo keju kaoshi shi* [A History of China's Imperial Examinations] (Hefei: Huangshan Publishing House, 1995), 212.

75. Ibid., 209, 238–39.

76. For the most important studies, see Edward A. Kracke Jr., "Region, Family, and Individual in the Chinese Examination System," in *Chinese Thought and Institutions*, ed. John King Fairbank (Chicago: University of Chicago Press, 1959; Chinese ed. 2008), 269–90; and Liu Chenglong, "Bei-Song nan-bei bang zhi zheng: guren de diyu qishi" [The Quarrel between the North and South in the Northern Song Dynasty: The Local Prejudice of the Ancients], *Culture and History Vision* 7 (2010): 58–59.

77. Kracke, "Region Family, and Individual," 284–85.

78. See Xie Qing and Tang Deyong, *Zhongguo keju kaoshi shi*, 212.

79. Even at the founding of the People's Republic of China in 1949, local representation was a consideration in the choice of the leaders of the people. Vice-Chairman Gao Gang was chosen largely because he came from the north. Cf. He Zaijin, "Xieshang jianguo: 1948–9 Zhongguo dangpai zhengzhi rizhi [Discussions at the Founding of the State:

A Diary of China's Party Politics 1948–9] (Beijing: People's Literature Publishing House, 2000), 354–55.

80. Many Chinese legal scholars take the U.S. Supreme Court case *Regents of the University of California v. Bakke*, 438 U.S. 265 (1978), to understand affirmative action. However, it should be noted that this was a constitutional action initiated by the U.S. administration and not by a judicial ruling. In 1961, President Kennedy signed Executive Order 10925, which not only forbade government employees from discriminating against any official or applicant for an official post on grounds of nationality, religious belief, skin color, or origin, but also called for affirmative action to guarantee that applicants could find jobs and that the persons employed would be subject to positive treatment during their time of service.

81. Ping-ti Ho, *The Ladder of Success in Imperial China: Aspects of Social Mobility, 1368–1911* (New York: Columbia University Press, 1964), 112–14.

82. If social mobility in the early Ming can be taken as representative, then 50 percent of the *jinshi* graduates came from ordinary families. Modern Western societies find it difficult to achieve such a ratio even today. See Ho, *Ladder*, 256.

83. *Mencius* 4 *Li Lou* A 1, Legge 2:289; *Xunzi* 12 *The Way of the Prince* 1; Mao Zedong, "Zhongguo Gongchandang zai minzuzhanzheng zhong de diwei" [The Role of the Chinese Communist Party in the National War] (14 October 1938), https://www.marxists.org /reference/archive/mao/selected-works/volume-2/mswv2_10.htm.

84. Translator's note: Fan Jin finally passed the exam at the age of fifty-four, and on returning home, he laughed hysterically. Fearing he was going mad, his father-in-law slapped him in the face.

85. "The examination system . . . has been part of China's . . . good tradition. . . . Within our republic, I hope to resurrect these good institutions, with a separation of five powers, and create a political theory that has not been seen anywhere else and create an amazing political plan in which each institution can develop fully and effectively." *Collected Works of Sun Yatsen*, vol. 1 (Beijing: Zhonghua Book Company, 1981), 219.

86. The last line of a poem by Mao Zedong (*Beidaihe* 1954); see https://www.marxists .org/reference/archive/mao/selected-works/poems/poems22.htm.

Chapter Four: The Mixed
Han-Tang-Song Structure and Its Moral Ideal

1. Su Li, "Introduction," 20.

2. Su Li, "Introduction," 20–26.

3. People have often believed that the theory of the five elements comes from Zou Yan, but based on much new material, Rao Zongyi shows that it actually comes from Zi Si. See Rao Zongyi, *Zhongguo shixueshang zhi zhengtonglun* [Orthodoxy in China's History Studies] (Shanghai: Shanghai Far East Press, 1996), 10–16.

4. Gu Jiegang, *Qin-Han de fangshi yu rushing* [Diviners and Scholars in the Qin and Han Dynasties] (Shanghai: Shanghai Classics Publishing House, 1998), 2–4.

5. Chen Mengjia, "Shangdai de shenhua yu wushu" [Myths and Magic of the Shang Dynasty], *Yenching Journal of Chinese Studies* 20 (December 1936): 485–576, 535, quoted in K. C. Chang, *Art, Myth, and Ritual* (Cambridge, Mass.: Harvard University Press, 1983), 47.

6. Needham: "all depict a dancing thaumaturgic shaman, holding plumes, feathers, or other ritual objects in his, or her, hands." Joseph Needham, *History of Science and Technology in China* (Cambridge: Cambridge University Press, 1954–2008), 2:134.

7. Ibid., 2:132.

8. Li Zehou, "Shuo wu shi chuantong" [On the Tradition of Shamans and Historians], in *Bozhai xinshuo*, ed. Li Zehou (Taiwan: Asian Culture, 2000), 43.

9. *Record of Rites* 1A *Qu Li* 74, http://ctext.org/liji/qu-li-i.

10. *Record of Rites* 9 *Jiao Te Sheng* [Sacrifices at the Border] 34, http://ctext.org/liji/jiao-te-sheng.

11. Ibid., 34.

12. *Record of Rites* 25 *Zhongni yanju* [Confucius Quietly at Home] 7 and 6, http://ctext.org/liji/zhongni-yan-ju.

13. Zhang Xuecheng, *Wenshi tongyi* [On Literature and History], ed. Ye Ying (Beijing: Zhonghua Book Company, 1985), 1:1.

14. Gong Zizhen, "Gushi juchen lun er," in *Gong Ding'an quanji leipian* [Collected Works of Gong Zizhen] (Beijing: Cathay Bookshop, 1991), 99.

15. There are many studies of the *Luxuriant Gems of the Spring and Autumn Annals*. For a clear and succinct study of the text, see Steve Davidson and Michael Loewe, "Ch'un ch'iu fan lu," in *Early Chinese Texts: A Bibliographical Guide*, ed. Michael Loewe (Berkeley: Society for the Study of Early China, 1993), 77–87.

16. J. G. Frazer, *The Golden Bough* 3 *Sympathetic Magic*, http://www.gutenberg.org/files/3623/3623-h/3623-h.htm.

17. Needham, *Science and Civilisation in China*, 2:282–83, https://monoskop.org/images/e/e4/Needham_Joseph_Science_and_Civilisation_in_China_Vol_2_History_of_Scientific_Thought.pdf.

18. Editors' note: Yi Shu refers to the *Book of Documents* (尚书) in pre-Qin scripts rediscovered in the wall of Confucius's house in the Han dynasty. At that time, the *Book of Documents* had another version transmitted by scholars' memory and written in post-Qin scripts.

19. If Laufer's view is right, it might well be that we should find some early transliteration of "shaman" in Chinese. Although I have not seen the suggestion made, we might perhaps recognize it in the term *hsienmen*, which does occur, in very significant contexts, in the Chin and Han periods. Both the *Records of the Historian* and the *Western Han History* list a certain Xianmen Gao as among the followers of Tsou Yen's magical-scientific *yin-yang* school. He came from the state of Yen in the far north, and appears in the former text as Xianmen Zi Gao, which might mean that Xianmen was a family name and his given names were Zi Gao, or that he was Gao the Xianmen Master. He would date from the latter half of the fourth century. Needham, *History of Science and Technology*, 2:133. Sima Qian, *Records of the Historian* 28 *Treatise on the Feng and Shan Sacrifices*; see Watson, *Records of the Grand Historian: Han Dynasty II*, 3–52; Sima Qian, *Records of the Historian* 6 *Annals of the First Emperor of Qin*; *Han History* 5 *Treatise on Sacrifices* A28, all speak of Xianmen Gao as a disciple of Zou Yan and of his magical practices. Needham thinks that the word "xianmen" is the origin of the word "shaman." Needham, *History of Science and Technology*, 2:148–49.

20. See http://www.gutenberg.org/files/3623/3623-h/3623-h.htm.

21. Quoted in Needham, *History of Science and Technology*, 2:280.

22. Translator's note: This theory is ascribed to late-night speculation. It posits the universe as an amorphous body beyond the scope of measurement.

23. *Han History: Treatises* 1 *Treatise on the Calendar* A19.

24. Xu Fuguan writes: "Many scholars in the two Han dynasties understood the classics according to *Mr Lu's Spring and Autumn Annals*. They read the great influence *Mr Lu's Spring and Autumn Annals* had on the development of politics as pertaining to the influence of classical studies. Outside *Mr Lu's Spring and Autumn Annals* it is impossible to understand the special features of Han scholarship" (Xu Fuguan, *Lianghan sixiangshi*

[History of Thought in the Han Dynasties] [Shanghai: East China Normal University Press, 2001], 2:1).

25. For the numerological significance and divisions of *Mr Lü's Spring and Autumn Annals*, see the clear exposition in Loewe, *Early Chinese Texts*, 324–30.

26. Cf. Xu Fuguan, *Lianghan sixiangshi*, 2:11–12. Xu Fuguan also says the five elements were originally five materials used in state planning and the people's livelihood. Later they evolved into five basic elements in the cosmos and were joined to the two *qi* of *yin* and *yang*. This process may be traced back to Zou Yan (ibid., 2:182). Also see Needham, *History of Science and Technology*.

27. Translator's note: In the *Zuo Zhuan* this comment is ascribed to Master Ji Wei. See *Zuo Zhuan 6 Duke Wen*, year 15, 11th month, Legge 5:272.

28. "The way of the *Spring and Autumn Annals* is marked by both permanence and change. What changes is used for what is changeable and what is permanent for what remains unchanged. Each has its own sphere; they do not interfere with each other." Dong Zhongshu, *Luxuriant Gems of the Spring and Autumn Annals 3 Bamboo Forest 2.*

29. Fan Ye, *Later Han History: Treatises 28 Treatise on the Hundred Officials Part 5,* http://ctext.org/hou-han-shu/bai-guan-wu/zh.

30. Dong Zhongshu, *Luxuriant Gems of the Spring and Autumn Annals 10* Menghui-yao 1, http://ctext.org/chun-qiu-fan-lu/meng-hui-yao/zh.

31. Dong Zhongshu, *Luxuriant Gems of the Spring and Autumn Annals 15 Erduan 1,* http://ctext.org/chun-qiu-fan-lu/er-duan/zh.

32. Feng Youlan writes: "Although he [Emperor Gao of the Han] . . . gave fiefs to his relatives and meritorious ministers, these fiefs from this time on had only political and not economic significance. By the middle of the Han, the new political and social order had already gradually become stabilized, and in the sphere of economics the people had become accustomed to the changed conditions arising from the natural economic tendencies of the time. The *History of the Former Han* says: 'among the common people, though all were (theoretically) of equal rank, some by the power of their wealth could become masters of others, while even should they become slaves, they were without resentment.'" Feng Youlan, *A History of Chinese Philosophy*, 2 vols., trans. Derk Bodde (Princeton, N.J.: Princeton University Press, 1952–53), 1:18–19.

33. Fu Sinian, "Lun Kongzi xueshuo suoyi shiying yu Qin Han yilai de shehui de yuangu" [A Discussion of the Reasons Why Confucius's Theories Were Appropriate for Society from the Qin-Han Onward], in *Fu Sinian Quanji* [Collected Works of Fu Sinian] (Changsha: Hunan Education Press, 2000), 483.

34. Dong Zhongshu, *Luxuriant Gems of the Spring and Autumn Annals 3 Bamboo Forest* 1.

35. *Selections from the Records of the Historian*, trans. Yang Hsien-yi and Gladys Yang (Beijing: Foreign Languages Press, 1979), 71–72. Translator's note: Out of respect for Yang Hsien-yi and Gladys Yang and remembering the afflictions they went through, I retain their translation.

36. Zou Yan's ideas on the size of the nine states were revived in the late Qing by classical scholars such as Liao Ping (1852–1932). Their aim was to set out the relationship between China and areas outside China on a geographical basis.

37. Dong Zhongshu, *Luxuriant Gems of the Spring and Autumn Annals 24 Offices Imitate Heaven* 1, quoted by Feng Youlan, *History of Chinese Philosophy*, 1:49–51.

38. Dong Zhongshu, *Luxuriant Gems of the Spring and Autumn Annals 28 Ranks in the State* 1. The best discussion of the relationship between the *Luxuriant Gems of the Spring and Autumn Annals* and numerology is found in Xu Fuguan, "Zhouguan chengli zhi shidai ji qi sixiang xingge" [The Time of Composition of the Zhou Officialdom and the

Characteristics of Its Thought], in *Xu Fuguan lun jingxueshi er zhong* [Two Articles by Xu Fuguan on the History of Classical Studies] (Shanghai: Shanghai Bookshop, 2002), 224–26.

39. *Han History*: *Biographies* 26 *Biography of Dong Zhongshu* 13: "On Elevating the Worthy and Good."

40. *Han History*: *Treatises* 4 *Treatise on Food and Goods* A23.

41. *Luxuriant Gems of the Spring and Autumn Annals* 29 *The Norm of Benevolence and Justice* 1. See Feng Youlan, *History of Chinese Philosophy*, 2:39.

42. Cf. Bai Gang, ed., *Zhongguo zhengzhi zhidushi* [A History of China's Political Institutions] (Tianjin: Tianjin People's Press, 1991), 246.

43. Zou Changlin thinks that after the Spring and Autumn period there was a conflict between old and new rites. The old rites were based on an amalgamation of the *Rites of Zhou* and the *Ceremonial* (*Yili*) and formed a unified body of rites. From the Han dynasty onward, there were new rites that were determined by what was just. This brought conflict among the rites. "In the structure of the *Ceremonial*, ancestral power is at the centre and everything revolves around this. In the combined *Ceremonial* and *Rites of Zhou*, the power of the ruler is at the centre. It is the norm for the state and is based on a rigid hierarchy between prince and minister, noble and base." See Zou Changlin, *Zhongguo guli yanjiu* [A Study of China's Ancient Rites] (Beijing: Wenjin Publishing House, 1992), 165.

44. The summary in the *Index to the Four Repositories of All the Books, juan* 19, states: "The *Rites of Zhou* was compiled in the early Zhou dynasty . . . some three hundred years before the capital was moved east. As offices changed and some books were damaged while others developed, the old ones were laid aside and new ones read. This happened innumerable times. . . . [A]s a result later norms were interpolated and the book was a muddle." On the authorship and time of composition of the book, Sima Guang (1019–86), Hu Anguo (1074–1138), Hong Mai (1123–1202), and Su Che (1039–1112) held a very peculiar opinion. They ruled it was a forgery by Liu Xin. This opinion was a prelude to that voiced by the late Qing reformer Kang Youwei. This theory originated when Wang Anshi used the *Rites of Zhou* as a justification for changing the law. The theory lacks any real scholarly historical proof.

45. Xun Yue (148–209) thought that the name of this book was changed from the *Officialdom of Zhou* to the *Rites of Zhou* by Liu Xin.

46. See Sun Yirang, ed., *Zhouli zhengyi* [Correct Interpretation of the "Rites of Zhou"] (Beijing: Zhonghua Book Company, 1987), 1.

47. In his essay on "The Time When the Rites of Zhou Were Established and the Characteristics of Their Thought," Xu Fuguan gives a very perceptive analysis:

> Offices express a political thought. They are a special form which develops in the history of political thought. From the *Book of Poetry*, the *Book of History*, *Zuo's Commentary*, the *Sayings of the States* and the *Book of Zhou*, the philosophers of the hundred schools from Confucius onwards made comments on the classics. These comments were content with rules of thumb such as "the ruler should know men and appoint good ones" and "be close to a gentleman and far from a mean-spirited man." They very rarely looked at the ideal of the offices in themselves or developed any political ideals. It was only in the mid-Warring States period that offices began to express a political ideal. My hunch is that it began with the phrase "the three dukes."

He concludes, "Wang Mang and Liu Xin followed the tradition of using the system of officials to represent the political ideal. When Wang Mang initiated his authoritarian rule as the Great Minister of War, he took this common political ideal and steered the body of the Confucian scholars and, having succeeded in uniting both in one system, he was able to write the blueprint for a practical political ideal." Xu Fuguan, *Xu Fuguan lun jingxueshi er zhong*, 213 and 245.

48. Xu Fuguan, *Xu Fuguan lun jingxueshi er zhong*, 228–32.

49. *Later Han History: Biographies 42 Biographies of Wang Chong, Wang Fu, and Zhong Changtong* 48.

50. Liu Zongyuan, "Shiling Lun" (Part I) [Discourse on Seasonal Commands], in *Liu Zongyuan Ji* [Anthology of Liu Zongyuan] (Beijing: Zhonghua Press, 1979), 85–86.

51. Translator's note: The terms are borrowed from the *Record of Rites 3 Royal Rule*, http://ctext.org/liji/wang-zhi #7 (trans. Legge).

52. Liu Zongyuan, "Fengjian Lun" [Discourse on Feudalism], in *Liu Zongyuan Ji*, 70.

53. In *The Original Way*, Han Yu ascribes "the way of mutual generation and growth" to the sages and not to the decree of heaven. It is the sages who taught us how to dress, eat, and make houses, and also it is they who taught us crafts, trade, medicine, funeral rites, ceremonies, music, politics, law, and other tasks of society. In his "Letter to Wei Zhongxing," Han Yu writes, "Whether one is worthy or unworthy is decided by one's own conduct; whether rich or poor, enjoying good fortune or suffering hard times is a matter for heaven. Whether one has a good or bad reputation is decided by one's own conduct. What pertains to the self is something I can exert myself to achieve, what is determined by heaven or by other people I leave to them and do not force myself." See Han Yu, *Han Changli wenji jiaozhu* [The Annotated Collection of Han Yu], annotated by Ma Qichang (Shanghai: Shanghai Classics Publishing House, 1986), 194.

54. Han Yu, "Reply to Liu Xiucai," in *Han Changli wenji jiaozhu*, 667.

55. Han Yu, "Preface to Meng Dongye," in *Han Changli wenji jiaozhu*, 235.

56. Han Yu, "Original Nature," in *Han Changli wenji jiaozhu*, 21.

57. Han Yu, "The Root of Government," in *Han Changli wenji jiaozhu*, 50–51.

58. The second circle of the Diagram of the Supreme Ultimate comes from the Diagram of Water and Fire, and its central portion, representing the interplay of the five elements, was likewise derived from the Diagram of the Three and Five Supreme Essences, which were both in the *Can Tongqi* (Akinness of the Trio). Feng Youlan, *History of Chinese Philosophy*, 2:440–41.

59. Zhou Dunyi, *Penetrating the Book of Changes*, chap. 11, in Wing-Tsit Chan, *A Source Book in Chinese Philosophy* (Princeton, N.J.: Princeton University Press, 1969), 470.

60. Shao Yong, *Supreme Principles Governing the World*, chaps. 7A–8B, *Outer Chapters on the Observation of Things* (Shanghai: Shanghai Classic Press, 1992), 33.

61. Zhu Xi, *Conversations of Master Zhu Arranged Topically*, ed. Wang Xingxian (Beijing: Zhonghua Book Company, 1986), 1611.

62. The first statement quoted is from Zhu Xi ("Discourse on the Changes by Zhu Xi"), *juan* 1, http://ctext.org/wiki.pl?if=gb&chapter=753396; the second is from Hu Wei (*Yitu mingbian* 易图明辨 [A Clear Appraisal of the Diagram of the Changes]), *juan* 5, http://ctext.org/wiki.pl?if=gb&chapter=297283. On the *River Chart* and the *Luo Writing*, see Jin Chunfeng, *Handai sixiangshi* [History of Thought in the Han Dynasty] (Beijing: China Social Science Press, 1997), 380–85.

63. See Feng Youlan, *History of Chinese Philosophy*, 2:440 and 460.

64. Shao Yong, *Supreme Principles Governing the World*, in Chan, *Source Book*, 485.

65. Ibid., 17.

66. Ibid., 41.

67. Ibid., 57.

68. Ibid., 49.

69. Cheng Hao, *Collected Works of the Two Chengs* (Beijing: Zhonghua Book Company, 2004), 45.

70. Shao Yong, *Supreme Principles Governing the World*, 49.

71. This requirement denies individual experience in the application of knowledge and seeks to be one with the union of heaven and earth "to be able to integrate the true state

of one's mind into harmony, to broaden the scope of the mind and raise the status of man and overcome the division of subjective and objective and so begin to go on the way of Zhu Xi in investigating things and extending knowledge." Qian Mu, *Lianxi, Baiyuan, Hengqu zhi Lixue* [The School of Principle of Zhou Dunyi, Shao Yong, and Zhang Zai] (Taipei: Dongda Book Company, 1978), 60, 63–64.

72. *Song History, juan* 427 *Daoxue zhuan* (Beijing: Zhonghua Book Company, 1977), 12, 724. The philosophers of the School of Principle rated the ritual system highly, but in terms of theory they linked morality to cosmology. This is a reflection of the transitory nature of Song society. As the aristocratic structure broke down, it was hard to know how to construct a true moral spectrum that would include a political component. The Cheng Brothers often spoke about ancestral law and called for it to be reinforced. Zhang Zai also acknowledged its necessity but was more concerned with its function rather than seeing it as part of the inherited tradition of the nobles. See Zhang Zai, *Zhang Zai Ji* [Collected Works of Zhang Zai] (Beijing: Zhonghua Book Company, 1978), 259.

73. Zhang Zai, *Correcting Youthful Ignorance* 17 *Qiancheng*, in Zhang Zai, *Zhang Zai Ji*, 63.

74. Zhang Zai, *Correcting Youthful Ignorance* 1 "Great Harmony," in Chan, *Source Book*, 501.

75. Chen Junmin, *Guanxue sixiang liubian* [On the Song-Ming School of Principle] (Hangzhou: Zhejiang People's Press, 1983), 109.

76. In reply to the Cheng brothers, who said, "When discussing the topics from learning to administration, from administration to the learning of rites, music, military, and criminal justice, few among the literati of the central Shaanxi plain were good at studying," Zhang Zai said, "If they are sincere, then they will have high aspiration and know that learners are laudable for applying their learning well in practice." See Cheng Hao, *Collected Works of the Two Chengs*, 1196.

77. This is how Zhang Shi assessed Sun Zhaoyuan; see Zhang Shiping, *Zhang Nanxuan xianshegn wenji* [Collected Works of Mr. Zhang Nanxuan] (Beijing: Commerce Press, 1936), 109.

78. As Li Ye says: "If one understands arts as commensurable with affairs, even rites and music are no more than an art; but if one understands arts as commensurable with Dao, can't we say even Lun Bian's art of making wheels is vested by the sage?" Li Ye, "Introduction," in *Ce Yuan Haijing* [Sea Mirror of the Circle Measurements] (Shanghai: Wenwu SKQS, 1936), 1. And as Li Fu says: "Things are generated and have shape; shape grows and they have a number." "Number arises naturally from heaven and earth. If there is a thing it has a form and what has form has a number." See Li Fu, "In Response to Xiucai Cao Yue," in *The Yu River Collection* (Shanghai: Wenwu SKQS, n.d.), 5 and 2. This view is the opposite of that set out by Shao Yong in his *Outer Chapters on the Observation of Things*: "Spirit produces numbers, the numbers produce emblems, and emblems produce implements" (Feng Youlan, *History of Chinese Philosophy*, 2:458). Zhou Hanguang, "Qianlun Song-Ming daoxue dui gudai shuxue fazhan de zuoyong he yingxiang" [A Brief Discussion of the Role and Influence of the Study of the Way of the Song and Ming Dynasties on the Development of Ancient Mathematics], in *Lun Song-Ming lixue* [A Discussion of the Song-Ming School of Principle] (Hangzhou: Zhejiang People's Press, 1983), 544.

79. Li Ye says: "It is right to say that numbers are knowable, and it's wrong to say numbers are unknowable. Why? There is something essentially luminous in the obscure. The luminous is the number of nature. But it is even better to be called the principle of nature, rather than the number of nature. . . . [I]f one can infer from the principle of nature to manifest the number of nature, even the furthest and the obscurest could be in tune" (Li Ye, "Introduction," 3). In talking about disasters brought about by errors in the calendar, Li Fu says, "This is the principle of nature. Heaven circulates without ceasing; sun and

moon alternate without stop. All are moving things. Things do not all move in the same way. Although one can make a fairly accurate general measurement, yet as to how many days make up a month and how many months a year it is impossible to avoid a few slight miscalculations. A small miscalculation is not evident, but over time it will build up into a considerable mistake." See Li Fu, "In Response to Xiucai Cao Yue," 5–6.

80. Zhu Xi continues Zhang Zai's theory of *qi* but critically. In his *Explanation of the Supreme Ultimate* and elsewhere he sets out a cosmogony, where the initial nebula is the principle of the supreme ultimate.

81. Wang Fuzhi, *Notes on Master Zhang's Correcting Youthful Ignorance, juan* 8, in *Chuan-shan Quanji* [Complete Works of Wang Chuanshan] (Changsha: Yuelu Press, 1992), 335.

82. Zhang Zai says, "The name 'heaven' comes from supreme vacuity; the name 'the Way' from the transformation of *qi*; the name 'nature' from the union of vacuity and *qi*; and the name 'mind' from the joining of nature and consciousness." *Correcting Youthful Ignorance* 1 "Great Harmony," in Chan, *Source Book*, 504.

83. Zhang Zai's theory of human nature still tends to be too heavily turned toward cosmology, so it is put in his *pian Chengming*. There is no specific discussion of the topic. This is generally accepted to be the case. For a discussion of the origin of his ideas, see Chen Junmin, *Zhang Zai zhexue yu guanxue xuepai* [The Philosophy of Zhang Zai and the School of Official Learning] (Taipei: Taiwan Student Bookshop, 1990), 7–14. On Zhang Zai's ideas of mind and human nature and their relationship to his cosmology, see Lao Sze-Kwang, *Xinbian zhongguo zhexueshi* [A New History of Chinese Philosophy] (Taipei: Sanmin Publishing House, 1981), 179–83.

84. Chan, *Source Book*, 568; Cheng Yi, *The Complete Works of the Two Chengs* (Beijing: Zhonghua Book Company, 2004), 19:1a.

85. Cheng Yi criticizes Shao Yong for his use of symbolic numbers: "The learning of Yao Fu (Shao Yong) begins with 'principle' and extrapolates from there to talk about symbolic numbers and says that the principles in the world all come in fours. . . . This makes it difficult to govern the states of the world. His personality is quite disrespectful and contemptuous" (Cheng Yi, *Complete Works of the Two Chengs*, 45).

86. Chan, *Source Book*, 541; Cheng Yi, *Complete Works of the Two Chengs*, 11:11b.

87. As Cheng says, "the decree of heaven talks about nature; it talks about the principle of nature. . . . In the principle of nature there is nothing that is not good. Speaking of 'heaven' it is the principle of nature" (Cheng Yi, *Complete Works of the Two Chengs*, 24).

88. "Nature is principle. It is what is called 'rational nature.' When traced to its origin there is no principle under heaven which is not good." Chan, *Source Book*, 569; Cheng Yi, *Complete Works of the Two Chengs*, 22A:11a.

89. Cheng Yi, *Complete Works of the Two Chengs*, 25.

Chapter Five: The Symbolic and the Functional

1. Su Li, *Fazhi jiqi bentu ziyuan.*

2. Su Li, "Dangdai zhongguo fali de zhishi puxi jiqi quexian: cong huangdie'an toushi [The Intellectual Spectrum of Jurisprudence in Contemporary China: A Perspective on the Pornography Watching Case], *Peking University Law Journal* 3 (2003): 287–306.

3. Zhu Suli, "Political Parties in China's Judiciary," *Duke Journal of Comparative and International Law* 17 (2007): 533–60.

4. *Marbury v. Madison*, 5 U.S. 137 (1803). In this case, the U.S. Supreme Court assumed the power of reviewing the constitutionality of laws passed by the federal legislature. In constitutional law discourse, it is often regarded as the first case in world history that established the institution of judicial review.

5. Su Li, "Introduction," 28–29.

6. Hannah Arendt, *On Revolution* (London: Penguin, 1973), 148.

7. See Su Li, "Zuowei zhidu de huangdi."

8. Thomas Hobbes, *Leviathan*, ed. Richard Tuck (Cambridge: Cambridge University Press, 1993), 89.

9. Xu Weiyu, ed., *Collected Annotations to Master Lü's Spring and Autumn Annals* (Beijing: Zhonghua Book Company, 2009), 296.

10. Francis Fukuyama, *The Origins of Political Order: From Prehuman Times to the French Revolution* (New York: Farrar, Straus and Giroux, 2011), 92–93.

11. And this was not only a Chinese political pathology. The same problem, for example, worried the Founding Fathers of the United States, especially the Federalists. Let it be remembered that the Federalist Party was one of the factions in the debate over the adoption of the Constitution of 1787. See Hamilton, Madison, and Jay, *Federalist Papers*, doc. 10.

12. Yuri Pines, *The Everlasting Empire* (Princeton, N.J.: Princeton University Press, 2012), 44–45.

13. John Neville Figgis, *The Divine Right of Kings* (1914; repr., London: Forgotten Books, 2012).

14. Joseph R. Fornieri, ed., *The Language of Liberty: The Political Speeches and Writings of Abraham Lincoln* (Washington, D.C.: Regnery, 2009), 33.

15. Su Li, "Gangchang, liyi, chenghu yu shehui guifan."

16. In ancient China, the governing rules were accepted because they were the edicts of the emperor, the Son of Heaven. Now, the laws are obeyed because they are the voice of the people under the leadership of the pioneering party. The people have replaced Heaven, and the Party has replaced the emperor.

17. It is quite rare for a modern, written Constitution to begin with a historical account of thousands of years. Even in China's past Constitutions, in both the Republic of China and the People's Republic of China (e.g., the 1954 Constitution), ancient China was never present.

18. There was a call for a "constitutional Party-archy" (*dangzhu lixian* 党主立宪), a parody of "constitutional monarchy" (*junzhu lixian* 君主立宪) from a Chinese constitutional scholar in the 1990s.

Chapter Six: The Ideal of Civilization and Formation of Institutions in Ancient China

1. Kang Youwei, "Request to Establish a Constitution and Call a National Assembly," in *The Complete Works of Kang Youwei*, vol. 4, ed. Jiang Yihua and Zhang Ronghua (Beijing: Renmin University Press, 2007), 424.

2. See Cao Yuanzhong, *Liyi (Rites)* [Autumn, Year 53 of the ROC], vol. 1 (Huzhou: Nanlin Mr Liu Qiushu Studio, 1916).

Chapter Seven: History, Culture, Revolution, and Chinese Constitutionalism

1. Cf. Zhao Xiaoli, "Ziran yu lishi: Meiguo xianzhengde bolun" [Nature and History: The Paradox of American Constitutionalism], *China Law Review* 2 (2014): 118.

2. Cf. Zhao Xiaoli, "Meiguo xianfazhongde zongjiao yu shangdi" [Religion and God in the American Constitution], *Peking University Law Journal* 4 (2003): 506.

3. See the following texts: The Provisional Constitution of the Republic of China (1912), Constitution of the Republic of China (Yuan Shikai's Constitutional Compact) (1914), Constitution of the Republic of China (Cao Kun Constitution) (1923), Constitution of the

Republic of China for the Political Tutelage Era (1931), and Constitution of the Republic of China (1947).

4. Mao Zedong, "Renmin yingxiong yongchuibuxiu" [Eternal Glory to the Heroes of the People], https://www.marxists.org/reference/archive/mao/selected-works/volume-5 /mswv5_03.htm.

5. In fact, Mao Zedong's name already appeared in the 1982 Constitution, because by that time he had already died and had entered into history.

6. 1982 Constitution of the People's Republic of China, http://www.npc.gov.cn/english npc/Constitution/2007-11/14/content_1372974.htm.

7. Qiang Shigong, *Lifazhe de falixue* [The Jurisprudence of the Legislator] (Hong Kong: Joint Publishing Company, 2007), 93–101.

8. *Book of Poetry* 260 *King Wen*, Legge 4:427.

9. Schmitt, *Constitutional Theory*, 75–76.

10. Liu Han, "'Erci geming' lianxu geming yu Meiguo xianfa Lianxuxing de xiang-xiang" ["A Second Revolution," Continuous Revolution and Imagination of Continuity of the American Constitution], *Politics and Law Review* 1 (2010): 127.

11. *District of Columbia v. Heller*, 554 U.S. 570 (2008). See Jiang Yan, "Qiangzhi tia-okuan haishi Minbing tiaokuan: Meiguo xianfa di er xiuzhengan yanjiu" [The Article of "the Right to Bear Arms" or of "Militia": A Study on the Second Amendment of U.S. Constitution] (master's thesis, Qinghua University Law School, 2013).

12. Zhao Xiaoli, *Meiguo xianfa de yuanzhi jieshi* [Interpreting the Original Intent of the American Constitution] (Shanghai: Shanghai People's Press, 2004).

13. Chen Ruihong, *Zhixianquan yu genbenfa* [Drawing Up a Constitution and the Basic Law] (Beijing: China Legal Publishing House, 2010), 213.

14. Ibid., 233.

15. Ibid., 245.

16. On the distinction between the absolute and relative senses of the Constitution, see Schmitt, *Constitutional Theory*, 4.

17. The speech referred to is Mao Zedong, "Lun Zhonghua Renmin Gongheguo Xianfa de qicao" [On the Draft Constitution of the People's Republic of China] (14 June 1954), https://www.marxists.org/reference/archive/mao/selected-works/volume-5/mswv5_37. htm. But the actual text quoted here comes from CCCPC Party Literature Research Office, ed., *Mao Zedong nianpu 1949–1976* [Chronology of Mao Zedong 1949–1976] (Beijing: Central Party Literature Press, 2013), 2:280–81.

18. See Su Li, "Introduction," 234.

19. Ibid.

20. *Cunmin weiyuanhui zuzhifa* (The Organic Law of the Villagers' Committees).

Chapter Eight: Response to My Critics

1. Tan Qixiang, "Lishishang de zhongguo he zhongguo lidai jiangyu" [Historical China and China's Historical Boundaries], *China's Borderland History and Geography Studies* 1 (1991): 1–9.

2. Mao Zedong, "Qilui: du 'fengjianlun' cheng Guo-lao," 361. Also, Tan Sitong says, "The government of the last two millennia is that of the Qin." Cai Shangsi and Fang Xing, eds., *Complete Works of Tan Sitong*, rev. ed. (Beijing: Zhonghua Book Company, 1981), 337.

3. Ban Gu, *Han History: Biography of Emperor Gao*, pt. 2, 46, http://ctext.org/han-shu /gao-di-ji-xia.

4. Later, it was discovered that the Qin coins differed considerably in weight. See *Records of the Historian* 30 *Book of Measures* 50, available at http://ctext.org/shiji/ping-zhun

-shu. Therefore there are scholars who think that the Qin, which was overthrown three years later, had not in fact unified the currency. It is not even certain whether the Qin actually made their own coins. See, e.g., Peng Xinwei, *A History of Chinese Coinage* (Shanghai: Shanghai Press, 1958), 48; and Xiao Maocheng, "Qin tongyi huobi de xingzhi ji qi lishi yiyi" [The Form of the Qin Unified Coinage and Its Historical Significance], *Journal of Financial Management and Research* 4 (2005): 63–64.

5. Douglass C. North and Robert Paul Thomas, *The Rise of the Western World: A New Economic History* (Cambridge: Cambridge University Press, 1976).

6. Ludwig Wittgenstein argues that to describe a broom as a brush joined to a matching broomstick or to describe an international chessboard as composed of a certain number of black squares and a certain number of white squares may be more "accurate" but in another sense betrays a failure to comprehend (*Philosophical Investigations* [London: Macmillan, 1953], aphorism 60).

7. Sima Qian, "Letter to Ren'an," in Ban Gu, *Han History* 32 *Biography of Sima Qian* 26, http://ctext.org/han-shu/si-ma-qian-zhuan.

8. Ronald H. Coase, "The New Institutional Economics," *Journal of Institutional and Theoretical Economics* 140 (1984): 230.

9. The idea of the costs of exchange in Coase's theory does not come directly from one or more items of empirical data or even a lot of data. Rather, it is something Coase hit on by speculation and later found a mass of empirical data to verify it. In the course of his argument, Coase even uses hypothetical examples. See Ronald H. Coase, "The Problem of Social Cost," *Journal of Law and Economics* 3 (1960): 1–44.

10. Su Li, "Daguo ji qi jiangyude zhengzhi goucheng" [A Large State and the Political Formation of Its Borders], *Jurist* 1 (2016): 26–44.

11. Ibid., sec. 2.

12. Su Li, "Jingying zhengzhi yu zhengzhi canyu," sec. 4.

13. *The Great Learning* in the *Record of Rites*, http://ctext.org/liji/da-xue (trans. Legge).

14. *Analects* 16 *Ji Shi* 2, Legge 1:310.

15. *Analects* 3 *Ba Yi* 1, Legge 1:154.

16. *Book of Poetry* 205 "North Mountain" 2, Legge 4:360.

17. Many scholars support this view. In the Qing dynasty, Zhang Xuecheng held that the rites were what "the worthies learnt from the sages and the sages learnt from the ordinary people." The person who made the greatest contribution to them was therefore the Duke of Zhou and not Confucius. Zhang Xuecheng, *Wenshi tongyi*, 1:141. In modern times, there is Liu Shipei, who held that "in ancient times the rites came from customs." Liu Shipei, "Guzheng yuanshi lun" [A Discussion of Primary Government], in *Liu Shenshu yishu* [The Collected Works of Liu Shipei] (Nanjing: Jiangsu Guji Press, 1997), 683. Also see Kuang Yaming, *Kongzi pingzhuan* [A Critical Biography of Confucius] (Nanjing: Nanjing University Press, 1990), 362; Li Zehou, *Zhongguo gudia sixiangshi lun* [A Discussion of the History of China's Ancient Thought] (Beijing: People's Press, 1986), 11; and Li Anzhai, *'Yili' yu 'liji' zhi shehuixue de yanjiu* [A Sociological Study of the "Ceremonial" and the "Record of Rites"] (Shanghai: Shanghai Century Publishing Group, 2005), 3.

18. *Analects* 1 *Xue Er* 2.

19. "In serving one's parents with filial piety, you will be loyal, and this can be adapted for the prince. Therefore in looking for loyal ministers you must seek among filial sons." Fan Ye, *Later Han History: Biographies* 16, 66, http://ctext.org/hou-han-shu/fu-hou-song -cai-feng-zhao.

20. Su Li, "Zaoqi rujia de renxingguan"; Su Li, "Gangchang, liyi, chenghu yu shehui guifan."

21. Bagehot, *English Constitution.*

22. Albert Venn Dicey, *Introduction to the Study of the Law of the Constitution* (Whitefish, Mont.: Kessinger, 2008).

23. "The constitutionality of Acts of Parliament and treaties shall not be reviewed by the courts." Constitution of the Kingdom of the Netherlands (2008; English version), art. 120.

24. Louis Favoreu, "Constitutional Review in Europe," in *Constitutionalism and Rights: The Influence of the United States Constitution Abroad,* edited by Louis Henkin and Albert J. Rosenthal (New York: Columbia University Press, 1989), 38–59.

25. *Texas v. White* 74 U.S. 700, 725 (1868), italics added.

26. On the relevant background, see Robert Allen Rutland, *The Birth of the Bill of Rights, 1776–1791* (New York: Collier Books, 1962).

27. The earliest judicial case citing this act is that of *McCulloch v. Maryland,* 17 U.S. 316 (1819). The case established the point that in international and interstate trade, federal power was supreme, thus overriding state regulations.

28. A mark of this is the famous Carolene case (*United States v. Carolene Products Co,* 304 U.S. 144 [1938]); see note 4 of the case.

29. *Katzenbach v. McClung,* 379 U.S. 294 (1964); *Heart of Atlanta Motel, Inc. v. United States,* 379 U.S. 241 (1964).

30. "We should have a European code of law, a European supreme court, a unified European currency, unified weights and measures, unified legislation." Georges Bordonove, *Napoleon* (Paris: Editions Pygmalion, 1978), 223.

31. Montesquieu, *Spirit of the Laws,* pt. 1, bk. 8, chap. 20; Rousseau, *Social Contract,* 99. Hamilton, Madison, and Jay, *Federalist Papers,* docs. 9–10. The focus is on democracy in small states; in discussing large states that establish a federal system, it points out the various advantages of republicanism.

32. Plato, *Statesman,* 54; Aristotle, *Politics,* 186–90.

33. "August Heaven has no special love; it helps only the virtuous. The people's hearts have no unchanging attachment; they cherish only kind persons." *Book of Documents: Zhou* 17 *Charge to Zhong of Cai* 2 (trans. Legge), available at http://ctext.org/shang-shu /charge-to-zhong-of-cai. This is not only an opinion, but proof that shows the consensus in society, at least around the time of the Qin-Han era. In the *Records of the Historian,* Sima Qian notes that the three most powerful politicians toward the end of the Qin dynasty, Chen Ying, Xiang Yu, and Liu Bang, all shared the view that anyone could rise to high office. As Chen Ying said, "Are kings, lords, generals, and ministers all born such?" (*Records of the Historian* 7 *Annals of Xiang Yu,* Yang and Yang, *Selections from the "Records of the Historian,"* 207, and *Records of the Historian* 8 *Annals of Emperor Gaozu*).

34. "Tang and Wu changed the decree; they obeyed heaven and responded to humankind." *Book of Changes* 49 *Ge Hexagram: Tuan Commentary* (trans. Legge), http://ctext .org/book-of-changes/ge. Also see *Mencius* 1B *King Hui of Liang* 18 (trans. Legge), http:// ctext.org/mengzi/liang-hui-wang-ii.

35. John Locke, *Two Treatises of Government,* ed. by Peter Laslett (Cambridge: Cambridge University Press, 1960), 364–66.

36. Ho, *Ladder,* 112–14.

37. Cf. Derek Heater, *A Brief History of Citizenship* (New York: New York University Press, 2004); and Peter Riesenberg, *Citizenship in the Western Tradition: Plato to Rousseau* (Chapel Hill: University of North Carolina Press, 1992).

38. "There is no greater chaos than to be without a Son of Heaven. Without a Son of Heaven the strong overcome the weak, the majority oppress the minority. They fight with weapons and there is no gaining any respite." *Mr Lü's Spring and Autumn Annals* 66 *Careful Listening,* http://ctext.org/lv-shi-chun-qiu/jin-ting.

39. Karl Popper, *The Open Society and Its Enemies* (London: Routledge, 1945). For another similar view, see Wittgenstein, *Philosophical Investigations*, no. 297.

40. On 28 July 2007, Queen Elizabeth II's grandson and the tenth in line to the throne, Peter Phillips, announced his engagement to a Canadian Catholic, Autumn Kelly. According to the Act of Succession of 1701, unless Kelly renounces her faith, Phillips will lose his right of succession. Reports suggest that he may do so. See "Peter Phillips May Renounce Succession," *Daily Telegraph*, http://www.telegraph.co.uk/news/uknews/1559322/Peter -Phillips-may-renounce-succession.html. At the time this act played an indispensable, necessary, and legitimate role in ensuring political stability for the English constitution. See Israel Tarkow-Naamani, "The Significance of the Act of Settlement in the Evolution of English Democracy," *Political Science Quarterly* 58, no. 4 (1943): 537–61. But with the passage of time this stipulation no longer has any constitutional significance, such that a constitutional advisor to the prime minister, Lord Lester, commented that this centuries-old prohibition is an injustice and should be abolished. See "Ancient Royal Marriage Law 'Should Be Changed,'" *Daily Telegraph*, http://www.telegraph.co.uk/news/uknews/1559425/An cient-royal-marriage-law-should-be-changed.html. In 2011, a summit of Commonwealth heads of state unanimously agreed to revise the Act of Succession and abolish this requirement. The United Kingdom later took steps to revise the legislation. See http://services .parliament.uk/bills/2012-13/successiontothecrown.html, art. 1, secs. (1) and (2).

41. Su Li, *Songfa xiaxiang: zhongguo jicheng sifa zhidu yanjiu* [Sending the Law down to the Countryside: A Study of China's Grassroots Judicial Institution], rev. ed. (Beijing: Peking University Press, 2011), 9–10.

Arendt, Hannah. *On Revolution*. London: Penguin, 1973.

Aristotle. *The Politics*. Rev. ed. Translated by T. A. Sinclair, revised by Trevor J. Saunders. Harmondsworth: Penguin, 1981.

Bagehot, Walter. *The English Constitution*. Cambridge: Cambridge University Press, 2001.

Bai Gang 白鋼, ed. *Zhongguo zhengzhi zhidushi* 中国政治制度史 [A History of China's Political Institutions]. Tianjin: Tianjin People's Press, 1991.

Bao Jiang 鲍江. "Yunnan de guanhua fangyan cong he erlai?" 云南的官话方言从何而来? [Where Did the Mandarin Dialect of Yunnan Come From?]. *Wenshi Monthly* 文史月刊, February 2011, 79–80.

Birch, Cyril, ed. *Anthology of Chinese Literature*, vol. 1: *From Early Times to the Fourteenth Century*. New York: Grove Press, 1965. http://afe.easia.columbia.edu/ps/china /taoqian_peachblossom.pdf.

Bolingbroke, Henry St. John. *Political Writings*. Edited by David Armitage. Cambridge: Cambridge University Press, 1997.

Brest, Paul, Sanford Levinson, J. M. Balkin, Akhil Reed Amar, and Reva B. Siegel. *Processes of Constitutional Decision Making: Cases and Materials*. 5th ed. New York: Aspen, 2006.

Cai Shangsi 蔡尚思 and Fang Xing 方行, eds. *Complete Works of Tan Sitong* 谭嗣同全集. Rev. ed. Beijing: Zhonghua Book Company, 1981.

Cai Yan 蔡琰. "Resentment" 悲愤诗. In *Gushiyuan* 古诗源 [The Origin of Ancient Poetry], edited by Shen Deqian 沈德潜. Beijing: Zhonghua Book Company, 1963.

Cao Yuanzhong 曹元忠. *Liyi (Rites)* 礼仪 [Autumn, Year 53 of the ROC]. Vol. 1. Huzhou: Nanlin Mr Liu Qiushu Studio, 1916.

CCCPC Party Literature Research Office, ed. *Mao Zedong nianpu 1949-1976* 毛泽东年谱 (1949-1976) [Chronology of Mao Zedong 1949-1976]. Beijing: Central Party Literature Press, 2013.

Chan, Wing-Tsit. *A Source Book in Chinese Philosophy*. Princeton, N.J.: Princeton University Press, 1969.

Chang, K. C. *Art, Myth, and Ritual*. Cambridge, Mass.: Harvard University Press, 1983.

Chen Junmin 陈俊民. *Guanxue sixiang liubian* 关学思想流变 [On the Song-Ming School of Principle]. Hangzhou: Zhejiang People's Press, 1983.

——. *Zhang Zai zhexue yu guanxue xuepai* 张载哲学与关学学派 [The Philosophy of Zhang Zai and the School of Official Learning]. Taipei: Taiwan Student Bookshop, 1990.

Chen Mengjia 陈梦家. "Shangdai de shenhua yu wushu" 商代的神话与巫术 [Myths and Magic of the Shang Dynasty]. *Yenching Journal of Chinese Studies* 20 (December 1936): 485-576.

Chen Ruihong 陈端洪. *Zhixianquan yu genbenfa* 制宪权与根本法 [Drawing Up a Constitution and the Basic Law]. Beijing: China Legal Publishing House, 2010.

Chen Shou 陈寿. *San Guo Zhi* 三国志. [Records of the Three Kingdoms]. Beijing: Zhonghua Book Company, 2006.

Cheng Hao. *Collected Works of the Two Chengs*. Beijing: Zhonghua Book Company, 2004.

Cheng Yi. *The Complete Works of the Two Chengs*. Beijing: Zhonghua Book Company, 2004.

Cicero. *On the State*. Translated by Shen Shuping. Beijing: Commerce Press, 1999.

Coase, Ronald H. "The New Institutional Economics." *Journal of Institutional and Theoretical Economics* 140 (1984): 229–31.

———. "The Problem of Social Cost." *Journal of Law and Economics* 3 (1960): 1–44.

Davidson, Steve, and Michael Loewe. "Ch'un ch'iu fan lu." In *Early Chinese Texts: A Bibliographical Guide*, edited by Michael Loewe, 77–87. Berkeley: Society for the Study of Early China, 1993.

Dershowitz, Alan M. "Torture of Terrorists: Is It Necessary to Do and to Lie about It?" In *Shouting Fire: Civil Liberties in a Turbulent Age*, 470–77. Boston: Little, Brown, 2002.

———. "Wiretaps and National Security Surveillance." In *Shouting Fire: Civil Liberties in a Turbulent Age*, 457–69. Boston: Little, Brown, 2002.

Diamond, Arthur Sigismund. *Primitive Law, Past and Present*. London: Methuen, 1971.

Diamond, Jared. *Guns, Germs, and Steel: The Fates of Human Societies*. New York: Norton, 1997.

Dicey, Albert Venn. *Introduction to the Study of the Law of the Constitution*. Whitefish, Mont.: Kessinger, 2008.

Du You 杜佑. *Tongdian* 通典. Vol. 1. Edited by Wang Wenjin 王文锦 et al. Beijing: Zhonghua Book Company, 1988.

Dworkin, Ronald. "The Threat to Patriotism." *New York Review of Books*, 28 February 2002, 44–49.

Editorial Committee of Series of Researches on Chinese Minorities' Society and History, Editorial Section of Sichuan Province, ed. *Sichuansheng Ganzizhou Zangzu Shehui Lishi Diaocha* 四川省甘孜州藏族社会历史调查 [Research on the Society and History of Tibetan Nationality in Prefecture of Garzê, Sichuan]. Beijing: Ethnic Publishing, 2009.

Eskridge, William N., Jr., and Sanford Levinson, eds. *Constitutional Stupidities, Constitutional Tragedies*. New York: New York University Press, 1998.

Fairbank, John K., ed. *The Chinese World Order: Traditional China's Foreign Relations*. Cambridge, Mass.: Harvard University Press, 1968.

Fan Wenlan 范文澜, *Zhongguo tongshi jianbian* 中国通史简编 [A Simple Edition of the General History of China]. Shijiazhuang: Hebei Educational Press, 2000.

Fan Zhongyan 范仲淹. "Yueyanglou ji" 岳阳楼记. In *Fan Zhongyan quanji* 范仲淹全集 [Collected Works of Fan Zhongyan], vol. 1., 194–95. Chengdu: Sichuan University Press, 2007.

Fang Tie 方铁. "Lun jimi zhice xiang tuguan tusi zhidu de yanbian" 论羁縻治策向土官土司制度的演变 [A Discussion of the Shift from the Slack-Rein Prefectures to Native Administrative and Military Rule]. *China's Borderland History and Geography Studies* 中国边疆史地研究 2 (2011): 68–80.

Fang Xuanling, et al. *Jin History*. Vol. 4. Beijing: Zhonghua Press, 1974.

Favoreu, Louis. "Constitutional Review in Europe." In *Constitutionalism and Rights: The Influence of the United States Constitution Abroad*, edited by Louis Henkin and Albert J. Rosenthal, 38–59. New York: Columbia University Press, 1989.

Fehrenbacher, Don E. "The Dred Scott Case." In *Quarrels That Have Shaped the Constitution*, rev. ed., edited by John A. Garraty, 86–99. New York: Harper & Row, 1987.

Fei Xiaotong 费孝通. "Lun zhishi jieji" 论知识阶级 [On the Intelligentsia]. In *Huangquan yu shenquan* 皇权与绅权 [Imperial Power and the Power of the Gentry], edited by Wu Han 吴晗, Fei Xiaotong 费孝通, et al. Shanghai: Shanghai Guanchashe, 1948.

———. "Sunshi chongxi xia de xiangtu" 损蚀冲洗下的乡土 [Native Soil under Erosion]. In *Xiangtu Zhongguo* 乡土中国 [Rural China], 295–303. Shanghai: Shanghai Century, 2007.

——. "Wenzi xiaxiang" [How Writing Moved into the Countryside]. *Xiangtu Zhongguo* 乡土中国 [Rural China] (2007): 18.

——. "Xiangtu chongjian" 乡土重建 [Rural Reconstruction]. In *Xiangtu Zhongguo* 乡土中国 [Rural China], 253–67. Shanghai: Shanghai Century, 2007.

——. "Zailun wenzi xiaxiang" 再论文字下乡 [A Fresh Look at How Writing Moved into the Countryside]. *Xiangtu Zhongguo* 乡土中国 [Rural China] (2007): 22.

Fei Xiaotong, Gary G. Hamilton, and Wang Zheng, trans., *From the Soil: The Foundations of Chinese Society* (Berkeley: University of California Press, 1992).

Feng Xiang 冯象. *Zhengfa biji* 政法笔记 [Notes on Politics and Law]. Nanjing: Jiangsu People's Press, 2004. Rev. ed., Beijing: Peking University Press, 2012.

Feng Yan 封演 [Tang dynasty]. *Fengshi wenjianji xiaozhu* 封氏闻见记校注 [Annotated Edition of the Memoirs of Feng Yan]. Beijing: Zhonghua Book Company, 2005.

Feng Youlan [Fung Yu-Lan] 冯友兰. *A History of Chinese Philosophy.* 2 vols. Translated by Derk Bodde. Princeton, N.J.: Princeton University Press, 1952–53.

Ferguson, Adam. *An Essay on the History of Civil Society.* Cambridge: Cambridge University Press, 1995.

Figgis, John Neville. *The Divine Right of Kings.* 1914. Reprint, London: Forgotten Books, 2012.

Fornieri, Joseph R., ed. *The Language of Liberty: The Political Speeches and Writings of Abraham Lincoln.* Washington, D.C.: Regnery, 2009.

Fu Sinian 傅斯年. "Lun Kongzi xueshuo suoyi shiying yu Qin Han yilai de shehui de yuangu" 论孔子学说所以适应于秦汉以来的社会的缘故 [A Discussion of the Reasons Why Confucius's Theories Were Appropriate for Society from the Qin-Han Onward]. In *Fu Sinian Quanji* 傅斯年选集 [Collected Works of Fu Sinian], 301. Changsha: Hunan Education Press, 2000.

Fukuyama, Francis. *The Origins of Political Order: From Prehuman Times to the French Revolution.* New York: Farrar, Straus and Giroux, 2011.

Gao Jingting 高静亭. *Zhengyin cuoyao* 正音撮要 [The Essence of Standard Pronunciation]. Vol. 2 卷二: *Guanhua biesu* 官话别俗 [Uncommon Customs of Mandarin]. 1834.

Ge Jianhong 葛剑雄. *Zhongguo lidai jiangyude bianqian* 中国历代疆域的变迁 [Border Shifts in the Course of Chinese History]. Hong Kong: Commercial Press, 1997.

Ge Jianxiong 葛剑雄. *Tongyi yu fenlie: Zhongguo lishi de qishi* 统一与分裂 : 中国历史的启示 [Unity and Division: Lessons from Chinese History]. Hong Kong: Commercial Press, 2013.

Geng Zhensheng 耿振生, ed. *Jindai guanhua yuyin yanjiu* 近代官话语音研究 [A Linguistic Study of Modern Mandarin]. Beijing: Languages & Culture Press, 2005.

Giddens, Anthony. *The Nation-State and Violence: Volume Two of a Contemporary Critique of Historical Materialism.* Oxford: Polity, 1985.

Gong Yin 龚荫, et al., eds. *Zhongguo tusi zhidu* 中国土司制度 [China's Headman System]. Kunming: Nationalities Publishing House of Yunnan, 1992.

Gong Zizhen 龚自珍. "Gushi juchen lun er" 古史钩沉论二. In *Gong Ding'an quanji leipian* 龚定庵全集类编 [Collected Works of Gong Zizhen], 99. Beijing: Cathay Bookshop, 1991.

Goody, Jack, ed. *Literacy in Traditional Societies.* Cambridge: Cambridge University Press, 1975.

Greenidge, A. H. J. *A Handbook of Greek Constitutional History.* London: Macmillan, 1914.

Gu Jiegang 顾颉刚. *Qin-Han de fangshi yu rusheng* 秦汉的方士与儒生 [Diviners and Scholars in the Qin and Han Dynasties]. Shanghai: Shanghai Classics Publishing House, 1998.

Gu Jiegang 顾颉刚 and Shi Nianhai 史念海. *Zhongguo jiangyu yangeshi* 中国疆域沿革史 [A History of the Evolution of China's Borders]. Hong Kong: Commercial Press, 2000.

Gu Yanwu 顾炎武. *Rizhilu Jishi* 《日知录集释》(上) [Explanations Collected by Huang Rucheng 黄汝成]. Vol. 1. Shanghai: Shanghai Classics Publishing House, 2006.

Gu Zuyu 顾祖禹. *Dushi fangyu jiyao* 读史方舆纪要 [Important Notes on Reading the Geography Treatises in the Histories]. Edited by He Cijun 贺次君 and Shi Hejin 施和金. Beijing: Zhonghua Book Company, 2005.

Guo Moruo 郭沫若. "Gudai wenzi zhi bianzheng de fazhan" 古代文字之辩证的发展 [The Dialectic Development of Ancient Characters]. *Acta Archaeologica Sinica* 考古学报 1 (1972): 9–10.

———. *Zhongguoshi gao* 中国史稿 [A Draft History of China]. Beijing: People's Publishing House, 1979.

Guo Zaiyi 郭在贻. *Xunguxue* 训诂学 [Phonetics]. Beijing: Zhonghua Book Company, 2005.

Hamilton, Alexander, James Madison, and John Jay. *The Federalist Papers*. 1788. Reprint, Watertown, Wis.: Tribeca Books, 2010.

Han Yu. "Four Poems on Various Subjects." In *Han Changli wenji jiaozhu* [The Annotated Collection of Han Yu], annotated by Qu Shouyuan and Chang Sichun, 2709. Chengdu: Sichuan University Press, 1986.

———. *Han Changli wenji jiaozhu* [The Annotated Collection of Han Yu]. Annotated by Ma Qichang. Shanghai: Shanghai Classics Publishing House, 1986.

He Xuefeng 贺雪峰. *Cunzhi moshi: ruogan anli yanjiu* 村治模式: 若干案例研究 [The Village Model: A Study of Some Key Cases]. Jinan: Shandong People's Press, 2009.

———. *Xin xiangtu Zhongguo: zhuanxingqi xiangcun shehui diaocha biji* 新乡土中国 ： 转型期乡村社会调查笔记 [New Rural China: Notes from a Survey of Rural China at a Time of Transition]. Guilin: Guangxi Normal University Press, 2003.

He Zaijin 郝在今. "Xieshang jianguo: 1948–9 Zhongguo dangpai zhengzhi rizhi 协商建国: 1948–1949 中国党派政治日志 [Discussions at the Founding of the State: A Diary of China's Party Politics 1948–9]. Beijing: People's Literature Publishing House, 2000.

Headland, Thomas N., Kenneth Pike, and Marvin Harris, eds. *Emics and Etics: The Insider/Outsider Debate*. Newbury Park, Calif.: Sage, 1990.

Heater, Derek. *A Brief History of Citizenship*. New York: New York University Press, 2004.

Ho, Ping-ti. *The Ladder of Success in Imperial China: Aspects of Social Mobility, 1368–1911*. New York: Columbia University Press, 1964.

Hobbes, Thomas. *Leviathan*. Edited by Richard Tuck. Cambridge: Cambridge University Press, 1993.

Hou Jingyi 侯精一. "Bainianqian de Guangdong renxue 'guanming' shouce 'zhengyinjuhua'" 百年前的广东人学'官话'手册《正音咀华》[*Correct Pronunciation* as a Handbook for Cantonese People a Hundred Years Ago Studying Mandarin]. *Wenzi gaige* 文字改革, December 1962.

Hou Suqin 侯素琴. "Mading-Lude yu xiandai deyu" 马丁·路德与现代德语 [Martin Luther and Modern German]. *Shanghai Technical University Journal* (Social Sciences) 上海理工大学学报 2 (2006): 53–55.

Hou Xiaorong 后晓荣. *Qindai zhengqu dili* 秦代政区地理 [Administrative Division in the Qin Dynasty]. Beijing: Social Sciences Academic Press, 2009.

Hsu, Cho-yun. *Ancient China in Transition: An Analysis of Social Mobility, 722–222 B.C.* Stanford: Stanford University Press, 1965.

Huang Renyu 黄仁宇. *Zhongguo da lishi* 中国大历史 [China: A Macro History]. Beijing: Joint Publishing, 1997.

Huntington, Samuel P. *The Clash of Civilizations and the Remaking of World Order*. New York: Simon & Schuster, 1996.

Institute of Chinese Administrative Divisions. *Woguo xingzhengqu gaigeshexiang* [A Reform Plan for China's Administrative Divisons]. Beijing: Chinese Society Press, 1991.

Jaffa, Harry V. *Crisis of the House Divided: An Interpretation of the Issues in the Lincoln-Douglas Debates.* 50th Anniversary ed. Chicago: University of Chicago Press, 2009.

Jiang Yan 蒋燮. "Qiangzhi tiaokuan haishi Minbing tiaokuan: Meiguo xianfa di er xiuzhengan yanjiu" '枪支条款'还是'民兵条款'：美国宪法第二修正案研究 [The Article of "the Right to Bear Arms" or of "Militia": A Study on the Second Amendment of U.S. Constitution]. Master's thesis, Qinghua University Law School, 2013.

Jin Chunfeng 金春峰. *Handai sixiangshi* 汉代思想史 [History of Thought in the Han Dynasty]. Beijing: China Social Science Press, 1997.

Jin Zheng 金诤. *Keju zhidu yu Zhongguo wenhua* 科举制度与中国文化 [The Imperial Examinations and Chinese Culture]. Shanghai: Shanghai People's Publishing House, 1990.

Kang Youwei. "Request to Establish a Constitution and Call a National Assembly." In *The Complete Works of Kang Youwei,* vol. 4, edited by Jiang Yihua and Zhang Ronghua. Beijing: Renmin University Press, 2007.

Kracke, Edward A., Jr. "Region, Family, and Individual in the Chinese Examination System." In *Chinese Thought and Institutions,* edited by John King Fairbank, 269–90. Chicago: University of Chicago Press, 1959. Chinese edition 2008.

Kuang Yaming 匡亚明. *Kongzi pingzhuan* 孔子评传 [A Critical Biography of Confucius]. Nanjing: Nanjing University Press, 1990.

Lao Sze-Kwang 劳思光. *Xinbian zhongguo zhexueshi* 新编中国哲学史 (三上) [A New History of Chinese Philosophy]. Taipei: Sanmin Publishing House, 1981.

Legge, James. *The Chinese Classics,* vol. 1: *Confucian Analects, The Great Learning and the Doctrine of the Mean.* 2nd ed. Oxford: Clarendon, 1893.

——. *The Chinese Classics,* vol. 2: *The Works of Mencius.* 2nd ed. Oxford: Clarendon, 1893.

——. *The Chinese Classics,* vol. 3: *The Book of Historical Documents.* 2nd ed. Oxford: Clarendon, 1893.

——. *The Chinese Classics,* vol. 4: *The Book of Poetry.* 2nd ed. Oxford: Clarendon, 1893.

——. *The Chinese Classics,* vol. 5: *The Ch'un Ts'ew with the Tso Chuen.* 2nd ed. Oxford: Clarendon, 1893.

Lepore, Jill. "The Rule of History, *Magna Carta,* the Bill of Rights, and the Hold of Time." *New Yorker,* 20 April 2015.

Li Anzhai 李安宅. *'Yili' yu 'liji' zhi shehuixue de yanjiu* 〈仪礼〉与〈礼记〉之社会学的研究 [A Sociological Study of the "Ceremonial" and the "Record of Rites"]. Shanghai: Shanghai Century Publishing Group, 2005.

Li Dalong 李大龙. *Han-Tang fanshu tizhi yanjiu* 汉唐藩属体制研究 [A Study of Barbarian Administrative Areas under the Han and Tang]. Beijing: China Social Science Press 中国社会科学出版社, 2006.

Li Dandan 李丹丹. "Guanhua de xingzhi" 官话的性质 [The Nature of Mandarin Chinese]. *Xinjiang Social Sciences* 新疆社会科学 5 (2011): 105–11.

Li Rong 李荣. "Guanhua fangyan de fenqu" 官话方言的分区 [The Area in Which the Mandarin Dialect Is Spoken]. *Dialect* 方言 1 (1985): 2–5.

Li Shiyu 李世瑜. *Tianjin de fangyan liyu* 天津的方言俚语 [Slang in the Tianjin Dialect]. Tianjin: Tianjin Classics Publishing House, 2004.

Li Shu 黎澍. "Sun Zhongshan shangshu Li Hongzhang shiji kaobian" 孙中山上书李鸿章事迹考辨 [A Study of the Account of Sun Yat-sen's Letter to Li Hongzhang]. *Historical Research* 历史研究 3 (1988): 75–83.

Li Site 李斯特. "Qingdai difang falü shijian zhong de xiandai luoji: weirao 'fanjian' zhankai" 清代地方法律实践中的现代逻辑—围绕'犯奸'展开 [The Modern Logic of the Implementation of Local Laws in the Qing Dynasty: Revolving around Adultery]. *Peking University Law Review* 北大法律评论 14, no. 1 (2014): 212–13.

Li Ye. *Ce Yuan Haijing* 測圓海镜 [Sea Mirror of the Circle Measurements]. Shanghai: Wenwu SKQS, 1936.

———. *The Yu River Collection*. Shanghai: Wenwu SKQS, n.d.

Li Zehou 李泽厚. "Shuo wu shi chuantong" 说巫史传统 [On the Tradition of Shamans and Historians]. In *Bozhai xinshuo* 波斋新说, edited by Li Zehou, 43. Taiwan: Asian Culture, 2000.

———. *Zhongguo gudia sixiangshi lun* 中国古代思想史论 [A Discussion of the History of China's Ancient Thought]. Beijing: People's Press, 1986.

Lin Bai 林白 and Zhu Meifang 朱梅芳. *Zhongguo keju shihua* 中国科举史话 [A Brief History of China's Civil Service Examinations]. Nanchang: Jiangxi People's Press, 2002.

Lin Tao 林焘. "Cong guanhua, guoyu dao putonghua" 从官话、国语到普通话 [From Mandarin, the National Language to Putonghua]. *Language Planning* 语文建设, October 1998, 6.

Liu Chenglong 刘诚龙. "Bei-Song nan-bei bang zhi zheng: guren de diyu qishi" 北宋南北榜之争—古人的地域歧视 [The Quarrel between the North and South in the Northern Song Dynasty: The Local Prejudice of the Ancients]. *Culture and History Vision* 文史博览 7 (2010): 58–59.

Liu Haifeng 刘海峰 and Li Bing 李兵. *Zhongguo keju shi* 中国科举史 [A History of China's Civil Service Examinations]. Shanghai: Orient Publishing Centre, 2004.

Liu Han 刘晗. "'Erci geming' lianxu geming yu Meiguo xianfa Lianxuxing de xiangxiang" '二次革命'、连续革命与美国宪法稳定性的想象 ["A Second Revolution," Continuous Revolution and Imagination of Continuity of the American Constitution]. *Politics and Law Review* 政治与法律评论 1 (2010): 127.

Liu Jinqin 刘金勤. "Yuanqu ciyu fangyan jinzheng" 元曲词语方言今证 [A Modern Study of the Dialect Terms in Yuan Operas]. *Chinese Knowledge* 语文知识 4 (2012): 41–43.

Liu Shipei 刘师培. "Guzheng yuanshi lun" 古政原始论 [A Discussion of Primary Government]. In *Liu Shenshu yishu* 刘申叔遗书 [The Collected Works of Liu Shipei], 663–86. Nanjing: Jiangsu Guji Press, 1997.

Liu Xu 刘昫. *Jiu Tang Shu* 旧唐书 [Old Tang History]. Beijing: Zhonghua Book Company, 1975.

Liu Zongyuan 柳宗元. *Liu Zongyuan Ji* 柳宗元集 [Anthology of Liu Zongyuan]. Beijing: Zhonghua Book Company, 1979.

Locke, John. *Two Treatises of Government*. Edited by Peter Laslett. Cambridge: Cambridge University Press, 1960.

Lodge, R. Anthony. *French: From Dialect to Standard*. London: Routledge, 1993.

Lu You 陆游. "Bingqi shuhuai" 病起书怀 [In *Lu You Shi Xuan* 陆游诗选 [Selected Poems of Lu You], selected and annotated by You Guo'En and Li Yi, 41. Beijing: People's Literature Publishing House, 1997.

Luo Xianglin 罗香林. *Kejia yanjiudaolun* 客家研究导论 [A Guide to Research in Hakka]. 1933. Reprint, Shanghai: Shanghai Literature and Art Publishing House, 1992.

Mao Zedong 毛泽东. "Jinggangshan de douzheng" 井冈山的斗争 [The Struggle in the Jinggang Mountains] (25 November 1928). https://www.marxists.org/reference/archive /mao/selected-works/volume-1/mswv1_4.htm.

———. "Lun shida guanxi" 论十大关系 [On the Ten Major Relationships]. https://www .marxists.org/reference/archive/mao/selected-works/volume-5/mswv5_51.htm.

———. "Lun Zhonghua Renmin Gongheguo Xianfa de qicao" 论《中华人民共和国宪法》的起草 [On the Draft Constitution of the People's Republic of China] (14 June 1954). https://www.marxists.org/reference/archive/mao/selected-works/volume-5/mswv5_37.htm.

———. *Mao Zedong Wenji* 毛泽东文集 [Collected Works of Mao Zedong]. Beijing: Peoples' Press, 1999.

———. "Qilui: du 'fengjianlun' cheng Guo-lao" 七律·读《封建论》呈郭老 [Seven-Character Poem: On Reading "A Discourse on Feudalism" for Guo Moruo]. In *Mao Zedong's Writings after 1949*, vol. 13, 361. Beijing: Central Party Literature Press, 1998.

———. "Renmin yingxiong yongchuibuxiu" 人民英雄永垂不朽 [Eternal Glory to the Heroes of the People]. https://www.marxists.org/reference/archive/mao/selected-works/volume-5/mswv5_03.htm.

———. "Xingxingzhihuo keyi Liaoyuan" 星星之火可以燎原 [A Single Spark Can Start a Prairie Fire] (5 January 1930). https://www.marxists.org/reference/archive/mao/selected-works/volume-1/mswv1_6.htm.

———. "Zai bada erci huiyi daibiaotuan tuanzhang huiyi shangde jianghua" 在八大二次会议代表团长会议上的讲话八大二次会议代表团长会议上的讲话 [Speech at the Conference of Heads of Delegations to the Second Session of the 8th Party Congress: The Elites Are the Most Ignorant and the Lowly the Most Intelligent] (18 May 1958). https://www.marxists.org/reference/archive/mao/selected-works/volume-8/mswv8_11.htm.

———. "Zhongguo Gongchandang zai minzuzhanzheng zhong de diwei" 中国共产党在民族战争中的地位 [The Role of the Chinese Communist Party in the National War] (14 October 1938). https://www.marxists.org/reference/archive/mao/selected-works/volume-2/mswv2_10.htm.

———. "Zhongguode hongse zhengquan weishenme nenggou cunzai?" 中国的红色政权为什么能够存在? [Why Is It That Red Political Power Can Exist in China?] (5 October 1928). https://www.marxists.org/reference/archive/mao/selected-works/volume-1/mswv1_3.htm.

Miller, William Ian. *Bloodtaking and Peacemaking: Feud, Law, and Society in Saga Iceland*, Chicago: University of Chicago Press, 1990.

Miyazaki Ichisada 宫崎市定. *A Study of the Law of the Nine Ranks of Officials: Before the Imperial Examinations* [九品官人法 : 科举前传]. Translated by Han Sheng 韩昇 and Liu Jianying 刘建英. Beijing: Zhonghua Book Company, 2008.

Montesquieu. *The Spirit of the Laws*. Translated and edited by Anne M. Cohler, Basia C. Millers, and Harold S. Stone. Cambridge: Cambridge University Press, 1989.

Müller, Ingo. *Hitler's Justice: The Courts of the Third Reich*. Translated by Deborah Lucas Schneider. Cambridge, Mass.: Harvard University Press, 1991.

Needham, Joseph. *History of Science and Technology in China*. Cambridge: Cambridge University Press, 1954–2008.

Nietzsche, Friedrich. *Beyond Good and Evil: Prelude to a Philosophy of the Future*. Translated by Judith Norman. Cambridge: Cambridge University Press, 2002.

———. *The Gay Science*. Edited by Bernard Williams, translated by Josefine Nauckhoff. Cambridge: Cambridge University Press, 2001.

———. *The Will to Power*. Edited by Walter Kaufmann, translated by Walter Kaufmann and R. J. Hollingdale. New York: Vintage, 1967.

North, Douglass C., and Robert Paul Thomas. *The Rise of the Western World: A New Economic History*. Cambridge: Cambridge University Press, 1976.

Ocko, Jonathan K. "I'll Take It All the Way to Beijing: Capital Appeals in the Qing." *Journal of Asian Studies* 47, no. 2 (1988): 291–315.

Ouyang Xiu and Song Qi. *Xin Tang Shu* [New Tang History]. Beijing: Zhonghua Book Company, 1975.

Pang Zhuoheng 庞卓恒. "Guanyu xi Zhoude laodong shengchan fangshi, shengchanlü he renkou guce" 关于西周的劳动生产方式、生产率和人口估测 [Methods of Production, Productivity and an Estimate of the Population of the Western Zhou]. *Journal of Tianjin Normal University (Social Sciences)* 天津师范大学学报（社会科学版）5 (1998): 41–50.

Peng Xinwei 彭信威. *A History of Chinese Coinage*. Shanghai: Shanghai Press, 1958.

———. *Zhongguo huobi shi* 中国货币史 [Chinese Monetary History]. Shanghai: Shanghai Press, 1958.

Pines, Yuri. *The Everlasting Empire*. Princeton, N.J.: Princeton University Press, 2012.

Plato. *Laws*. Translated by Wang Xiaochao. Beijing: People's Press, 2003.

———. *Statesman*. Edited by Julia Annas and Robin Waterfield. Cambridge: Cambridge University Press, 1995.

Popper, Karl. *The Open Society and Its Enemies*. London: Routledge, 1945.

Posner, Richard A. "The Homeric Version of the Minimal State." In *The Economics of Justice*, 119–45. Cambridge, Mass.: Harvard University Press, 1983.

———. *Law, Pragmatism, and Democracy*. Cambridge, Mass.: Harvard University Press, 2003.

———. *Not a Suicide Pact: The Constitution in a Time of National Emergency*. Oxford: Oxford University Press, 2006.

———. *Problems of Jurisprudence*. Cambridge, Mass.: Harvard University Press, 1990.

———. "Review of Ingo Müller, *Hitler's Justice: The Courts of the Third Reich*." *New Republic* 36 (17 June 1991).

———. "What Is Law, and Why Ask?" In *Problems of Jurisprudence*, 220–44.

Pye, Lucian W. "China: Erratic State, Frustrated Society." *Foreign Affairs*, Fall 1990. http://nfgworld.com/files/China-ErraticState.pdf.

Qian Mu 钱穆. *Guoshi xinlun* 国史新论 [A New Account of Chinese History]. Hong Kong: Joint Publishing Company, 2001.

———. *Qin-Han shi* 秦汉史 [A History of the Qin and Han]. Hong Kong: Joint Publishing Company, 2004.

———. "Zailun zhongguo shehui yanbian" 再论中国社会演变 [A Second Discussion of the Evolution of Chinese Society]. In *Guoshi xinlu* 国史新论 [A New Discussion of Chinese History], 43–64. Hong Kong: Joint Publishing Company, 2001.

———. "Zhongguo lidai zhengzhi deshi 中国历代政治得失 [The Experiences and Lessons of China's Politics throughout the Centuries]. Hong Kong: Joint Publishing Company, 2001.

Qian Mu 钱穆. *Lianxi, Baiyuan, Hengqu zhi Lixue* 濂溪百源横渠之理学 [The School of Principle of Zhou Dunyi, Shao Yong, and Zhang Zai]. Taipei: Dongda Book Company, 1978.

Qian Zengyi 钱曾怡, ed. *Hanyu guanhua fangyan yanjiu* 汉语官话方言研究 [A Study of the Mandarin Dialects of Chinese]. Jinan: Qilu Press, 2010.

Qiang Shigong 强世功. *Lifazhe de falixue* 立法者的法理学 [The Jurisprudence of the Legislator]. Hong Kong: Joint Publishing Company, 2007.

———. "Zhongguo xianfa zhong de buchengwen xianfa: lijie zhongguo xianfa de xinshijiao" 中国宪法中的不成文宪法：理解中国宪法的新视角 [The Unwritten Constitution in China's Constitution: A New Way of Understanding China's Constitution]. *Open Times* 开放时代 12 (2009): 10–39.

Qiu Xikui 裘锡圭. *Wenzixue gaiyao* 文字学概要 [An Introduction to Chinese Characters]. Shanghai: Commercial Press, 1988.

Rao Zongyi 饶宗颐. *Zhongguo shixueshang zhi zhengtonglun* 中国史学上之正统论 [Orthodoxy in China's History Studies]. Shanghai: Shanghai Far East Press, 1996.

Rawls, John. "Justice as Fairness: Political Not Metaphysical." *Philosophy and Public Affairs* 14 (1985): 223–51.

———. "Kantian Constructivism in Moral Theory." *Journal of Philosophy* 77 (1980): 515–72.

———. *A Theory of Justice*. Cambridge, Mass.: Harvard University Press, 1971.

Riesenberg, Peter. *Citizenship in the Western Tradition: Plato to Rousseau*. Chapel Hill: University of North Carolina Press, 1992.

Rousseau, Jean-Jacques. *The Social Contract*. Translated by Willmoore Kendall. Washington, D.C.: Henry Regnery, 1954.

Rutland, Robert Allen. *The Birth of the Bill of Rights, 1776–1791*. New York: Collier Books, 1962.

Schmitt, Carl. *Constitutional Theory*. Translated by Jeffrey Seitzer. 1928. Reprint, Durham, N.C.: Duke University, 2008.

Sepinwall, Alyssa Goldstein. *The Abbé Grégoire and the French Revolution: The Making of Modern Universalism*. Berkeley: University of California Press, 2005.

Shao Yong. *Supreme Principles Governing the World*. Chaps. 7A–8B, *Outer Chapters on the Observation of Things*. Shanghai: Shanghai Classic Press, 1992.

Shen Changyun 沈长云. "Xi Zhou renkou lice" 西周人口蠡测 [A Rough Estimate of the Population of the Western Zhou]. *Journal of Chinese Social and Economic History* 中国社会经济史研究 1 (1987): 100.

Shen Deqian 沈德潜, ed. *Gushi yuan* 古诗源 [The Origin of Ancient Poems]. Beijing: Zhonghua Book Company, 1963.

Sichuan Province Editorial Group. "Zhongguo shaoshu minzu shehui lishi diaocha ziliao congkan." In Editorial Revision Committee, *Sichuan sheng ganzi zhou zangzu shehui lishi diaocha* [A Survey of Social History in Ganzi Tibetan Region, Sichuan Province]. Beijing: Nationalities Publishing House, 2009.

Sima Guang. *Zi Zhi Tongjian* [Comprehensive Mirror to Aid in Government]. Beijing: Zhonghua Book Company, 1956.

Song Zhenhao 宋镇豪. *Xia-Shang shehui shenghuo shi* 夏商社會生活史 [A History of Social Life under the Xia and Shang Dynasties]. Beijing: Chinese Academy of Social Sciences, 1994.

Su Li 苏力. "Daguo ji qi jiangyude zhengzhi goucheng" 大国及其疆域的政制构成 [A Large State and the Political Formation of Its Borders]. *Jurist* 法学家 1 (2016): 26–44.

———. "Dangdai Zhongguo de zhongyang yu difang fenquan: chongdu Mao Zedong 'Lun shida guanxi' diwujie" 当代中国的中央与地方分权: 重读毛泽东《论十大关系》第五节 [Contemporary China's Separation of Power between Central and Local Governments: Rereading Section 5 of Mao Zedong's "On the Ten Major Relationships"]. *Chinese Social Sciences* 中国社会科学 2 (2004): 42–55.

———. "Dangdai zhongguo fali de zhishi puxi jiqi quexian: cong huangdie'an toushi [The Intellectual Spectrum of Jurisprudence in Contemporary China: A Perspective on the Pornography Watching Case]. *Peking University Law Journal* 3 (2003): 287–306.

———. *Daolu Tongxiang Chengshi* [The Road to the City]. Beijing: Law Press, 2004.

———. *Fazhi jiqi bentu ziyuan* 法治及其本土资源 [Rule of Law and Its Indigenous Resources]. Beijing: China University of Political Science and Law Press, 2004.

———. "Gangchang, liyi, chenghu yu shehui guifan: zhuiqiu dui rujiade zhiduxing lijie" 纲常、礼仪、称呼与社会规范: 追求对儒家的制度性理解 [Morality, Rites, Titles and Social Norms: In Search of an Institutional Understanding of Confucianism]. *Chinese Journal of Law* 中国法律评论 5 (2007): 39–51.

———. "Hewei xianzhi wenti?" 何为宪制问题? [What Are Constitutional Questions?]. *Journal of East China University of Political Science and Law* 华东政法大学学报 5 (2013): 90–111.

Su Li 苏力. "Jingying zhengzhi yu zhengzhi canyu" 精英政治与政治参与 [Elite Politics and Participation in Politics]. *Chinese Journal of Law* 法学研究 5 (2013): 77–92.

——. "Qi Jia: Fucizixiao yu Zhangyouyouxu" [Governing the Family: Let the Father Be Affectionate and the Son Be Dutiful and Let Elders and Juniors Each in Their Places]. *Fazhi yu Shehui Fazhan* [Law and Social Development] 2 (2016): 100–113.

——. *Song Fa Xia Xiang* [Sending Law to the Countryside]. Beijing: China University of Law and Political Science Press, 2000.

——. *Songfa xiaxiang: zhongguo jicheng sifa zhidu yanjiu* 送法下乡: 中国基层司法制度研究 [Sending the Law down to the Countryside: A Study of China's Grassroots Judicial Institution]. Rev. ed. Beijing: Peking University Press, 2011.

——. "Wenhua zhidu yu guojia goucheng: yi 'shu tongwen' he 'guanhua' wei shijiao" 文化制度与国家构成——以'书同文'和'官话'为视角 [Cultural Institution and Structure of State: In the Light of Unified Script and Mandarin Chinese]. *Chinese Social Sciences* 中国社会科学 12 (2013): 78–95.

——. "Xianzheng de Junshi Suzao" [How the Military Shapes the Constitution]. *Faxue Pinglun* [Law Review] 1 (2010): 1–16.

——. "Xianzhi de junshi suzao" 宪制的军事塑造 [The Constitution Shaped by Military Affairs]. *Law Review* 法学评论 1 (2015): 1–16.

——. "Xiucixue de zhengfa jiamen" 修辞学的政法家门 [Rhetoric in Its Legal Branch]. *Open Era* 开放时代 2 (2011): 38–53.

——. "Zaoqi rujia de renxingguan" 早期儒家的人性观 [The Early Confucian View of Human Nature]. *Law and Social Development* 法制与社会发展 5 (2010): 3–14.

——. "Zuowei zhidu de huangdi" 作为制度的皇帝 [The Emperor as an Institution], *Law and Social Sciences* 法律与社会科学 13 (2013): 153–92.

Suerna 素尔纳, et al. *Xuezheng Quanshu* 学政全书 [Collection of Administration of Schools and Examinations]. Vol. 65 (1793). In *Lidai keju wenxian zhengli yu yanjiu congkan. Qinding Xuezheng Quanshu Jiaozhu* 历代科举文献整理与研究丛刊. 钦定学政全书校注 [A Series of Editions and Study of Literature on Imperial Examinations in All Dynasties: Notes on the "Collection of Administration of Schools and Examinations" Made by Imperial Order]. Wuhan: Wuhan University Press, 2009.

Sun Yat-sen 孙中山. *Collected Works of Sun Yatsen*. Vol. 1. Beijing: Zhonghua Book Company, 1981.

Sun Yirang 孙诒让, ed. *Zhouli zhengyi* 周礼正义 [Correct Interpretation of the "Rites of Zhou"]. Beijing: Zhonghua Book Company, 1987.

Tan Qixiang 谭其骧. "Lishishang de zhongguo he zhongguo lidai jiangyu" 历史上的中国和中国历代疆域 [Historical China and China's Historical Boundaries]. *China's Borderland History and Geography Studies* 中国边疆史地研究 1 (1991): 1–9.

——. "Tangdai jimizhou shulun" 唐代羁縻州述论 [A Description of the Slack-rein Prefectures in the Tang Dynasty]. In *Changshui cuipian* 《长水粹编》 [Selections from Changshui Collections]. Shijiazhuang: Hebei Educational Press, 2000.

Tang Deyong 汤德用, ed. *Zhongguo keju kaoshi shi* 中国科举考试史 [A History of Imperial Examination in China]. Hefei: Huangshan Press, 1995.

Tarkow-Naamani, Israel. "The Significance of the Act of Settlement in the Evolution of English Democracy." *Political Science Quarterly* 58, no. 4 (1943): 537–561.

Tian Yuqing 田余庆. *Dongjin menge zhengzhi* 东晋门阀政治 [Noble-Family Politics in the Eastern Jin]. 5th ed. Beijing: Peking University Press, 2012.

——. *Qin-Han-Wei-Jin Shi tanwei* 秦汉魏晋史探微 [A Study of the Qin, Han, Wei and Jin Histories]. Rev. 3rd ed. Beijing: Zhonghua Book Company, 2011.

Upham, Frank K. "Who Will Find the Defendant if He Stays with His Sheep? Justice in Rural China." *Yale Law Journal* 114 (2005): 1675.

Wang Dingbao 王定保. *Tang Zhiyan* 唐摭言 [Collected Sayings of the Tang]. Beijing: Zhonghua Book Company, 1959.

Wang Hui 汪晖. "Liuqiu yu quyu zhixu de liangci jubian" 琉球与区域秩序的两次巨变 [The Ryuykyu and Two Major Shifts in Regional Order]. In *Dongxi zhijian de "Xizang wenti"* 东西之间的"西藏问题"（外二篇）[The Tibetan Question between East and West (with 2 Additional Chapters)], 207–60. Beijing: SDX Joint Publishing Company, 2011.

———. "Liuqiu: zhanzheng jiyi, shehui yundong yu lishi jieshi" 琉球：战争记忆、社会运动与历史解释 [Ryukyu: War Memories, Social Movements and Historical Interpretation]. In *Yazhou shiye: Zhongguo lishi de xushu* 亚洲视野：中国历史的叙述 [An Asian View: An Account of Chinese History], 185–236. Beijing: Oxford University Press, 2010.

Wang, Rui. *The Chinese Imperial Examination System: An Annotated Bibliography*. Plymouth: Scarecrow, 2013.

Wang Shuo 王朔. *Wuzhizhe wusi* 无知者无畏 [The Ignorant Is the Brave]. Liaoning: Chunfeng Wenyi Press, 2000.

Wang Yumin 王育民. *Zhongguo lishi dili gailun* 中国历史地理概论 [An Introduction to the Historical Geography of China]. Beijing: People's Education Press, 1987.

Watson, Burton, trans. *Han Feizi: Basic Writings*. New York: Columbia University Press, 2003.

———, trans. *Records of the Grand Historian: Qin Dynasty* (Hong Kong: Columbia University Press, 1993).

Weber, Max. *Economy and Society: An Outline of Interpretive Sociology*. 2 vols. Berkeley: University of California Press, 1978.

Wittfogel, Karl A. *Oriental Despotism: A Comparative Study of Total Power*. New Haven, Conn.: Yale University Press, 1967.

Wittgenstein, Ludwig. *Philosophical Investigations*. London: Macmillan, 1953.

Wu Han 吴晗 and Fei Xiaotong 费孝通. *Lun shenquan, Zailun shenquan, lun shi daifu* 论绅权，再论绅权，论士大夫，皇权与绅权 [On the Power of the Gentry, A Second Look at the Power of the Gentry, On Officials, and Imperial Power and the Power of the Gentry]. Shanghai: Shanghai Guanchashe, 1948.

Xiao Maosheng 肖茂盛. "Qin tongyi huobi de xingzhi ji qi lishi yiyi" 秦统一货币的形制及其历史意义 [The Form of the Qin Unified Coinage and Its Historical Significance]. *Journal of Financial Management and Research* 金融管理与研究 4 (2005): 63–64.

Xie Qing 谢青 and Tang Deyong 汤德用, eds. *Zhongguo keju kaoshi shi* 中国科举考试史 [A History of China's Imperial Examinations]. Hefei: Huangshan Publishing House, 1995.

Xin Delin 信德麟. *Ladingyu he xilayu* 拉丁语和希腊语 [Latin and Greek]. Beijing: Foreign Language Teaching and Research Press 外语教学与研究出版社, 2007.

Xu Fuguan 徐复观. *Lianghan sixiangshi* 两汉思想史 [History of Thought in the Han Dynasties]. Shanghai: East China Normal University Press, 2001.

———. "Zhouguan chengli zhi shidai ji qi sixiang xingge" 周官成立之时代及其思想性格 [The Time of Composition of the Zhou Officialdom and the Characteristics of Its Thought]. In *Xu Fuguan lun jingxueshi er zhong* 徐复观论经学史二种 [Two Articles by Xu Fuguan on the History of Classical Studies], 224–26. Shanghai: Shanghai Bookshop, 2002.

Xu Shen 许慎. *Shuowen Jiezi* 说文解字 [Explanation of Words and Characters]. Beijing: Zhonghua Book Company, 2004.

Xu Tongqiang 徐通锵. *Lishi yuyanxue* 历史语言学 [Historical Linguistics]. Hong Kong: Commercial Press, 1991.

Xu Zhuoyun 许倬云. *Xizhou shi* 西周史 [A History of the Western Zhou]. Rev. ed. Hong Kong: Joint Publishing Company, 1993.

Yanfu 严复. "Xianfa dayi" 宪法大义 [The Essence of Constitution], in *Yan Fu Ji* 严复集 [The Collected Works of Yan Fu]. Edited by Wang Shi. Beijing: Zhonghua Book Company, 1986, 239.

Yan Gengwang 严耕望. *Zhishi sanshu* 治史三书 [Three Books on the Study of History]. Vol. 2. Shanghai: Shanghai People's Press, 2011.

———. *Zhongguo zhengzhi zhidu shigang* 中国政治制度史纲 [A Historical Outline of Chinese Political Institutions]. Shanghai: Shanghai Classics Publishing House, 2013.

Yan Zhenqing 颜真卿. (封演: 《封氏闻见记校注》. Beijing: Zhonghua Book Company, 2005.

Yang Lien-sheng. "Historical Notes on the Chinese World Order." In Fairbank, *Chinese World Order*, 20–33.

Zang Jinshu 臧晋叔. *Yuanqu xuan* 元曲选 [An Anthology of Yuan Poetry]. Beijing: Zhonghua Book Company, 1958.

Zhang Shilu 张世禄 and Yang Jianqiao 杨剑桥. *Yinyunxue rumen* 音韵学入门 [Introduction to Phonetics]. Shanghai: Fudan University Press, 2009.

Zhang Shiping 张栻. *Zhang Nanxuan xianshegn wenji* 张南轩先生文集 [Collected Works of Mr. Zhang Nanxuan]. Beijing: Commerce Press, 1936.

Zhang Xiaozheng 张晓政. "Gudai zhouxian zhuguan de xuanren" 古代州县主官的选任 [The Selection of Heads of the Prefectures and Counties in Ancient Times]. *Study Times* 学习时报, 15 October 2012, 9.

Zhang Xuecheng 章学诚. *Wenshi tongyi* 文史通义 [On Literature and History]. Edited by Ye Ying 叶瑛. Beijing: Zhonghua Book Company, 1985.

Zhang Yulai 张玉来. "Ming-Qing shidai hanyu guanhua de shehui shiyong zhuangkuang" 明清时代汉语官话的社会使用状况 [The Social Use of Mandarin in the Ming and Qing Dynasties]. *Language Teaching and Linguistic Studies* 语言教学与研究 1 (2010): 90–93.

Zhang Zai 张载. *Zhang Zai Ji* 张载集 [Collected Works of Zhang Zai]. Beijing: Zhonghua Book Company, 1978.

Zhang Zhongkui 张中奎. *Gaitu guiliu yu miao jiang zaizao* 改土归流与苗疆再造 [Reforming the Barbarians and Remaking the Miao Region]. Beijing: China Social Science Press, 2012.

Zhao Dingxin 赵鼎新. "Warfare in the Eastern Zhou and the Rise of the Confucian-Legalist State" [东周战争与儒法国家的诞生]. Presentation at the University of California, Los Angeles, 10 October 2006. http://web.international.ucla.edu/institute/event/5207. Published in Chinese by East China Normal University, 2011.

Zhao Erxuan 赵尔巽. *Qing Shi Gao* 清史稿 [Draft Qing History]. Beijing: Zhonghua Book Company, 1977.

Zhao Xiaoli 赵晓力. *Meiguo xianfa de yuanzhi jieshi* 美国宪法的原旨解释 [Interpreting the Original Intent of the American Constitution]. Shanghai: Shanghai People's Press, 2004.

———. "Meiguo xianfazhongde zongjiao yu shangdi" 美国宪法中的宗教与上帝 [Religion and God in the American Constitution]. *Peking University Law Journal* 中外法学 4 (2003): 506.

———. "Ziran yu lishi: Meiguo xianzhengde bolun" 自然与历史 ：美国宪政的悖论 [Nature and History: The Paradox of American Constitutionalism]. *China Law Review* 中国法律评论 2 (2014): 118.

Zhao Yi 赵翼. *Nianershi zhaoji* 廿二史劄记 [Notes on the 22 Dynastic Histories]. Edited by Cao Guangfu 曹光甫. Nanjing: Phoenix Publishing House, 2008.

Zhou Hanguang 周瀚光. "Qianlun Song-Ming daoxue dui gudai shuxue fazhan de zuoyong he yingxiang" 浅论宋明道学对古代数学发展的作用和影响 [A Brief Discussion of the Role and Influence of the Study of the Way of the Song and Ming Dynasties on the Development of Ancient Mathematics]. In *Lun Song-Ming lixue* 论宋明理学 [A Discussion of the Song-Ming School of Principle], edited by the Zhejiang Academy of Social Sciences, 544. Hangzhou: Zhejiang People's Press, 1983.

Zhou Zhenhe 周振鹤. *Zhongguo difang xingzheng zhidushi* 中国地方行政制度史 [A History of Local Administration in China]. Shanghai: Shanghai People's Press, 2005.

Zhu Suli. "Political Parties in China's Judiciary." *Duke Journal of Comparative and International Law* 17 (2007): 533–60.

Zhu Xi. *Conversations of Master Zhu Arranged Topically.* Edited by Wang Xingxian. Beijing: Zhonghua Book Company, 1986.

Zhu Yongjia 朱永嘉. *Shang Yang bianfa yu Wang Mang gaizhi: Zhongguo lishishang de liangci zhuming gaige* 商鞅变法与王莽改制: 中国历史上的两次著名改革 [Shang Yang's Reforms and Wang Mang's Regime Change: Two Famous Revolutions in Chinese History]. Beijing: China Chang'an Press, 2013.

Zou Changlin 邹昌林. *Zhongguo guli yanjiu* 中国古礼研究 [A Study of China's Ancient Rites]. Beijing: Wenjin Publishing House, 1992.

CONTRIBUTORS

SU LI is the pen name of Zhu Suli, a professor of jurisprudence at the School of Law of Peking University. He publishes widely in law and economics, law and literature, and the sociology of law. E-mail: zhusuli@pku.edu.cn.

DANIEL A. BELL is dean of the School of Political Science and Public Administration of Shandong University and a professor of ethics and political philosophy at Tsinghua University (Department of Philosophy and Schwarzman College). He has published eight books (including four edited volumes) on East Asian politics and philosophy with Princeton University Press. E-mail: daniel.a.bell@gmail.com.

LIU HAN is an associate professor at the School of Law, Tsinghua University. He holds a J.S.D degree from the Yale Law School. He specializes in Chinese and comparative constitutional law, legal theory, and political philosophy. He has published widely in both Chinese and English. Email: liuhan@tsinghua.edu.cn.

WANG HUI is a professor of literature and history at the School of Humanities, Tsinghua University. He began his career as an expert on Lu Xun (鲁迅) and is widely known for his reinterpretation of Chinese intellectual history and critique of neoliberalism. He has published more than a dozen books on modern Chinese literature and intellectual history. Many of his works have been translated into English, Italian, Japanese, Korean, and other languages. Email: wanghui1010@gmail.com.

WU FEI is a professor in the Department of Philosophy, Peking University. He specializes in Confucian and Christian ethics and political philosophy, anthropology of religion, and other topics. He is widely known in China for his research on suicide, Confucian rituals, and cardinal relationships. Email: wufeister@pku.edu.cn.

ZHANG YONGLE is an associate professor at the School of Law, Peking University. He specializes in modern Chinese constitutional history and intellectual history, history of western political/legal thought, and Graeco-Roman historiography. He has published widely in both Chinese and English. Email: kairos98@pku.edu.cn.

ZHAO XIAOLI is an associate professor at the School of Law, Tsinghua University. His research fields include legal theory, modern Chinese constitutional history, history of western legal thought, law and literature, and other topics. He has published numerous articles in Chinese. E-mail: zhaoxiaoli@mail.tsinghua.edu.cn.

A NOTE ON THE TYPE

{〜⟩⟨〜}

THIS BOOK has been composed in Miller, a Scotch Roman typeface designed by Matthew Carter and first released by Font Bureau in 1997. It resembles Monticello, the typeface developed for The Papers of Thomas Jefferson in the 1940s by C. H. Griffith and P. J. Conkwright and reinterpreted in digital form by Carter in 2003.

Pleasant Jefferson ("P. J.") Conkwright (1905–1986) was Typographer at Princeton University Press from 1939 to 1970. He was an acclaimed book designer and AIGA Medalist.

The ornament used throughout this book was designed by Pierre Simon Fournier (1712–1768) and was a favorite of Conkwright's, used in his design of the *Princeton University Library Chronicle.*